Blair, Labour and Palestine

Blair, Labour and Palestine

Conflicting Views on Middle East Peace After 9/11

Toby Greene

BLOOMSBURY

NEW YORK • LONDON • NEW DELHI • SYDNEY

Bloomsbury Academic

An imprint of Bloomsbury Publishing Plc

1385 Broadway	50 Bedford Square
New York	London
NY 10018	WC1B 3DP
USA	UK

www.bloomsbury.com

First published 2013

www.tobygreene.net

ISBN: HB: 978-1-4411-4372-3
ePDF: 978-1-4411-5951-9

Library of Congress Cataloging-in-Publication Data
A catalog record for this title is available from the Library of Congress.

Typeset by Deanta Global Publishing Services, Chennai, India

Contents

Acknowledgements

I would like to thank Dr Neill Lochery, for giving me the opportunity to pursue the doctoral research on which this book is based, and for his guidance over the past few years. I also owe a debt of gratitude to the late Professor John Klier for providing timely advice and encouragement in the early stages of my research. My doctoral examiners, Professor Colin Shindler and Professor Rosemary Hollis, provided insightful comments, which helped considerably to strengthen the work, and I am grateful to Professor Shindler in particular for his advice on how to bring this work to publication. My thanks are due also to several anonymous reviewers for their helpful comments. I wish to thank the Hebrew and Jewish Studies Department at UCL for their support while I was affiliated with the department, including through the award of an Ian Karten Scholarship. Two employers, Labour Friends of Israel and the Britain Israel Communications and Research Centre, generously allowed me the flexibility to pursue my research while under their employment. I wish to thank all those who gave their time to be interviewed or to discuss these issues with me informally. I am also very thankful for the material and moral support provided by my parents, Diane and Philip Greene. My gratitude goes also to Marie-Claire Antoine, formerly of Continuum Books, who was extremely supportive in bringing this book to publication and all those at Bloomsbury who worked so professionally on its production. Above all, I wish to thank my wife, Talya, without whose constant encouragement, limitless patience and constructive editing, over many long years, I would never have completed this work.

This book is dedicated to Talya, Sivan and Lielle.

Introduction

'The policy choices from 9/11 onwards were and are immensely difficult. But eventually, they come down to this: do we confront this extremist ideology in order to change it, or do we manage it and hope in time it changes itself?'

Tony Blair[1]

The scope of the book

This book is an attempt to explain British policy in the Israeli-Palestinian arena during the premiership of Tony Blair, particularly in the wake of the attacks by Al Qaeda on New York and Washington of 11 September 2001 (9/11). The events of 9/11 shocked the world with the scale of death and destruction. One of their consequences was to bring greater urgency to the debate within Europe and the United States over the role played by Western foreign policies in engendering hostile feeling towards the West among Muslims.[2] An important part of this debate was the extent to which British and other Western government's policies in the Israeli-Palestinian arena were a contributory factor. Part of the question was, as Lochery has framed it, 'whether Israel was the front line against global terror or was at the root cause of it.'[3]

Western support for Israel and the fate of the Palestinians had long been cited by Islamists as a major grievance against the West, and the Israeli-Palestinian question had widespread prominence in the discourse of politicized Muslims. Al Qaeda, the orchestrators of 9/11, and their sympathizers, spoke of Israel as part of a 'Zionist-Crusader' alliance against the Islamic world and referred to the violence in the Palestinian territories in justifying their actions.[4] Though most Muslims, including many Islamists, condemned the 9/11 attacks, leaders in the Islamic world widely linked the attacks to what they considered America's unbalanced policies in the region, particularly with regard to the Israeli-Palestinian conflict.[5]

British policy makers began to link foreign policy issues, including the Israeli-Palestinian issue, directly to British national security. In trying to understand the drivers of radicalization, officials considered whether taking greater account of concerns in the Islamic world when formulating Middle East policy would reduce the risk of Islamic anti-Western radicalization and violence, both among Muslims in the Middle East and in the United Kingdom. In May 2004, for example, Cabinet Secretary Sir Andrew Turnbull wrote to Permanent Secretary of the Home Office John Gieve, and other senior officials, about the concern that, 'parts of the Muslim community, particularly younger men, are disaffected', and asking the question, 'should our stance (e.g. on MEPP [Middle East Peace Process] or Kashmir) be influenced more by these concerns?'[6] Yet Tony Blair, in increasingly strident terms during his time in office, rejected the idea that Western foreign policies caused radicalization as 'nonsense'.[7] He showed far greater sympathy for Israel, as a democratic state at threat from extremism, than many of his European counterparts, much to the dismay of many of his colleagues in his own party.

Though there has been an enormous amount written about Tony Blair's Middle East policy, the predominant focus has been his decision to commit British forces to the US-led invasion of Iraq. However, the Blair government's approach in the Israeli-Palestinian arena deserves its own account. Britain under Blair was no passive bystander with regard to this issue, nor did it hide in the chorus of international declarations and condemnations. Britain was unusually proactive, with Tony Blair more than once describing the conflict as the world's most pressing challenge. Blair visited the region on numerous occasions and twice organized international conferences in London in an attempt to generate progress. Moreover, British policy was distinct, with clear differences of approach between Britain and other major European powers on the one hand, and the United States on the other.

This policy area also draws attention because of the extent to which it divided the ruling Labour Party, with many in the party particularly perturbed by an approach they perceived as too sympathetic to Israel. Blair's policy decisions in the Israeli-Palestinian arena were among his most controversial and politically damaging. His responses to the Second Intifada and the Second Lebanon War alienated his party more than any foreign policy issues aside from the Iraq War. Blair's refusal to call for an unconditional ceasefire during the Second Lebanon War in 2006 was one of the factors that triggered a backbench rebellion which forced him to announce the date of his departure from office. According to Blair's own account, his response to the Second Lebanon War, 'showed how far I had swung from the mainstream of conventional Western media wisdom and from my own people.'[8] The differences were not only between Blair and the grassroots. Differences of opinion between ministers were at times manifested as inconsistencies in position and policy from different representatives of the same government, both with regard to the Israeli-Palestinian arena and to the challenge of how to relate to Islamism and Islamists.

Given that the period in question is so recent, there is limited scholarly writing which focuses on it. Existing accounts, such as those of Rynhold and Spyer, Hollis, Miller, and Lochery all provide valuable insights, but only address the Blair government's policy in the Israeli-Palestinian arena as part of wider studies.[9] There is a tendency in existing accounts to view Blair's policy in the Israeli-Palestinian arena as an attempt to find a middle way between the position of the United States on the one hand and the positions of Britain's EU partners, and Blair's own political party on the other. Rynhold and Spyer argue that Blair sought to synthesize the post-9/11 Bush approach to the Middle East, which focused on confronting Saddam's Iraq, and the predominant view of the British left, which put the priority on the Palestinian issue.[10] Hollis emphasizes how New Labour positioned itself in the first term as the 'principal European facilitator of US diplomacy' and after 9/11 tried to 'straddle the divide between Washington's increasingly uncritical support for Israel and the continental European consensus on Israeli and Palestinian rights.'[11] Rory Miller claims that 'Blair's primary goal was to minimize the increase in tension between the United States and the EU due to the Israel-Palestine conflict.'[12] Indeed Blair's manoeuvring on the international stage to try and maintain a transatlantic common ground was an important factor in determining his policy. The need to balance between the position of the United States and his own sceptical party rank and file was also significant. But the tendency to reduce Blair's position to one of balancing or bridging between the positions of others has left underexplored Blair's distinct personal view of the Israeli-Palestinian conflict and its relationship to the broader challenge of political Islam.

By contrast, the significant role played by Blair's personal world view has been highlighted in the far more extensive literature relating to the decision to participate in the Iraq War. There is a significant theme in the academic and wider literature, which presents Blair's decision to back the war in Iraq as being shaped predominantly by a concern to maintain the special relationship with the United States, and thereby the United Kingdom's influence with the world's strongest power. Put simply, this is the image of Blair expressed in more popular discourse as George Bush's 'poodle'.[13] A belief in the importance for Britain's interests of maintaining a very close relationship with the United States was undoubtedly very significant in Blair's thinking. However, the view that this was the principal reason for Britain's involvement in Iraq has been convincingly challenged by those who have emphasized Blair's own perception of global challenges as key to his decision-making. Coates and Krieger wrote, for example, in their analysis of why Blair and his government chose to join the war in Iraq that, 'the key to his foreign policy, like the key to the foreign policy of Labour leaders in the past, lies in the overall world view that he and they bring to the totality of their policy agenda'.[14] Lawrence Freedman argued while Blair was still in power that, 'Bush's conviction limited Blair's options, but it by no means turned Blair into a poodle. His approach to the "war on terror" has been wider and in many respects more ambitious than Bush's'.[15]

This book uncovers Blair's unique position on the Israeli-Palestinian issue in the context of his overall world view and foreign policy, and in particular, his response to the challenges presented by 9/11 and his views on political Islam. According to the account presented here, the distinctive character of British policy in the Israeli-Palestinian arena after 9/11 was influenced considerably by Tony Blair's view of the Middle East. This view, which hardened over time in response to events, conflicted with the opinions of much of his party, based on a set of assumptions they did not share. Blair's evolving ideas about the nature of political Islam, rooted in a world view blending Christian Socialism, Atlanticism and neoliberalism, led Blair to regard the relationship between the Israeli-Palestinian issue and Islamic extremism very differently from many political colleagues, as well as officials within the Foreign Office and other branches of government. Even New Labour loyalists who broadly shared Blair's world view did not tend to share his consistent level of personal interest in the Israeli-Palestinian issue. On close examination, had any other individual in the Labour Party been leader, it is hard to imagine their approach would have been the same. In particular, Blair's fully fledged neoliberalism and Atlanticism, though shared among the New Labour loyalists, were not shared by many of the party rank and file, many of whom held some degree of attachment to post-colonialism and were far more suspicious of America's global role.

Blair's underlying ideological predispositions contributed significantly to his being considerably more sympathetic to the Israeli position than many in his party. Indeed, in the period of his leadership, attitudes to the Israel-Palestinian conflict came to express the political identities of politicians and activists in different wings of the party. After 9/11, and even more so after 7/7, Blair's overall world view also underpinned his view of what he termed 'radical Islam' as an inherently anti-liberal threat to Western values and interests that needed to be confronted. This 'confrontationalist' approach to the challenge of political Islam was in contrast to the more 'accommodationist' instincts of many others within his party, and within the Foreign Office, who tended to see the anti-Western sentiment of Islamists as driven by specific political grievances which could potentially be ameliorated.[16] These differences were increasingly significant after 9/11, as British policy makers attempted to understand the causes of Islamic anger against the West and determine how best to respond.

At the same time, Blair believed that the Israeli-Palestinian conflict was exploited by radical Islamists to rally support for their anti-Western ideology and that resolving the conflict was key to overcoming the opposition they presented to Western interests and values. The importance of addressing, and being seen to address, the conflict, therefore, became a perennial source of tension in the UK–US relationship under Blair. The British Prime Minister consistently tried to persuade the Bush administration to focus greater attention on the issue.

Methodology and terminology

This book examines the domestic sources of foreign policy. Researchers in the field of foreign policy analysis have convincingly challenged the belief that state behaviour in the international arena can largely be understood by looking at the international system. They have sought to add to the understanding of state behaviour by studying the internal processes within the state. Foreign policy analysis, as described by Christopher Hill, works on the hypothesis that 'the outputs of foreign policy are to some degree determined by the nature of the decision making process.'[17] As such, this field of study is interested in the interaction of domestic politics and international affairs, and studies the actors and structure of decision-making within states, which generates a state's foreign policy. Though many domestic factors influence foreign policy outcomes, the emphasis in this book is the significance of the distinct ideas about the world held by the central decision maker, Tony Blair, and the extent to which those ideas contrasted with many of those around him.[18] This is an interpretative study, which attempts to construct a narrative that best explains the motivations, beliefs and actions and of those involved. This is based on the assumption that however much the decisions of Blair and others involved were shaped by material factors beyond their control, including the structure of the international system and Britain's place within it, there was sufficient space for their own distinct beliefs to significantly shape their decisions and actions within those constraints.[19] British policy in the Israeli-Palestinian arena was certainly not solely determined by the world view of the Prime Minister or a narrow clique of aides and political allies. Structural factors, realist considerations, bureaucratic factors, domestic political bargaining and electoral considerations are among the factors that played a role. The claim is that the distinctive world view of the Prime Minister shaped his perception of the threat emerging from the Middle East and was the dominant factor explaining his position, and consequently UK policy, in the Israeli-Palestinian arena at key junctures after 9/11.

There are advantages and disadvantages to studying such recent events. Among the advantages is that key players are accessible to be interviewed, and their memories relatively fresh. In researching this book, I conducted numerous in-depth interviews with a wide range of politicians, officials, journalists and experts who were personally involved in the events or who followed them closely. This fieldwork supplemented an analysis of existing literature including scholarly studies, memoirs and diaries and an analysis of official records, statements and documents. These included not only publicly available government policy papers, parliamentary reports, press conferences, interviews and speeches, but also previously unpublished documents acquired through the Freedom of Information Act or from interviewees. I have also analysed a number of documents which were originally part of the hidden diplomatic or policy-making process but which have come to light either through leaks or public inquiries. Though the full documentary record will not be available for some time, this limited snapshot nonetheless provides fascinating glimpses of the policy-making process as it was underway. I have used these various sources to try and determine the policy choices made and to interpret the understandings and motives of the decision makers.[20]

There are three terminological issues to highlight. First, the term 'Palestine' in the title of this book is used as shorthand for what might be called 'the Palestine question', or my preferred term, 'the Israeli-Palestinian arena'.

Second, terms such as 'Middle East peace process' and 'Middle East conflict' are ambiguous. The term 'Middle East' can be defined in a number of ways but typically refers to the greater part, if not all, of the Arab states in addition to Israel, Iran and sometimes Turkey.[21] However, the term 'Middle East peace process' is often used by politicians and policy makers to refer specifically to the Israeli-Palestinian peace process. From the use of the term 'Middle East peace process' to refer to the Israeli-Palestinian peace process, it could be inferred that resolving the Israeli-Palestinian conflict is central to bringing peace to the whole of the region. Though the Israeli-Palestinian conflict is undoubtedly linked to relations between Israel and the wider Arab world, I do not believe that peace between Israel and the Palestinians is equivalent to comprehensive peace in the Middle East. For this reason, I prefer to refer less ambiguously to the Israeli-Palestinian arena, conflict or peace process, meaning the ongoing clash between rival Jewish and Palestinian–Arab national movements in the area which was known as Palestine under the British Mandate ending in 1948.[22] However, I have repeatedly quoted individuals referring to the Middle East peace process, where they are often referring primarily to the Israeli-Palestinian arena.

Third, I regard 'political Islam' and 'Islamism' as equivalent terms to refer broadly to the 'contemporary movement that conceives of Islam as a political ideology',[23] or more explicitly, that seeks to apply Islamic law and text to the organization of state and society.[24] This can conceivably include non-violent and violent groups, and democratic and non-democratic groups. 'Islamism' and 'political Islam' have at times been used interchangeably with other terms including 'Islamic fundamentalism', 'radical Islam', 'Islamic extremism' and others. I regard the tendency to use the term 'radical Islam' interchangeably with 'political Islam' as generally indicative of a view that all forms of political Islam are ultimately anti-liberal and anti-democratic. Towards the end of his term in government, Tony Blair began to refer freely to 'radical Islam' or 'reactionary Islam' somewhat ambiguously. For reasons explained in Chapter 9, I do not believe he meant necessarily to refer to all expressions of Islamism, but principally to those he regarded as anti-liberal or anti-democratic.

Book outline

Chapter 1 provides a historical context in order to introduce the broad themes of how the Israeli-Palestinian issue has interacted with British politics and foreign policy. It then draws out the patterns of interests, alliances and institutional factors which remained relevant when Blair entered office.

Chapter 2 examines the diverse attitudes towards the Israeli-Palestinian arena within the Labour Party prior to coming to power in 1997. It looks at the history of Labour's relations with the issue, and explains how when Blair became party leader, attitudes to the Israeli-Palestinian issue came to be emblematic of ideological rifts between New Labour and the Labour left.

Chapter 3 shows how foreign policy in the Israeli-Palestinian arena was made prior to 9/11, during Labour's first term, and how Blair's first term established key elements of his approach to foreign policy in general and his approach to the Israeli-Palestinian arena in particular.

Chapter 4 sets the context for examining the response of policy makers in the West to 9/11. It places the events of 9/11 in the context of the wider challenge of political Islam, the role the Israeli-Palestinian conflict played in the rhetoric of Islamists and the debate about the causes of Islamic anger against the West. It reviews contrasting interpretations of 9/11 and its causes, including the Clash of Civilizations thesis, the neoliberal interpretation and the grievance-based interpretation. The chapter then expands on the debate about how Israel is seen – as the cause of the Islamist extremism or an ally against it – and frames that debate within the context of the Labour Party.

Chapter 5 describes Blair's initial response to 9/11 and how he viewed the place of the Israeli-Palestinian issue in the War on Terror – which was distinct from many others in his party – based on his belief in the need to confront the threat of terrorism and its ideological sources, coupled with a steadfast commitment to supporting the United States in the War on Terror.

Chapter 6 examines how the debate about the Israeli-Palestinian issue in the United Kingdom intensified in the context to the build-up to war in Iraq and the escalation of violence in the Second Intifada, and shows how focusing on the Israeli-Palestinian conflict became not only a diplomatic imperative for Blair, but also a domestic political imperative.

Chapter 7 examines how, following the end of major combat operations in Iraq, Blair tried to establish the Israeli-Palestinian issue as the first priority in the War on Terror, but how his fundamental view of the nature of the conflict and how to resolve it remained distinct from many in his party and in diplomatic circles. In particular, it explores how Blair's overall approach guided his positive response to Israel's disengagement plan in 2004, in the face of considerable domestic and international criticism.

Chapter 8 examines the impact of 7/7 on Britain's domestic counter-radicalization policy. It shows how, as a result of the London bombings, Blair steered the approach away from focusing on foreign policy grievances, such as Western support for Israel, and moved it onto a more confrontational footing, based on the belief that Islamic extremism was an ideology that had to be defeated, rather than accommodated.

Chapter 9 examines how Blair's increasingly confrontationalist approach to the challenge of 'radical Islam' informed his response to challenges in the Israeli-Palestinian arena in his third term, in particular, the election of Hamas and the Second Lebanon War. It further shows how Blair's increasingly strident position created a political crisis within his party which forced him to announce the date of his departure from government.

The conclusion brings together all the elements of my research and looks at the wider implications of the findings. It also indicates how the debates explored in this book have continued among Western policy makers in the years since Blair ended his premiership, with the challenges evolving again in the wake of the 'Arab Spring', which has given Islamist parties an opportunity to take power in several Arab states.

Roots of British Policy in the
Israeli-Palestinian Arena

The Mandate period

Whether they like it or not, British policy makers do not travel lightly in the Middle East. They carry baggage. As well as the various, often conflicting interests they have to balance in their hands, they take on their backs the legacy of Britain's historic role in the region; what Elizabeth Monroe called 'Britain's Moment in the Middle East'.[1] It was Britain, along with France, that drew the map of the post-Ottoman Arab world, and when dissatisfaction arose, they were always liable to having the finger pointed at them by Arab leaders.

Divergent trends in Britain's policy towards the Israeli-Palestinian arena predate General Allenby's conquest of the territory from the Ottoman Turks in 1917. During World War I, support for Zionism – the movement to create a Jewish state in Palestine – grew within the British government, though the reasons for this have been contested over the decades. Some emphasize the sentimental sympathies of British leaders for the Zionist cause rooted in a Christian attachment to the Bible. An alternative interpretation focuses on the largely false belief of Lloyd George and others that Jews had global power, including influence in Russia and the United States, that could be harnessed in the context of the war, through support for Zionism. Another version has it that Britain acted on the basis of its strategic considerations and a belief that a Jewish presence under British protection on the eastern Mediterranean would strengthen Britain's position in the region against the French and the Russians, giving protection to the Suez Canal and access to India. Others emphasize the significance of the skill and influence of the Zionist leadership, in particular, Chaim Weizmann.[2]

Whatever the dominant cause of the British cabinet's pro-Zionism, there was always a strong countervailing sympathy for the Arabs in the British establishment during and after World War I. This pro-Arab sympathy also stemmed from varied sources. These included a belief that the far more numerous Arabs were of greater importance as a strategic ally for Britain, a romantic attraction to Arab culture and society, and the belief that Britain's adoption of the Zionist movement's aims in the issuing of the Balfour Declaration in 1917 was an injustice to the Arabs.[3] These views were often shot-through with anti-Semitic beliefs about the Jews as either grasping capitalists or dangerous Bolsheviks.[4]

Prior to World War I, Britain had acquired a number of protectorate Arab territories in the Persian Gulf, military and economic domination in Egypt, a colony in Aden, and a strategically vital oil concession in Persia. After World War I, Britain was mandated by the League of Nations to administer Iraq and Palestine. Britain promised Hussain ibn Ali, the Sharif of Mecca, in a 1915 letter from British High Commissioner in Cairo Sir Henry McMahon, that it would support Arab national aspirations in return for Hussain's support for the British war effort against Turkey. Arabs subsequently claimed that this agreement included Palestine, something later denied by the British.[5] Whether or not it contradicted its promises to the Arabs, in 1917 Britain issued the 'Balfour Declaration', expressing support for 'a national home for the Jewish people in Palestine . . . it being understood that nothing shall be done which may prejudice the civil or religious rights of existing non-Jewish communities in Palestine.'[6]

In January 1919, Faisal Ibn Husain, the leader of the Arab delegation to the post-war Paris peace conference, and Chaim Weizman, leader of the Zionist movement, signed an agreement in London to support each other's national aspirations in the Middle East. Faisal wrote in a letter to another Zionist representative, Felix Franfurter, two months later, 'We Arabs, especially the educated amongst us, look with the deepest sympathy on the Zionist movement . . . We will do our best, in so far as we are concerned, to help them through: we will wish the Jews a most hearty welcome home.'[7]

However, this spirit of cooperation was not felt widely, and the Arab world soon became implacably opposed to a Jewish homeland in the region. As a result, for most of the twentieth century, British policy makers have worked in a context whereby to support Arab aspirations in Palestine was to undermine the interests of the Jews, and vice versa. Both Arabs and Jews have sources of resentment against the British dating back to the Mandate period. In 1922, Britain restricted the area designated for a Jewish national home to the smaller part of Mandate Palestine west of the River Jordan, establishing to the east the Emirate of Transjordan, ruled over by Abdullah, one of the four sons of the Sharif of Mecca and a brother of Faisal. Nonetheless, the Arabs and their sympathizers regarded a national home for the Jews even in the area West of the Jordan unjustified, given that the Jews were at the time a small minority in the territory, and believing that the policy inevitably diminished the rights of the Arab majority. For Arabs, Britain carries considerable blame for helping establish Israel with the Balfour Declaration and its support for Jewish immigration into Palestine prior to World War II. As both Jewish and Arab societies developed in Palestine in the 1920s and 1930s, and as the Jewish population rapidly expanded, tensions and violence between the communities, and between the Arab population and the British authorities, increased. This peaked with a major Arab uprising against the British and the Jews between 1936 and 1939. In 1937, the Peel Commission established by the British government to investigate the Palestine problem concluded that there was no way to reconcile conflicting Arab and Jewish demands. The Commission proposed the partition of Palestine into Jewish and Arab states. The principle of partition was accepted by the Zionist movement, though they objected to the proposed borders. Any idea of partition which would create a Jewish state was rejected by the Arabs.[8]

In 1939, in an attempt to appease the Arabs and gain their support on the eve of World War II, the British issued the MacDonald White Paper, which heavily restricted Jewish immigration into Palestine, thus denying European Jews a refuge from the Nazis.[9] Just as Arabs recall with rancour the Balfour Declaration, Jews recall the 1939 White Paper with great lament. Regardless of the White Paper, the Palestinian leader Haj Amin al Husseini made an alliance with Hitler, spending the war years in Berlin and recruiting Bosnian Muslims to the Nazi SS. During World War II, approximately six million Jews, the majority of Europe's Jewish population, were murdered by the Nazis and their accomplices in the Holocaust. At the end of the war, up to 300,000 survivors passed through Jewish refugee camps in Europe. Robbed of all property and rights, many wished to move to Palestine and there was a surge of international sympathy for the Zionist demand for an independent state. The Jewish Agency, the representatives of the Jewish community in Palestine, called on Britain to allow 100,000 Jews to enter. The proposal was backed by the United States, and by the report of a joint Anglo-American Committee of Inquiry published in 1946, but the British resisted.

The Labour government, led in its policy by Foreign Secretary Ernest Bevin, had to contend with a number of issues in the Middle East. The United Kingdom had a large military installation in the Suez Canal zone in Egypt and the Abadan oil refinery in Iran, as well as, at its peak, 100,000 troops stationed in Palestine. Britain was heavily in debt, both to the United States and to its

colonial territories and protectorates including Egypt. Britain could not afford
to maintain its military control over large parts of the Middle East. However, the
United Kingdom wished to maintain as much influence as possible and protect its
strategic position.[10] This was for the sake of important trade routes, the reliability
of oil supply from the Gulf and the value of military bases in the region for any
future war against the Soviets. Britain, along with the United States, also feared
the spread of Communism and Soviet influence into the region.[11] These interests
created a need to maintain good relations with the Arabs and contain the rising
tide of anti-Western, pan-Arab nationalism.[12]

According to a famous critique by Elie Kedourie, Britain's intellectual and
official classes were also influenced by a particular view of the region Kedourie
termed the 'Chatham House Version'.[13] Kedourie attributed the 'Chatham House
Version' to the influence of Arnold Toynbee, the historian who was appointed
the first head of the Research Analysts department in the Foreign Office in 1943,
and was for 30 years the Director of the British foreign policy research centre
Chatham House. Toynbee acknowledged himself to be a 'Western spokesman
for the Arab cause'.[14] He saw the Arabs as a naturally unified entity that had
been artificially suppressed by the Ottomans and then divided up by oppressive
Western powers. He felt the Middle East's malaise to be a consequence of this
Western interference in the region, including support for Zionism. Toynbee
believed that Zionism itself was little better than Nazism, and in supporting it,
Britain had cheated the Arabs of Palestine out of their promised independence
and burdened the region with the Arab–Israel conflict.

The refusal of the British Government to allow Jews to enter Palestine after
World War II intensified both illegal Jewish immigration and the confrontation
between the British authorities and the Jews of Palestine. In November 1945,
the Haganah, the Jewish armed force established to defend Jewish communities,
joined forces with the radical Jewish Lechi and Irgun armed groups in an alliance
to conduct armed actions against the British. With Jewish violence against the
British intensifying, the Mandate forces heavily suppressed Jewish militancy,
arresting 3000 people in an operation at the end of June 1946. The violence
peaked when the Irgun bombed the British headquarters at the King David
Hotel on 22 July 1946, killing more than 90 people. This event, and the hanging
and booby trapping of the bodies of two British servicemen by the Irgun, led to
considerable anti-Jewish feeling in Britain, including anti-Jewish riots.

The mounting violence within Palestine, and international pressure to resolve
the Jewish refugee crisis in Europe, forced the British to turn the problem over

to the UN and hastened their desire to withdraw from the territory. Fearing that the Haganah was not ready for war with the Arabs, the Jewish leader in Palestine, David Ben Gurion, tried to delay Britain's departure and persuade Bevin that Britain should stay longer. He reasserted the case, made by Herzl and Weizmann before him, that the Jews in Palestine represented a foothold of European values in the Middle East. His efforts were to no avail.[15] Bevin was preoccupied with maintaining British influence in the wider Middle East and was personally unsympathetic to the Jews and the Zionist movement. The UN's commission, UNSCOP, recommended portioning the territory into two states, one Jewish and one Arab. In November 1947, the UN General Assembly approved the proposal, with Britain abstaining in the vote.

The Jewish Agency accepted the partition plan, but Palestinian and other Arab representatives rejected it. War broke out between Jews and Arabs in Palestine, with the fighting leading many Arabs to flee their homes to neighbouring countries or other parts of Palestine. In May 1948, the British pulled out the last of its troops and David Ben Gurion declared the independence of the State of Israel as a Jewish state. Simultaneously, the armies of Jordan, Syria, Egypt, Iraq and Lebanon, with additional forces from Saudi Arabia, invaded the nascent Jewish state. By 1949, Israel had repelled the Arab armies, had negotiated armistice agreements with their governments and was admitted to the UN. Its borders exceeded those that had been allotted to it by the UN, but the bulk of the territory intended for the Arab state by the partition plan was in the hands of Jordan, which annexed the West Bank, and Egypt, which occupied the Gaza Strip. Jerusalem was divided between Israeli and Jordanian control, with the Old City and its holy sites in Jordanian hands. The war resulted in a situation where between 500,000 and 940,000 Palestinian Arabs became refugees in neighbouring Arab countries.[16] In the first years of its existence, Israel's population was swelled by hundreds of thousands of Jewish refugees from Europe, and by Jews fleeing persecution in Middle Eastern countries.

After Israel's establishment

After Israel's establishment, British strategic priorities shifted. While maintaining good relations with the Arab states remained the first priority, the United States and the United Kingdom were also keen to ensure that the new Jewish state turned to them for support rather than to the Soviet Union. Britain recognized Israel in 1949. In 1950, Britain, France and the United States made the 'Tripartite

Agreement', committing to defend the integrity of the Israeli-Arab armistice and to coordinate arms supplies to Israel and the Arabs for their defence and to repel Soviet influence.[17] In the decades that followed, the readiness to supply heavy weaponry was often the key benchmark by which Israel measured its relations with the great powers, including Britain.[18]

However, the fear that Israel might fall under Soviet influence soon subsided.[19] In the early 1950s, Britain's policy in the region was determined largely by its desire to retain influence and prestige with Arab states.[20] Britain, along with the United States, was anxious not to encourage the rising tide of Arab anti-colonial nationalism and to prevent Communist inroads to the region.[21] In addition, between 1948 and 1960, the Middle East's oil rose as a proportion of global supply from one eighth to one quarter.[22] Britain also sought to maintain its exports to the Arab world, particularly in arms. The desire to maintain favour in the Arab world grew in the face of a developing relationship between the new Arab nationalist regime of Gamal Abdel Nasser in Egypt and the Soviet Union. The priority given to relations with the Arabs was reflected in an imbalance of arms sales between Israel and its Arab neighbours.[23] It led Conservative Prime Minister Anthony Eden to call in 1955 for the 1947 partition plan borders to be a factor in establishing a permanent peace between Israel and its Arab neighbours, a proposal which deeply soured the UK–Israel relationship at the time.[24]

Suez and the British exit from the Middle East

The Suez crisis of 1956 was a watershed moment in precipitating British withdrawal from the Middle East, with Britain attempting to force its will on Egypt, a state that had hitherto been under its influence, but without US support proving unable to do so. That year the United States and Britain, perturbed at the growing relationship between Egypt's Arab nationalist president, Nasser, and the Soviet Union, withdrew financial support for the Egyptian Aswan Dam infrastructure project. Nasser responded by nationalizing the Suez Canal, which was British and French-owned and a vital conduit for their oil supplies. At the same time, Israel was concerned about Nasser's military build-up and his support for raids by Palestinian armed groups into Israel from the Sinai desert. This led to a secret military pact between Britain, France and Israel to attack Egypt. Israel attacked the Sinai, while Britain and France captured the Canal Zone under the guise of peacemakers.[25] While the operation was a military success for Israel, it was a diplomatic disaster for Britain. The United Kingdom did not win the support of President Eisenhower who was entering an election campaign and feared alienating the Arab world. The United States withdrew financial support for Britain, creating an immediate and severe economic and political crisis in the United Kingdom, and forcing it to abandon the operation.[26] In early 1957, Israel acceded to American demands and withdrew from the Sinai.

The Suez episode was a key turning point after which the United States took over Britain's role as the dominant Western power with responsibility for repelling Soviet influence and protecting pro-Western regimes in the Middle East.[27] Furthermore, the story of Suez was etched deep into Britain's foreign policy culture, symbolizing the dangers of pursuing a foreign policy that contradicted the will of the United States. In the wake of this debacle, as Britain sought to distance itself from Israel's actions and repair its image in the Arab world, UK–Israel relations fell to a very low ebb.[28] Relations recovered gradually, including through cooperation to assist King Hussein of Jordan in the wake of the coup in Iraq in 1958. But while Britain sold arms to Israel in the 1950s and 1960s, its fear of being accused of pro-Israel bias by the Arabs limited the closeness of the relationship.[29] In 1959 and 1960, Britain also provided Israel with heavy water for its French-built plutonium reactor in Dimona, but it appears that any assistance this gave to Israel's development of nuclear weapons was inadvertent.[30]

During the 1960s, the region became increasingly polarized, with the Soviets arming Israel's Arab neighbours and Britain, the United States and France arming Israel to maintain the balance of power. Britain shared the US agenda to balance Soviet military support for Arab states, but it was far more dependent than the United States on its relations with the Arabs for its supply of oil and for its bases and influence in the region.[31] The underlying British national interest after Suez was in gradually withdrawing from its Gulf dependencies, thereby disengaging from its role in the region, while maintaining stability.[32] To the extent that Britain supplied arms to Israel, it was motivated by a desire to maintain a balance of power to prevent war, as opposed to a principled commitment to Israel. As a cable from the British Embassy in Tel Aviv to the Foreign Office in 1960 put it:

> We do not give the Israelis arms because they are pro-Western or because we admire their achievement. We give them arms because our interests in the Middle East are to keep the place quiet and to prevent war. Anything, which makes war in the Middle East more likely, is against the interests of the Western powers.[33]

While Britain became established as an important trading partner for Israel,[34] it did not, for example, condemn the Arab trade boycott of Israel. However, neutrality became harder to sustain as tensions between Israel and its Arab neighbours increased over the course of the 1960s.

The 1967 and 1973 Wars

The Six Day War added another significant layer to British policy considerations in the Israeli-Palestinian arena. A gradual increase in tensions, including a struggle for control of water sources between Israel and Syria, came to a head in 1967. In May of that year, Egypt expelled the UN separation force that had been in the Sinai Peninsula since the 1956 war and sent its own troops into the desert. Nasser threatened Israel's destruction, made a military pact with Syria and Jordan, and announced the closure of the Straits of Tiran to Israeli shipping. Three weeks of international diplomacy failed to resolve the crisis. An effort led by the Harold Wilson government to mobilize an international flotilla that would secure free passage through the Tiran Straits failed to get off the ground. Facing war on three fronts, Israel launched a pre-emptive attack against Egypt on 5 June 1967. Over the course of six days, Israel captured the Sinai Desert and Gaza Strip from Egypt, East Jerusalem and the West Bank from Jordan, and the Golan Heights from Syria.

Britain was sympathetic to Israel's position during the war. Wilson in particular, and much of his cabinet, was personally warm towards Zionism and its democratic socialist character and enjoyed good personal relations with Israeli leaders. Britain also welcomed a defeat for Nasser's radical, anti-Western Arab nationalism, which threatened the stability of oil-producing allies in the Gulf. The perception of sympathy for Israel damaged Britain's image in the Arab world.

However, the outcome of the war proved a turning point in the way Israel was viewed in Britain and elsewhere. For one thing, the extent of Israel's victory transformed Israel's image from a small and embattled state to that of a strong and victorious power, removing any doubts among the Western powers about the threats to its existence.[35] Furthermore, the status of the territories captured by Israel in the war, and the circumstances under which they should be traded for peace treaties with the Arab states, became a bone of contention not only between Israel and the Arabs, but also between Israel and Western governments, including Britain. London had a hand in the drafting of UN Security Council Resolution 242, reflecting Britain's interest in seeing a balanced overall settlement which would reduce tensions in the region.[36] The resolution set out the basis for resolving the conflict based on the twin principles of 'withdrawal of Israeli armed forces from territories of recent conflict' and 'respect for and acknowledgement of the sovereignty, territorial integrity and political independence of every state in the area'. While Israel formally accepted the principle of a peace agreement based on UNSC 242, perceiving itself to be in a position of strength it was content to wait for the Arabs to 'pick up the phone'.[37] Israel's apparent unwillingness to offer concessions that would get the ball rolling frustrated Britain.[38]

In this tense environment, while Britain remained committed to Israel's independence and security, maintaining good relations with the Arab states was the priority. One Foreign Office official wrote another in an internal correspondence in 1972:

> As Lord Janner once said: "Oil is thicker than Jewish blood." In our calculation it will have to remain so. If there is no real settlement of the Arab-Israeli conflict (and no one can be optimistic about the prospects) we cannot afford not to ensure that our very considerable interests in the Arab world are not, as a result, put at risk.[39]

The Foreign Office under Heath's Conservative government, from 1970 to 1974, was already concerned with the long-term problems being created by the consolidation of Israeli control in the West Bank.[40] While the Israeli development of infrastructure in the Occupied Territories created jobs and improved the economy for its Palestinian–Arab residents, British officials even then believed it was making a future peace settlement harder to achieve.[41]

This underlying frustration with Israel, and the perpetual concern not to alienate the Arab world – on which Britain was dependent for 30% of its oil – was the backdrop to the Heath government's policy of neutrality when Egypt and Syria launched a surprise attack on Israel in October 1973.[42] Also highly significant was Prime Minister Edward Heath's wider agenda of reorienting British foreign policy more in line with Europe. Britain had joined the European Economic Community (EEC) earlier in the year, committing it to the framing of a common European foreign policy and calling into question Britain's 'special relationship' with the United States. When the Arab world decided to pressure European countries not to support Israel by cutting back oil supplies, Britain secured a place on a coveted list of 'friendly countries' in Europe, along with

France and Spain. The desire to avoid the oil boycott ensured that Britain did not follow the United States by helping Israel to rearm after suffering heavy early losses in the war. Heath, under protest from Harold Wilson's Labour opposition, refused to supply spare parts for Israel's Centurion tanks or to provide landing rights in Cyprus for US military supply planes en route to Israel. Britain was also party to the EEC's first foreign policy declaration on the Middle East, made shortly after the war, which distinguished itself by explicitly recognizing the 'legitimate rights of the Palestinians', angering both the United States and Israel.[43]

Israel responded to the vulnerability of its military supplies exposed by the 1973 war by developing greater self-sufficiency in arms. Israel also became much more dependent on the United States as a supplier of arms and as a strategic partner, a trend that was already developing in the wake of the 1967 war, and in the face of large-scale Soviet supply of arms to the Arab states. From that time, British supply of heavy weapons to Israel declined in importance in the bilateral relationship, though Israel continued to be concerned about what Britain supplied to the Arabs.[44]

For the United States, the second defeat of Soviet-backed Arab nationalist forces in 1973 paved the way for them to exert greater influence over the Arab world, particularly Egypt. The success of the US-brokered Egypt–Israel peace process further raised US prestige as a power broker in the region, and the only power with significant sway over Israel. The US rewarded both Israel and Egypt for signing the treaty in 1979 with economic and military aid. The UK Labour government of Jim Callaghan played a marginal but supportive role in the Israel–Egypt peace process, hosting, for example, a round of talks in 1978.[45] This was in contrast to the French who were more openly suspicious of a separate peace between Egypt and Israel which left the Palestinian issue and the conflict with the wider Arab world unresolved. When Menachem Begin, the leader of the right-wing Likud party, and former head of the Irgun, displaced the centre-left Alignment block to become Israel's Prime Minister in 1977, the Callaghan government set aside the widespread British perception of Begin as a terrorist and duly welcomed him to Number Ten.[46]

Overall, the period saw a further evolution in Britain's diplomatic position, from being an independent player at the end of World War II, and subsequently a supporting actor behind the United States. After entry into the EEC, Britain found itself at the pro-American end of a European pack trying, and frequently struggling, to shape a common European position that did not compromise its special relationship with the United States, without angering the oil-producing Arab states.

The impact of the 1982 Lebanon War

This trend continued after the Conservatives returned to government in 1979. Britain's bilateral relations with Israel were helped by the perception of Margaret Thatcher – who represented a sizeable Jewish community in her Finchley constituency – as being sympathetic to Israel.[47] In a manner that prefigured Blair, Thatcher entered office with known personal sympathies for Jews in general, and a suspicion for the establishment Foreign Office. Thatcher's attitudes also prefigured Blair's in other ways. She was an Atlanticist who, in the mould of Churchill, saw Britain as in alliance with the United States for the protection of liberty. Though this was primarily in the face of the Communist threat, it also applied to the threat posed by Islamic radicalism following the Iranian revolution in 1979.[48]

Nonetheless, Britain's position on the Arab–Israeli conflict was increasingly coordinated with its European Community colleagues. British Foreign Secretary Lord Carrington was closely involved in the drafting of the EEC's 1980 Venice Declaration. This recognized the Palestinian rights to self-determination and the necessity of a role for the Palestine Liberation Organization (PLO) as representatives of the Palestinian people. It also called for an end to the occupation and criticized the construction of Israeli settlements in the Occupied Territories as a serious obstacle to peace.[49] Endorsement of the PLO was at odds with United States policy. The PLO, under the leadership of Yasser Arafat, was regarded by the United States and Israel as a terrorist organization. One of the effects of this position was to increase Israeli suspicion of European engagement in the peace process.[50]

While the Israel–Egypt peace treaty had brought international praise, and a Nobel peace prize for Begin as well as Anwar Sadat in 1978, a number of Israeli actions in the early 1980s attracted international criticism. These included the bombing of Iraq's Osirak nuclear reactor, the annexation of the Golan Heights captured from Syria and the acceleration of new settlement construction in the West Bank. However, it was Israel's 1982 invasion of Lebanon, triggered by the attempted assassination of Israeli Ambassador Shomo Argov in London by Palestinian Terrorists, that particularly alienated Thatcher from the Likud-led government in Jerusalem. Israel invaded initially to confront PLO forces in the south of the country responsible for shelling towns in northern Israel. It went on to besiege Beirut, expel the PLO from Lebanon and attempt unsuccessfully to install a friendly Christian-led government. Israel's actions which led to many civilian deaths, were widely condemned and led to a British arms embargo on Israel.[51] An Israeli state inquiry found that Israeli Defence Minister Ariel Sharon was indirectly responsible for the massacres of Palestinian civilians in the refugee camps of Sabra and Shatilla, carried out by Israel's Maronite Christian Lebanese allies in revenge for the assassination of their leader Bashir Gemayel.[52]

Thatcher privately pushed the Americans to take a tougher line towards Israel and urged them on in their efforts to promote peace.[53] Over time, she increasingly saw Israel less as an ally in containing the Soviets, and more as a liability, with its uncompromising policies increasing the threat of radical Soviet and Islamist forces expanding their influence.[54] Putting pressure on the Americans to, in turn, pressure Israel, was a clear sign that Britain did not consider itself to have an independent role or leverage over Israel. However, for some in the Foreign Office, the importance of European trade with Israel did give the United Kingdom and other European states leverage that they decided not to use. Oliver Miles recalled:

> I can remember in my day in the office, having draft submissions put up to me, putting recommendations to ministers saying, "we don't really have any effective means of putting pressure on Israel." And I said, "You can't say that. We may decide not to put effective pressure on Israel but there are ways we can do it. Who eats their grapefruit? We do . . . and the other Europeans do."[55]

The Thatcher government even made its own brief, independent attempt to promote the peace process by inviting a joint Jordanian–Palestinian delegation, including PLO representatives, to London for talks in 1985. The initiative collapsed when the Palestinian delegation was unwilling to endorse a statement recognizing Israel.[56]

While Thatcher expressed frustration with Israel in private, she did not allow this to dim her publicly expressed admiration.[57] She was angered when Foreign Office Minister David Mellor publicly upbraided an Israeli officer, an act she saw as undermining the relationship of trust which allowed Britain to mediate.[58] A symbol of Thatcher's desire to maintain warm relations with Israel, despite frustrations at Israeli policies, was Thatcher's visit to the country in 1986, the first by a serving British Prime Minister.[59] Nonetheless, the international perception of Israel, damaged by the 1982 Lebanon War, was further harmed by Israel's attempts to suppress the First Intifada, a spontaneous grass roots uprising by Palestinians living under Israeli occupation in the Gaza Strip and West Bank in December 1987.[60]

The era of the peace process

The end of the Cold War and the successful US-led coalition to expel Iraqi forces from Kuwait in 1991 made possible the Madrid peace conference. This brought Israel and many of its Arab neighbours, including a Palestinian delegation, around the table for the first time. However, relations between Britain and Israel remained difficult so long as a right-wing Israeli government, hostile to the peace process, was in power. A Labour-led coalition government under Yitzhak Rabin replaced the Likud-dominated government of Yitzhak Shamir in 1992.

Rabin saw advancing the peace process as being in Israel's strategic interests. He understood the immense cost to Israel of continuing to rule over the increasingly restive Palestinian population in the Occupied Territories, and he recognized the limitations in the use of force to protect Israel's vital interests. He believed it was necessary for Israel to secure its relationship with the United States, including American economic support in the form of loan guarantees. Rabin was aware that in a post-Cold War era in which the United States was the undisputed global hegemonic power, Israel's status as a strategic asset was in question due to the friction its conflict with the Palestinians caused with the Arab world. He also wanted to transform Israel's relations with pro-Western Arab states in the face of the growing threat posed by the radical states of Iraq and Iran, with their development of long-range missiles and weapons of mass destruction (WMD).[61]

The breakthrough of the Oslo accords, signed between Israel and the PLO in 1993, made it much easier for Britain to build closer relations with Israel, reducing the usual concerns about alienating the Arab world. Under the Oslo process, Israel and the PLO recognized each other and negotiated a series of agreements which created Palestinian self-rule over the major Palestinian population centres in the Gaza Strip and the West Bank. The plan was that a series of interim agreements would build confidence before the reaching of a comprehensive agreement which would end the conflict.

Britain's ambassador in Tel Aviv from 1993 to 1995, Andrew Burns, remembered the two years following the signing of the Oslo Accords as a very positive time. The election of an Israeli government committed to the peace process created the context for John Major's government to lift the arms embargo on Israel, end a ban on the sale of North Sea oil to Israel and work within the European Union (EU) to end the Arab boycott on British and European firms doing business with Israel.[62] Even though Rabin did not comprehensively freeze settlement construction, because of his progressive attitude to the peace process, the United Kingdom and the United States were willing to give him more leeway than they did for Shamir before him.[63] Israel's relations with the European Union as a whole took a significant step forward with the signing of the EU–Israel Association Agreement in 1995. John Major travelled to Israel the same year with a large British trade delegation.[64] In the same visit, Major became the first British Prime Minister to meet with PLO leader Yasser Arafat. According to historian Martin Gilbert, who accompanied Major, the Prime Minister conducted his meeting very much in line with the wishes of the Israelis, with whom he consulted beforehand, by pressing, in particular, for elections to be held in the Palestinian Territories.[65]

The manner in which US President Bill Clinton took ownership of the Oslo process further cemented US dominance in the role of Arab–Israeli peace broker. The European Union became increasingly involved, but mainly as financial backers to the newly formed Palestinian Authority. This position also developed a British stake in the task of Palestinian institution-building.[66]

The period of optimism was ended by the deeply shocking assassination of Yitzhak Rabin by a Jewish extremist and the subsequent term of Benjamin Netanyahu as Prime Minister from 1996 to 1999. Netanyahu was instinctively conservative, deeply suspicious of the Palestinians, reluctant to make territorial compromise and politically hamstrung. With the Israeli Prime Minister being such an unenthusiastic partner in the Oslo process, progress slowed. Though Netanyahu did sign an agreement with Arafat to hand over control of most of Hebron in early 1997, by the time Francis Cornish became British Ambassador in Tel Aviv in 1998 he recalled, 'The huge expectation was that it [the peace process] was likely to fall apart with dangerous consequences.'[67]

Blair's and Labour's inheritance

What legacy did the history of Britain's involvement in the region leave by the time Blair came to power in 1997? What imprint had it left on institutions such as the British foreign office and on Britain's perception of its interests? The inherited memory of the Mandate, and a sense of British responsibility, was still present in the Foreign Office in the Blair period. Retired Arabist Basil Eastwood, who was Ambassador to Syria during Blair's first term, recalled:

> When I first joined the foreign office in 1967, one of my first bosses, who joined in 1947 said, "Basil there is now this thing called the Arab-Israel dispute." He had been told by his first boss that this would see him through to the end of his career and he turned to me and said, "Basil I think it will see you through to the end of your career."[68]

Even in the Blair era, British diplomats were, to a surprising extent, conscious of the historic responsibility Britain carried for the Israeli-Palestinian dispute. Jeremy Greenstock, ambassador to the UN from 1998 to 2003, considered historic British support for Zionism and the Balfour Declaration to be one of the roots of Britain's ongoing tendency to be more pro-Israel than other European states.[69]

UK officials were also conscious of how Britain's historic involvement in the Middle East also impacted on how it was seen by people in the region. Oliver Miles, a senior Arabist who retired from the Foreign Office in 1996, said that Arabs were cognizant of Britain's role in the creation of a Jewish state, meaning there was 'an historical responsibility there which you can't escape'.[70] For Israelis too, memories of the Mandate occasionally coloured how they responded to British involvement in the region. In an unusually angry confrontation between Tony Blair's envoy Lord Levy and Israeli Prime Minister Ariel Sharon in 2002, sparked by a disagreement over a meeting Levy had just held with Yasser Arafat, Sharon apparently left Levy with the words, 'The British mandate is now finished.'[71]

However, beyond creating a special sense of British involvement in the issue, it is hard to discern a concrete impact the historic legacy of the Mandate period had for British policy in the Israeli-Palestinian arena in the Blair era. By the time Labour came to power, 50 years of history had passed. The sum pattern of development in the relationship was an uneven but marked process of normalization in the relationship between Britain and Israel.[72] Neither Blair nor his ministers, nor the officials of the Foreign Office, had personal memories of the Mandate period. There is little evidence that the second- and third-hand memories of the Mandate period had a significant impact on policy makers. Indeed, soon after coming to power, Blair specifically rejected the notion that Britain should feel guilty about its imperial history.[73] Events that took place after the mandate, including the 1967 War, the 1982 Lebanon War and the peace process, were more significant factors defining the context of British policy making in the Blair period. As discussed in more detail in Chapter 2, these events had a distinct significance for sections of the Labour Party and British Left.

However, Britain's imperial history in the region left an important institutional legacy in the Foreign Office. Though British military presence in the Gulf ended in 1971, Britain maintained very close relations with Gulf Arab rulers, and there remained large numbers of diplomats learning Arabic and spending much of their careers in one of Britain's 22 missions to Arab states. By contrast, there were relatively few diplomats with experience of Israel. Given the importance of contacts in the Arab world, a posting in Israel was for many years regarded as an unhelpful career move for a British diplomat.[74] This structural factor, which meant that far more Foreign and Commonwealth Office (FCO) officials had experience of working in the Arab world than of working in Israel, remained a factor in the Blair period. Arabic remained one of the FCO's four most frequently taught languages, with an average of 63 officers trained in Arabic each year between 2004 and 2008.[75]

However, it is important to note that senior officials from the Blair period saw the pro-Arab inclination of the Foreign Office as being in relative decline. Francis Cornish, Ambassador to Israel from 1998 to 2001, explained:

> To this day there is a big group of people who understand the Arab world. Many of them love the Arab world. [But] they are dying out now . . . until quite recently you had people who were involved with the Gulf States and so on [which] were British protectorates, so they had a more than ordinary relationship with these people.[76]

Not only had the generations of diplomats who had direct experience of the period when Gulf States were British protectorates died out, but the advent of the peace process began to erode the straightforward divisions of the past. As Andrew Burns, who served as Ambassador to Israel from 1992 to 1995, stated:

> There was undoubtedly a point at which no Arabist would want to be posted to Israel because it would compromise their career elsewhere . . . If you have learned Arabic you don't want to be prevented from postings in the Arab world and you would not accept a posting in Israel.

But over time, things changed, as Burns explained:

> On the one hand the Arab countries concerned are more realistic and don't blackball people, and on the other it has become so central to British policy.

It's been more important for people's careers to engage in these issues of central political concern than not.[77]

The latter point made by Burns was reinforced by the Blair government. With the Arab-Israeli conflict being such a high-profile issue, and one of increasing personal priority to the Prime Minister, the post of Ambassador to Israel became a place to get noticed. David Manning was handpicked by Tony Blair to be his personal foreign policy chief in 2001, having impressed while in the post in Tel Aviv. Sherard Cowper-Coles went to the post in 2001 from being Robin Cook's Principal Private Secretary (PPS) and went on to serve in other key postings in Saudi Arabia and Afghanistan. Simon McDonald went from being Ambassador to Israel from 2003 to 2005 to leading Jack Straw's Private Office and then to being Gordon Brown's foreign policy adviser in Number Ten. This point was acknowledged by Israeli official Roey Gilad who noted the increasing tendency of top FCO officials to have served in Israel, saying, 'I do not think the FCO these days are Arabists as such. If you will check the Middle East directorate one can see that the senior people there . . . may speak Hebrew.'[78] A posting in Tel Aviv became increasingly attractive also for younger officials, providing not only the chance to serve in an area of very high international interest, but also to live in a highly westernized Mediterranean city, widely regarded as a vibrant and comfortable place to live.[79]

It should also be noted that in any period, officials are individuals affected by their own independent views and experiences. Foreign Office officials noted that experience of the Arab world did not automatically translate into unquestioning sympathy for it. FCO Arabists sometimes talked of their relationship with the Arab world as 'love-hate', believing the Arabs to sometimes be their own worst enemies.[80] The Blair period, therefore, saw the traditional perception of pro-Arab inclination in the FCO still holding some validity, but somewhat diminished.

The importance for Britain's strategic and commercial interests of retaining good relations with Arab states remained a constant. Britain developed its own sources of oil in the North Sea in the 1970s. However, ensuring stability in the region for the sake of reliable global oil markets remained key, as did the maintenance of the stability and prosperity of oil-rich Arab states, which provided lucrative export markets and were important for the stability of global financial markets. The 'Al Yammamah' arms deal with Saudi Arabia, initiated in 1985, was once described as the 'largest single defence deal in history'.[81] By 1997, of a total $16Bn in British exports to the Middle East, $11.4Bn were to Gulf Cooperation Council (GCC) states.[82]

In other ways, the Middle East itself, and Britain's place in it, had changed dramatically with the end of the Cold War, the events of First Gulf War, the increased influence of the United States in the region, and, in particular, the peace process. The Oslo process made dealing with Arabs and Israelis less of a zero-sum game for Britain. The mutual recognition of Israel and the PLO led to an initial thawing of Arab hostility to Israel. By 1997, full diplomatic relations had been established between Israel and Jordan, and Israeli interest offices had opened in Oman, Qatar, Morocco, Tunisia and Mauritania. At the same time, the peace process intensified a dynamic whereby the warmth of bilateral relations between Britain and Israel was linked to the perceived enthusiasm of the Israeli government to advance the peace process. In the 1990s, Britain was far better disposed to dealing with the Labour governments of Yitzhak Rabin and Shimon Peres than Benjamin Netanyahu's government. Former Chair of Labour Friends of Israel (LFI) and cabinet minister James Purnell said that a good predictor of how people within the Labour Party feel about Israel was, 'whether they are seeing Israel as making the first move for peace or resisting peace. So when they think that there is someone there who is willing to make sacrifices for peace then they are less critical.'[83]

With respect to Britain's wider foreign policy strategy, the US–UK special relationship remained an important and enduring feature when Labour came to power in 1997.[84] It had deep roots in the two World Wars and the Cold War which left a legacy of close military and intelligence cooperation.[85] The relationship also had a very strong economic dimension, with very high levels of investment travelling both ways across the Atlantic.[86] In the post-war era, British leaders have seen the 'special relationship' with the United States, the primary global economic and military power, as a way to maximize Britain's own global influence. The quality of the relationship has often been judged by the quality of the relationship of the Prime Minister with the US President.[87] Being close to the President of the United States brings the British Prime Minister prestige on the world stage and a special role as the self-appointed bridge between Europe and the US. There has been a tendency for the special relationship with the US to pull the Prime Minister in a more Israel-sympathetic direction than the officials of the Foreign Office might like.[88]

This desire to be close to the US has generally led Britain to resist a fully independent European role in the peace process, with the Heath government the most obvious exception. The US, like Britain, has a legacy of balancing its relationship with Israel with its relations with Arab states.[89] However, US support for Israel is much more deeply rooted in its political culture. America's pro-Israel consensus is anchored not only by the influence of America's sizeable Jewish community or the strategic value of Israel as a counterweight to anti-Western elements in the region, but also by a broader American view of Israel as a like-minded liberal democracy.[90] The UK–US special relationship has contributed to Britain's unique position, balancing its support for US diplomacy with the typically more pro-Arab positions taken by others in Europe, particularly France.[91]

The significance of the challenge of balancing between the United States and the European Union was increasing as the Blair government came into power. The EU's engagement in the Israeli-Palestinian arena as a single unit increased considerably from the 1970s.[92] Other European states shared many of the UK's interests in the Middle East, including maintaining stability, promoting trade interests, ensuring reliable supplies of oil and gas and addressing the threat posed by radical anti-Western elements. For European states close to North Africa, there was an additional motivation to maintain stability and promote prosperity so as to avoid waves of immigrants from North Africa.[93] In 1995, the European Union launched the European-Mediterranean 'Euromed' process, also known as the Barcelona process. The programme aimed to extend the EU's principles of free trade and regional cooperation to the Middle East, through bilateral dialogue and agreements between the European Union and individual states, and cooperative multilateral institutions. For Israel, the most open and developed of the regional economies, this represented an important opportunity to increase its integration with the European market, which was vital for its economic success. Furthermore, the multilateral institutions were the only forums in which Israeli officials could interact with some of their counterparts from regional nations with which they had no diplomatic relations.[94] Israel also welcomed EU financial support for the nascent Palestinian Authority. The European Union collectively, and through the bilateral donations of its member states, was enthusiastic to make a success of the peace process, and became a key financial prop for Palestinian institutions. A Spanish diplomat, Miguel Moratinos, was appointed as an EU envoy to the Middle East, and in 1997, a British initiative led to the creation of an EU–Israel dialogue on development of the Palestinian Economy.[95]

Overall however, attempts to develop a common European foreign had not by 1997, significantly affected the independence of British policy-making in the Israeli-Palestinian arena. 'Normal' foreign policy considerations of member states – in the UK's case its more pro-US inclinations – prevented a united EU position emerging beyond a long-term commitment to assisting a negotiated solution.[96] Britain tended to consider its own role, and that of the European Union, to be secondary to the US, while other states, particularly France, consistently sought to balance overwhelming American power.[97]

Turning to domestic political interests, the Blair government inherited a dynamic situation. Throughout the history of British involvement in the Israeli-Palestinian arena, there have always been influential members of the British Jewish community working to press Israel's case with the country's political leadership.[98] In the early years of the Zionist movement, Zionism was highly divisive for British Jews,[99] but from 1945, most British Jews have had a strong affiliation with Zionism and Israel.[100] At least since the late 1970s, from both right and left-wing perspectives, British Jews have engaged critically with Israel's policies,[101] but British Jewry has remained on the whole strongly supportive of Israel.[102]

The Board of Deputies, a representative body of Jewish synagogues and communal organizations, formally represents the British Jewish community. But beyond this formal representation, well placed individuals within the community with personal connections in high levels of government have played an important role in promoting sympathy for Israel in the British establishment.[103] The long-standing role of British Jews promoting support for Zionism and Israel among the country's political and social elite continued to be relevant in the Blair period. Aside from individual relationships developed between leading members of the community and political leaders, Jewish donors funded the secretariats of pro-Israel caucuses in the major political parties – Labour Friends of Israel and Conservative Friends of Israel. These groups took MPs on study trips to Israel, briefed MPs for parliamentary and public debates and built connections between British politicians and their Israeli counterparts. After the outbreak of the Second Intifada, British Jews also established the Britain Israel Communications and Research Centre (BICOM) to promote 'a more supportive environment for Israel in the UK' principally through work with the media.[104] Then, in 2003, the Jewish Leadership Council was formed to better co-ordinate the political activities of various Jewish leaders and organizations on behalf of the community.

Evaluating the significance of British Jews on British policy in the middle East, Andrew Burns, former British Ambassador to Israel and former Chair of the Anglo-Israel Association, said:

> [The role of British Jews has been] in terms of Britain-Israel [bilateral relations], very, very important. In terms of Britain-Middle East or peace process generally,

important but obviously matched by comparable expressions of views coming from all sort of other society.[105]

There is a history of British Jews working directly to try and promote reconciliation between Israel and the Arab world. Perhaps the most prominent example was the failed 1987 London agreement to establish an international peace conference, drafted by King Hussein of Jordan and then Israeli Foreign Minister Shimon Peres, at a secret meeting hosted in London by Lord Mishcon. The initiative ultimately foundered due to the objections of the hawkish Israeli Prime Minister Yitzhak Shamir.[106]

While the British Jewish community had long played a role in promoting support for Israel, the increased political mobilization of British Muslims was a new factor which became relevant in the Blair period. Britain's diverse Muslim population mainly originated from the Asian Subcontinent. However, in the late 1980s and 1990s, a phenomenon developed in the United Kingdom and elsewhere in Europe, of second- and third-generation Muslims identifying politically with international causes involving Muslims, including the Israeli-Palestinian issue.[107]

A watershed moment in the politicization of British Muslims was the publication of 'The Satanic Verses', a novel by British-Indian writer Salman Rushdie, which many Muslims felt was highly offensive to Islam.[108] The Rushdie affair succeeded in politically mobilizing British Muslims, many of whom protested, with some participating in public burnings of the book. The affair created an opportunity for British Muslims originating from South Asia, and influenced by the Islamist ideology of Sayyid Abul A'la Maududi and the Pakistani Jamaat-e-Islami party, to position themselves as leaders and spokesmen for British Muslims, through the formation of the UK Action Committee on Islamic Affairs (UKACIA). The presence on British shores of radical Islamist preachers such as Abu Hamsa al-Masri, exiled from their Arab home countries, and the presence of Saudi-funded religious scholars, also contributed to the politicization and, in some cases, radicalization of British Muslims.[109]

By the mid-1990s, the Conservative government saw the need for a recognized national body to politically represent British Muslims.[110] The Muslim Council of Britain (MCB) was established in 1997 in response to this call. UKACIA was the precursor for the MCB.[111] The MCB counted among its numerous affiliates the Muslim Association of Britain (MAB), an organization aligned with the Muslim Brotherhood. When the Blair government came to power in 1997, the MCB became its vehicle of choice for engaging with British Muslims.[112]

The question of Palestine was not a central concern to most British Muslims up until the 1980s.[113] The issue of Kashmir had greater resonance for many British Muslims with roots in South Asia.[114] Oliver Miles recalled:

> When I was head of the [Middle East and North Africa] department in the Foreign Office [from 1980–1983] I was very much aware of the Arab community in London, but the Arab community in London at that time was relatively small. It was very influential, it was an important community. For example, it controlled probably some of the most influential newspapers in the Arab world – it still does – but it was not a major sector of the British population and it did not have any obvious links – obvious to me, maybe there were links that I was not aware of – with other Muslims groups, like people from the sub-continent and so on.[115]

The issue began to come on to the British Muslim agenda following the outbreak of the First Intifada in 1987.[116] Subsequently the response of some British Muslims to the First Gulf War in 1991 indicated the growing place Palestine had on their agenda. Foreign Office Minister Douglas Hogg was heckled at a conference of British Muslims for supporting the war in Iraq while rejecting similar action to end Israeli occupation of Arab lands.[117]

While the main focus for the newly established MCB in Labour's first term was domestic issues such as legislation on race relations, it also had a strong foreign policy agenda. When Tony Blair addressed an MCB event for the first time in 1999, he spoke about Kosovo, but remarkably, did not mention the Israeli-Palestinian issue at all. However, speaking in response, the MCB's leader, Iqbal Sacranie, called on Blair to bring 'the courageous, moral and humanitarian stand' he had taken on Kosovo to bear on the issues of 'Palestine, Jammu and Kashmir and the continuing suffering of the civilian population of Iraq'. In October 2000, shortly after the outbreak of the Second Intifada, Sacranie wrote, 'the question of Palestine and the status of Jerusalem is the foremost international concern on the agenda of Muslims', adding that the MCB would 'exert all its moral, financial and political influence upon the British government to pressure Israel into accepting a fair and just solution of the Jerusalem issue.'

The politicization of British Muslims had particular significance for a Labour government. With constituencies containing large Muslim populations tending to be represented by Labour MPs, the formation of a Labour government in 1997 meant that for the first time, a significant number of government MPs and ministers represented constituencies with large and politically conscious

Muslim populations. Jack Straw, Home Secretary in Blair's first government, had 25,000 Muslims in his constituency, and was a strong supporter of the MCB.

This changing pattern of domestic interests added another layer of complexity to the considerations of British policy makers with regard to the Israeli-Palestinian arena. This layer was in addition to Britain's underlying strategic interests in the region and Britain's broader set of global alliances, in particular, with the US and the European Union. At the same time, another factor which cannot be ignored is the significance of the views and predispositions of individual decision makers. At important moments, individual decision makers contributed to the shape and substance of British policy through their personal attitudes to the Israeli-Palestinian issue, often shaped by their personal experiences and the wider world views they brought to both their domestic and foreign policy agenda.

New Labour and the Israeli-Palestinian Issue

Labour up to the end of the Mandate

The British Labour Party which Blair came to lead in 1994 had its own distinctive history in terms of its relationship to the Israeli-Palestinian conflict. The European left in general has had a conflicted view on the Zionist enterprise throughout the twentieth century. In the wake of the Balfour Declaration, there were those who saw Zionism positively as a way to transform Jewish society and to bring progress to Palestine. Others, particularly on the far left, saw Zionism as a colonial settler movement and a tool of British imperialism.[1] The pro-Zionist inclination was supported by personal ties between the Labour Party and the Zionist movement. There was an ideological sympathy and admiration for the Zionist aspiration to create a socialist state that would give justice and a homeland to the Jewish masses of Eastern Europe.[2] There was also an ideological inclination to the Jewish national movement which was regarded as bringing progress and civilization to the region.[3]

The Labour Party reaffirmed its support for the Jewish National Home promised in the Balfour Declaration on 11 occasions between 1917 and 1945 and it opposed the 1939 MacDonald White Paper which severely restricted Jewish immigration to Palestine, thereby denying Jews a refuge from the Holocaust.[4] The horrors of the Holocaust intensified Zionist sympathy within the Labour Party; a sentiment reinforced by the Palestinian Arab leadership's decision to ally itself with Hitler and support the Nazi war effort. In 1944, the Labour Party was so concerned for the plight of European Jews that it backed a National Executive Committee (NEC) policy statement that called for transferring Arabs out of Palestine in order to allow for Jewish immigration.[5]

The pro-Zionist leaning in the Labour Party had a particularly articulate standard bearer in the voice of Member of Parliament Richard Crossman, who had seen the horrors of the death camps shortly after their liberation, and who was appointed by the Labour government to the Anglo-American committee in 1946. In an astute and clear-sighted personal account of his experiences serving on the commission, in the displaced persons camps of Europe and in Palestine, Crossman wrote, 'I had reached the conclusion that Zionism, whether we liked it or not, was a bare necessity for the existence of eastern European Jewry.' The desire shared by Jews in Britain and the United States for a Jewish state was a fact that 'must be accepted as a political force by the Gentile world whose anti-Semitism was its main cause.' The demand of the survivors of the Holocaust to move to Palestine was, he felt, 'not the product of Zionist organization, but the expression of the most primitive urge, the urge for survival.' He believed that the influx of 100,000 Jewish Holocaust survivors and the creation of a Jewish state in part of Palestine was an injustice to the Arab population, but that it was a lesser injustice than denying the Jewish people their national rights. He was influenced in this conclusion by his view of the Jews in Palestine that, 'no Western colonist in any other country had done so little harm, or disturbed so little the life of the indigenous people.' Moreover, he added, in the name of social progress, 'the Jews had set going revolutionary forces which, in the long run, would benefit the Arabs.' The Jews, Crossman perceived, had created in Palestine not only a national home, but also 'something more, a socialist commonwealth, intensely democratic, intensely collectivist, and strong enough to fend for itself.'[6]

However, Labour's Foreign Secretary Ernest Bevin felt very differently. Bevin believed firmly in the maintenance of British power overseas and saw the Middle East to be second in importance to British interests only to the United Kingdom itself. These interests created a need to maintain good relations with the Arab states and contain the rising tide of anti-Western, pan-Arab nationalism. For Bevin, in his attempts to maintain Britain's influence in the Arab world, the Palestine problem was a severe irritation. Moreover, Bevin was staunchly anti-Communist and feared that a Jewish state, dominated by the Socialist Zionist movement, could turn into a Communist state under Soviet influence.[7]

But Bevin's hostility towards Zionism was not derived purely from the *raison d'état*, it was also mixed in with his view of Zionism and the Jews. Bevin sympathized with the Arab view of Zionism as a colonial invasion, believing that Palestine was rightfully an Arab territory, and that a solution to the Jewish refugee problem ought to be found in Europe. His principal experience of Jews, in the East End of London, led him to see Jews as a religious group, rather than a nation. Though the question of whether Bevin hated Jews *per se* is disputed, it can be said at least that he frequently expressed anti-Semitic remarks and resorted to anti-Jewish stereotypes.[8] Anti-Semitism is not required to explain Bevin's anti-Zionism, given that his position was in line with the predominant realist view of the Foreign Office. But it was very much under Bevin's influence that the Attlee government ultimately abstained from the UN vote on the 1947 partition plan. The US State Department was similarly against partition, but was overruled by President Truman who instructed the US delegation to vote in favour.[9]

Israel's collusion with Empire

Once Israel was established, fears that it might ally with the Soviet Union proved unfounded, allowing for the re-establishment of a pro-Zionist consensus in the Labour Party.[10] The first major challenge to this consensus was the 1956 Suez-Sinai war. The year 1956 was an important one in the linking of pro-Arab sentiment and anti-imperialism on the left across Europe. This was due both to distaste at the actions of Britain and France as imperial powers against Egypt in the Middle East and the Algerian war for independence against the French. The British Labour Party was fiercely opposed to British military action in Suez on the basis that legal, rather than military means should have been pursued in response to Egypt's nationalization of the Suez Canal. Labour MPs argued that military action contravened the charter of UN, that there had been no declaration of war and that Parliament had been deceived.[11]

Overall, however, the war did not lead to a loss of Labour support for Israel. Labour politicians distinguished between the motives of Israel, with which they sympathized, and those of the Conservative government, whose actions they opposed.[12] However by placing itself on the same side as the colonial powers, Israel did put a dent in its image for some on the left.[13] The war also led Labour MPs to give more serious consideration to the cause of Arab nationalism.[14]

The year 1956 was also significant for the brutal Soviet repression of the Hungarian uprising against Communist rule and the emergence of Krushchev's 'secret speech' denouncing Stalin. These events combined were important in the development of the New Left movement in Europe, which was disillusioned with the repressive Soviet Union, but hopeful for the socialist potential of post-colonial states.[15] This later paved the way for a strong left identification with the Palestinian cause as an anti-colonialist national liberation movement, as it rose to prominence in the late 1960s and 1970s. This was particularly the case for a new generation of left wing political activists who had no personal memory of the fight against fascism and anti-Semitism, the horrors of the Holocaust, or the establishment of Israel, and lacked the sympathy for the Jewish cause that was prominent for many of their forebears. Nevertheless, when Labour returned to power in 1964, there were still warm ties between the ruling Labour Party in Israel and the British Labour Party based on strong personal connections and enduring social-democratic ideological affinities.[16] Harold Wilson was a particular admirer of Israel, and considered most of his cabinet to be supportive.[17]

The era of occupation

The 1967 Six-Day War triggered major changes in the relationship of the left with Israel. During the conflict itself, the Wilson-led Labour government was largely sympathetic to Israel's position.[18] Labour's ideological sympathies for Zionism dating back to the 1940s remained strong. There was still limited sympathy for Arab nationalism in the party, which was seen as backward, feudalistic and sometimes fascistic. The Palestinian national movement had yet to make an impact as a political movement independent of pan-Arab nationalism. Wilson's government also pursued more broadly an Atlanticist policy, which meant firm opposition to the Soviet Union which supported the Arab states.[19] Labour's position also reflected widespread public sympathy for Israel. However, Israel's dramatic and overwhelming military victory in the 1967 war led to the transformation of Israel's image from an embattled social-democracy and a victim of Arab aggression to an occupying and expansionist power.

After the 1967 war, criticism of Israel and sympathy for the Arabs grew more prominent on the Labour left. This was in the context of the increasing radicalism of New Left politics in Europe and the United States, partly fuelled by America's controversial war in Vietnam. The view of Israel as an ally to imperial US power suppressing anti-colonial Arab nationalism gained greater traction. A marked increase in US support for Israel predated the 1967 war, with the US beginning to arm Israel under Kennedy. This growing strategic relationship between Israel and the US contributed to the perception on the left of Israel as a 'hegemonic regional power closely allied with the USA.'[20] There was also social change in the United Kingdom. There was a shift among British Jews from the political left to the right as their social conditions improved. At the same time, left-wing groups sought increasingly to appeal to Black and Asian immigrants who were expected to be attracted to third-world causes.[21]

Criticism of Israel also flowed from the state's policies. Shortly after the Six-Day War, Israel annexed East Jerusalem, in a move that no other country recognized. Then it began a series of other measures to change the status quo in the territories it had captured from its Arab neighbours. Israel established military bases and subsequently civilian settlements within all the territories captured in 1967, in an attempt to establish a permanent hold on key strategic locations. This retrospectively changed the complexion of the 1967 war. Israel had gone to war believing its survival was at stake, and not for the sake of territorial expansion. However, its settlement activities, undertaken once the land was in its hands, lent credence to the charge that Israel had acted as an aggressive imperial power seeking territorial aggrandizement.

Meanwhile, Arab nationalists, led by Nasser, made greater use of socialist terminology. In the 1970s, the PLO brought to prominence the Palestinian cause as a national independence movement fighting for liberation from Israeli occupation. The Palestinian cause garnered recognition initially through violent attacks on Israeli civilians in Israel and around the world, and subsequently through a successful diplomatic campaign.[22] This led to the PLO gaining observer status at the UN in 1974 and the passing of a General Assembly resolution equating Zionism with racism in 1975. These achievements came with the support of the Soviet Union and the Non-Aligned Movement. Nonetheless, the Labour leadership, under Wilson and then Callaghan, retained its deep-rooted sympathy for Israel. They were Europe's most outspoken critics of the PLO and Callaghan was more openly supportive of the Israel–Egypt peace agreement than his French and German counterparts.[23]

Labour's turn against Israel

After 1977, political change within Israel became an increasingly important factor in further alienating the British left. The displacement of the left-of-centre Alignment bloc that year by the right-wing Likud party led by Menachem Begin removed an important factor which bonded the British Labour Party with the Israel government. However, it was the 1982 Lebanon War which did most to precipitate a collapse of the pro-Israel consensus within the British Labour Party.[24] Israel's invasion of Lebanon, which had become a base for the PLO to attack northern Israel, did enormous damage to Israel's international standing. Particularly damaging were massacres of Sunni Muslims in Sabra and Shatila by

Israel's Christian Phalange allies. Gerald Kaufman, shadow Foreign Secretary from 1987 to 1992, described the change from sympathy to scepticism thus:

> Forty years ago, at the time of the Six Day War, the Labour Party was overwhelmingly pro-Israel . . . But over the years and particularly since '82 and Lebanon the Labour Party has come to the view, which I share . . . That it's one thing for the Israelis to fight to defend their country, it's another thing to wage a series of aggressive wars within Lebanon, and secondly to refuse to make peace with the Palestinians.[25]

The impact of these events on the Labour Party, however, was amplified by a changing political context in the British and wider European left. During the 1980s, the generation of politicians influenced by New Left politics, who entered the Labour Party in the years after the Six-Day War, were reaching political maturity. The anti-colonial influence of the New Left had, by the 1980s, become influential in the Labour Party and in wider liberal discourse.[26] Labour attracted more middle-class members, less concerned with traditional working-class issues and more interested in global issues, such as anti-racism and nuclear disarmament. Grassroots Labour activists began to actively campaign on behalf of Palestinian nationalism and against Israel. Edmunds notes an important development whereby:

> The Palestinian cause became closely associated with the new kind of left activist. The party's policy in favour of Palestinian statehood in the early 1980s was part of the wider process which led to the adoption of unilateralism and a policy of withdrawal from the EC.[27]

A notable exemplar of this trend was Ken Livingstone who actively promoted the Palestinian cause from his position as head of the Greater London Council to which he was elected in 1981. Labour's national leadership swung sharply to the left after the general election defeat of 1979, electing Michael Foot as leader in 1980. Foot, wrote Naughtie, 'gave voice to a worldview based on the premise that the United States was the greatest threat to peace.'[28] The Labour left's anti-imperialism and suspicion of US power and global capitalism fed into its criticism of Israel, as Israel came to be seen as a lingering example of colonialism, and ever-increasingly associated with the United States. Left-wing leaders like Tony Benn, who has been supportive of Zionism in the 1940s, became harsh critics of Israel. This process of disillusionment was fed by the development of Israel, not into a socialist utopia characterized by the kibbutz, but into a society similar economically to those of Western Europe.[29]

Guilt at Britain's historic role, and the support Labour politicians once showed for Israel, may also have animated the growing hostility of Labour and the British left to Israel. As Jonathan Freedland suggested, for a politician like Tony Benn, who in the 1940s was passionately pro-Zionist, and for a left-wing newspaper like the Guardian, which was pro-Zionist before the establishment of the state, there was a sense of personal or institutional responsibility for the conflict. Freedland said, 'I think there is a view that history plays a part here and Britain most certainly, and Labour, feel some kind of responsibility for that conflict. There is a sense of guilt that, "we were on the wrong side of this." '[30] It was not just the left of the party that became more critical of Israel. While there were always those who remained staunch supporters of Israel, as Edmunds wrote, 'most of the party's sections began to challenge Labour's traditional loyalty to Israel and to advocate a policy in favour of Palestinian national rights.'[31] The perception of Israel, damaged by the Lebanon War, was further harmed by Israel's forceful attempts to contain the First Intifada, a spontaneous grass roots uprising that broke out in the Gaza Strip and the West Bank in December 1987.[32]

For parts of left, the end of the Cold War made the Israeli-Palestinian issue even more of a priority. As has been argued by Anthony Julius, among others, the ideological and political collapse of the left which culminated in the demise of the Soviet Union at the end of the 1980s resulted in leftists in the West rallying around specific causes, rather than the 'general transformation of society that was socialism's goal'. Anti-Zionism was one of these causes and according to Julius, 'perhaps now even the principal one'. Julius claims: 'The 'fight for Palestine' appears to some to be the successor to the 'fight for socialism'.[33]

In sum, it can be said that between the 1940s and 1980s, the perception of Israel and Zionism on the left changed from being an anti-colonial movement for national emancipation and a human rights imperative to being an archetypal, colonial movement and agent of US-led neo-imperialism. This was a position held most determinedly on the left of the party, but which also came to influence the party more widely. Numerous developments led to this change. There was an international change in left-wing politics unrelated to the Middle East, whereby the New Left emerged with a focus on global issues such as post-colonialism, as opposed to traditional working-class concerns. There were changes within Britain and the British Labour Party, with the party shifting sharply to the left and coming under the increasing influence of New Left politics. There were also significant changes in the Israeli-Palestinian arena, including the entrenchment of the occupation after 1967, the successful PLO campaign for international recognition in the 1970s and 1980s and the shift to the right in Israel and the Lebanon war.

The politics of Blair and New Labour

In 1983, the year Blair was first elected to Parliament, the Labour Party had drifted to the left of mainstream public opinion. Its radical agenda, including unilateral nuclear disarmament, withdrawal from the EEC and renationalization, was heavily defeated in the general election. The party was internally divided on foreign policy. Atlanticists on the right believed Britain's role in the world was to be in close alliance with the US. They were opposed by those on the left who were suspicious of capitalist America and who were more in sympathy with international socialism.[34] Under the leadership of Neil Kinnock and Roy Hattersley, from 1983 to 1992, the Labour Party made a considerable journey away from its left-wing positions of the early 1980s. This included shifting Labour policy to take a more sympathetic position on Israel and to rebuild bridges with the British Jewish community.[35] However, the party still failed to win the trust of enough of the electorate and stuttered to a fourth consecutive election defeat in 1992.

After the sudden death of Kinnock's successor, John Smith, in 1994, the Labour Party chose Tony Blair as its leader, not because he best represented the views of the party members, but because it accepted the need for further modernization and reform to make the party electable.[36] In the words of John Rentoul, 'it wanted to win the next general election badly enough to give the Blair the benefit of its many doubts.'[37] Tony Blair was 41 when he became party leader. He was the son of a law lecturer and barrister, Leo Blair, whose political ambitions in the Conservative party were cut short by a stroke. Born in Edinburgh, Blair attended Fettes, a public boarding school in Scotland, before reading law at Oxford and practising as a barrister.[38] Though it would be wrong to suggest that the Labour Party was socially or culturally homogenous, Blair's personal and political profile made him something of an outsider within the party.[39] He came relatively late to party politics, not getting involved until after university. He was not driven by a personal connection with the working class, a trade union background or Marxist ideology. He was motivated by a sense of personal responsibility to engage with the problems of society, linked to a religious conviction which began to develop while he was at university. He was also influenced by his ideologically driven partner Cherie Booth.[40] Blair began to adopt a Christian socialist political philosophy at university, influenced by the moral philosophy of twentieth-century British thinker, John MacMurray.[41] The key elements of Blair's emerging philosophy were a strong sense of moral absolutism, combined with a feeling of responsibility to society and social causes.

Blair wrote about his Christian Socialist thinking in the foreword to a 1992 compilation of Christian Socialist essays, declaring:

> Christianity is a very tough religion. . . . There is right and wrong. There is good and bad. We all know this, of course, but it has become fashionable to be uncomfortable about such language. But when we look at our world today and how much needs to be done, we should not hesitate to make such judgements. And then follow them with determination.[42]

This passage was indicative of Blair's readiness to make definitive moral judgements, his belief that it is possible to change the world and his sense of personal responsibility to try and do so. Blair openly cited William Gladstone, the Christian moralist, Liberal Prime Minister of the Victorian era, as one of his political heroes.[43] Both the tendencies of idealist moral certainty and activism would feature prominently in Blair's approach to foreign policy as Prime Minister.

Blair's brand of religious moralism was not of the exclusive kind. While he was confirmed as a Christian at university, he was never a 'Bible bashing' or evangelical Christian.[44] Blair showed admiration for the 'Abrahamic religions'.[45] Blair developed an interest and respect for the Jewish faith before he became party leader through friendships with British Jews.[46] He spoke more than once about his admiration for the Jewish community and its values, for example, telling a Labour Friends of Israel annual lunch in 2004:

> I've certainly made no secret of the fact that Labour has drawn tremendous inspiration from the Jewish community. Jewish values – based on the importance of family, community and justice – are shared by all of the most successful communities in Britain.[47]

After becoming leader, Blair and his close group of modernizers, including fellow MPs Gordon Brown and Peter Mandelson, communications director Alistair Campbell and strategist Philip Gould, had a focused determination to transform the Labour Party and make it electable.[48] They rebranded the party as 'New Labour' and distanced it from the unpopular policies of the past. A key symbol of reform was the rewriting of Clause IV of the party's constitution to replace the socialist commitment to 'common ownership of the means of production' with a commitment to creating a community in which 'wealth and opportunity are in the hands of the many, not the few'.[49]

While Blair was a believer in moral absolutes, he rejected traditional political dogmas and dichotomies. This was in part an application of the tactical device of 'triangulation' learnt from the Clinton campaign team in the United States. The principle was to adopt policy positions that cut between left and right-wing poles on an issue.[50] The goal was to stay in the political centre-ground, where polling showed that the majority of the voters were. Blair's famous sound bite, 'Tough on crime, tough on the causes of crime,' with which he came to be associated as Shadow Home Secretary in 1993, was an early example. Blair rejected the traditional dichotomy between blaming the individual for crime and blaming society by arguing that there were two sides to the problem, both of which had to be addressed.[51] Blair adopted a similar sound bite with regard to his foreign policy, rejecting the dilemma of Britain choosing between loyalty to the European Union and loyalty to the US, by declaring that Britain would be, 'Strong in Europe and strong with the US'.[52]

Over time, Blair sought to define his approach as the positive political philosophy of the 'Third Way'. As Blair set out in a 1998 pamphlet, the Third Way meant a modernized approach to social democracy that was above all pragmatic. While the goal of 'a distribution of the benefits of progress' remained fixed, means should be constantly revised in the light of changes taking place in industrialized societies.[53] Over time, the notion of the Third Way was criticized as lacking in content, and gradually fell from use.[54] Nevertheless, it is an important indication of the general approach of Blair and New Labour to problem solving. Blair was a moral activist who believed it was possible to change the world. At the same time, he was pragmatic and rejected traditional polarities and dogmas, prioritizing ends over means.

New Labour's turn to Israel

Foreign policy was relatively marginal to New Labour.[55] Nonetheless, the New Labour reforms did include foreign policy. New Labour embraced economic globalization and interdependence,[56] and explicitly subscribed to Atlanticism and neoliberalism.[57] As Williams wrote, 'the party's elite articulated (consciously or otherwise) the Fukuyaman argument that liberal capitalist ideas represented the "end of history."[58]

The New Labour world view also included a more positive attitude towards Israel for a number of reasons. Blair's own personal sympathy for Israel was clearly a factor. Blair's Israel-sympathetic tendency was rooted initially in his friendships in the British Jewish community and his overarching political tendencies, rather than in a detailed knowledge or analysis of the situation.[59] His interest in the Israeli-Palestinian arena developed, in particular, during his time as leader of the opposition. A fervent interest grew from Blair's first visit to Israel in 1993 on a trip organized by the Israeli Embassy in London.[60] An important facilitator in this was his close associate and chief fundraiser Michael Levy (later Lord Levy). Levy was closely connected to Israel, where he kept a home and was well networked within the Israeli establishment due to his involvement with British Zionist charities.[61] He was particularly well connected on the Israeli left. His son Daniel moved to Israel and served as an official in the governments of Yitzhak Rabin and Ehud Barak.

Levy met Blair shortly before he became leader of the party and raised money for Blair's leadership campaign.[62] With Blair as leader, Levy widened the funding base of the party to include wealthy businessmen. This not only increased the party's resources and reduced its financial dependency on trade unions but also positioned it as more pro-business.[63] A number of those that Levy turned to for donations were wealthy Jewish philanthropists. Levy quickly developed a personal relationship with Blair and positioned himself as the Jewish community's gateway to the Labour leader.[64] Levy also helped to deepen and frame Blair's understanding of the Israeli-Palestinian arena. While in Israel for the funeral of Yitzhak Rabin, after Rabin's assassination in November 1995, Levy arranged meetings between Blair and senior Israeli political figures, including Labour ministers Yossi Beilin and Ephraim Sneh.[65] Blair spoke on the phone with Rabin's successor, Shimon Peres.[66] According to Levy, Blair returned to Britain 'animated' by the issue and the prospects for peace, and with an enhanced determination to play a role in the peace process.[67] Given the relative insignificance of the British role in the peace process, it might seem odd that even as leader of the opposition Blair might have hoped to play a role. James Purnell explained that Blair's desire to be involved in the Israeli-Palestinian issue fitted with his personality, saying, 'Temperamentally, Tony never wants to be on the sidelines, bleating about things, he wants to be in there trying to resolve them.'[68]

Levy's dual role as Blair's fundraiser and as his conduit to the Israeli political establishment left Blair open to the suspicion that he was influenced in his support for Israel by the party's financial dependence on Levy and his network of donors. However, Andrew Hood, who was a special adviser to Robin Cook as foreign Secretary in Blair's first term, believed that ultimately, Blair's attitude towards the issue, 'was something that he believed deep down irrespective of anything else and if we'd been looking to get support from the Muslim community, Tony would still have had the same view because it was his view of where things were right'.[69] Diplomats who worked closely with Blair concurred that Blair's attitudes were rooted in deeply held convictions and were very much his own. Francis Cornish, Britain's Ambassador in Tel Aviv from 1998 to 2001, who was later a critic of Blair's Middle East policy, said: 'Levy is not a strategic thinker, he is a fixer, a contacts man . . . The strategic thinking came from Blair'.[70]

When Blair became Prime Minister in 1997, his knowledge of the issues in the Israeli-Palestinian arena was still, according to Levy, 'pretty flimsy'.[71] However, despite still not having a complete grip on all the details, Blair's broad view on the issues was fixed. Andrew Hood summarized it as follows:

> Tony's view was that Israel is a democracy in a region that has been besieged. That there are of course injustices that have resulted from the Occupied Territories which need to be resolved. That in practice the way to resolve those is by taking the heat out of the argument; stopping people standing on soap boxes and calling one another names and getting them to sit down with each other and work out a solution. So to move away from absolutism to try and find pragmatic ways forward. So he starts from being a committed friend who believes deep down in Israel's right to exist, has huge respect for the struggle that's gone on there to set up a young nation, and for the history that led to Israel being established. But at the same time is equally committed to trying to find a pragmatic way forward where they can put aside the pressures of their extremists and try and create a consensus and a coalition of the centre ground.[72]

At the Labour Friends of Israel annual lunch in 2004, Blair said, 'When people ask me why I'm a friend of Israel, I give them a simple answer: because I admire Israel, her people and what they have achieved since her creation'.[73] In more spontaneous remarks to an LFI reception in 2006, Blair said:

> I have never actually found it hard to be friend of Israel, I am proud to be a friend of Israel. Whatever differences there are with whatever government is in power from time to time, it is a democracy; it has a right to exist. It is actually a country

that if only we could change the conditions in the region, could live willingly in peace and be in many ways particularly in economic development and indeed in some ways political development, a model for the region.[74]

For Blair, therefore, Israel's existence was not only a legal and political reality, but also a moral right and an admirable ongoing endeavour. It is significant that his early exposure to the issue, though directed from the Israeli perspective, also came through the prism of the Oslo Accords and the process to address the demands of the Palestinian people. In effect, Blair's early schooling in the issues came from the perspective of the Israeli Zionist left. His position never wavered from the approach of trying to reach an agreement that gave Palestinians their rights while protecting Israel's security.

According to Francis Cornish, not only did Blair have a clear view about the Israeli-Palestinian issue when coming into power, but also he had a strong sense of its wider importance. According to Cornish, 'right from the word go', Blair was of the opinion, 'that this was a running sore that was extremely difficult to heal, but as long as it continued to fester it ran the risk of doing untold damage to all sorts of indirectly related issues.'[75] David Manning, who was Britain's Ambassador in Tel Aviv when Blair came into office, and subsequently Blair's foreign policy adviser in Number Ten, agreed. According to Manning, 'From the very beginning of his time as PM in my experience he has been very involved with this and very exercised by it.'[76]

It was also significant that other key New Labour modernizers had warm views towards Israel. Gordon Brown was the next most important figure in the party after Blair, and his most significant rival in the cabinet. The sharp rivalry between Blair, Brown and their two camps of supporters was the most fraught internal division within the party during the Blair premiership. But Brown, like Blair, had strong sympathies for Israel, inherited form his father, who had been a Chair of the Church of Scotland's Israel committee, and visited the country frequently.[77] So while the Israeli-Palestinian issue divided the party, it was not a feature of the most significant rift in the party, between Blairites and Brownites. The third key architect of New Labour was Peter Mandelson, who was credited with rebranding the party, and who mentored Blair and Brown on their dealings with the media. Mandelson's father was Jewish and worked for the Jewish Chronicle. Mandelson visited and wrote about Israel as a young man, and spoke publicly in support of Israel during the Second Intifada.[78]

While Blair's personal interest in the issue and the pro-Israel sympathies of other key New Labour figures were significant, there were wider reasons for New Labour's pro-Israel position. The shift to a more positive attitude to Israel was part of a general desire to distance the party from the unpopular Labour policies of the past, including the foreign policy positions of the 1980s.[79] According to journalist Jonathan Freedland, 'What defines New Labour is a desire to be everything old Labour wasn't . . . Part of that package was Israel.'[80] In reality, New Labour's warmth to Israel was not a one hundred and eighty degree turn. As already mentioned, there were always some in the party who maintained their long-held support for Israel, and the process of consciously rebalancing the party's policy on Israel began under the leadership of Kinnock and Hattersley. However, Blair's modernizing reforms and rebranding of the party as 'New Labour' was more radical and more calculated in defining itself in opposition to positions claimed by the left.

Whereas the left was anti-American, New Labour was Atlanticist. Labour was determined to reaffirm Britain's special relationship with America, which had been strained under the Major government.[81] Whereas old Labour was suspicious of global capitalism, New Labour had total faith in liberal market democracy as the ultimate form of sociopolitical organization, and a commitment promoting this overseas.[82] Consistent with this reorientation was a rejection of the post-colonial guilt that affected parts the British left and the Foreign Office. In his first Guildhall speech, an annual foreign policy address given by the Prime Minister, Blair declared, 'There is a lot of rubbish talked about the Empire. In my view, we should not either be apologizing for it or wringing our hands about it. It is a fact of our history. It was, in many ways, a most extraordinary achievement.'[83] Engagement with the Israeli-Palestinian issue was also consistent with New Labour's broader agenda to 'restore Britain's pride and influence as a leading force for good in the world.'[84] Blair and New Labour espoused the principle that Britain could play a unique role in global affairs as a leading power in the European Union that acts as a bridge between Europe and the US.[85]

The more pro-Israel stance was also made possible by the changed situation in the region itself. Blair became leader in 1994 at the height of the Oslo peace process which was made possible by the mutual recognition of Israel and the PLO in 1993. During this period, support for Israelis or Palestinians was much less of a zero-sum game than it had been previously, and it was considerably more comfortable for politicians on the left to show warmth to Israel. MPs from Labour Friends of Israel (LFI), the pro-Israel caucus within the Parliamentary

Labour Party (PLP), and the Labour Middle East Council (LMEC), the pro-Arab caucus in the party, travelled together to the region on joint delegations.[86] Such cooperation ceased completely when the peace process broke down after 2000.[87]

Against the backdrop of these factors, a pro-Israel position became part of the political identity of the modernizing New Labour wing of the party. From 1997 onwards, it became commonplace for LFI to be chaired by rising, Blairite backbench MPs, firmly affiliated with the modernizing wing of the party, and on their way into ministerial ranks. The chairs included Kim Howells, Jim Murphy, Jane Kennedy, Stephen Twigg, James Purnell, David Cairns and Iain Wright, all of whom subsequently enjoyed ministerial careers. Vice-chairs who went on to become ministers included Meg Munn, Ivan Lewis and Barry Gardiner. Another vice-chair, Mike Gapes, became Chair of the Foreign Affairs Select Committee. Other MPs picked out for ministerial careers, who identified with LFI and were members of its Parliamentary Executive, included Andy Burnham, Jim Knight and Huw Irranca-Davies. Some of the most active LFI supporters were either Jewish themselves or had a significant Jewish population in their constituency. Louise Ellman was a prominent example of the former and Andrew Dismore of the latter. However, most of the leading LFI MPs were neither Jewish themselves nor had many Jewish constituents.

In September 1997, Siôn Simon claimed that a pro-Israel leaning was, 'an infallible admission test' for the 'sect of Labour modernisers'. Simon, a journalist who himself went on to become a Labour MP active in LFI, argued that what made the modernizing wing of the Labour Party instinctively sympathetic towards Israel was a deep distrust for the dogmatic, 'politically correct Left orthodoxy of the Eighties'. Sympathy for Israel became a clear identifying badge for Labour modernizers in part because Israel was such a 'bogeyman' for the Labour Party of the 1980s.[88] The re-emergence of a strong pro-Israel caucus in Labour was made possible by the Oslo process. But it was also fuelled by individuals in the party wanting to take positions that associated them with Blair and New Labour. The LFI reception became one of the largest and most well-attended events at the Labour Party's annual conference, with Blair routinely making an impromptu speech at the event, and other key front benchers also attending.[89] This link between New Labour and a pro-Israel stance endured through the first two terms of Blair's government and survived the breakdown of the peace process. By June 2004, journalist Rob Blackhurst was still able to refer to LFI's 'status as a favoured club for young Blairites'.[90]

For some MPs, the roots of their attachment to Israel predated New Labour and went back to their experiences of student politics. Stephen Twigg went to university already with a positive predisposition to Israel, based on his contact with left-wing Zionists in the Labour Party when growing up in Southgate, but he acknowledged that:

> Student politics gave those of us who went through it a certain kind of grounding and set of relationships. A lot of it is quite a personal thing and you get to know people who were involved in UJS [Union of Jewish Students] when we were involved in Labour students and on a lot of things we had alliances and formed friendships.[91]

In a number of cases, rising Blairites had their first contact with Israel and the Israel-Palestine question through Jewish friends at university or even from travelling to Israel on a trip sponsored by the Union of Jewish Students (UJS).[92] Three consecutive Presidents of the National Union of Students, Stephen Twigg (1990–1992), Lorna Fitzsimons (1992–1994) and Jim Murphy (1994–1996), went on to become MPs active in LFI. Fitzsimons, having narrowly lost her seat in 2005, became Chief Executive of the pro-Israel Britain Israel Communications and Research Centre (BICOM).

Countervailing factors: The Labour left and the Muslim lobby

While there was a clear association between New Labour and a pro-Israel inclination, it would be a mistake to think that pro-Israel attitudes dominated the party. John Rentoul wrote that 'The weakness of New Labour . . . was the lack of committed "Blairites" at any level in the party except the very top.'[93] This gap in perspectives between Blair and much of his party was apparent with regard to the Israeli-Palestinian issue. While the hard left of the party was relatively small and marginalized, there remained a significant soft left element in the PLP.[94] Former political editor of the New Statesman Martin Bright described how the Israeli-Palestinian issue continued to be seen by a sizeable bulk of Labour MPs:

> At quite a high level of the Parliamentary Labour Party, once you raise the issue of either the Middle East peace process in general or questions around

radicalization and Islamism, if they have had a past either within revolutionary politics themselves, i.e. as Trotskyites generally or Communists, or if indeed they've been involved in the left of the Labour Party at any point, they will generally have a sympathy for the Palestinian cause. They will be sceptical if you start to raise questions about the nature of Islamic radicalism . . . And they will often relate it as well to the Northern Ireland situation. So you will have a scenario where if someone argues that you should tread very carefully when talking to militants they will invoke the Northern Ireland peace process as an example of why one must always keep lines of communication open to revolutionary movements.[95]

Bright further argued that the romantic association with the Palestinian cause did not just affect the left-wing of the party or those that identified with it. He speculated that some MPs who largely accepted Blair's modernization of the Labour Party and the swing to the right also took pro-Palestinian positions as a way of asserting their 'leftist' credentials with the party grass roots. It is, he said:

> a relatively easy position on the left to say . . . 'You may think that I have kowtowed too much to the Blairite agenda, you make think that New Labour is meaningless and I no longer have any principles, but look at my position on Israel. That's where you can test if I am genuinely a person of the left.

While Blair and his cohort were able to largely determine the direction of the party, Labour remained a coalition in which individuals representing a wide range of political views maintained an important stake. In Blair's first cabinet, two of the most prominent left-wing figures in the party held foreign policy portfolios. Robin Cook became Foreign Secretary, and Clare Short, Secretary for International Development.

Short was one of the members of Blair's government most obviously identified on the left of the party.[96] Short resigned from the Labour front bench in 1991 over the conduct of the First Gulf War, declaring:

> The background to this conflict and the major cause of the disaster is United States policy in the Middle East . . . which has basically been to prop up the state of Israel, to back it in all its intransigence and its gross breaches of international law in terms of its behaviour towards the Palestinians in the occupied territories.[97]

She argued that Israel's treatment of the Palestinians in the Occupied Territories was the cause of anger in the Arab world against America, and that it was for fear of Israel's military might that Arab states felt the need to arm themselves. In a speech made one month after Labour came to power, she caused controversy by saying, 'I am very conscious of the historical wrongs done to the Palestinian people – and the unfairness of the world's expectation that they should make sacrifices to make up for the evil done by Europeans during the Holocaust.'[98]

While Short was the most vocal supporter of the Palestinian cause in the cabinet, Robin Cook was the highest-ranking representative of the left-wing. Born the grandson of a miner and the son of a teacher near Glasgow, he had old left roots.[99] Cook followed Labour's path towards the political centre ground under Neil Kinnock, dropping opposition to Britain's nuclear arsenal, the role of NATO and membership of the EEC. Nonetheless, under Blair's leadership he was still considered, in the words of Andrew Rawnsley, 'the custodian of the party's conscience from the Blairites.'[100]

As well as the continuing influence of the left-wing ideological causes within the party, another factor which increasingly influenced the Labour Party during the period in question was the growing political activism of British Muslims. Britain's growing Muslim population concentrated in inner cities was more inclined to vote Labour, and constituencies with large Muslim populations tended to be represented by Labour MPs. According to the 2001 census, there were 39 constituencies in which Muslims constituted more than 10% of the population and 101 constituencies in which Muslims were at least 5% of the population. In Birmingham, Sparkbrook and Small Heath, the percentage of Muslims was 48.8%.[101] All of those with more than 10% Muslim population were Labour. By contrast, the Jewish population of Britain declined rapidly following World War II, dropping 40% to just 275,000 in 2005.[102] By 2001, there were just four constituencies in which Jews constituted more than 10% of the population, and 11 constituencies in which Jews were at least 5% of the population. The highest Jewish population of any constituencies were the neighbouring districts of Hendon and Finchley and Golders Green, each with 18%.[103]

The views of MPs are affected by many factors, and no direct correlation can be drawn between the ethnic demographics of their constituency and positions taken on foreign policy. However, MPs are clearly sensitive and responsive to the concerns of their constituents. Organizations like the Muslim Council of Britain (MCB) and the Muslim Public Affairs Committee (MPAC) became progressively more organized in mobilizing the Muslim vote to lobby MPs, and to judge them on their stance on 'Muslim issues'.

Inayat Bunglawala, a senior official of the MCB, asserted that, 'Certainly those MPs who had a sizeable Muslim constituency tended to know more about the

MCB and politics generally among British Muslims than other MPs.' He noted further that, 'Those ministers who had over a number of years extensive contact with their local Muslim communities brought that experience with them into government.'[104] As will be noted in later chapters, Jack Straw, who represented a constituency with a 25% Muslim minority, and served in Blair's cabinets as Home Secretary and then as Foreign Secretary, was a significant example.

3

'Patient and Quiet Diplomacy' in Labour's First Term

Who made policy?

A widely noted feature of policy-making during the Blair premiership was the centralization of decision-making in the hands of the Prime Minister and his personal circle of advisers. The enthusiasm of Blair and his clique of New Labour modernizers to rebrand the party included a desire to create strong leadership, in place of the divisions that had damaged the party in the past. Blair's own persona was an important part of the rebranding of New Labour. A close-up image of his face beamed from the cover of the 1997 manifesto. His huge electoral landslides in 1997 and 2001 were each interpreted as a strong personal mandate, enhancing his power over party colleagues. This gave him the power not only to override objections from the weakened Conservative opposition, but also frequently to disregard objections from within his own party. Blair's was a 'command and control' premiership, according to Peter Hennessy, in which he functioned as a chief executive, rather than the traditional 'primus inter pares'.[1] The main exception was Gordon Brown, who had considerable control over economic and domestic policy. But this, if anything, freed up Blair to focus on foreign affairs.

The Prime Minister often agreed policies bilaterally with individual ministers or with small groups. As a result, the role of Cabinet was downgraded as a forum for discussing policy, a factor criticized by the Butler Report with regard to the Iraq War. This shift in political power was reflected in the changing nature of governing institutions. The staff in the Prime Minister's Office multiplied, in particular, with a profusion of politically appointed policy advisers with considerable powers and influence. Blair trusted in his close advisers, including Jonathan Powell, his chief of staff, Alistair Campbell, his director of communications, and Sally Morgan, his political secretary. Powell, a former diplomat, had a unique overview of all policy areas and was a key adviser to the Prime Minister on Foreign Policy.[2]

Another feature of government for which Blair was criticized in the Butler Report was the informality of his style, in particular, the tendency to make decisions in informal groups of close advisers.[3] Michael Foley wrote of Blair during his first term that, 'Adherence to institutional restrictions and social conventions has a far lower priority than the pursuit of a theme, or the need to adapt patterns of behaviour and thought to achieve objectives.'[4] A significant example of this in the Israeli-Palestinian arena was the appointment of Lord Levy as Blair's personal envoy. A consequence of the proliferation of personal advisers and the informality in decision-making was a loss of clarity about the process and outcomes of foreign policy-making.[5] As Hollis wrote,

> Blair had a formal, an informal and a semi-formal network of personal confidants, including professional diplomats as well as political allies, whose influence on policy derived from their access to the Prime Minister. Thus there were different layers in the foreign policy-making process that could not be understood by simply examining the chain of command at the Foreign Office and its formal dealings with No. 10.[6]

An important consequence of the centralization of foreign policy was a downgrading of the role of the Foreign and Commonwealth Office (FCO). The FCO's prestige as a source of expertise on the Middle East was already in decline when Blair came to power.[7] There was an overall shift in the nature of foreign policy-making from an approach orientated around geographical regions and alliances to one based on global themes and challenges, which were disseminated from the top down. Andrew Burns remarked on the change that came about at the end of his FCO career:

> We used to pin everything on our alliance, because it's the Cold War against the Soviets. What we have moved to now is concerns about climate change, human rights, and various other issues which are of a generic kind, where you are pursuing a broader cause rather than relationships with specific countries.[8]

In an environment of increasing globalization, Blair and New Labour were taken with the idea of branding Britain as a 'force for good in the world'.[9] When reflected in foreign policy, this meant an increasing focus on worldwide issues like the environment, terrorism, conflict prevention, human rights and development.[10] This shift to a more thematic, rather than geographical, view of foreign policy was also reflected in Labour's creation of a Department for International Development (DfID) in 1997. Established with Clare Short as its first Secretary of State, the department siphoned off the functions of the Overseas Development Agency in the FCO, with the goal of promoting sustainable development and tackling global poverty. As part of this role, it spent tens of millions of pounds every year on programmes in the Palestinian Territories. Clare Short herself was a consistent and vocal advocate of the Palestinian cause to the Prime Minister and in Cabinet. Her threats to resign around the run-up to the Iraq War put pressure on Blair to generate progress on the Israeli-Palestinian track. But as was illustrated with regard to the War in Iraq, her overall impact on the direction of policy was limited.

The influence of Blair's first Foreign Secretary Robin Cook was not helped by early problems he encountered in his role. On entering government as foreign secretary, Cook declared: 'Our foreign policy must have an ethical dimension and must support the demands of other peoples for the democratic rights on which we insist for ourselves.' He claimed his new direction, 'supplies an ethical content to foreign policy and recognizes that the national interest cannot be defined only by narrow realpolitik'.[11] Diplomats steeped in the realist institutional code of the FCO, including Blair's chief of staff Jonathan Powell, were dismissive of the notion of an 'ethical foreign policy'.[12] The Prime Minister's office proved resistant to some of the applications of the ethical foreign policy, and was concerned that proposals by Cook for new restrictions on arms trade would damage the industry and cost British jobs.[13] The idea of an 'ethical foreign policy' was soon undermined, among other things, by controversial arms sales to countries with poor human rights records, including Indonesia, damaging the credibility of the Foreign Secretary.[14]

In the Israeli-Palestinian arena, the extent to which the Prime Minister dominated decision-making was accentuated by the fact that Blair had a strong personal view about Israel. Andrew Hood, special adviser to Robin Cook as Foreign Secretary during Blair's first term, recalled that on coming to power, 'Tony was completely and utterly fixed in his view on what the right thing was to do for Britain on the issue.'[15] Andrew Burns felt that Cook, by contrast, though holding a strong view on settlements, was initially fairly cautious in his approach to the Middle East.[16] Andrew Hood recalled that it was part of his role to ensure that Cook's and Blair's positions were aligned, and that in Hood's words, the 'Foreign [Office] officials understood the alignment.'

While other ministries touched on the Israeli-Palestinian arena at points, none significantly influenced the direction of policy. The Department for Trade and Industry, for example, was responsible for granting arms export licenses, but it was the Foreign Office that was supposed to set the policy on arms exports, and the FCO was at times overruled directly by the Prime Minister when he was unhappy with their decision.

A steep learning curve

Given Cook's roots on the left of the Labour Party, there was clear potential for him to diverge from Blair's position on the Israeli-Palestinian issue. However, it would be wrong to assume a sharp policy divide between Cook and the Foreign Office taking a pro-Arab line, and Blair being pro-Israel. From the perspective of former British Ambassador to Israel, Francis Cornish, there was no marked gap between the Prime Minister's office and the Foreign Office.[17] The avoidance of policy gaps between Blair and Cook on the Israeli-Palestinian issue was helped by the fact that when they entered office, there was a strong international consensus supporting the continuation of the Oslo process. The Clinton administration was intensively engaged in trying to push Israel to give more territory over to Palestinian control in the West Bank, and refrain from settlement construction. The leadership of the Palestinian Authority (PA) under Yasser Arafat was expected to clamp down on Hamas and other violent Palestinian groups opposed to the peace process. However, this was a frustrating time for British diplomats. Cornish recalled:

> Tensions were not terribly high by Israeli standards. But there was a sense that this is not going very far; Bibi [Benjamin Netanyahu] does not want it to. The huge expectation was that it was likely to fall apart with dangerous consequences.[18]

In 1996, Benjamin Netanyahu narrowly defeated Labour leader Shimon Peres following the assassination of Yitzhak Rabin. Netanyahu was reluctant to make territorial concessions and was unwilling to confront coalition partners by stopping settlement construction. Periodic suicide bombings, carried out by armed Palestinian Islamist groups Hamas and Islamic Jihad against Israeli civilians, helped him to justify his approach.

When Middle East Minister Derek Fatchett toured the region in May 1997 and January 1998, he balanced criticism of both sides for the stalls in the peace process. He forcefully criticized Israeli settlement building and movement restrictions in the West Bank and called for implementation of Israeli withdrawals that had been agreed by Rabin and Peres under the 1995 Interim Agreement. He also challenged Arafat's Palestinian Authority on the question of financial accountability, raised questions over the Palestinian's record on human rights and focused attention on Palestinian efforts on security. At this stage, Netanyahu was demanding assurances from the PLO that it had revised its charter to remove clauses inconsistent with the peace process. Fatchett secured a letter to the Prime Minister from Arafat detailing the clauses that had been removed to try and resolve the issue.[19]

In January 1998, the United Kingdom took over the six-month rotating presidency of the European Union. The organization had been seeking a more active engagement in the Middle East with the appointment of a special envoy in 1996. Leading an active European engagement in the peace process, in support of the US, fitted well with Blair's view of Britain as being a leading power in Europe and a bridge between the European Union and the United States. Britain listed promoting the Middle East peace process as one of its priorities for the presidency. However, Blair stressed that it was strictly in a role that supported and did not compete with US leadership.[20] Blair was asked by the Arab daily Al Hayat newspaper if there was a danger for Britain's standing in the Arab world of being associated too closely with the US, and he responded:

> We support US efforts to revive the peace process because we believe that the US are best placed to broker a deal which will provide a firm basis for a resumption of negotiations . . . At the same time, the European Union clearly has an important role to play alongside the US . . . and in my view that role could be more active.[21]

He was also asked about the perception that his government was pro-Israel, following an address he had made to a Labour Friends of Israel event, and replied:

> I am aware of the perception in the Arab world that the Labour government is somehow more pro-Israeli or less well-disposed toward the Arab world than its predecessors. I am keen to dispel that impression. It is true that the Labour Party has long-standing ties with the Israeli Labour Party, based on our common membership of the Socialist International. We also have good friends in the Arab world . . . I do not see any tension between these friendships; indeed I believe they can help us to play a constructive role in the search for peace and reconciliation in the Middle East.

He added, in true third-way form, 'Our policy is neither pro-Israeli nor pro-Arab, but pro-peace.'

Yet, it remained a period of relative stagnation for the peace process, with Clinton's personal authority and engagement being diminished by the Lewinsky scandal which broke out in January 1998.[22] The vacuum created more opportunities for European involvement. Foreign Secretary Robin Cook visited in March 1998. Prior to his visit, Cook made a speech launching an European Union plan to reinvigorate the peace process through mutual confidence-building measures, EU assistance for the Palestinians in economy and security fields, and renewed European diplomacy.[23] However, Cook's trip was marred when a planned visit to an Israeli housing project in East Jerusalem, intended to express disapproval, led to the Foreign Secretary being jostled by protesting settlers, causing a row with the Israeli government and the cancellation of a planned dinner with Netanyahu. An editorial in the *Times* described it as a 'Diplomatic Disaster'.[24] Though Cook had wanted to make a political point with the visit, he was clearly not seeking the kind of public confrontation that his actions created. British officials who were there claimed that the incident was caused more by Israel reneging on a pre-agreed itinerary, than by the posturing of the Foreign Secretary. Whatever the cause of the incident, the events left a legacy in the collective memory of the Foreign Office, including a cloud of ill-feeling towards Netanyahu, and reinforced the view that the Israeli-Palestinian arena was full of 'minefields', and that the settlements issue was a central problem.[25]

Cook travelled again to the region in October 1999. The itinerary was successfully planned to rebuild trust with the Israelis and avoid flashpoints.[26] Nonetheless, Cook had shown an abrasive style that was out of step with Blair's preferred approach.[27] The tensions he generated on his first visit likely contributed to the development of Lord Levy's role as Blair's personal envoy.

Blair lays down a marker in the peace process

While Cook struggled to gain credibility as Foreign Secretary, Blair quickly grew in confidence on the international stage. His pragmatism found ways to make progress in the Northern Ireland peace process. Blair played a critical role in securing the Good Friday Agreement, which was signed in April 1998. He won praise from all sides, having been personally involved, not only in negotiating compromises, but also in personally drafting the wording of the agreement. The

American envoy, George Mitchell, who brokered the agreement, said of Blair, 'He understands the extent to which both communities see themselves as victims, and he has a remarkable ability to identify with and calm their fears.'[28] Blair saw parallels between the Northern Ireland dispute and the Israeli-Palestinian conflict. He saw the Unionists as the Israelis, the Republicans as the Palestinians, and his role like that of the US trying to bring the two parties together.[29] According to Andrew Hood, his approach to dealing with the Middle East peace process was identical to that of Northern Ireland, in that, 'if you took the right risks, on your own reputation, and political risks personally, then there was a way to get the people around the table talking and to get the right outcome.'[30]

Shortly after signing the Good Friday Agreement, Blair went to Israel and the Palestinian Territories. The visit was promoted ambitiously by Number Ten as a mission to unblock the peace process.[31] Blair's success in Northern Ireland raised expectations that he personally could make an impact. In sharp contrast to the visit of Cook, Blair's trip was well received. David Manning, Britain's Ambassador to Israel at the time, recalled that Blair 'managed with enormous skill to talk to both the Israeli government and Arafat and made it very clear to both sides that he absolutely was committed to trying to find some kind of peaceful settlement', and that he 'got enormous respect from both sides'.[32] The goodwill surrounding Blair's trip contrasted not only with that of Cook a month earlier, but also with the first official visit of President Chirac of France in 1996, who caused friction with Israel with an impromptu walkabout in the Arab Quarter of the Old City. Blair met with Arafat and Netanyahu and made high-profile visits both to Yad Vashem and to a refugee camp in Gaza. He secured an agreement from both sides to meet in London in early May. Another outcome of the visit was signing with Arafat the 'Joint Declaration on E.U./Palestinian Security Cooperation', which increased European support for promoting the Palestinian's security capacity.[33]

Blair took care to emphasize that the London talks were to be led by US Secretary of State Madeleine Albright and that he did not want to 'cut across' the role of the US. However, the Foreign Office did not hesitate to claim that the meeting was a British achievement, even though the proposals for talks in London were already advanced by the US before Blair's visit.[34] The US had an interest in holding talks in Europe, which avoided diluting the impact of a visit to the region by the secretary of state.[35] The London talks proved inconclusive. For two days, the Americans led by Albright, with Blair in support, flitted between Israeli and Palestinian delegations ensconced in separate London hotels, without a single meeting between the protagonists themselves. Nevertheless, Blair's first major foray into the Israeli-Palestinian arena showed his ambition to be personally involved, and it was interpreted by commentators as an indication of the trust that the American administration had in Blair.[36]

The period demonstrated Blair's support for the idea of Europe having an independent international role, albeit to complement, rather than rival the United States. The same sentiment was behind the Anglo-French St. Malo summit in September 1998, which laid the groundwork for the European Union to be able to conduct coordinated military operations. The period was also very significant in establishing Blair's standing as a statesman committed to developing personal capital with Israelis and Palestinians and to contributing to the search for a solution.

From Kosovo to Chicago: Blair's foreign policy activism develops

Blair developed a close personal relationship with President Clinton, helped by ideological affinities in domestic and foreign policies, somewhat marginalizing the role of the Foreign Office in the transatlantic relationship.[37] A unified position over Iraq helped cement the UK–US strategic relationship, particularly when Britain's consistent support for US-led military action put him at odds with his EU colleagues, including the French.[38] Iraq was an issue on the Prime Ministerial and parliamentary agenda from the beginning of Blair's premiership. In February 1998, the issue came to a head when Saddam refused to cooperate with UN inspection teams to oversee the decommissioning of Iraqi WMD, part of the ceasefire terms of the First Gulf War. Just 25 MPs voted against using 'all necessary means' to bring Iraq into compliance.[39] Twenty-three were Labour, principally from the left-wing Campaign Group, including Tony Benn, Ken Livingstone, Tam Dalyell and George Galloway. They were all fierce critics of Israel and became synonymous with the anti-war movement in 2003. Among their objections to military action in 1998 was that it constituted double standards, in that Israel, which they claimed was also in breach of UN resolutions, did not receive similar treatment. They also argued that it was difficult to get support in the Arab world for action against Saddam because of anger at Israel's intransigence in the peace process.[40] In 1998, they were an isolated group.

In February, when Saddam gave way, Blair was convinced that this was only because of the credible threat of force.[41] The issue rose again in December 1998, leading to Operation Desert Fox, a four-day US and UK bombing campaign. Operation Desert Fox was an early indication of Blair's willingness to link progress on the peace process with winning Arab support for an interventionist policy in the Middle East – an important theme that would be developed further after 9/11. In Parliament Blair dismissed the comparison, made by George Galloway, between Israel and Iraq. However, he acknowledged that to maintain Arab support it was important to be 'even-handed in our approach' to the application of UN Security Council Resolutions in the Middle East.[42] The operation also demonstrated Blair's readiness to speak in value-laden terms about foreign policy, describing Saddam's regime as 'evil'.[43] Blair's biographer Anthony Seldon claims that the biggest impact of Desert Fox on Blair was on his self-confidence.[44] He had followed through on what he thought was morally right, in the face of sceptical international opinion.

Blair used similarly moralistic language in dealing with the Kosovo conflict a few months later, when Serbian President Slobodan Milošević began a campaign of ethnic cleansing against Albanians in the Kosovo region of Serbia.[45] After a series of failed negotiations, Blair determined that only the credible threat of force would stop the atrocities. The United States and the United Kingdom led a NATO bombing campaign to stop Serbian attacks on ethnic Albanians. There was no UN resolution to give the war legal basis, but within the UK Parliament, opposition to the conflict was even smaller than to the bombing in Iraq. A left-wing group of just 11 Labour MPs opposed the conflict. As John Rentoul wrote, it was a case in which 'for many on the left, righteous interventionism superseded anti-Americanism'.[46]

When the air campaign did not have the desired effect and the refugee crisis sped up, Blair tried to persuade a reluctant Clinton to back the use of ground troops.[47] In the midst of this effort, on a trip to the US in April 1999, Blair made his most celebrated foreign policy speech, setting out what became known as the 'doctrine of the international community'.[48] The speech argued that in a world where local conflicts could have global security implications, it was sometimes necessary to intervene. This was a challenge to the 'Westphalian order' and the traditional principles about non-intervention in the internal affairs of another state.[49] In this context, Blair stressed the importance of the US as the world's strongest state and criticized the fact that 'If anything Americans are too ready to see no need to get involved in affairs of the rest of the world.' Blair argued that after the Cold War, NATO was called to act not only to defend the existence of its member states, but also by 'a more subtle blend of mutual self-interest and moral purpose in defending the values we cherish'. He added, 'If we can establish and spread the values of liberty, the rule of law, human rights, and an open society then it is in our national interest too.'

This was a personal statement of policy devised by Blair and his team. The key passage defining the terms under which intervention would be justified was drafted by Lawrence Freedman, Professor of War Studies at Kings College London.[50] Neither the Foreign Office nor the Ministry of Defence had been informed, despite its significant implications.[51] It was a speech in the strongly Atlanticist and liberalist tradition of Churchill and Thatcher. Blair was not consciously identifying with the neoconservative thinkers in the United States who believed in using America's overwhelming economic and military power to actively promote democracy and oppose its enemies across the globe. Blair's belief that intervention to promote liberty might be necessary for the sake of global security was arrived at independently based on his own set of principles.[52] This did not stop prominent neoconservatives later claiming his thinking to be consistent with their own.[53] Blair's approach to the Kosovo conflict was a major departure for him. Rather than the cautious politician of triangulation, Blair acted as driven moral crusader. He set a highly ambitious public goal of allowing Kosovo Albanians to return to their homes, with no guarantees that it could be done. In his Chicago speech, he seemed to channel the spirit of Churchill himself in declaring, 'Success is the only exit strategy I am prepared to consider.'[54] It was an important sign that though Blair was a politician who instinctively sought a consensus position, this had not dimmed his religiously rooted sense of moral purpose and activism.

There were sobering lessons from the Kosovo campaign. It confirmed the weakness of Europe's armed forces, even when operating in their own backyard, and confirmed the ongoing importance of US leadership in the post-Cold War era. It also left a mark for Blair and his team on the best way to handle their American allies. Blair's Chief of Staff Jonathan Powell recalled:

> By being so in their face we really, really irritated Clinton. He thought we were briefing the papers, trying to make him look like a wimp . . . So you have to be incredibly careful, particularly with the Americans. There is a trade off between what you say publicly and how seriously your advice will be listened to in private.[55]

Blair and his staff took away from the experience the lesson that publicly criticizing the Americans might come at the cost of influence that could be achieved through friendly persuasion behind closed doors.

The growing threat from Islamist violence

The threat of violence from extreme Islamist groups grew over the course of Blair's first term. Of particular note were the attacks orchestrated by Osama Bin Laden on the US embassies in Kenya and Tanzania, on 6–7 August 1998, in which over 200 people were killed. US intelligence agencies had been tracking Osama Bin Laden and his network for several years when the attacks took place. They were aware that Bin Laden had relocated his organization to Afghanistan in 1996 and they knew he operated in a relationship of mutual support with the fiercely traditionalist and extremely repressive Taliban regime. The Clinton administration responded to the bombings with cruise missile strikes on Bin Laden's camps in Afghanistan and the Al Shifa pharmaceutical factory in Sudan. They believed the factory was being used to manufacture chemical weapons and that Bin Laden wanted to carry out a mass casualty attack in the US. The attacks were widely criticized either as a feeble, 'pinprick' response or as an overly aggressive act motivated by a desire to draw attention away from the Lewinsky scandal.[56] Blair nonetheless defended the US strikes.

A special session of the House of Commons was called in early September 1998 to pass emergency anti-terror legislations after a bombing by the Real IRA which killed 28 people in Omagh. The legislation made it an offence to conspire to commit terrorist attacks outside the United Kingdom. Tony Blair said during the debate: 'Countries that are state sponsors of terrorism must recognize that action will be taken if they sponsor terrorism and if terrorists based in their country take action against their nationals abroad.'[57] The African embassy attacks brought Bin Laden and his network to the attention of media and politicians alike, and helped to develop his image as a shadowy, villainous threat.[58] Blair demonstrated a growing awareness of transnational terror threats when towards the end of 2000, in his annual foreign policy speech at the Guildhall, he referred to the dangers of WMD proliferation and international terrorism. He was apparently influenced in his thinking by among others Robert Cooper, a senior British diplomat, who argued that 'The twin dangers of terrorism and weapons of mass destruction present us with a radically altered security environment.'

In February 2001, the Terrorism Act 2000 came into force, making possible the proscription of foreign Islamist terror groups. The list of foreign groups to be proscribed, drawn up by the Home Office under then-Home Secretary Jack Straw, was passed into law in March 2001. As well as Bin Laden's international Al Qaeda network, the list included the 'Hizballah External Security Organisation', the 'Hamas Izz al-Din al-Qassem Brigades' and 'Palestinian Islamic Jihad'. It was notable that in the case of Hamas and Hezbollah, the Home Office chose to specify the military arms of the organizations, as opposed to proscribing each of the organizations in full. Leaked correspondence between Home Office and Foreign Office officials from 2005 indicated that this was a policy decision made by ministers and that the intelligence services did not support making a distinction between political and military wings.[59] Hamas in its entirety had appeared on the US list of foreign terrorist organizations since 1997. It is not clear, therefore, why a political decision was made to draw a distinction between military and political wings.

The Muslim Council of Britain (MCB) lobbied against proscribing Hamas. Whether this opposition had any bearing on the Home Secretary's decision not to ban the group in full, three months before a general election, is unknown. Straw, whose Blackburn constituency had a 25% Muslim population, had a particularly close relationship with British Muslim leaders. The Home Secretary met with Muslim groups before announcing the list.[60] The MCB along with other British Muslim groups opposed the act altogether. In a press release, they asked, 'Why have Palestinian organizations been proscribed, but not the state-sponsored terrorists?' They found it 'baffling' that they had not been consulted in the drawing up of the list. The MCB's then Secretary General, Yousuf Bhailok, said, 'The Home Secretary has failed to distinguish between legitimate resistance movements who fight against the illegal occupation of their own land and organizations like the IRA which have targeted mainland Britain.'[61] This was a significant example of attempts by British Muslim representatives to influence the UK's policy in the Israeli-Palestinian arena. It was also an indication of the government's difficulties in working out how to relate to Hamas and Hezbollah.

Barak's election and the role of Lord Levy

In October 1998, Netanyahu and Arafat signed the Wye River Memorandum determining the next Israeli withdrawals from the West Bank and a timetable for final status talks. In trying to implement the plan, Netanyahu lost the support of his coalition, and his government fell. This created a six-month period of stagnation until the Israeli election. There was concern that the Palestinians might unilaterally declare independence, since 4 May 1999 was the deadline in the Oslo Accords for concluding final status issues. They lobbied European governments and the US to support the Palestinian right to statehood. The Americans asked the Europeans not to support any unilateral moves. The result was the Berlin declaration of March 1999, in which Britain claimed a leading role.[62] The statement unequivocally supported the rights of the Palestinians to a state, and the belief that a Palestinian state was the best way to solve the conflict and address Israeli concerns. It also made it clear that this could only be part of an agreement.

In Israeli elections in May 1999, Ehud Barak, leader of the Israeli Labour Party, rebranded as 'One Israel' for the election, defeated Netanyahu. Barak was a former chief of staff of the Israel Defence Forces and Israel's most decorated soldier. His platform included a pledge to follow in the path of Rabin and continue the Oslo process, and explicitly accepted the possibility of a Palestinian state. Barak was welcomed with gushing enthusiasm in the United Kingdom. Blair told the Commons, 'His victory offers the Middle East peace process a chance to move forward,' and in a joint Downing Street press conference in July 1999, he gave Barak his '101 per cent support for all that he is doing for Israel and the Middle East peace process.'[63] In a subsequent press conference with Barak, Blair said, 'What a beacon of hope he has raised for people the world over facing conflicts.'[64]

It might be thought that the centre left party affinity between British and Israeli Labour parties accounted for the goodwill. It was common ideological affinity that helped forge the relationship of the governments of Harold Wilson with their Israeli Labour counterparts. It is true that there was some affinity between the parties in the 1990s. Senior figures in the Israeli party visited the British Labour Party headquarters to seek advice before their election victory in 1992, and did so even more in 1999.[65] The team of American political consultants that was put together to run the Barak campaign, Stanley Greenberg, Bob Shrum and James Carville, were the same consultants who had helped rebrand Labour in the United Kingdom before 1997 and Clinton's Democrats in the US. However, party affinity was not the primary factor explaining the goodwill that Britain had for Barak. It was due far more to the new hope he offered the peace process. Under John Major's Conservative government, Britain's relations with Israel improved when there was a switch from a hawkish Likud government to a more dovish Labour government in 1992.[66] As a result of the promise Barak offered in the peace process, concerns that the British had about other issues were kept under the surface. There were, for example, growing concerns in the European Union that goods produced in the Occupied Territories were taking advantage of the EU-Israel free trade agreements, even though EU states considered those settlements illegal. In the opinion of Francis Cornish, the reason this issue did not come to a head during Barak's premiership was the desire to encourage and support him.[67] This motivation also likely kept in check any criticisms and concerns Blair had about ongoing settlement construction.

The election of a left-wing government in Israel made more significant the role of Lord Levy, as Tony Blair's personal envoy to the Middle East. Levy was already acting unofficially as an envoy for Blair by the time Cornish took over from David Manning as Ambassador in October 1998.[68] Levy made efforts to smooth over the diplomatic tensions caused by the Cook visit in March 1998, and met with Netanyahu in advance of Blair's visit to the region in May 1998.[69] With Levy's contacts mainly in the Israeli Labour camp, his utility to engage with the key players in the Netanyahu government was relatively limited. After Ehud Barak's election, Levy's personal connections on the Israeli left became more significant. The intensification and formalization of Levy's appointment, in August 1999, reflected the new opportunities created by the election of Barak. Levy made increasing visits not just to Israel, but to Arab leaders, indicating the extent to which Blair wanted to have a greater personal involvement in the peace process. Lord Levy gave Blair a chance to engage directly with the relevant leaders, bypassing the formal machinery of the Foreign Office, and the posturing of the Foreign Secretary, which had proven so counterproductive. His primary role was as networker and fixer, rather than policy adviser.[70]

Not surprisingly, there were those in the Foreign Office who were uncomfortable at the appointment of a prominent Zionist Jew as a go-between in the Arab-Israeli conflict. One former Foreign Office Arabist likened the appointment to having 'a very green Catholic Irishman to represent him [Blair] in Northern Ireland'.[71] Levy's role was also attacked in the Commons as an example of Blair's 'cronyism', and critics claimed Levy was incapable of earning trust in the Arab world.[72] However, Blair valued Levy's first-hand knowledge of the issues and personalities in the Israeli-Palestinian arena.[73] As for whether Levy's role alienated Arab leaders, the picture was mixed. Britain's Ambassador to the US from 1997 to 2003, Christopher Meyer, claimed that Jordanian and Saudi royalty told him that Levy was 'not terribly welcome' to them.[74] However, Britain's Ambassador to Syria at the time, Basil Eastwood, was impressed at the personal rapport Levy created with both President Hafez al-Assad and his son

Bashar. Levy was able to brief the Syrian president first-hand about Ehud Barak and the Israeli political scene.[75] After a series of visits, he helped to convince Assad that Barak was serious about peace with Syria.[76]

Blair's increasing use of Levy as an envoy indicated the extent to which Blair considered the peace process a personal priority even before 9/11. In addition, it shows that Blair believed that problems could be solved by his own direct intervention and persuasion. The fact that Levy could credibly claim that he spoke for the Prime Minister directly and unlike Blair's ministerial colleagues, had no political ambitions of his own, contributed to the added value he brought to Blair's engagement in the Middle East.

Responding to the peace process crisis

The extent to which the Prime Minister personally drove policy before 9/11 varied to some extent according to what other factors were dominating the domestic political agenda. When the Camp David peace talks between Israel and the Palestinians collapsed in the summer of 2000, and the Second Intifada erupted a few months later, various international parties, with the US in the lead, tried to stop the violence. However, foreign policy was sidelined for Blair during this period as he worked to maintain his domestic authority amidst major domestic crises over fuel prices and severe flooding.[77]

Israeli and Palestinian negotiating teams, led by Barak and Arafat, spent two weeks in July 2000 at Camp David trying to resolve core issues including the future borders, a solution for refugees and the sharing of Jerusalem. The summit failed to reach agreement. Negotiations continued in the months following, and Britain contributed to maintaining the diplomatic momentum with Lord Levy and then Middle East Minister Peter Hain travelling to the region at the end of August. Blair met with Barak, Arafat and Clinton on the margins of the UN in September 2000. In discussions with the Palestinians, UK ministers backed Clinton's position that this was the best opportunity the Palestinians would get.[78]

Dialogue between Israelis and Palestinians was continuing when at the end of September, a wave of violent demonstrations broke out across the Palestinian Territories. The Palestinians blamed the violence on Israeli opposition leader Ariel Sharon, who made a provocative visit to the Temple Mount/Haram al-Sharif, the site of the first and second Jewish temples between the Tenth

Century BCE and First Century CE, and the location since the Seventh Century of Islam's third holiest Mosque. Israelis claimed that the Palestinians, led by Arafat, used this as an excuse to launch a premeditated and centrally coordinated violent uprising. While talks continued, so did the violence, making prospects of reaching an agreement even harder.

Robin Cook took the lead as Britain assumed for itself a role in trying to control the crisis. Cook claimed credit on behalf of British officials for brokering UN Security Council Resolution 1322, which placed the weight of criticism for the violence on Israel.[79] The US abstained on the resolution. Cook, accompanied by Levy, was also among a host of international figures who flew to the region to try and calm the situation and he shuttled between Arafat and Barak from 11 to 13 October 2000.[80] Clinton eventually secured a ceasefire agreement at a summit in Sharm el Sheikh in a few days later, but it failed to hold. By the end of October, Israel's efforts to suppress violent Palestinian demonstrations had led to the deaths of 115 Palestinians, with 11 Israelis killed.[81] US efforts to close the gaps on final status issues in the weeks before leaving office also failed when the Palestinian side rejected Clinton's bridging proposals.[82]

The Second Intifada started principally as Palestinian riots against Israeli military positions and shootings of Israeli civilians and soldiers within the West Bank and Gaza. It soon developed with mortar attacks on Israeli settlements and bombings targeting civilians inside Israel. Israeli actions against the Palestinians escalated to include armed ground incursions into Palestinian-controlled areas, targeted assassinations of leaders of armed groups, tight restrictions on Palestinian movement and the suspension of tax revenues transfers to the Palestinian Authority – an arrangement that was part of the Oslo Accords. Palestinian workers stopped being able to enter Israel to work, cutting off another major source of revenue for the Palestinian economy. The European Union increased its funding to the PA to compensate and formally criticized Israel's security policies.[83]

The weight of Cook's blame for the spiral of violence increasingly leant on Israel.[84] He resisted calls in Parliament to criticize the Palestinian leadership for encouraging the violence and denied that they were in a position to 'turn off violence as if it were a military general commanding troops'.[85] He focused instead on what he saw as the roots of the violence – the lack of hope among the Palestinian people – and called on Israel to relax internal restrictions on movement. Cook's frustration at Israel's policies in the territories was consistent with the views of the Ambassador and his staff in Tel Aviv. Francis Cornish recalled:

All of us in the embassy were extremely concerned about the effect on the ground on ordinary Palestinians of what in those days was . . . the endless roadblocks and burns and cutting off of individual villages, and the cutting off of mothers from the hospital, children from the school, farmers from their olive groves and all the rest of it . . . It struck us the whole time that a continuation of the myriad incidents day in day out, simply raises the temperature, makes retaliation more likely, stokes up the fury, makes it much more difficult to persuade these people to calm down.[86]

However, despite not being closely involved in the policy area, the Prime Minister avoided being led by the language of the Foreign Office and continued to articulate a distinct position. When the Prime Minister answered questions on the situation in Parliament, he stressed that the responsibility to restore security 'applies not simply in respect of the Israeli forces, but also in respect of people from the Palestinian Authority'. He declared, 'I have taken the view throughout that our best way to influence the situation is by patient and quiet diplomacy'.[87] The phrase aptly summed up Blair's approach. He preferred to measure his tone in public in order to maintain his influence in private.[88]

In February 2001, Ehud Barak was defeated in an election for Prime Minister by Ariel Sharon. The cool British response to the election of Sharon could barely have contrasted more sharply with the welcome given to Barak less than two years earlier. For the Foreign Office, the memory of Sharon was tied up with the events of the First Lebanon War and the massacres carried out by Israel's Christian allies at Sabra and Shatila.[89] This was also the case for the left of the PLP. Sixteen Labour MPs did not wait to see what kind of government Sharon would form, and signed an Early Day Motion (EDM) tabled by George Galloway, the day after Sharon's election, accusing him of 'involvement in war crimes' and calling for the government 'to freeze all sales of military equipment to Israel and to recall Her Majesty's ambassador from Tel Aviv for consultations'.[90] Pro-Israel Labour MPs also expressed disappointment, though there was some relief when Labour joined Sharon's Likud in a national unity government.[91] Blair and his Foreign Office Ministers were more careful not to pass judgement on Sharon in public.

However, one area where parliamentary pressure forced the government's hands after the outbreak of the Second Intifada was with regard to arms sales. The IDF's efforts to suppress the violent Palestinian uprising resulted in a growing Palestinian death toll and attracted considerable international criticism. Although the UK government did not reimpose the embargo on the sale of military equipment to Israel, Britain did become more stringent about arms export licenses. It would be a mistake to overstate the significance of British arms sales to Israel in this period, given that the value of British military equipment sold to Israel was worth less than £0.5m a year between 1997 and 1999, and £1.35m in 2000.[92] But even though the scale was small, it was sensitive politically. After the outbreak of the Second Intifada, Labour member of the Foreign Affairs Select Committee, Phyllis Starkey, won assurances from ministers that the government would not knowingly allow British equipment to be used by Israel in the Occupied Territories.[93] The Foreign Office secured a letter from the Israeli government promising that 'no UK-originated equipment nor any UK-originated systems/sub-systems/components are used as part of the IDF's activities in the territories'.[94] In reality, it was extremely difficult for the Israeli assurance about the use of British equipment in the Territories to be verified.[95] The only way for the British government to control where its equipment was used was at the supply end, and there was a jump in the number of export licenses refused or revoked, particularly in 2001 and 2002.[96] In practice, the government avoided providing actual armaments, but allowed continued provisions of ancillary military equipment. Francis Cornish recalled that, 'We decided pretty artificially to draw this line between armaments and other equipment.'[97]

The licenses were issued by the Department of Trade and Industry, but the FCO was the lead department deciding if the sale of particular equipment served UK policy goals. However, the Prime Minister retained his aversion to steps that would antagonize either side and was receptive to appeals from Israel to overrule the Foreign Office and get certain licenses approved. An example given by Cornish was the supply of radio aerials. He recalled, 'The Foreign Office tried to block it. The Israelis kicked up, I kicked up, it went to Number Ten, and they went.' For Cornish, this approach reflected, 'An instinctive Tony Blair feeling that you are just not going to get anywhere by encouraging the Israelis, yet again, to circle the wagons and to get all defensive.' Cornish recalled, Blair saying, '"We mustn't be silly about this. Just tell the Foreign Office not to be silly." Meaning don't be so purist that you end up denying the Israelis just about everything.'[98] According to Cornish, this avoidance of direct confrontation with the Israelis was typical of Blair's diplomatic style. When urged by Foreign Office officials to raise specific concerns on subjects like settlements or house demolitions in a phone call or face-to-face meeting, he would 'touch on the subject very lightly, and then ran away'. Lord Levy also claimed that Blair's light touch was a source of frustration.[99] It was, however, in tune with the approach Blair had defined as 'patient and quiet diplomacy.'

After George Bush became US President in January 2001, his administration decided to be much less involved in the peace process, perceiving Clinton to have wasted time and political capital on the issue. Some neoconservatives in the administration shared the Israeli right's scepticism towards the peace process in general. While President Bush welcomed Prime Minister Sharon to the White House, he showed no interest in talking to Arafat. In the absence of US engagement, the European Union tried to mediate. Blair continued to engage with both sides via Lord Levy who met with Sharon and Arafat in April 2001. At the ground level, a small group of European Union officials, led by Alastair Crooke, seconded from MI6, talked to all the Palestinian factions to try and persuade them to keep a ceasefire.[100] These attempted interventions had no effect.

Israel responded to a suicide bombing in Netanya in May 2001 with airstrikes against PA security installations. It was around this time that the White House reconsidered its hands-off policy.[101] In May 2001, US Senator George Mitchell published a report commissioned at the Sharm el Sheikh summit, into the outbreak of the Intifada. The report called on the Palestinians to make '100% effort' to prevent terror attacks and on Israel to freeze settlement construction.[102] Sharon responded to international pressure from the European Union and the United States by declaring a policy of restraint towards the end of May. Then on June 1, Hamas and Islamic Jihad claimed responsibility for a suicide bombing in the Tel Aviv Dolphinarium disco which killed 20, mainly teenagers. Until that point, Sharon had been using his son Omri as an unofficial envoy to Arafat. After the Dolphinarium bombing, he no longer dealt with the Palestinian leader at all.[103] Scrambling to prevent a heavy Israeli response, the Bush administration sent CIA Director George Tenet as his special envoy, and the ceasefire plan he negotiated took effect on June 13.

However, violence continued on both sides, including attacks and provocations by extremist Jewish settlers. The response of the British government followed a familiar pattern. When Sharon stopped over in London to meet with Blair in June 2001, he reportedly received a sympathetic hearing.[104] Foreign Office ministers, on the other hand, took a more critical line on Israel's closure policies. Junior Minister Ben Bradshaw declared the following month:

> We have serious concerns with the Israeli policy of closures on political, legal and humanitarian grounds. It is hard to justify the closures, even on the narrow security grounds which Israel presents. The closures radicalise the Palestinian population and fuel violence in the occupied territories. They cannot, therefore, achieve their stated purpose.[105]

By August 2001, the US administration increasingly accepted the need to engage more substantially, under pressure not only from European allies but also, and perhaps more significantly, from an alarmed Saudi government.[106] Bush privately committed to the Saudis his support for a Palestinian state.[107] However, plans to announce this publicly were put on hold by the events of 9/11.

Radical Islam, 9/11 and the Israeli-Palestinian Issue

Grappling with 9/11

On the morning of 11 September 2001, four commercial airliners were hijacked in the United States. Two were flown into the twin towers of the World Trade Center in New York and a third into the Pentagon. The fourth, on its way to target the White House or Capitol Hill, crashed when the cockpit was stormed by its passengers. The entire world watched in horror at the sight of the twin towers collapsing, killing close to 3000 people. These unprecedented events changed everything. They brought front and centre an issue that hitherto had been growing in importance but had not been top of the international agenda. This problem was transnational sub-state groups motivated by an extreme and violent strain of Islamist ideology that was virulently anti-Western. It was quickly established that the attacks were carried out by Arab Islamist extremists, mostly of Saudi nationality, and was orchestrated by Osama Bin Laden's Al Qaeda network based in Afghanistan. The stated goals of Bin Laden were the removal of US troops from Arabia, Jews from Palestine and the overthrow of corrupt Arab regimes. He claimed to oppose the oppression of the Islamic world at the hands of the 'Zionist-Crusader Alliance'.

The events of 9/11 immediately sparked an intense discussion in the United Kingdom and elsewhere about the causes of the event and how Western governments should respond. The discourse after 9/11 was not centred primarily on the Israeli-Palestinian question. Many issues entered the debate. Part of the discussion focused on the world of the terrorists and what caused them to be so radicalized as to carry out their suicidal acts of mass killing. The social, economic, political, religious, ideological and psychological milieu of the perpetrators was the object of keen interest, as people in the West tried to understand what drove them to carry out their acts in the name of the Islamic faith. The discussion included assessing the role that social, economic and political failures of states in the Middle East played in creating a breeding ground for extreme radicalism. There was also interest in the role of globalization, which had created unprecedented levels of interaction between cultures, and had created circumstances in which the means to cause mass casualty terror attacks across the world had greatly proliferated. The organizational nature of Al Qaeda, the character of its leaders and how it conducted its operations were also of considerable interest.

Much of the discourse was orientated on questions of security, including why security services had failed to stop the attacks and what needed to be done to prevent their recurrence. The primary policy focus in Britain and the United States was on the need to target terrorists and their supporters wherever they were in the world and to tighten up domestic security to protect against future attacks. As time went on, the question of domestic security evolved into a debate about the balance to be struck between the preservation of liberalism and human rights and the sometimes conflicting demands of maintaining security.

At the same time, there was a considerable focus on the actions of the West in general and the United States in particular, and a debate about the extent to which past policy errors or ongoing policies and actions were responsible for what had happened. Some commentators charged the US with creating the specific circumstances in Afghanistan which allowed Al Qaeda to base itself there, through its support for Mujahideen Islamist fighters against the Soviet occupation in the 1980s. More generally, there were many, particularly on the left, who pointed the finger at the US for its 'imperialist' policies around the world, and specifically in the Middle East. It was America's own actions, they claimed, which generated an intense sense of grievance that was the root cause of hostility in the Islamic world towards the West. Among the most important supposed sources of grievance against the US was its support for Israel.

The rise of the challenge of political Islam

The debate in the West about the nature of the challenge posed by various strands of political Islam did not begin on 9/11. The contemporary political ideology of Islamism came about as a reaction against the dominance of Western powers over the Islamic world in the early part of the twentieth century.[1] Hasan al-Bana established the Muslim Brotherhood in 1928 to re-Islamize Egyptian society while it was under the political and military domination of the British. He was influenced by his contemporary, Sayyid Abul A'la Maududi, a Pakistani writer who founded the Jamaat-e-Islami party in 1941. Maududi associated the corrosive influence of the West with the Islamic world's state of ignorance of Islamic ways, which he called 'Jahaliyya',[2] a term that was previously used to refer to the time before the revelation of Islam.

A key turning point in the evolution of Islamist ideology was brought about by Sayyid Qutb, Hasan al-Bana's successor as leader of the Egyptian Muslim Brotherhood. Having initially supported Nasser's revolution in Egypt, the Brotherhood soon came into confrontation with the secular regime. Thrown in prison, Qutb developed an ideology based on a radical critique of the Nasserite regime, and its attachment to Western secular ideas of capitalism and communism, both of which he considered godless ideologies that rebelled against divine authority.[3] The need to overturn Jahaliyya was central for Qutb. He did not associate Jahaliyya with Western society alone, but with all societies that did not conform to his notion of the true Islamic way, including the Arab states of his day.[4] He articulated a revolutionary call to overthrow the secular regime and replace it with an ideal society based on Islamic law. Qutb transformed political Islam from a bottom-up movement for the reislamization of Islamic societies into an anti-regime revolutionary force. His impact as a thinker was augmented by his execution in 1965.[5] When the credibility of secular pan-Arab nationalism suffered a crippling blow as a result of the Arab defeat to Israel in 1967, Islamism came to surpass pan-Arab nationalism as an anti-Western movement with mass appeal in the Arab world which threatened Western interests in the Middle East.[6]

It was the Iranian revolution in 1979 and its attempts to export itself throughout the Muslim world which heralded to the West the emergence of political Islam as the primary challenge to its interests in the region. The Shia Islamists in Iran also rejected the negative influence of the West, and Qutb's Shia Iranian contemporary, a senior cleric named Ayatollah Khomeini, was similarly imprisoned by his country's government in the mid-1960s.[7] But whereas Qutb's attempts to create an Islamic state in Egypt ended with his hanging in an Egyptian prison in 1967, Khomeini was exiled by the Pahlavi regime. When the Shah's regime fell in February 1979 in the face of popular protest, Khomeini made a triumphant return to claim the leadership of a newly constituted Islamic Republic of Iran.[8] The replacement of the pro-Western Shah with an Islamist regime was a major blow to US and wider Western regional interests. In particular, the Islamic republic threatened the stability of Western-allied regimes, in particular, the Arab, oil-producing states in the Gulf. It also opposed the Arab-Israeli peace process and any acceptance of Israel's existence.

In the post-Cold War environment, understanding and responding to the challenge of political Islam became an increasingly important issue for the US and other Western policy makers.[9] Over the course of the 1980s and 1990s, political Islam rose in significance in numerous arenas beyond Iran. Egyptian President Anwar Sadat was assassinated by Egyptian Islamist extremists in 1981. Radical Shia Islam also became an important factor in the Lebanese political mire, with radical Shia Islamists under the direction of Iran blowing up 241 US servicemen in their barracks in Beirut, and a further 58 French troops, in simultaneous suicide bombings in October 1983. During the 1980s, the US itself covertly funded the Mujahideen Islamist fighters in their successful efforts to expel Soviet forces from Afghanistan. At the end of 1991, the Islamic Salvation Front won the first round of national elections in Algeria, before the military annulled the election with tacit American support. Fred Halliday wrote of Islamist movements in 1995 that they 'show no sign of going away: in the Islamic world, fundamentalists are in power in Iran and the Sudan; they threaten to come to power in Algeria and Egypt, and perhaps elsewhere'.[10] The successful Islamist insurgency against the Soviets in Afghanistan was significant in drawing together Jihadi fighters from around the Arab world, developing their experience and expertise, and creating important networks and training bases.

The growth in concern over Islamic fundamentalism in Britain during this period is reflected in the changing tone of parliamentary statements from Foreign Office ministers. In March 1989, backbench Labour MP Robert Wareing asked the government to 'make a statement on Her Majesty's Government's policy towards the consequences for international stability of Islamic fundamentalism in (a) Iran and (b) Afghanistan'. Junior Foreign Office Minister Lynda Chalker's entire response stated: 'We fully support the right of the Iranian and Afghan peoples to choose freely their own representative Governments and to run their own affairs. If they choose Islamic fundamentalist Governments that is their right.' By contrast, at end of 1996, when the Commons was debating the last Queen's speech of the Conservative government, then Foreign Secretary Malcolm Rifkind made a point of stressing that in the post-Cold War era, 'The worrying and disturbing growth in religious extremism has major political consequences.'

Fawaz Gerges helpfully framed the debate within US policy circles at the turn of the millenium about how to deal with the rising tide of political Islam and its threat to the existing political order in the Middle East. Gerges described US policy as swinging between two contrasting outlooks, analogous to contrasting approaches to the Soviet challenge during the Cold War. On the one hand, he identified confrontationalists who saw Islamism as a monolithic, ideologically driven anti-Western and anti-liberal threat that was inherently threatening to Western interests in the Middle East and had to be contained or rolled back. On the other hand were accommodationists who believed that Islamism's hostility to the West was more driven by grievances arising from specific Western policies or actions, including support for Israel. Accommodationists tended to believe that most Islamists would respond pragmatically and flexibly if they were allowed to enter the political process.[11]

However, already over the course of the 1990s the nature of the threat was evolving. In 1993, a group of Islamist extremists led by the Pakistan-born Ramzi Yousef detonated a huge bomb in the basement of the World Trade Center in New York.[12] This marked an evolution of the challenge of violent strains of political Islam from being a threat to the stability of pro-Western regimes in the region to the emergence of sub-state groups and individuals with the motivation and capacity to launch violent attacks directly at the US mainland. It also signalled the prominence of the Palestinian cause in their discourse and rhetoric. The first of Yousef's demands on claiming responsibility for the attacks was to 'stop all economic, political and military aids to Israel'.[13]

Awareness of the direct threat of extremist violence against the West and its significance as a national security issue grew with the emergence of Al Qaeda in the mid-1990s. Led by Saudi dissident Osama Bin Laden, Al Qaeda was a network of extreme radical Islamists with a violent anti-Western agenda, based in Afghanistan under the protection of the ultra-conservative Islamic Taliban regime. In 1996, Bin Laden issued a declaration of war directly against the United States and made the case that it had to be targeted before local Arab regimes could be overturned. The decision of some extreme Islamists to turn to violence directly against the United States did not necessarily imply the growth of Islamism's popularity in the Middle East. Indeed, Giles Kepel argued that this development was actually a consequence of the failure of Islamists to rally support for their ideology and win power in Arab states.[14] Focusing enmity on the United States created a unifying rallying call to unite disparate Islamist groups and overcome their local differences and identities, and resonated with wider public opinion in the Arab world which was hostile to Western political influence. Though the main focus for Bin Laden was the American military presence in Saudi Arabia, his call to arms went much further. He referred to a host of grievances in the Islamic world and tried consciously to articulate a message that transcended local issues to focus on a common enemy. In this context, the Israeli-Palestinian arena featured prominently. Bin-Laden repeatedly termed his enemy the 'Zionist-Crusader alliance' and railed against the 'Zionist state in Palestine'.[15]

A tendency of policy makers and commentators in the West to focus on Israel and the Israeli-Palestinian dispute in seeking to understand the threat of violent Islamism was fuelled by the prominent role the issue played in Islamist rhetoric. The notion that Jews are responsible for the oppression of the Islamic world is a notable element of Islamist thought. The history of Jew-hatred in the Islamic world is not as intense as that of the Christian world. Jews have generally had a tolerated and protected status in the Islamic faith, in contrast to the demonization of Jews as Christ-killers, which has been so much a feature of Christianity through the centuries. However, as Wistrich and Lewis among others have described, the subjugation of Jews and anti-Jewish prejudice nonetheless has a clear tradition in Islamic culture.[16]

In modern times, parts of the Islamic world have also been influenced by anti-Semitic conspiracy theories that have their origins in Christian Europe. In an essay written in the 1950s entitled, 'Our struggle with the Jews', Sayyid Qutb merged ancient prejudices against Jews in Islam with modern European forms of anti-Semitism.[17] Qutb depicted the rise of Jews from Dhimmi status to the position of a sovereign people as a symbol of Western success. Qutb described the Jews as a demonic threat to Islam, responsible for the decline of Muslims.

Not only did antipathy towards Jews and Israel have significant roots in Islamist ideology, but also rhetoric relating to the question of Israel–Palestine played a special role for Islamists in their campaign to rally Muslims in general to their point of view. Middle East scholar Beverly Milton-Edwards pointed out how the history of the Arab-Israeli conflict was particularly emblematic of Arab defeat and capitulation and the failures of the Islamic world. She noted that

> both internal and external Islamist elements have employed the Palestinian-Israeli conflict as a motif for an array of political issues that motivate and enliven a variety of Islamist discourses. In this sense Islamists ride the resurgence wave and the issues that define it.[18]

The status of Jerusalem, home to the third holiest site in Islam, being under the control of the Jews after 1967, enhanced the power of the Palestinian issue to rouse the emotions of Muslims around the world.[19] The historic struggle over the Holy Land waged between Christians and Muslims in the period of the Crusades has also played an important role in the way Muslims have viewed Western penetration into the Middle East in modern times.[20] Western imperialism was frequently depicted in Islamist discourse as a revival of the Crusades and a war against Islam itself. In Bin Laden's 1996 call to arms, Zionism represented not only the Jewish oppression of Muslims in Palestine, but also a partner in the Crusader alliance to oppress the Muslim 'Umma'. With the intensification of violence in the Israeli-Palestinian arena after 2000, Bin Laden increasingly saw the utility of the Palestinian issue in gaining legitimacy in the Arab and broader Islamic world.[21]

Al Qaeda and Bin Laden came to public attention with high-profile attacks on US embassies in Kenya and Tanzania in 1998, and on the USS Cole off the coast of Yemen in 2000. The events of 9/11 led both the United States and Britain to treat extremist Islamist violence, in combination with access to technology, including WMD, as their primary national security threat. Policy makers scrambled to try and understand this threat and its causes, including the role played by the Israeli-Palestinian issue.

The Clash of Civilizations interpretation

Within the public discourse about the nature of relations between the Islamic world and the West, perhaps the most cited and discussed idea was Huntington's Clash of Civilisations thesis.[22] Writing several years before 9/11, Huntington argued that the structure of the post-Cold War international system would be increasingly shaped by alliances and conflicts determined by the civilizational identity of states. He paid particular attention to conflict between the Islamic world and the Western world, which he viewed as an inevitable consequence of the very natures of those civilizations.[23] Huntington explicitly stated that the problem was with the whole of the Islamic world and the whole of the Western world. The phenomenon of Islamism as a political ideology was just one expression of a civilization-wide response to, and rejection of, Western culture.[24]

In explaining the culturally rooted character of the Islamic world's reaction against the West, Huntington drew on the analysis of Bernard Lewis. In a 1990 paper seeking to explain 'The Roots of Muslim Rage',[25] Lewis sought to identify why parts of the Islamic world had intense hatred of the West. He described the historic rivalry and military confrontation between Islam and Christian Europe, and noted that some specific political factors are often identified as causes of the ill-feeling. These specific grievances included American support for unpopular regimes in the Islamic world and especially American support for Israel. While acknowledging these as genuine sources of Islamic anger, Lewis argued that the deeper cause was the sense of humiliation felt due to the usurping of traditional values by alien Western ideas such as secularism and modernism. According to Lewis, certain groups of Muslims opposed Western secularism and modernity as not only evil but also corrosive to their traditional Islamic society which they considered to be superior.[26] They rejected the separation of religion and politics and the culture of modernity – not least the notion of gender equality.

As well as endorsing this explanation, Huntington accepted the school of thought which saw the failure of liberal democracy to take root in the Islamic world as due at least in part to 'the inhospitable nature of Islamic culture and society to Western liberal concepts'.[27] For Huntington, therefore, it was not specific political grievances such as Western support for Israel which were the cause of tension between the Islamic world and the West, but rather the inherent character of those civilizations. Huntington's stark conclusion was:

> So long as Islam remains Islam (which it will) and the West remains the West (which is more dubious), this fundamental conflict between two great civilisations and ways of life will continue to define their relations in the future even as it has defined them for the past fourteen centuries.[28]

Huntington wrote before 9/11, and his focus was on states, not on non-state actors. However, his analysis of the causes of political Islam and its negative attitude to the West as rooted in cultural differences was an important touchstone in the debate about the root causes of Islamist extremism after 9/11. Interviewed after 9/11, he encouraged this by suggesting that the actions of Osama bin Laden and the West's response had the potential to develop into a clash of civilizations.[29]

Though 9/11 sparked a resurgent interest in Huntington's thesis, it was in many cases cited by those who wanted explicitly to reject it. Revulsion in the Islamic world, as well as in the West, led many to want to explicitly stand against the notion that 9/11 confirmed Huntington's idea of an inevitable civilizational conflict. Most Western political leaders rejected the idea of a clash of civilizations in public and appeared to even regard it as dangerous. Even prior to 9/11, leading political figures in the West more frequently stressed a distinction between 'radicals' or 'extremists' who had manipulated Islam, which posed a threat, and 'moderate' Islam, which was an ally to Western values and interests.[30] Soon after coming into office, Tony Blair told an Arabic newspaper, 'Some academics, journalists and even politicians do talk in misguided terms of an "Islamic Threat" or a "Clash of Civilizations". But those of us who know Islam and who know the Islamic world reject such nonsense.'[31] When, after 9/11, Italian Prime Minister Silvio Berlusconi spoke of the superiority of Western values over those of the Islamic world, other Western leaders firmly rejected his comments.[32]

There were many specific criticisms of Huntington's thesis, but perhaps the most common was to reject Huntington's claim that there was sufficient unity of Islamic culture to render meaningful any talk of a coherent Islamic civilization that claimed the identity of Muslims and determined their choices. John Esposito and Fred Halliday were among those who argued that the notion of a unified Islamic civilization was a myth, given the complex diversity within the Islamic world and its plethora of different identities and interests.[33] Esposito further argued that for Turkey and Israel, in the absence of the Cold War, it was convenient to play up the notion of a monolithic Islamic threat against which they were the buffer. Huntington was also criticized by Basam Tibi, for example, for failing to make a distinction between the Islamic faith and Islamism as a political ideology rooted in Islam.[34] Edward Said argued that Huntington and Lewis's talk of a 'clash of civilizations' was typical of Western 'orientalist' misrepresentation of Islam. Said criticized both Lewis and Huntington for transmitting a generalized view of Islam that was out of touch with the varieties of Islam as lived and experienced by its myriad adherents.[35] Another important criticism of both Lewis and Huntington was that they overemphasized the extent to which distinct Islamic groups were driven by cultural identity or religious belief, and failed to pay sufficient attention to material grievances Muslims held against the West.

However, as a broad way to understand the cause of anger in the Islamic world towards the West – as a rejection of Western values and norms as opposed to a response to grievances deriving from Western actions – the idea of a civilizational clash remained highly salient and influential.[36] The phrase was used countless times in newspaper columns before, and especially after 9/11. Even those who criticized Huntington for failing to acknowledge the importance of contingent, political factors often acknowledged that Islamic cultural or civilizational identity did play some role in motivating radical Islamists' negative attitudes to the West.[37]

The neoliberal interpretation

While Western politicians and commentators tended to distance themselves from the idea of an inevitable clash of Western and Islamic civilizations, far more popular, particularly in Britain and the US, was the neoliberal idea that Western liberal values of democracy and free markets were universally applicable and should be promoted globally. Popular on both sides of the Atlantic was the idea that the spread of free trade, market capitalism and democracy would promote peace and prosperity, and that increasing globalization created interdependence which drove greater cooperation between states and between non-state actors, mediated by international institutions.[38]

Perhaps the most frequently cited case for the universality of the 'liberal idea' in the post-Cold War discourse was the claim of Francis Fukuyama that the end of the Cold War heralded the 'end of history'.[39] Fukayama's thesis was one to which the Clash of Civilizations idea was frequently contrasted.[40] While Huntington predicted a new basis for future confrontation in the world, Fukuyama claimed that the great ideological struggles were effectively over. He argued that liberal democracy and the free market had proven their superiority in their ability to meet human needs, and would eventually take over the whole world. For Fukuyama, writing in the early 1990s, the collapse of the Soviet bloc was clear evidence of this.

In terms of explaining Islamic rejection of Western norms, as Fukuyama himself pointed out, there was actually commonality between Huntington and Fukuyama.[41] Like Huntington, Fukuyama saw rejection of Western norms within the Islamic world as an expression of tension between local cultural identity and modernity. They both treated Islamic anger against the West as a reaction to Western ideals, values or cultural norms, as opposed to expressing underlying material grievances. The key difference was Fukuyama's belief that political and economic liberalism were universal in their applicability and ultimately unrivalled in their appeal. He rejected the essentialist position held by Huntington that Islamic or Arab culture was inherently inhospitable to democracy.[42]

The implication of Fukuyama's political and economic neoliberalism was that differences between Western and Islamic culture did not ultimately change the inevitable direction in which all societies were heading. While the West had already largely arrived at the 'end' goal of liberal economics and democratic governance, the Islamic world had some way to go. Nevertheless, the Islamic world was still being driven to liberalism and democracy by the necessary forces of human development. Fukuyama acknowledged that political Islam was preferred to Western-style liberalism in many parts of the Islamic world, and even that the spread of Western ideas has helped create an Islamic revival. However, he maintained that the choice of political Islam over liberalism was only contemplated where Islamic culture was already prevalent and was inconceivable outside of that sphere.[43] He also pointed out that in some cases, Islam as a system of political organization in competition with liberalism was artificially sustained by oil wealth.[44]

The belief in the superiority of liberal democracy was closely related to the 'democratic peace thesis', another important neoliberal theory of international relations which grew in popularity after the end of the Cold War. This thesis held that perhaps the closest thing to a law of international relations was that democracies do not fight wars with one another. Though the empirical truth of this claim has been the source of considerable dispute, the idea has proved popular and influential with Western politicians.[45] The policy implications of the belief in the universal spread of liberalism were clear. If the spread of democracy and the liberal idea led to the spread of peace, then it called for a Western policy of democracy promotion. These policy approaches found influential advocates in both US and British governments during the Blair period. Simon Murden described Fukuyama as 'the intellectual voice of a US mission to take the liberal idea to the unconverted world'.[46] As discussed in the previous chapters, faith in the superiority of the 'neoliberal market economy' was one of the central pillars of New Labour's foreign policy.[47] Blair clearly articulated this position in his 1999 Chicago speech on the doctrine of the international community, in which he stated: 'If we can establish and spread the values of liberty, the rule of law, human rights and an open society then that is in our national interests too. The spread of our values makes us safer.'[48] Advocates of this approach did not perceive it to be in any way anti-Islamic. Unlike Huntington, and indeed Islamist ideologues like Qutb, they rejected any suggestion of an inherent contradiction between Islamic culture and society, and the liberal democratic and economic systems.

In the Bush administration, a number of senior officials who subscribed to the neoconservative strand of thought advocated actively promoting the defence and spread of democracy and opposing its enemies through the strategic application of America's hegemonic, global, military and economic reach.[49] This ideological persuasion had its roots in the US policy debate of the 1970s about how to deal with the Soviets.[50] Early neoconservatives were figures on the American liberal-left who became disillusioned with, among other things, what they perceived as the left's inadequate response to the threat posed by the Soviet Union.[51] The end of the Cold War gave momentum to the neoconservative approach. The demise of the Soviet Union created an international arena in which the US stood unmatched as the world's only superpower. It was in a position to define its own foreign policy as never before and the neoconservatives advocated greater freedom of action abroad. In particular, from the late 1990s, neoconservatives called for using all means to remove Saddam Hussein from power in order to negate his threat to US interests, troops and allies in the region.[52] While not monolithic in their views, neoconservatives tended to the confrontationalist view of Islamism as a singular anti-liberal ideology which posed a threat to the West analogous to that of Communism during the Cold War.[53] Neoconservatives saw the active promotion of democracy as the correct American response to the Islamist threat. Their presumption was that the spread of liberty would transform Islamic society and bring peace.[54]

Neoconservatism was also associated with a policy position on Israel that was sympathetic to the Israeli right and sceptical about the Arab-Israeli peace process. This was based on a firm commitment to the defence of Israel as a democracy and a belief that the central barrier to peace was the unwillingness of Arab states to accept Israel's existence.[55] This contributed to a recurring charge against neoconservatives that they were in fact a Jewish cabal conspiring to direct US foreign policy to the benefit of Israel, rather than the United States. Critics frequently emphasized the influence of Jewish American officials in the Bush administration with neoconservative views such as Paul Wolfowitz, Richard Perle and Elliot Abrams. These individuals, particularly Wolfowitz, were strong advocates within the administration for attacking Iraq,[56] and critics frequently attributed the decision to invade Iraq to their influence. In 2003, veteran left-wing Labour MP Tam Dalyell claimed that a similar 'cabal' of Jewish advisers steered British government policy also.[57] Leading neoconservatives acknowledged that there are many Jews among their number. Joshua Muravchik suggested that, 'the Jewish affinity with the left may be one reason why neoconservatism boasts so many Jewish adherents: it is a movement whose own roots lie in the left.'[58] But, as Muravchik also pointed out, Jews were at the same time among the leading critics of neoconservatism.

The claim that a Jewish cabal steered the US and Britain into the Iraq war had more than a whiff of anti-Semitism about it.[59] It overlooked the fact that not one of the principal advisers and policy makers involved in the Bush administration's decision to go to war in Iraq was either Jewish or clearly identified as neoconservative.[60] The key figures were President George W. Bush, Vice-President Dick Cheney, Defence Secretary Donald Rumsfeld, National Security Adviser Condoleezza Rice, CIA Director George Tenet and Secretary of State Colin Powell.[61] The policy to topple Saddam, while broadly welcomed in Israel, was also not a central goal that Israel was lobbying for. While Saddam was considered a menace in Israel for funding Palestinian terrorism, and for firing Scud missiles at Tel Aviv in the 1991 Gulf War, Iran was considered the more prominent threat.[62]

The view of political Islam as an anti-liberal ideology that needed to be confronted or at least contained was most commonly associated with the right in the United States. However, influential American writer Paul Berman was a prominent example of one who made a similar case from a particular strand of anti-totalitarian left-wing thinking. He argued that Islamism was an anti-liberal and totalitarian reaction to liberal culture, which had commonalities with the twentieth-century anti-liberal ideologies of Nazism and Communism. He emphasized the importance of these ideological features over the material grievances of the Islamic world. Berman stressed the common ideological roots of all Islamists.[63] Shortly after 9/11, in attempting to explain the hostility to the US of both Islamists and Arab nationalists, Berman wrote:

> It is because America's crime, its real crime, is to be America herself. The crime is to exude the dynamism of an everchanging liberal culture. America is like Israel in that respect, only 50 times larger and infinitely richer and more powerful. America's crime is to show that liberal society can thrive and that antiliberal society cannot. This is the whip that drives the antiliberal movements to their fury.[64]

The grievance-based interpretation and its appeal to the left

The approaches discussed so far tended to treat Islamic anger against the West as arising from cultural, social or political factors within the Islamic world. A competing approach was to emphasize the significance of political grievances and injustices arising from the policies and actions of Western states.[65] Writing years before 9/11, John Esposito criticized Huntington for dismissing the anger towards the West as driven by 'a blind, irrational clinging to faith'.[66] Esposito, while acknowledging that Islam was a real motive force for politicized Muslims, argued that the Clash of Civilizations approach failed to give enough credence to the specific sociological and political grievances which drove these different groups. These include the legacy of Western imperialism in the region, Western support for repressive regimes and leaders who protect their economic and strategic interests in the region and, in particular, Western support for Israel. He wrote that, 'Differences between Western and Muslim societies can best be explained by competing political, socioeconomic, and cultural interests rather than a clash of civilisations.'[67]

Those stressing the importance of contingent political factors to explain Islamist hostility to the West also tended to highlight the importance of specific, local, social and political issues that fuelled radical Islamism. Writing in 1995, Graham E. Fuller, a former vice-chair of the CIA's National Intelligence Council and Ian Lesser, a former member of the Secretary's Policy Planning Staff at the US Department of State, stressed the dangers of the 'civilizational' approach, which missed the significance of specific local grievances. They concluded that such an approach could 'even be harmful over the long run, not so much because it is false in all cases but because that kind of emotive characterization leads to simplistic and damaging views on both sides'.[68] According to this view, it was misleading to view Islamism as a homogenous social phenomenon or ideological movement, rather it was a variety of groups and movements which varied considerably in their background, structures, beliefs, goals and methodologies.

The view of Islamism as driven primarily by legitimate grievances against injustice perpetrated or supported by the United States and its allies had greater appeal for many on the left who shared to some degree the hostility of the Islamists to the United States. There was a tendency for some to treat Islamism as a vehicle for revolutionary change.[69] Islamists generally rejected socialism and communism as secular, Western ideologies that were antithetical to Islam. This hostility was starkly illustrated by the war of the Mujahideen fighters against the Soviets in Afghanistan in the 1980s. Nonetheless, anti-capitalist and post-colonialist ideas heavily influenced Islamist discourse and self-justification, just as they influenced pan-Arab nationalists before them. This contributed to the affinity that parts of the British left, including some on the left of the Labour Party, felt for them.

Fred Halliday wrote in 2006 that sections of the left 'show every indication of appearing to see some combination of al-Qaida, the Muslim Brotherhood, Hizbollah, Hamas, and (not least) Iranian president, Mahmoud Ahmadinejad as exemplifying a new form of international anti-imperialism that matches – even completes – their own historic project'.[70] The attraction of Islamist movements for parts of the left came in spite of the Islamists' opposition to Western liberal ideas – including gender equality, democracy, free speech and gay rights – and in spite of armed Islamist groups resorting to the intentional killing of civilians on a large scale. Those leftists who viewed Islamism through the lens of anti-imperialism also shared with the Islamists a hostility for Israel, viewed by both as the most blatant and offensive expression of the West's malignant involvement in the politics of the Middle East.

Israel: The cause of Islamist extremism, or an ally against it?

Even aside from the variety of interpretations on the challenge of political Islam, Israel's unique history and diverse society, as well as the contested nature of Israeli identity and Zionist ideology, meant that Israel was open to being viewed in a range of different ways by policy makers in the West.[71] Israel from its outset identified itself as democratic and therefore Western in its political institutions, aligned itself strategically with Western powers, and was dominated, at least in the early decades of the State, by Ashkenazi Jews who were culturally more European than anything else.[72] The support Israel received from Western powers in its establishment and survival certainly contributed to the Arab world seeing it as a Western imposition in the region. However, Israel's unusual social makeup and history have always resisted any straightforward characterization of the state as Western. Indeed, internal complexities and tensions within Israeli society over the nature of the state and its identity have increased over time, including tensions between Jews of Ashkenazi (European) and Mizrachi (Middle Eastern) origin, between secular and religious conceptions of Zionism, and between Jewish and non-Jewish citizens of the state.[73] As has been discussed, the post-1967 era of occupation further complicated the perception of Israel in Europe: according to one conception, a besieged democracy and ally of the West against radical forces, according to another, a legacy of colonialism and an occupying power that denied the right to self-determination of the Palestinians.

Contrasting views about the nature of Islamism and the causes of its hostility to the West further complicated the variety of ways in which Israel and the Israeli-Palestinian arena was seen through Western eyes. For those tending to see negative Islamic reaction against the West as a rejection of Western culture, hostility to Israel in the Islamic world was best explained by Israel's association with the West and its embrace of Western values. Israeli politicians often promoted this idea. The words of Ehud Barak, for example, characterized the position often taken when he wrote following 9/11: 'The West is not hated by the terrorists because it supports Israel. It is the other way around: Israel is hated because it is perceived as an outpost of democratic values and the western way of life.'[74]

Furthermore, for those who believed in the active promotion of liberal democracy, there was a tendency to see Israel as a beacon for those values in a region where they had otherwise failed to take root. Since Fukuyama, like Huntington, saw the dominant cause of Islamic reaction against the West as rooted in cultural identity, as opposed to specific material grievances, he gave no special significance to the role of Israel and the Israeli-Palestinian conflict in explaining why some Muslims might want to attack the West. In some cases, neoliberals argued that Israel was an ally in promoting Western liberalism and in containing or confronting its enemies in the Middle East. After 9/11, Israeli leaders and supporters actively promoted the idea that Israel and the US were united by a shared struggle for Western values against terror.

This view of Israel as a democracy, inherently aligned to Western interests, in a region largely inhospitable to Western values, lent itself to the case for maintaining strong support for Israel as a strategic asset and ally.[75] Neoconservatives tended to articulate the most uncompromising versions of this approach, taking the view that promoting the Arab-Israeli peace process was futile so long as the Arab world failed to accept Israel's right to exist.[76] In 1996, Richard Perle and Douglas Feith, former staffers in the Reagan administration and prominent neoconservatives who became senior officials in the George W. Bush administration, were among the signatories of a paper produced for the incoming Likud government in Israel.[77] They rejected the Oslo process in favour of an approach which would confront terrorism and seek a balance of power based on containment, rather than negotiation with Israel's enemies. Through this shift they hoped a Likud-led Israeli government would create a better basis on which Israel could help actively promote Western values and 'better cooperate with the United States to counter real threats to the region and the West's security'.[78]

On the other hand, those who saw Islamist extremism as a phenomenon predominantly driven by material and political grievances against the West, rather than as a reaction against Western culture and values, tended to view support for Israel as a driving force behind Islamist hostility, rather than as an asset in trying to contain it. This was a view attractive to parts of the left but not exclusively so. Two leading neorealist scholars of international relations, John Meirsheimer and Stephan Walt, argued in 2007 that, 'Israel is a liability in both the "war on terror" and the broader effort to deal with so-called rogue states.'[79] Meirsheimer and Walt argued that, 'the United States has a terrorism problem in good part because it has long been so supportive of Israel.'[80] This approach carried echoes of the 'Chatham House Version', historically influential in the British Foreign Office, with its tendency to view Zionism as an artificial presence and a major cause of unrest, Arabs as victims of Western interference in the region, and to elevate the Palestine dispute as the key issue in the Middle East.

The view that support for Israel was a major cause in fermenting violent hostility towards the West among Muslims carried major policy implications for Western leaders. If policy makers adopted that view, then Israel looked less like a strategic asset in containing radical forces and more like a strategic liability in fuelling them. For those with a left-wing world view, drawn in some degree to anti-imperialism, post-colonialism and anti-Americanism, this logic had particular appeal. This position prompted an obvious question for other Western states that claimed to be supporters and friends of Israel, including the United Kingdom: to what extent should the threat of Islamic violence directed against the West be taken into account in formulating policy towards Israel and the Israeli-Palestinian conflict? It is clear from government documents that exactly this question was considered by officials at the highest levels of the British government in response to the threat of Islamist violence.[81] British policy makers during the Blair era asked themselves whether supporting Israel less, and the Palestinians more, would lessen Islamic anger against the West, and consequently the threat of violence against Western targets.

Framing Labour's response to 9/11

From the preceding discussion, and the overview of Labour's attitudes to the Israeli-Palestinian question provided in Chapter 2, it is possible to see why the relationship between 9/11 and the Israeli-Palestinian arena would generate a range of interpretations within the Labour Party. Labour assumed power in 1997 with a legacy of internal ideological divide between Atlanticists on the right who tended to see Britain's role in the world as in close alliance with the US and the defence of liberalism, and those on the left who were suspicious of capitalist America and its global influence.[82] The number of Labour MPs with serious ideological anti-capitalist commitment was considerably shrunken by 1997.[83] However, a larger number could be identified as 'soft left', and retaining some degree of attachment to the ideals of the left. These included anti-imperialism and post-colonialism, and an agenda which included sensitivity to third world and minority rights, inclining them to sympathize with Palestinian nationalism.[84]

Blair was firmly attached to the belief in the promotion of democratic and economic liberalism. He also entered office with a particularly sympathetic view of Israel as a democracy surrounded by dictatorships. But many people in the British Labour Party, including many Labour MPs, did not share his world view in this and many other respects. The Labour left had an underlying tendency to see the West's role in the region, including support for Israel, as a source of justified grievance in the Islamic world. Their world view inclined them to lean towards what Gerges labelled the 'accommodationist' interpretation of political Islam.[85] When Islamists after 9/11 claimed that Western support for Israel was one of the grievances which caused 9/11, there was a tendency on the left to agree. Tony Benn, for example, an icon of the Labour left, held the view that 'Palestine' was the direct cause for 9/11.[86]

The accommodationist approach was also attractive to British liberals, or the middle-class left, for whom the Israeli-Palestinian conflict also became a totemic issue. In his polemic against left-liberal anti-Westernism and sympathy for Islamism, Nick Cohen wrote that, 'The resurgence of fascistic ideologies in the Middle East was explained away by the liberal left and just about everyone else with the assertion that its "root cause" was the Israeli occupation of the West Bank and Gaza.'[87] As David Hirsh wrote, 'There is a left "common sense" in the United Kingdom that sees only one struggle going on [in the Israeli-Palestinian arena] – a war of the oppressed against the oppressors.'[88] An example of this thinking appeared in the British press immediately after 9/11. Self-defined left-wing columnist Suzanne Moore wrote in the Sunday Mail, five days after the 9/11 attacks:

> When I heard the dreadful news I was in the swimming pool with a bunch of mothers and their babies. Hardly a political gathering. Yet every one of them immediately murmured the word "Israel". This is the difference between the

British and the American public: we do not condone this attack but we at least have some idea of why it might have happened.[89]

One of the consequences of this world view was the belief that Britain should consider changing its foreign policy to take account of claimed grievances in the Islamic world. John Denham, a leading figure in the Labour soft left, told the *Spectator* in 2005, 'we may well need to . . . be prepared to change the emphasis of our foreign policy in order to safeguard our own security.'[90]

Some on the left regarded the Israel–Palestine issue not just as one grievance among several that Muslims had against the Islamic world, but the most important grievance, that above all other issues poisoned relations between the West and the Islamic world. This view led to a policy approach to the Middle East which put a very high priority on meeting Palestinian demands for justice ahead of other considerations. In the policy discussions in the wake of 9/11, the loudest advocate of what could be called a 'Palestine first' position in the British cabinet was Clare Short. After leaving government, she took this position to its furthest extreme, claiming in 2005 that, 'US backing for Israeli policies of expansion of the Israeli state and oppression of the Palestinian people is the major cause of bitter division and violence in the world.'[91] On a number of occasions after 9/11, Blair adopted a position that could be mistaken for the Palestine first position. He stressed in increasingly strong terms that the Israeli–Palestinian issue was the most pressing international issue and that the War on Terror could not be won without progress in that arena. In fact, as will be explored, his assumptions and policy were quite different from those of Short and others on the Labour left.

Blair and others subscribing to his world view were not affected by post-colonial thinking and anti-Americanism, and were more sympathetic to Israel as a liberal democracy and an ally against radical anti-Western ideologies. Blair's firmly Atlanticist and neoliberal commitments, and his sympathy for Israel, inclined him more towards what Gerges termed the 'confrontationalist' interpretation of political Islam. Rather than seeing Israel, and Western support for Israel, as causes of negative Islamic sentiment towards the West, he tended to see Israel as an ally in containing radical Islamist threats to Western interests in the Middle East.[92] Blair's position regarding the threat posed by Islamism hardened over the course of his term in office. After the July 2005 London bombings, he described the idea that the bombings were a result of British policy in Iraq or Afghanistan or support for Israel as 'nonsense'. In increasingly stark terms, he argued that 'reactionary Islam' was a single unified phenomenon encompassing terrorists in London and Madrid and Islamist groups in Palestine as well as those in Afghanistan and Iraq.

Blair was not alone. Home Secretary Charles Clarke, for example, said after the London bombings in 2005 that, 'There is not some particular government policy decision, or even some overall policy stance, which we could change and thus somehow remove our society from the al-Qaeda firing line. Their nihilism means that our societies would only cease to be a target if we were to renounce all those values of freedom and liberty which we have fought to extend over so many years. Our only answer to this threat must be to contest and then to defeat it.'[112]

Labour, therefore, encompassed within it the divergence between accommodationist and confrontationalist views on the relationship between the Islamist challenge and the Israeli-Palestinian question. These differences in world view, and their implications for Britain's approach to the Israeli-Palestinian arena, were the seeds of a bitter rift that grew within the party in the wake of 9/11.

5

The Israeli-Palestinian Issue
and the Response to 9/11

Blair and Labour in the second term

After four years in government, Blair had developed clear foreign policy principles and assumed a greater position of seniority on the world stage. His dominance of his party, his cabinet and the domestic political scene as a whole was at its zenith, and he believed that government should be run from a strong centre in the person of the Prime Minister. Having won a second landslide victory in June 2001, Blair was emboldened to pursue a more radical policy of public service reform than the cautious first-term programme. He further strengthened his own Prime Ministerial institutions to better control Whitehall, adding more units to the Cabinet Office to assist him in development of policy, strategy and delivery.[1] In this context, Blair's pre-eminence in foreign policy also grew.

However, Blair was also increasingly distant on ideological grounds from his cabinet and the membership of the Labour Party.[2] There was a drop in core working class support in the 2001 election. A restriction of democratization in the party led to declining influence and a drop in activism among the grass roots.[3] Within the parliamentary party, Blair was confronted by a series of major backbench rebellions, not only against the most controversial foreign policy decision to go to war in Iraq, but also on a series of public service reforms. The opposition to Blair on both domestic and foreign policy was not just from the hard left, which was an increasingly marginal and shrinking force in the party. It also came from the more substantial and enduring caucus of the 'centre' or 'soft' left, characterized by the pressure group Compass, founded in 2003.[4] Of great concern to many was the need to defend multilateralism in the face of what they perceived as the US exercise of 'unilateral power' to advance its own interests. The Compass founding document, for example, described the need for Britain to be part of a Europe which balanced US power and promoted 'social democratic principles.'[5] Blair consistently succeeded in overcoming internal party opposition and pushing forward both his domestic and foreign policy agendas. But in doing so he oversaw increased division within the party, a growth in disaffection among many traditional party activists and a decline in membership.[6]

In the Cabinet, Blair's colleagues remained dependent on his patronage, and had little independent power in the party to provide them with any leverage against him.[7] Clare Short, in her resignation speech in 2003, went so far as to charge that 'there is no real collective responsibility because there is no collective, just diktats in favour of increasingly badly thought through policy initiatives that come from on high'.[8] At the beginning of the second term, Blair made appointments to key ministries that consolidated his own position, including in the foreign policy portfolio. Robin Cook was replaced as Foreign Secretary by Jack Straw, who was not experienced in foreign affairs, and was willing to accept the Prime Minister's leadership.[9] This contributed to a situation whereby the Prime Minister defined Britain's response to 9/11, with Straw and the FCO relegated to a 'supporting role'.[10] The appointment of David Manning, an official at the level of a Permanent Secretary, to sit within Number Ten as Blair's personal foreign policy adviser was a significant attempt to increase the ability of the Prime Minister to lead the government's foreign policy.[11] The role of a senior diplomat functioning as an adviser within Number Ten, and bypassing the traditional diplomatic machinery, was a source of frustration for ministers and officials in the Foreign Office.[12]

The Israeli-Palestinian issue in Britain's response to 9/11

The events of 9/11 held the entire world transfixed in front of their television sets in a state of confusion and uncertainty, grappling to understand what had happened, what its implications might be and what would happen next. Britain's Ambassador in Tel Aviv, Sherard Cowper-Coles, reported in a telegram to the Foreign Office on the evening of the attacks, 'Like the rest of the world, Israel is in total shock. Sharon called by US colleague earlier this evening to express condolences: for the first time in anybody's recollection, Sharon was lost for words.' The Ambassador noted Israeli distaste at 'the signs of jubilation on the streets of Nablus and East Jerusalem'.[13]

Blair and his team lacked any detailed knowledge about the Taliban and the situation in Afghanistan prior to 9/11, though Blair had a general awareness of the threat of Bin Laden and the threat of attack from Al Qaeda. He had referred to the issues in a general way in his November 2000 speech to the Lord Mayor's Banquet and he claimed to have raised his concerns about Bin Laden and WMD proliferation with Bush in their first meeting in February 2001.[14] Nonetheless, as with the Kosovo crisis two years earlier, Blair responded to the events of 9/11 decisively. The first systematic expression of Blair's response to the challenges posed by 9/11 was a memo sent to President Bush on September 12.[15] He drew up proposals following briefings from his advisers, principally the intelligence chiefs, in the immediate wake of the attacks.[16] Fearing a rash US military strike, the memo called for Bush to focus on a measured response with international support, targeted at hitting Al Qaeda. Blair proposed that the Taliban in Afghanistan should be given an ultimatum to hand over Bin Laden. He noted that to facilitate military action, there was a need to improve relations with Pakistan and India. However, the memo further stressed the need to act against supporters of terrorism worldwide. It also emphasized the importance of getting public opinion onside, of creating international coalitions and of avoiding a 'war of civilizations' between Muslims and Christians. As an important part of an overall strategy, Blair stated from the outset that restarting the Middle East peace process should be a priority, in order to build Arab support for the War on Terror.

In the aftermath of the attacks, there were those on the hard left and the liberal left who argued that it was the actions of America or Israel that motivated the violence. John Pilger wrote, six days after the attacks, 'Far from being the terrorists of the world, the Islamic peoples have been its victims – that is, the victims of American fundamentalism, whose power, in all its forms, military, strategic and economic, is the greatest source of terrorism on earth.' More moderate versions of this case were heard within the discourse of policy makers, from a range of sources. On the day that Blair was producing his memo for Bush, one of his Arabist experts from the Foreign Office made the case to Blair that, 'the Americans should look to their own policy on the Middle East to understand why so many people don't like them.' The official, according to Alistair Campbell, 'came very close to saying the attack was justified'.[17] In a meeting of the Cabinet on September 13, Alistair Campbell recalled that Clare Short 'did her usual bit', stating that, 'the real problem was lack of progress in the Middle East, the fact that so many people were willing to be suicide bombers, and she asked if we had the will to improve life for the Arab world.' In an emergency debate in the House of Commons on 14 September, the point was voiced by Conservative

MP Jonathan Sayeed who said, 'There must be some understanding of why there is such hatred for so many institutions in the United States. Unless we deal with some of the deep-seated causes, more terrorists will come to the fore.'

Blair's response was to reject the idea that the attacks were in any way premised on a justified grievance, while acknowledging the importance of understanding the reasons for the hatred. He told the Commons:

> It is important to analyse some of the hatred of which the hon. Gentleman has spoken and to see what we can to do minimise it. We must never, however, find ourselves in a position of moral ambiguity. Nothing can ever justify what has taken place. Some comments from around the world have worried me on that score . . .
>
> We must also make common cause with decent, law-abiding peoples in the Islamic world in combating the threat of terrorism, of which they, too, are the victims. In so far as we can, we must move forward the process of peace in the Middle East. A balanced and sensible view must be taken, but we can never take any position other than to say that what happened in the United States of America can have no conceivable shred of justification . . . We have to consider how to push forward the process of peace and understanding in the world, but that should not draw us back in any way from pursuing those responsible for the atrocity.[18]

Blair did not believe that Al Qaeda was motivated by the Israeli-Palestinian issue. Rather he thought the conflict was used as a tool for them to exploit for their own ends. In an interview to the *Observer* published on 14 November, he argued:

> You're not dealing with reasonable people; you're not dealing with people you can negotiate with. Their demands are that we obliterate the state of Israel and the Arab world turns into a set of fundamentalist Taliban states. Well, what do you do with those people? You can't talk to them about it – you've got to go and beat them, I'm afraid; you've got to go and defeat them. Each time I search for what the alternative is, I can't see it.[19]

In making these remarks, Blair was echoing the intelligence assessments he had received. A Joint Intelligence Committee report on 18 September stated that Bin Laden 'has no interest in negotiation and there is no indication that he can be deterred.'[20]

At this stage, Blair spoke of Al Qaeda as a phenomenon on the extreme fringes of the Islamic world, which the vast majority of Muslims utterly repudiated.[21]

An important anchor for Blair's response to 9/11 was a personal view about the nature of Islam and of the relationship between the Islamic and the Western worlds. He had been reading the Koran prior to 9/11 and readily quoted parts of it in private to his colleagues.[22] He firmly rejected Huntington's notion of an inevitable conflict between the Islamic world and the West. His Christian faith informed a view that was, in general, sympathetic to religion and the positive role it can play in society. Instead of framing the problem as a struggle against Islamic extremism or fundamentalism, Blair described 'mass terrorism' as the evil of the age and the situation as a battle 'between the free and democratic world and terrorism'.[23] Blair framed the issue this way in his first Downing Street statement on the day of the attacks, even before Bush declared a 'war against terrorism', in his evening address from the Oval Office.

Later in his memoirs, Blair described this initial interpretation of the events of 9/11 as a mistake. He described his errors as failing to understand how widespread sympathy for extremism was in the spectrum of modern Islam and that there was a 'fundamental struggle for the mind, heart and soul of Islam'.[24] The evolution of Blair's views from the immediate aftermath of 9/11, to the end of his term in office, in a generally confrontationalist direction, can be identified clearly in speeches and statements he made in 2006, examined in Chapter 9.

In 2001, however, Blair sought to draw a clear line between the terrorists and the Islamic faith. In a statement on 27 September 2001, after meeting with British Muslim leaders at Downing Street, Blair rejected any connection between the 9/11 perpetrators and Islam. He said the attack on America 'was not the work of Muslim terrorists. It was the work of terrorists, pure and simple. We must not honour them with any misguided religious justification.'[25]

Blair was very keen to reach out to the Islamic world and build a Muslim coalition of support for the War on Terror. While Blair did not see the Israeli-Palestinian issue as a grievance that had caused the attacks, Blair considered advancing the Israeli-Palestinian peace process to be an important part of this coalition-building effort. In his speech to Parliament on September 14, he said:

> We do not yet know the exact origin of this evil. But if, as appears likely, it is so-called Islamic fundamentalists, we know that they do not speak or act for the vast majority of decent law-abiding Muslims throughout the world. I say to our Arab and Muslim friends: 'Neither you nor Islam is responsible for this; on the contrary, we know you share our shock at this terrorism, and we ask you as friends to make common cause with us in defeating this barbarism that is totally foreign to the true spirit and teachings of Islam.' I would add that, now

more than ever, we have reason not to let the Middle East peace process slip still further, but if at all possible to reinvigorate it and move it forward.

Furthermore, Blair believed that resolving the Israeli-Palestinian dispute would take away a tool that Al Qaeda used to rally support. According to Jonathan Powell, Blair believed that after 9/11, it was important

> to remove the excuses that were used by people like Al Qaeda. In other words it's not that we believe that Al Qaeda was motivated by any real concern about the people of Palestine, but it did provide them with a very good stick to beat the West and to beat Israel in Islamic communities.[26]

Lord Levy described Blair's position similarly, saying that he wanted to address the Middle East peace process 'not because this is the reason for the terror to have happened but by making progress, it dilutes one of the reasons they claim they are pursuing.'[27] In the *Observer* interview, Blair stressed the distinction. For him, the imperative to 'kick start' the peace process was not about trying to accommodate the demands of the terrorists, but was rather part of an agenda to isolate them:

> Nothing justifies this type of savagery and fanaticism, but I see strong parallels with the Northern Ireland peace process. What happens when the process breaks down is that the fanatics and extremists use the breakdown as an excuse to engage in more violence, because there's a vacuum, and when there's a vacuum these people move in and exploit it, in exactly the same way that bin Laden is exploiting the Palestinian cause. He planned this operation two to three years ago, when the peace process was going somewhere. He doesn't support the peace process at all. In fact he opposes it. He wants Israel wiped off the face of the earth.

When the cabinet convened on September 13, Blair told his colleagues he wished to focus on three things. They were: 'Whatever US military response is made, and our participation within it. Politics and diplomacy and in particular trying to get impetus into the Middle East peace process. And practical security arrangements.'[28] In a meeting with Italian Prime Minister Silvio Berlusconi on 17 September, Blair emphasized that it was important to have Arab countries as part of the coalition. According to Alistair Campbell, Blair told Berlusconi:

> The best signal of all would be a restart of the Middle East Peace Process. There was a real risk that Sharon sees this as an opportunity to say that Arafat equals OBL [Osama Bin Laden]. He said it was important we all made clear to Israel

this should not be an opportunity to settle scores but on the contrary we should have the objective of reinvigorating the peace process.[29]

According to David Manning, Blair believed making progress in the Israeli-Palestinian arena was not just about making common cause with the Arab and Muslim world, but about developing the Middle East. Blair felt the Palestinian issue provided Arab governments with an excuse not to modernize. Blair saw 9/11 as presenting an opportunity to promote new dialogue to help resolve problems. He believed that better prospects for the Middle East peace process would lead to greater inward investment and to political progress in the Arab world. Blair hoped that the impact of 9/11 would, in Manning's words, 'not only lead to a resolution of this problem but . . . would shake up the region and lead to modernisation'. As Manning put it:

He immediately understood, I think, the implications of 9/11 in terms of the West's relationship with the countries of the Middle East, with the Islamic world as a whole, and never wavered from the view that dealing with the problems of 9/11 geopolitically must involve trying to find a just settlement between Israel and Palestine. . . . You could not say, well we'll deal with Iraq, or we'll deal with Afghanistan as though somehow these things don't relate to a much wider picture. If you want stability, if you want to reach a much wider working relationship across the piece, he always believed that finding a settlement for Israel and Palestine was vital.[30]

Blair wrote in his memoirs that he saw the problems of the Middle East after 9/11 as interlinked and that the most basic challenge was the urgent need for modernization. He wrote that at the street level and among the educated commentariat:

[The Israeli-Palestinian issue] became a means of siphoning off the demand for change inside, by focusing political energy and commitment to an external cause, an injustice not just to Palestinians but to Muslims everywhere, a vital and persistent proof that the West was inimical to Islamic interests and to Islam itself.[31]

In this context, Blair believed, 'the Palestinian issue was of essential strategic importance to resolving this wider struggle' against extremism.

Given the emphasis Blair placed on the peace process after 9/11, it would be easy to confuse his position with that of the Palestine first accommodationists who were also stressing the need to resolve the Israeli-Palestinian issue. It is important to stress that their positions were in fact very different. First, Blair rejected anti-Americanism. His experiences of his first term in government only reinforced his instinctive pro-American orientation by convincing him of the need for the US to use its power as a leading force for good in the world. He did not accept the view, championed on the left by Noam Chomsky among others, of the United States as a malign and hypocritical force in the world, concerned only in advancing its own hegemonic interests, with Israel as its local beat policeman.[32] Blair told the annual Labour Party conference on October 2 that, 'Some of the reaction to September 11 betrays a hatred of America that shames those that feel it.'[33]

Second, he did not accept the notion that Israel was primarily responsible for the Israeli-Palestinian problem. While Blair subscribed fully to the belief that the Palestinians should be supported in their endeavours to secure a state, he had a deep-rooted sympathy with Israel's predicament as a democracy seeking to maintain its security in a deeply hostile environment. In addition, Blair's personal style inclined him to seek influence by building affinity and trust within his interlocutors. For this reason, he usually avoided publicly apportioning blame in the Israeli-Palestinian conflict to either side and typically sought to recognize the responsibilities and challenges on both sides. Another feature of the Palestine first position that had been expressed in the debate over Iraq in 1998 was the argument that focusing on the Security Council Resolution breaches by Iraq was showing double standards by the West. Blair rejected this equivalence.

Third, as discussed, Blair rejected the idea that US or other Western foreign policies, including support for Israel, were the root cause that led to terrorism. In the weeks after 9/11, he accepted the need to try to understand the hatred, but drew a sharp line between that and allowing for any justification. He did not believe that Bin Laden and his movement themselves were driven by the Palestinian cause.

Blair's immediate desire after 9/11 to put new impetus into the peace process was part of a broader sense that the events of 9/11, however awful in themselves, had created new opportunities. Lawrence Freedman, who spoke to officials in Number Ten in the days after 9/11, recalls that the mood there, rather than being one of panic or foreboding, was one of high excitement. For Blair and Jonathan Powell, 9/11 was 'a great opportunity in international relations as well as a terrible tragedy, because everything is churned upside down and you can be creative in ways that you couldn't be creative up to now.'[34]

This included a renewed effort to get the US to engage in the Israeli-Palestinian arena, an issue on which Blair had been frustrated by US inaction. David Manning recalled:

> He felt there was a moment when things were very plastic internationally and reforming and reshaping things was a real possibility and because the international situation changed so much it did give opportunities to tackle old problems in new ways. And I am sure he felt that was true of Israel-Palestine.

Blair expressed this approach in his address to the annual Labour Party Conference on 2 October, in a speech infused with Blair's activist spirit and reflecting the monumental scale of his personal ambition. He declared, 'This is a moment to seize. The kaleidoscope has been shaken. The pieces are in flux. Soon they will settle again. Before they do, let us re-order this world around us.'[35] Sections of the speech dealing with the response to the 9/11 crisis were somewhat defensive. It was an indication of the disquiet already developing within the party at Blair's response to the crisis. He defended his commitment of UK forces to support the US in attacking Afghanistan, stating: 'There is no compromise possible with such people, no meeting of minds, no point of understanding with such terror. Just a choice: defeat it or be defeated by it. And defeat it we must.' Blair also referred to the need to tighten up legislation at home to target terrorism and its supporters. He returned to the theme of global interdependence and the need for the world to act together to address international problems. As part of this, he declared, 'If we wanted to, we could breathe new life into the Middle East peace process and we must.' In attempting to seize what he saw as the opportunities created by 9/11, Blair wanted to build a wide international coalition and assumed for himself a role of winning global support for the War on Terror. In the first 60 days after the crisis, Blair held 59 meetings and 34 telephone calls with world leaders.[36]

On his way to visit New York on 20 September, he spoke with the President of Iran, the first such contact since the Iranian revolution. UK relations with Iran had returned to ambassadorial level during Blair's first term. However, advances had been cautious, with Robin Cook resisting the advice of his Permanent Secretary John Kerr to visit the country.[37] Blair, however, saw Iran as a party with a legitimate interest in the issues. He stressed to President Khatami that 'this was not a struggle between Islam and the West, but between civilisation and terror.'[38] The outreach to Iran indicated that while Blair was depicting the conflict at this stage as one between 'civilization' or 'freedom' and 'terror', he was clearly open-minded as to where the dividing line was. He was open to the possibility that the Iranian regime could become an ally in the struggle.

Blair travelled twice to the Middle East, in the months following 9/11, in October and November. Western-allied Arab leaders reinforced Blair's impression that the Palestinian cause was an urgent issue that had to be addressed after the war in Afghanistan.[39] Blair also travelled to Syria, where his coalition building hit a public and embarrassing barrier. In a joint press conference, Syrian President Bashar al-Assad defended Palestinian 'resistance', described Israeli actions as 'terrorist' and criticized the attack on Afghanistan.[40]

The UK's outreach to Iran greatly concerned the Israeli government. Foreign Secretary Jack Straw followed up on Blair's contact by arranging a visit to Tehran to be followed by a visit to Israel. On the day of his trip to Iran, he published an article in Iran which stated:

> I understand that one of the factors which helps breed terrorism is the anger which many people feel at events over the years in Palestine . . . On leaving Iran, I shall be visiting Jerusalem to make it clear to both sides that they must not squander this opportunity for peace. The international community will find it very hard to understand if the violence and brutality resume. The quest for peace has to be part of the war against terrorism.[41]

The message infuriated the Israeli government. As far as they were concerned, it was Iran that was supporting the terrorists. Sharon's spokesman Ra'anan Gissin said:

> I've never seen such a bunch of lies garbled together . . . I've no doubt that it's malicious. I would expect the foreign minister of Libya or Iran to write such an article, but not the foreign minister of Britain.[42]

Ephraim Sneh, a cabinet minister from the Israeli Labour Party, who generally enjoyed good relations with the British Labour Party, said, 'His trip to Tehran, co-ordinated by the Americans is sticking a knife in Israel's back.'[43] As a result of the article, Israel's President Moshe Katzav cancelled a meeting with Straw at Sharon's request. A formal banquet arranged by Foreign Minister Shimon Peres was downgraded to a simple meeting. A meeting with Sharon only went ahead after a personal intervention from Blair.[44]

Though the outreach to Iran had been led initially by Blair, Straw's personal visit, alongside his comments about suicide bombers, left a lasting negative impression of the Foreign Secretary in Israel. Sneh later said he considered

Straw's outreach to Iran nothing short of 'appeasement'.[45] This marked the beginning of an important development in British–Israeli relations. Whereas in the past, it was Britain's desire to maintain good relations with the Arab states that most impeded its relationship with Israel, now Israel perceived that the desire of Western states to have better relations with the entire Islamic world might come at its expense. Israelis had hoped the attacks in America would create greater understanding for its own 'war on terror'. The telegram sent by Sherard Cowper-Coles to the FCO on September 11 reflected this, stating, '[T]he Israelis will undoubtedly see today's attack as underlining in dramatic terms they [sic] warning they have been giving others about the need to take very firm action against terrorism in all its forms.'[46]

However, after Straw's visit to Iran, Israelis saw that the attacks had the potential to create the opposite effect and that Israel could be blamed as the cause of the terror. This came as a shock to many in Israel.[47]

In fact, Blair quickly began to lose patience with Iran. Challenged over Iran's support for Hamas, Blair told the Commons on 5 December that dialogue with Iran

> should be based on one clear understanding—that, in the end, there can be no new relationship with countries which, for a variety of reasons, have had a very poor relationship with the Western world over the past few years . . . except on the basis that they cease supporting activities of terrorism.[48]

However, there were gaps between the tone of the Prime Minister and his Foreign Secretary. Speaking the same day, Jack Straw insisted, 'That dialogue and engagement must continue.' Diplomatic efforts to persuade Iran to be more cooperative were maintained by the Foreign Office and Straw visited Iran for a second time before the end of 2001.[49] At the height of the Iraq War in April 2003, the Foreign Office announced a relaxation of export controls to Iran and Minister Mike O'Brien visited Iran and Syria.[50]

On his second visit to the Middle East after 9/11, at the beginning of November 2001, Blair met Sharon and Arafat and pressed both sides to stop the violence. It was an inopportune moment. Two weeks earlier, on 17 October, gunmen from the Palestinian Front for the Liberation of Palestine, an armed PLO faction, had assassinated a hard-right Israeli Cabinet Minister, Rehavam Ze'evi, in a Jerusalem hotel. The Israeli response was to send ground forces into 'Area A', Palestinian population centres normally under Palestinian security control. Sharon expressed his readiness to engage in negotiations, but only when terrorism stopped.[51] Arafat gave Blair unconvincing assurances about his commitment to apprehending those responsible for the assassination of Ze'evi.[52]

Two trips to the Middle East in a month was a clear illustration of Blair's approach to the War on Terror, which included building a coalition of support with the Islamic world. As Rosemary Hollis has highlighted, focusing on the Israeli-Palestinian issue became a means to an end for Britain in reducing Arab criticism of the War on Terror. This generated suspicion of British motives on both Israeli and Palestinian sides.[53] Israelis feared they would be asked to pay the price for the War on Terror being pursued by the US and Britain. Blair was also forced to try and persuade his Arab interlocutors that his focus on the Middle East peace process in the wake of 9/11 was not a cynical ploy to win over the Arab world in a time of need, but a continuation of a long-term involvement. He cited the Tenet ceasefire plan and the Mitchell Report as examples of US commitment to peace.[54] Blair was aware, however, that without full US engagement no amount of effort by him or others would significantly change the situation.

Trying to persuade Bush

The differences between Blair and the Bush administration on the salience of the peace process after 9/11 were among the most significant policy disagreements on how to conduct the War on Terror. In the US administration, the desire to strike back at the source of the attacks was the overwhelming consideration.[55] The administration thought that US responses to terror attacks in the past had been inadequate and that the best way to protect America was to go on the offensive.[56] In a statement on the evening of the attacks, Bush declared that the US would 'make no distinction between those who planned these acts and those who harbour them'. This principle, which became known as the Bush Doctrine, became the central and defining mission of the President.[57] According to Bob Woodward's account of the Bush administration in the first 100 days after 9/11, there was little if any discussion within Bush's team of the motives or reasons for the suicide bombers' acts. Bush was well aware of Arab concerns about the Israeli-Palestinian issue, in particular expressed by the Saudis. However, the dominant thinking among his senior officials was that the Israeli-Palestinian problem was perpetuated by Arab intransigence.[58]

Bush mirrored Blair's approach to building bridges with moderate Islam in rhetorical terms. Like Blair, in the immediate aftermath of 9/11 Bush drew a sharp distinction between Al Qaeda and 'the peaceful teachings of Islam'.[59] However, Blair struggled to convince Bush to prioritize the Israeli-Palestinian issue as an important part of building common cause with the Islamic world. In an address to Congress on September 20, with Blair in attendance, Bush did not spare even a word for the Middle East peace process. He mentioned Israel only in the context of Al Qaeda's desire to remove it from the region. There was also no great emphasis placed on the importance of coalition building stressed by Blair, merely an acknowledgement of the support of countries around the world and a call for 'every nation to join us'.[60] The Bush administration was more inclined to forego the support of allies than compromise on its objectives or principles. Bush believed the US should determine policy on its own terms and those that supported it would follow.[61] It was a constant effort on the part of Blair to try and persuade Bush to act in coordination with other states.

The US did not ignore the Israeli-Palestinian issue completely. American pressure brought about a temporary truce towards the end of September 2001. On 2 October, President Bush made a brief but significant statement endorsing the idea of a Palestinian state.[62] However, this was not simply a response to 9/11. An announcement in support of a Palestinian state and an upgraded diplomatic effort to address the conflict had been planned in any case as a direct result of Saudi pressure in August. Rather than giving greater impetus to this, 9/11 had in fact distracted from it.

In response to Bush's endorsement of a Palestinian state, Ariel Sharon expressed the fear that Israel would be asked to pay a price by Western governments as they sought to maintain good relations with the Arab world while pursuing the War on Terror. In a press conference following a terror attack by a Palestinian gunman in Afula, Sharon said:

> I call on the Western democracies and primarily the leader of the free world, the United States: Do not repeat the dreadful mistake of 1938 when enlightened European democracies decided to sacrifice Czechoslovakia for a convenient temporary solution. Do not try to appease the Arabs at our expense . . . This is unacceptable to us. Israel will not be Czechoslovakia. Israel will fight terrorism.[63]

While Sharon feared the US would lead a Western policy of appeasement, generally Bush and his team accepted the Israeli government's logic that Arafat and the Palestinian terrorists were part of the broader problem of terrorism. After 9/11, Blair saw resolving the Israel–Palestine issue as even more important than before. The US administration, however, found it difficult to engage in the

Israeli-Palestinian peace process because of their tendency, in the words of David Manning, to refract the issue, 'through the prism of terror'.[64] Bush adopted a Manichean view of the world in which every nation in every region was required to choose, 'Either you are with us or you are with the terrorists'.[65] He explicitly linked Hamas, Islamic Jihad and Hezbollah to the War on Terror, drawing no distinction between them and Al Qaeda.[66] He also increasingly held the view that because Arafat was complicit in Palestinian terrorism, he was an enemy of the US and its interests.[67]

By contrast, while Blair was critical of Arafat, he rejected the comparison between Palestinian militancy and Al Qaeda, saying in an interview at the end of October 2001:

> There is a big difference between a situation where there is a genuine source of conflict, a political disagreement, that it is best to try to resolve by dialogue and negotiation, and a situation where you have got terrorists who have no demands, other than completely unrealisable demands, who are prepared to slaughter innocent people to further their ends.[68]

The unwillingness of many in Bush's administration to accept the connection between the Middle East peace process and the War on Terror frustrated Blair's team. Manning said, 'There was often a reluctance, as we saw it, to join up the dots. There was a tendency, certainly in some parts of the Administration, to put issues into different silos as if they did not connect'.[69]

Despite these frustrations, central to Blair's response to 9/11 was his belief in supporting the US in public while keeping differences of opinion private. Jonathan Powell noted that it was a lesson reinforced by the experience of the Kosovo conflict that this was the way to ensure the greatest degree of cooperation and influence.[70] A relationship of partnership and trust with the United States was central for Blair's post-9/11 ambitions to 're-order' the world. The lines of communication with the White House went directly through Blair and his office.[71] Blair shared Bush's commitment to confront not just the perpetrators of 9/11 but all those who supported or harboured terrorists.[72] He accepted immediately after 9/11 that Afghanistan as a whole would have to be addressed.[73] At the same time, in private, Blair continuously tried to persuade Bush to do more on the peace process. Manning claimed that, 'I really don't think any serious conversation passed on the transatlantic network of any length that didn't raise this. He was completely convinced that we had to make a massive effort to solve this problem'.[74]

Blair met with Bush in Washington on 7 November 2001. The primary focus was the war in Afghanistan, which had begun with US and UK bombing on October 7, but Blair also wanted to know what the Americans were ready to do on the peace process. According to the account of Britain's then Ambassador in Washington, Christopher Meyer, Secretary of State Colin Powell was pushing to make a policy speech on the issue that had been planned since the Saudi intervention in August. But, according to Meyer, 'the President's antipathy towards Yasser Arafat was undisguised.'[75] While Powell supported greater US engagement in the issue, he was a relatively isolated figure in the administration.[76]

The Israeli-Palestinian issue entered the discussion about the strategy to deal with Afghanistan, but Blair and Bush differed about whether it was worthwhile to go on dealing with Arafat. Bush was not willing to divert attention away from his primary commitment to militarily confronting the perpetrators of 9/11. Standing alongside Blair in a press conference, Bush declared that Al Qaeda would be defeated, 'peace or no peace in the Middle East'.[77] At a speech to the UN, three days later, he reiterated his support for a two-state solution and declared, 'We will do all in our power to bring both parties back into negotiations.' But he added that, 'Peace will only come when all have sworn off forever incitement, violence and terror.'[78]

Limited US engagement

While Bush was a reluctant partner in promoting the peace process, Blair had a likeminded ally in Secretary of State Colin Powell. After Bush's statement to the UN, Powell was able to make the major speech on the Middle East peace process which he had planned before 9/11. Powell's thinking, as evidenced in this speech, was close to Blair's. He described making peace between Israel and the Arabs as America's 'central diplomatic challenge' in the Middle East. While calling for Palestinians to end violence and incitement, he also called for Israel to stop settlement activity and declared that 'the occupation must end'. He announced that Assistant Secretary of State for Near Eastern Affairs Bill Burns and Retired Marine Corps General Anthony Zinni, acting as a senior adviser to the Secretary of State, would meet with Israelis and Palestinians to bring about a ceasefire.[79]

The two US officials travelled to the region in 26 November 2001, but despite promises by Arafat to end the violence, in the following two weeks there were five suicide bombings and ongoing Israeli operations against Palestinian armed groups. In December, Israel intensified its response with airstrikes and shelling of PA targets including the airport in Gaza. Though Arafat promised he was acting to arrest Hamas and other militants and stop the terror, the Israeli cabinet blamed him for the bombings, declared him 'irrelevant' and cut off all contacts.[80]

Jonathan Powell recalled that a considerable part of the problem in getting Bush to agree to a more substantial intervention was the US President's acceptance of the Israeli position that 'Arafat was not a serious negotiator [and] that he wasn't going to get anywhere with him.'[81] The British were also highly critical of Arafat at this time. On 5 December 2001, in the wake of suicide bombings in Jerusalem and Haifa, Blair told the House of Commons:

> It is important in my view that the Palestinian Authority does everything it possibly can to ensure that those in the organisations responsible for those attacks are rounded up and put under proper lock and key. That is the very minimum that the international community needs to see from the Palestinian Authority.[82]

In a Commons debate the same day, Arafat was criticized from all sides. Jack Straw stated, 'My criticism of President Arafat and the Palestinian Authority is that they have not done sufficient to pick up the terrorists.'[83] In an interview on 21 December, Straw reaffirmed his impatience with Arafat and called for him to declare an end to the Intifada. He expressed sympathy with Israel's position and said:

> If there was an Omagh (bombing) happening every weekend, then this would place any government under the most astounding pressure . . . Israel has the same population as Scotland. The pressures on any government would be unbelievable.[84]

A particular source of both Israeli and international concern was the Palestinian Authority's 'revolving door', whereby members of armed groups would be arrested by Arafat's security services and interned in Palestinian prisons, before being released after a short time. However, both Blair and Straw consistently defended maintaining contact with Arafat on the basis of his being the legitimately elected representative of the Palestinian people.

International lack of confidence in Arafat was greatly reinforced by the capture of the *Karine-A* ship by Israeli forces in early January 2002, carrying 50 tonnes of weapons purchased from Iran by the Palestinian Authority. Senior members of the US administration treated this as a smoking gun linking the Palestinian Authority and Arafat both to Iran and to Palestinian violence, and it reinforced the view of Israel as being on the front line in the War on Terror.[85] The capture of the ship took place just a few weeks before Bush made a speech in which he named Iran, alongside Iraq and North Korea, as part of an 'axis of evil' that threatened to support terrorists with WMD.

The capture also took place just as Zinni was returning to renew his efforts to reach a ceasefire, effectively ending his efforts before they began. The complete lack of faith on the part of the US in Arafat effectively ended the short-lived US efforts to intervene diplomatically in the Israeli-Palestinian arena. More violence followed at the beginning of 2002, with Israeli tanks moving into the heart of Ramallah to besiege Arafat's compound. Despite Blair's desire to see progress in the Israeli-Palestinian peace process, it was hard to see where to begin.

The Israeli-Palestinian Issue
and the Iraq War

The agenda turns to Iraq

The campaign in Afghanistan to remove the Taliban and destroy Al Qaeda's bases was largely concluded by the end of 2001. Thereafter, the central focus for the War on Terror became Iraq. It had been an express concern for the United States and United Kingdom during Blair's first term that WMD materials could fall into the hands of terrorists, intent on mass casualty attacks on Western targets. There was also a cohort within the US administration who strongly believed that toppling Saddam would be a catalyst for development and democratization in the region. But whereas Afghanistan was a clear and easily justifiable target after 9/11, targeting Iraq was far more controversial. The Labour Party was sharply divided as the build-up to war gained momentum in 2002 and early 2003. Blair's views diverged from many members of his government and party over the relationship between confronting Iraq, making progress on the Israeli-Palestinian peace process and addressing the threat of extreme Islamist violence directed at the West.

In January 2002, President Bush made a state of the union speech in which he defined states that threatened to support terrorists with WMD as an 'axis of evil', singling out North Korea, Iran and Iraq, with particular emphasis on the latter. In that context, he laid out a policy of pre-empting threats before they could develop. In the immediate aftermath of 9/11, the US administration suspected Iraqi involvement and considered Iraq as a target in the War on Terror.[1] Some senior officials in the Bush administration, led by the neoconservative Deputy Defence Secretary Paul Wolfowitz, had long advocated an active policy of regime change in Iraq.[2] The Clinton administration had adopted a formal policy of regime change in 1998, but in effect, UK and US policy was one of containment. In early 2001, the FCO's assessment was that this policy was failing. Saddam was able to circumvent sanctions to maintain his regime and, British officials feared, acquire WMD materials. Britain also assessed that he was restoring his standing in the Arab world through his support for the Palestinian Intifada.[3]

The new climate of uncertainty created by the 9/11 attacks raised fears in Britain and the US about the potential combination of terrorists bent on mass killing and the proliferation of WMD. After 9/11, Blair spoke of the realization of how destructive terrorists were willing to be, which created a situation whereby threats of WMD proliferation could not be tolerated. He later recalled: 'What changed for me with 11th September was that I thought then you have to change your mindset . . . you have to go out and get after the different aspects of this threat.'[4]

On 6 March 2002, Blair published an article in *The Express* arguing that Saddam's ongoing possession of WMD posed a direct threat to Britain.[5] This led to the voicing of concerns in Cabinet, with a number of ministers stating that the Middle East peace process was 'the real concern'.[6] Among them was Robin Cook, who believed that Blair was 'out on a limb', and that confronting Iraq would diminish hope for the peace process.[7] Home Secretary David Blunkett related the issue to 'social cohesion at home and the obvious issues that had arisen over 11 September, where the real message was: Why aren't you doing something about the Palestine-Israeli conflict? Why are you just backing the Americans?'[8] Expressing similar concerns, 162 MPs from all parties signed a House of Commons Early Day Motion tabled on 4 March expressing 'deep unease . . . at the prospect that Her Majesty's Government might support United States military action against Iraq', in the belief that it would 'disrupt support for the anti-terrorism coalition among the Arab states'.[9] On 25 March, Jack Straw sent Blair a personal memo in which he opined that there was no majority support in the Parliamentary Labour Party for war in Iraq. He pressed on the Prime Minister the fact that, 'The whole exercise is made much more difficult to handle as long as conflict between Israel and the Palestinians is so acute.'[10]

Policy advice from officials also stressed the link between Iraq and the Middle East peace process, though often in ill-defined and sometimes contradictory terms. An SIS assessment on regime change in Iraq in December 2001 stated that, 'Working for regime change could be a dynamic process of alliance building which could effect climatic change in the Arab-Israeli conflict.' Yet, the paper simultaneously noted that one of the risks involved in military action against Iraq included 'Boost to the Intifada and damage to MEPP efforts'.[11] A few months later, in March 2002, the Overseas and Defence Secretariat of the Cabinet Office issued a policy options document for ministers which stated:

Even a representative government [in Iraq] could seek to acquire WMD and build up its conventional forces, so long as Iran and Israel retain their WMD and conventional armouries and there was no acceptable solution to Palestinian grievances.[12]

Among the document's conclusions was that, 'an effort to engage the US in a serious effort to re-energize the MEPP would greatly assist coalition building.' John Sawyers, Director General for Political Affairs at the FCO from 2003 to 2007, explained his view to the Iraq Inquiry that, 'there was a link because having an unpopular policy on Iraq was one thing but our wider interests in the Middle East could be best addressed if we had at least some active policy on the Middle East.'[13]

During March 2002, UK officials made the case to their US counterparts that advancing the peace process was a vital accompaniment to confronting Iraq. David Manning told Bush's National Security Adviser, Condoleezza Rice, that the Prime Minister fully supported regime change but that he 'had to manage a press, a Parliament and public opinion that was very different to anything in the States.'[14] Manning told Rice that to gain coalition support for military action against Iraq, the US would have to first address the issue of Iraqi WMD through the UN, and secondly recognize 'the paramount importance of tackling Israel/Palestine'. Manning told Rice, 'Unless we did [take account of this concern], we could find ourselves bombing Iraq and losing the Gulf.' British Ambassador Christopher Meyer met Deputy Defence Secretary Paul Wolfowitz a few days later and reinforced the same message.[15]

The importance of the peace process to maintaining cooperation from Arab states was also stressed to the US by its allies in the Arab world. When Vice President Dick Cheney met with Blair on 11 March 2002, on his way to tour Arab states, he resisted any link between Iraq and the Israeli-Palestinian issue.[16] However, Bob Woodward claimed that the preoccupation of his Arab interlocutors with the Middle East peace process 'was something of a wake-up call for the vice president'.[17]

Circumstances on the ground, however, were not conducive to progress, after the *Karine-A* incident in January 2002 effectively ended efforts by US envoy Anthony Zinni to secure an Israeli-Palestinian ceasefire. Bush was unwilling to deal with Arafat and was not inclined to restrain Sharon, a position that dismayed many European diplomats. French Foreign Minister Hubert Vedrine said at the time: 'Europeans do not agree with the White House's Middle East policy and believe it's an error to blindly support Ariel Sharon's policies of pure repression.'[18] In the absence of committed US diplomacy, the French tried to rally EU members behind their own plan. They proposed elections in the Palestinian Authority in which the Palestinians would be able to affirm their commitment to peace, followed by the establishment of a Palestinian state in advance of final status negotiations.[19] However, during a visit to Israel on 13 February 2002, Straw, mindful of his problematic visit in September 2001, was sympathetic to Israeli security concerns. He called for Arafat to deliver on security and stressed the need for a common diplomatic approach with the US.[20] Blair resisted condemning Israel's military actions as fatalities rose on both sides in March.[21]

Then on 27 March 2002, the deadliest suicide bombing of the Intifada was carried out with 30 killed in a Netanya hotel during a festive Passover meal. This brought the number of Israeli civilians killed that month to 83, with 238 Palestinians killed by Israeli security forces in the same month.[22] On 28 March, the Arab League endorsed a Saudi-led plan which offered full normalization of relations with Israel in return for full withdrawal from the Occupied Territories and a 'just solution' to the refugee problem. Coming immediately after the Netanya attack, neither Israel nor the US issued any immediate response. On 29 March, Israel launched Operation Defensive Shield with major incursions into Palestinian population centres in the West Bank. The deadliest fighting took place in Jenin between 3 and 11 April, where 52 Palestinian militants and civilians and 23 Israeli soldiers were confirmed killed.[23] False Palestinian claims of a massacre with 500 Palestinian dead were widely and repeatedly quoted by *The Guardian* among others, whose editorial on 17 April described it as a 'crime of especial notoriety', which was, they believed, 'every bit as repellent' as the 9/11 attacks themselves.[24]

Amidst growing international outcry, Bush made a speech at the White House on 4 April in which he took the unusual step of calling for Israel to halt incursions and begin to withdraw. He declared that he was sending Colin Powell to seek a ceasefire and re-establish the peace process.[25] It came on the eve of a visit by Blair. Given the scale of the violence, the British wanted to take a firmer position against Israel and Christopher Meyer lobbied in Washington so that there would be no gaps between Britain and the US when Blair arrived. When Blair and Bush held their joint press conference in Crawford, Texas, the position had been hardened to a withdrawal 'without delay'.[26]

In Crawford, Blair pushed for the US to follow the UN route in confronting Saddam and to promote the Middle East peace process.[27] Then-Permanent Secretary at the FCO John Kerr believed that British support for war in Iraq at this stage was conditioned on progress in the peace process. At the same time Blair was in Crawford, Kerr was at a conference in Washington where he met senior US officials. He recalled what he believed to be the Prime Minister's position at the time as being, 'yes, you are probably right, one day we will have to do something about this [threat of WMD in Iraq],' with two conditions. The first was the 'multilateralisation' of the dispute through a UN Security Council Resolution. The second was

> That the Middle East Peace Process, the Oslo process, must again be seen to be on the road. You, Americans, have to correct the impression, held by all in the Middle East, that you are not interested in the peace process, that you are in Mr Sharon's pocket, that since he is not interested in the Peace Process, therefore you aren't either, and that nothing is going to happen except that the luckless Palestinians will suffer more and more. Unless that impression is corrected, we will have no bases or public allies, many will privately support us, but we will have no Middle East regimes, even the Saudis or Mubarak.[28]

Kerr recalled that

> When I argued . . . along the lines being taken in Texas by the Prime Minister, all the Wolfowitzes and the Perles jumped on me arguing that I had got the sequence the wrong way round, that there would never be a peace process while Saddam Hussein was in power in Baghdad. They maintained that it was he who was training, arming, rewarding the terrorists and the suicide bombers . . . I told them I thought you were absolutely wrong, that what was motivating these young people to strap on the bombs and get in the bus, was not the fact that Saddam might send a cheque to their father – if he remembered – once they had blown themselves up, but the huge and understandable sense of grievance at the way they were being treated, the building of the wall, and the knocking down of their towns. So the Neocons genuinely believed that you had to take out Iraq in order to get the peace process on the road.

The argument of the neoconservatives in the US administration that removing Saddam was a prerequisite for progress in the peace process was in fact broader than characterized by Kerr. Wolfowitz believed that by removing Saddam's totalitarian regime and installing democracy, a domino effect would be triggered spreading democracy in the region. He and like-minded thinkers believed democratization would ameliorate the social conditions in which extremism flourished and weaken the forces of radicalism which undermined the peace process.[29]

Kerr argued that it was an 'understandable sense of grievance' that was driving Palestinian suicide bombers. Though claiming to be representing Blair's views, the head of the diplomatic service had in fact justified Palestinian violence in a way that Blair consistently avoided doing. Furthermore, in his memoirs, Blair made it clear that behind closed doors, he actually agreed with the view that regime change in Iraq would contribute to a much broader agenda of transforming the region. As a result of 9/11, Blair believed in bringing a 'revolutionary' change to the region that would promote modernization and help overcome extremism.[30] His view was that leaving Saddam in power in Iraq lessened the chances of the region progressing gradually in a positive direction. He recalled coming to the conclusion that, 'The region needed a fundamental change.'[31] Instead of simply seeking to manage and contain threats in the region as Western governments had done in the past, Blair wrote, 'This time we would bring democracy and freedom.' Where Blair believed he differed from the neoconservatives was in seeing the Palestinian issue as being 'of essential strategic importance to resolving this wider struggle'. Blair wrote, 'It hadn't caused the extremism, but resolving it would enormously transform the battle lines in defeating it.' He saw the issues of Iraq and Israel-Palestine connected in the 'broader context of the Middle East as a region in transition'.

Blair did not describe in a very clear and systematic way how the issues were connected, or the way in which either regime change in Iraq or resolution of the Israeli-Palestinian conflict would bring wider regional reform. Rather, a number of interrelated themes emerge from his memoirs. One is the view that for those in the region opposed to Western influence, including both Al Qaeda and Saddam Hussein, peace between Israel and the Palestinians was a threat. It would mean 'coexistence', which was anathema to Al Qaeda and a threat to Saddam since, 'A calm region, on a path to change, would not be an easy region for the likes of him and his sons.' Related to this, Blair wrote that addressing the Israeli-Palestinian issue was important in order to confront Iraq 'without a revolt on the Arab streets and upset across the Muslim world'. Furthermore, as already mentioned, Blair believed the Israeli-Palestinian conflict fuelled popular anti-Western sentiment among Arab publics, and thereby drew 'political energy' away from the 'demand for change', even though, according to Blair, Arab leaders actually wanted peace.[32]

Blair stressed in his memoirs that these broader discussions about the future of the region were part of the case he made to Bush in April 2002 for addressing the Israeli-Palestinian issue alongside confronting Iraq. For these various reasons, Blair wrote, addressing the Israel-Palestine peace process was 'utterly crucial to creating the conditions in which the tougher, harder measures could be taken'. He similarly testified to the Iraq Inquiry in 2010 that he told Bush he thought progress on the Israeli-Palestinian issue was 'vital'. The thinking is also reflected in a memo Jonathan Powell wrote to Blair in July 2002, in which he set out steps that Blair should propose to Bush as part of a 'road map to getting rid of Saddam'. This included the assertion that, 'We need at least *neutrality in the region* before we can act . . . If we want to base our troops in the region this will mean a real effort on the MEPP (for example difficult to believe Jordan could allow basing without progress)' [emphasis in the original].[33]

Did this mean that progress on the Israeli-Palestinian issue was a condition set by Blair for Britain supporting US military action in Iraq? Then-Permanent Secretary John Kerr clearly thought so. Other senior officials also thought it was a condition,[34] as did Foreign Secretary Jack Straw, and Defence Secretary Geoff Hoon according to the evidence they gave the Iraq Inquiry. Straw wrote to Blair on 8 July to express his concerns at the failure of the US to address in their military planning 'your three conditions for UK involvement (preparation of public opinion, UN route exhausted, and some MEPP improvement)'.[35] The Director of the Middle East and North Africa Department of the Foreign Office reaffirmed in a submission to the Foreign Secretary's office a few days later the necessity for 'visible improvement in the Israel/Palestine situation, to give us some protection against the argument of double standards'.[36] But despite the fact that Blair did link the issues, the belief in a strong conditional link between the two policy areas appears to have been an exaggeration of his position. Jonathan Powell told the Iraq Inquiry that Blair did not place conditions on his support for confronting Iraq but rather argued for a framework within which to conduct the policy.[37] In his own evidence to the inquiry, Blair stated that his view of the importance of the Israeli-Palestinian peace process did not translate into specific conditions on British support for military action in Iraq. Blair told the inquiry, 'I think we should certainly, in order to understand my mindset, avoid this language of trading this policy for that policy. I would not have done Iraq, if I hadn't have thought it was right, full stop, irrespective of the Middle East [peace process]'.[38]

From these sources, the motivation to press the Middle East peace process both in Number 10 and in the Foreign Office was to create a permissive diplomatic environment in the Arab world to make regime change in Iraq possible. But what accounts for the different understandings even among key cabinet colleagues of the government position on the issue of conditionality between the policy areas – Israel-Palestine and Iraq? In part, the lack of clarity appears rooted in a lack of precision about what progress in the peace process actually meant on the ground, how it was to be measured and why it mattered.

The vagueness of the position may also have reflected Blair's diplomatic style. He was not keen to set clear conditions or ultimatums with allies, and certainly not with the US. Blair was accused in various quarters of not being firm enough in pressing his position. Lord Levy's view was that this was a consistent trait of Blair's. He said, 'In all my experiences with him, he's very non-confrontational. And I don't believe really pushed the agenda he wants to pursue in a tough enough way.'[39] Then-US Secretary of State Colin Powell, whose views were close to the British position, told Blair's biographer Anthony Seldon, 'Blair would express his concerns, but he would never lie down on the railroad tracks.'[40]

Blair's Chief of Staff Jonathan Powell defended Blair's approach with the Americans, saying:

> I think that is essentially a misunderstanding of the way he saw his role. There are different ways you can have influence on other leaders. You can do it by banging them over the head and bullying them and forcing them into doing things. Or you can try and cajole them, sweet talk them, explain to them why it's in their interests to do something. Tony was in the latter camp. It would have been completely out of character for him to try and bully Sharon or bully Bush into doing things and frankly I don't think he would have got very far. Because Britain as Britain had very little locus in all of this . . . I always think that people criticising Tony like that would rather have had a different sort of leader. But a different sort of leader probably wouldn't have made it into the Oval Office or Sharon's office as often as Tony did. Did Tony have influence by cajoling? Yes he did. If he'd been a different sort of person hectoring and bullying would he have had more influence? No I doubt it.[41]

It transpires, therefore, that while there was a consensus between Blair and his senior officials and ministers, that addressing the Israeli-Palestinian conflict was an important accompaniment to confronting Iraq, Blair preferred to try and persuade Bush to act, rather than attempt to force him through an ultimatum.

Managing the Israeli-Palestinian problem

Operation Defensive Shield contributed to concern and anger already building in parts of the British media and in Parliament over Israel's actions. British Ambassador to Israel, Sherard Cowper-Coles, told the *Jerusalem Post* in March 2002 that the 'centre of gravity in the chattering classes has shifted against Israel'.[42] Jonathan Freedland described how as a result of the outbreak of the Second Intifada, Israel had come on the UK public agenda to a greater extent than at any time since the First Intifada. Even before 9/11, Israel was increasingly seen as 'the bad guy'.

> Certainly Labour activists would have been feeling shocked and horrified by images of Israel hitting back and that reached an absolute peak with the Jenin episode in spring 2002. This is where I see a divergence of narratives between America and Israel on the one hand, and Britain and Europe on the other.[43]

In the US administration, Israel was seen as the country on the front line in the War on Terror, fighting the same enemy as the United States. But in the United Kingdom, Freedland stated, people thought, 'It's Western countries beating up Muslims: no wonder they are so angry they are prepared to go to extreme lengths or undertake extreme acts like 9/11.'[44] Labour MP Richard Burden, Chair of the pro-Arab Labour Middle East Council, tabled a parliamentary motion accusing Israel of collective punishment in breach of the Geneva Convention. It was signed by 152 MPs, many of them Labour.[45] It was around this time that a movement began to gain ground among certain British trade unions, led by British academics, to boycott Israel.[46]

It is remarkable, therefore, that on returning to the United Kingdom, Blair resisted calls in Parliament to condemn Sharon for Israel's actions, and was typically pragmatic. While he had worked on Bush to engage the US in improving the situation, he took a distinctive position about how the Europeans should engage. Rather than focusing on Israel's need to withdraw its forces, as many on the British liberal left, and his European colleagues did, he focused on Palestinian reform. He proposed that the EU intervene to ensure the Palestinian Authority was able to provide basic security guarantees for Israel, for example, by monitoring Palestinian jails to provide assurances that captured terrorists were not released again by the PA. He expressed European readiness to help the Palestinians rebuild their infrastructure and 'establish an accountable and transparent security structure'.[47]

In the same speech, on 10 April, Blair acknowledged the difference between himself and other European leaders. His approach can be understood to be a function of his convictions, political style and political calculations. Blair thought publicly upbraiding the Israelis would diminish his influence with them. He did not want to reduce his sway with the Americans by distancing himself from their approach. At the same time, he sympathized genuinely with Israel's security concerns and shared to some extent the US disdain for Arafat. His pragmatism also led him to a position whereby he saw the key to progress not on trying to persuade Israel to relax its security measures, but on getting the Palestinians to reform.

While Blair agreed with his European colleagues, and the Mitchell report, that settlements were a barrier to peace, he consistently sought to balance criticism on both sides. He told the Commons:

> I understand the anger of the Palestinians, who see the steady encroachment of Israeli settlers who take their land from them in defiance of international law and successive UN Security Council resolutions. That must stop, but so must the appalling suicide bombings that have taken so many Israeli lives in the past few months. Palestinians have supporters the world over for their cause, but that support is weakened every time the suicide bombers act.

Some may have considered that Blair's relatively soft touch on settlements lacked principle, and was counterproductive. Blair's approached, as described above by Jonathan Powell, reflected a belief that Britain had no power of compulsion over either side. Therefore, rather than try forlornly to 'force them into doing things,' the best way Britain could have influence was to 'sweet talk them'. This approach was heavily criticized by the Palestinian side. Afif Safieh, the Palestinian Authority's senior representative in Britain, told a BBC documentary that, 'Britain within Europe remains our weakest link.'[48]

Colin Powell's mission to the region was undermined by other senior members of the US administration.[49] Senior Foreign Office officials believed that while Blair had helped to persuade Bush of the importance of addressing the Israeli-Palestinian issue, a combination of the hawks in the administration, the Sharon government, the pro-Israel lobby and the Republic right 'swung the President back again.'[50] This was despite more pressure from Saudi Arabia to intervene.[51]

British officials on the ground continued to mediate between Israel and the Palestinians. The siege of Arafat's compound was ended by an agreement that the assassins of Rehavam Ze'evi, who were sheltering there, would remain in custody overseen by US and UK security monitors. British MI6 agent, Alistair Crooke, seconded to the EU envoy's office, was involved with brokering the deal which ended the siege of the Church of the Nativity where another group of Palestinian militants was sheltering.[52]

On 24 June 2002, Bush made another speech on the Middle East. It set out a process whereby Palestinian elections, accompanied by political and security reform, would make possible the establishment of a state in provisional borders, before addressing the remaining disputes with Israel. In some respects it echoed the earlier French proposal for Palestinian elections and some of Blair's proposals in April on Palestinian reform. The main difference was that Bush called for the Palestinians to elect new leaders 'not compromised by terror'.[53] Bush was making Arafat's replacement a clear condition on progress. Christopher Meyer described this statement as a reversal of the position taken in April, and one which put the US policy on the peace process on a 'care and maintenance basis' until the Palestinians got rid of Arafat.[54] Jonathan Powell noted that Bush's view of Arafat was critical in stopping him making any significant commitment to the peace process. He argued:

> In the end Bush had made the decision that Arafat was not a serious negotiator that he wasn't going to get anywhere with him . . . He only wanted to invest political capital where it could make a difference. I don't think for much of that period that he thought that investing political capital in the Middle East was worth doing because he wasn't going to get anywhere. We tried to persuade him that we should but we didn't succeed.[55]

Blair agreed that Arafat needed to be replaced and suggested to Bush that Arafat could remain as a titular head, with someone else managing negotiations. Alistair Campbell recorded in his diary after the Bush speech:

> TB didn't really want to end up in a US/UK rift situation, but we said it was up to the Palestinian people to elect their leaders, which was taken as an attack on Bush so we were heading for the rift headlines, even though TB was really in agreement that Arafat was weak, and that there had to be more sympathy for the Israelis.[56]

Despite Blair's feelings about Arafat, the United Kingdom, unlike the United States, continued to maintain contact with him. Lord Levy explained the British reasoning by saying, 'For the UK to have been able to play any role . . . would not have been possible yet alone viable unless they were able to meet with the leadership on both sides.'[57] For the Americans, he recalled, it 'was actually rather helpful because we were able to report back to them.' Britain's ongoing readiness to engage with Arafat marked a clear difference from the US approach. Blair believed in trying to actively manage the conflict, even if it could not be immediately solved. John Sawyers told the Iraq Inquiry:

> One of Tony Blair's maxims in foreign policy was that if you can't solve a problem, you have to manage it. So he thought we needed to have active measures in place to manage the Middle East even if it wasn't solvable at that time. And that was certainly very important to our main Arab partners, the Saudis, the Egyptians, the Jordanians, the Gulf Arabs and so on.[58]

Overall, however, concerns were growing within the UK government that British backing for the US position was damaging its international reputation. Alistair Campbell referred in his diary to the perception that Blair slavishly followed Bush's line on the Middle East as the 'poodle position'.[59] Meyer observed that the British 'conditions' were losing traction and warned London that 'the UK risked being taken for granted'.[60]

Blair commits to confronting Iraq

A Cabinet Office briefing paper to ministers in July 2002 reiterated that the 'conditions necessary for military action in Iraq' included a 'quiescent Israel/Palestine'. It stated that, 'Saddam would use continuing violence in the Occupied Territories to bolster popular Arab support for his regime.' It confirmed that the UK government was 'using the Palestinian reform agenda to make progress, including a resumption of political negotiations'.[61] Around the same time, Blair sent a note to Bush, making the case both for going down the UN route in confronting Iraq and for addressing the Middle East peace process.[62]

However, over the course of the summer, Blair became more decided on his readiness to use military force against Iraq, and his emphasis on the policy linkage between confronting Iraq and making progress on the Middle East peace process diminished markedly. In an extensive press conference given in September 2002, Blair emphasized that though he wanted to advance the Iraq issue and the peace process, they were not, in his view, 'connected directly'. He told the press,

They are different issues in the sense that it is important that we deal with the threat posed by weapons of mass destruction and the breach by Saddam Hussein of the United Nations resolutions. It is important that we deal with that and that is a separate issue from the issue of the Palestinians.[63]

Blair held another summit with Bush at Camp David in early September 2002. John Kerr's view was that 'when the Prime Minister went to Camp David in September, our Middle East peace process condition had been dropped, and we were maintaining only the UN condition.'[64]

According to Blair's memoirs, the sole objective of the British at that meeting was 'to get George to go down the UN route'.[65] Blair, working closely with Straw and US Secretary of State Powell, convinced Bush to seek the renewal of UN weapons inspections in Iraq, against the advice of Vice President Cheney and other more hawkish US advisers.[66] Nonetheless, Blair also continued to push the issue of the peace process and extracted a promise from Bush that he would, according to the account of Alistair Campbell, 'get something on the Middle East'.[67] According to David Manning, Blair pushed, in particular, for a Middle East peace conference and offered London as a venue.[68]

Bush did not take up the idea of a peace conference, but the following week, representatives of the Quartet, consisting of the UN, United States, European Union and Russia, announced that they were 'working closely with the parties and consulting key regional actors on a concrete, three-phase implementation roadmap that could achieve a final settlement within three years.'[69] The Quartet was an innovation which sought to coordinate international engagement in the Israeli-Palestinian arena and which gave the European Union a more established role as a partner to the US in the process. The three-phase plan, which was being led by the US State Department, echoed the proposals in Bush's Rose Garden speech of 24 June 2002 and elements of the Mitchell Report. The first phase was an Israeli pullback of forces and reform of the Palestinian Authority, the second was the option of establishing a Palestinian state in temporary borders and the third was final status negotiations.

Focus on the Iraq issue intensified in the United Kingdom in September 2002 with the publication by the government of a dossier setting out concerns regarding Iraq. At a Cabinet meeting on 23 September 2002, concerns were voiced from across the political spectrum about confronting Iraq without significant efforts to advance the Israeli-Palestinian peace process. According to Alistair Campbell, the issue of 'double standards' was raised not only by Clare

Short, but also by loyal Blairite health secretary Alan Milburn.[70] In 1998, the double standards argument had been raised by a small and isolated group of left-wing MPs. In the period before the Iraq War, and with the Second Intifada at its height, this argument was being repeated by ministers with a range of political views within the Cabinet.

Speaking in the Commons the following day, Blair resisted making a direct link between Iraq and the Israeli-Palestinian issue but acknowledged that, 'there is genuine resentment at the state of the Middle East peace process, which people want to see the international community pursue with the same vigour.'[71] He reiterated his call for Palestinian security and political reform, a 'new conference on the Middle East peace process' and 'a massive mobilisation of energy to get the peace process moving again'. However, he rejected that the policy of confronting Iraq, and not Israel, over the breach of Security Council resolutions was double standards. He argued that the central UN resolutions relating to the peace process, resolutions 242 and 338, placed obligations not just on Israel but on 'all the states in the region'. They could only be addressed, therefore, through a peace process. Jack Straw similarly recognized the double standards argument as one of the four main concerns expressed by MPs about confronting Iraq. The others were whether Iraq really was a threat, whether there were other countries that equally posed a threat and whether use of force was justified. Straw reiterated the Prime Minister's reasoning for rejecting the 'double standards' case.[72]

Another way some MPs linked Israel into the debate was by arguing the accommodationist line that anger in the Islamic world at the Palestinian situation was the primary cause of radicalization and terrorism. Because the Palestine issue fuelled extremism and hatred of the West, it was argued, the way to combat terrorism was to address this issue, rather than by confronting Iraq.[73] Conversely, some on the Conservative benches echoed the arguments of the hawks in the US administration. They claimed that because Saddam directly funded Palestinian terrorism, removing him could only help the peace process,[74] or alternatively argued that a democratic Iraq would spread democratization in the region.[75] Sixty-four MPs, most of them Labour, registered their objections to confronting Iraq by voting against the adjournment motion in the House.[76]

Having faced his critics within the government and in Parliament, Blair had to face the Labour Party grass roots at its annual conference. Such was Blair's concern at the pressure from the party over the Israeli-Palestinian issue that in his conference speech he made a highly uncharacteristic statement that clearly contradicted US policy.

> Some say the issue is Iraq. Some say it is the Middle East peace process. It's both . . . I agree UN resolutions should apply here as much as to Iraq. But they don't just apply to Israel. They apply to all parties . . . By this year's end we must have revived final-status negotiations.[77]

The phrasing, which was aimed directly at the double standards argument, was typical of Blair's third-way style. However, the call for final status talks by the end of the year was a departure from Blair's principle not to publicly contradict the US agenda on the peace process. Blair's call for final-status talks was sharply different from the Quartet's three-phase Roadmap, which deferred final status talks to the third phase, not expected to be reached before 2004–05. Though Blair had called for a peace conference in Parliament, he had done so only in very general terms. According to journalist John Kampfner, Blair decided at the last minute, along with Jonathan Powell, to insert the passage without any consultation with other ministers or officials. The statement was not coordinated with the US. Bush, who had domestic political considerations prior to midterm elections, did not want to impose an artificial timeline.[78] Blair's aim, Kampfner reported, was to answer directly the double standards argument and to 'sweeten the pill of Iraq'.[79] Intense pressure from his party does indeed seem to be the best explanation for Blair's out-of-character statement.[80]

This unusual step by Blair marked a significant development. Whereas before Blair had seen addressing the Middle East peace process as an important part of a broad strategy to deal with the problems in the region, now he also saw it as vital for maintaining domestic political support. Journalist Jonathan Freedland agreed that, 'It's his congenital intellectual habit to look for a third way, but it's also in this case absolutely pragmatic . . . He was caught between his own party and government at home and this administration in Washington, and he needed to find some kind of balance.'[81] It has been argued that Blair's intense focus on the Israeli-Palestinian arena was driven primarily by a desire to bridge gaps between the United States and the European Union.[82] Though his self-assumed role of 'transatlantic bridge' certainly influenced Blair's thinking, as this incident shows, domestic political pressure tended to have a more tangible and immediate impact on the Prime Minister's position than the desire to maintain common ground with France or other EU partners.

War in Iraq causes strains in UK–Israel relationship

It might be expected that Blair's commitment to back the US in confronting Iraq would enhance Britain's relations with Israel. Saddam was one of Israel's most implacable enemies, who funded Palestinian suicide bombers and had fired Scud missiles at Tel Aviv during the First Gulf War. There were many who believed that at least part of the US motivation for going to war was to advance Israel's interests, as opposed to those of the United States or the United Kingdom.[83] Sometimes this belief took on a conspiratorial character, as in the case of veteran left-wing Labour MP Tam Dalyell. In the summer of 2003, he claimed that both British and American governments acted under the influence of a 'cabal of Jewish advisers'.[84]

In fact, Blair's growing political need to address concerns within his party over the Palestinian issue, in the context of the party's misgivings over the war in Iraq, caused considerable tension in the Israel–UK bilateral relationship. His call for immediate peace talks drew criticism from Israeli ministers.[85] A series of specific incidents deepened the rift. In the summer of 2002, the government came under heavy parliamentary criticism for allowing the sale of a component for the F16 fighter to the US, which was in turn sold to the Israeli Air Force. The government had established a principle in its first term of not selling equipment that was used against the Palestinians in the territories. The government had to revise its export rules to allow the F16 component to be exported.[86] Subsequently, in the second half of 2002, the government decided not to allow the export of a particular part for the ejector seat of the aging Phantom F4 combat aircraft. According to Ephraim Sneh, this grounded the aircraft and poisoned the bilateral relationship. Israel eventually retired the plane from service entirely in 2004.[87]

Tensions flared at the beginning of 2003 in a meeting between Lord Levy and Prime Minister Sharon. As part of his strategy to isolate Arafat, Sharon insisted that European leaders who wanted to see Arafat should not visit Israel in the same visit. Part way into a meeting with Levy, Sharon discovered that the British envoy had just come from seeing Arafat, and became very angry, ending the meeting on the spot.[88] This event left a legacy of distrust between Sharon and his advisers and Lord Levy.[89]

The situation was exacerbated shortly before Israel's general election at the end of January 2003. In the context of an ongoing Israeli election campaign, the US delayed the publication of the finalized Roadmap document, to the frustration of the European Union.[90] With no prospect for the peace conference Blair had been calling for, the Prime Minister announced an event in London to focus international support for Palestinian reform.[91] The event was scheduled for 14 January 2003. The week before, a double suicide bombing in Tel Aviv carried out by the Fatah-affiliated Al Aqsa Martyrs Brigades killed 22. Israel declared Palestinian leaders would not be allowed to travel. The announcement dismayed the Foreign Secretary, who was chairing the event, and was not informed in advance of the decision.[92] David Manning recalled that the decision also angered Blair.[93] The Palestinians participated by teleconference and the event produced only a statement by the Foreign Secretary summarizing the consensus on Palestinian reform, including the appointment of an 'empowered Prime Minister'.[94]

Insisting on holding a conference at that moment, despite it being unwelcome to the Israelis and out of step with the US president, was again motivated in part by Blair's concern to manage domestic public opinion. David Manning stressed that Blair was driven primarily by his desire to see progress on the issue. However, he acknowledged that in the lead up to the Iraq War, being seen to be active on the Israeli-Palestinian front also 'had a political management value for him inside his government, inside his party, certainly in presentational terms domestically in Britain but also internationally'.[95] Veteran British journalist, Simon Henderson, writing in April 2003, linked Blair's overt focus on the peace process to the 'the strength of feeling in the governing Labour Party against military action in Iraq', and the 'party members' unhappiness with the closeness of Blair's relationship to Bush'.[96]

Stephen Twigg, a minister in Blair's government at the time and a former Chair of Labour Friends of Israel, saw Blair's intense focus on the Israeli-Palestinian issue in this period similarly. He said:

> I think he certainly did have a really core conviction that this was something important both in terms of justice but also in terms of the long-term prospects for peace and stability of the region and internationally. But also obviously he is a very canny politician and could see that putting a very big emphasis on this alongside standing shoulder to shoulder with Bush on Iraq would take at least some of the heat off him on the Iraq issue so I think both considerations were there.[97]

Another incident contributed to tensions between Britain and the Sharon government. Two weeks before the Israeli election, Blair granted a high-profile meeting at Number Ten to Amram Mitzna, leader of the Israeli Labour Party and Sharon's rival for the post of Prime Minister. Shortly before, Blair had declined a

meeting with Israeli Foreign Minister Benjamin Netanyahu.[98] Israel's anger had
been increased by seeing Syrian president Bashar al Assad, in December 2002,
welcomed by the Prime Minister and even meeting the Queen, while continuing
to ignore calls to close the offices of Palestinian terror groups in Damascus.[99]
Israel accused Britain of interfering in the election. Ephraim Sneh recalled
that because of this event, Amir Peretz was refused a meeting with Blair when
running as Labour leader in the 2006 election.[100]

Blair's rhetoric also shifted to reflect the concerns of his critics. In early
January 2003, he made a major foreign policy speech to an unusual conference
of senior Foreign Office staff, including Ambassadors who had gathered from all
over the world. Blair stressed the need to 'reach out to the Muslim world', stating
that, 'The reason there is opposition over our stance on Iraq has less to do with
any love of Saddam, but over a sense of double standards. The MEPP [Middle
East peace process] remains essential to any understanding with the Muslim
and Arab world.'[101] In the Commons, Blair, backed up by Straw, had forcefully
rejected accusations of double standards. Here, without accepting that the West
was in fact applying double standards, he acknowledged that the perception that
such was the case was damaging the West's relations with the Islamic world.

In this period, Blair also made a separate argument that, 'absence of a sense
of real progress on the Israel-Palestine issue is a far bigger worry in terms of
recruiting people to terrorism than is the pursuit of Iraq over weapons of mass
destruction.'[102] In making this statement, he sought to rebuff those who claimed
that going to war in Iraq would make the threat of terrorism worse, by arguing
that the Israeli-Palestinian issue was a more important issue in the Islamic world.
However, he still avoided accepting the position that the Israeli-Palestinian
conflict, or Western support for Israel, was a legitimate grievance that motivated
Al Qaeda. His statement was consistent with the view that the ongoing conflict
was exploited by Al Qaeda to rally mainstream Islamic opinion to their cause.

Meanwhile, Blair continued to try and free the blockage in the peace process
by exerting pressure on Arafat to appoint a Prime Minister, a key US condition
for publishing the Roadmap. David Manning recalled that Blair pushed Arafat,
'very, very hard' on this issue, including through direct phone calls. According
to Manning, 'Blair was absolutely clear that it was essential for Arafat to have a
Prime Minister . . . who was acceptable internationally as a point of reference in
a way that Arafat had ceased to be.'[103] Informed that Arafat was finally ready to
give this commitment, Lord Levy was sent to Ramallah to receive the promise
in writing.[104]

Domestic pressure on Blair continued to build over Iraq. On February 15, the Stop the War coalition organized one of the largest political demonstrations in British history in central London. The Stop the War movement was formed by the far left Socialist Workers Party (SWP) prior to the war in Afghanistan. In the course of 2002, the movement joined forces with the Muslim Brotherhood-linked Muslim Association of Britain (MAB).[105] Despite having very different world views, the leftists and the Islamists were able to unite under a common banner. The priority for the SWP was Iraq. For the MAB, it was Palestine. An estimated one million people marched under the dual slogan, 'No War on Iraq; Freedom for Palestine.' The campaigners succeeded in attracting support well beyond their own core constituencies of fringe leftists and Muslims. Numbers were swelled with educated, middle-class professionals of the liberal left.[106]

It could be argued that Blair's refusal to criticize Israeli government policy left a vacuum which was filled by the far left. However, it is not clear that if Blair had been more critical of Israel, there would have been any less of an opportunity for the far left to promote anti-Zionism. Most people who rallied under the SWP-MAB 'Stop the War' banner in 2003 came out onto the streets because of the Iraq War. It was the political opportunism of the MAB to create a join slogan which put 'Freedom for Palestine' on the same level as 'No War in Iraq'. The masses who attended the rally appeared to accept without question the unification of these issues because the 'oppression' of the Palestinians at the hands of Israel had already become, in Hirsh's phrase, 'left "common sense"'. Had Blair been more openly critical of Israel, he may only have further reinforced the widely field belief within the left that Israel's behaviour was reprehensible.

The focus of political pressure within Blair's Cabinet was to get a second UN resolution to authorize the use of force that would ensure the legality of the war. However, Clare Short demanded the publication of the Roadmap as a condition for not resigning.[107] On 10 March, President Chirac of France declared that he would veto a second UN resolution, marking a major diplomatic setback for Britain and a political setback for Blair. However, a few days later, under intense British pressure, Bush finally gave the Roadmap his public backing. On 14 March, he announced that as soon as the Palestinian Prime Minister was appointed, the Roadmap would be presented to the parties for their consideration.[108] Jonathan Powell felt Blair's pressure was instrumental. He said: 'Getting the Roadmap coughed up, I think that was important. If we hadn't been pushing I'm not sure Bush would have announced willingness to go ahead with that.'[109]

The House of Commons debated war in Iraq on the evenings of 17 and 18 March 2003. The significance of the Israeli-Palestinian issue was indicated by the fact that the motion to support military action included a welcome for the publication of the Roadmap and an endorsement of the Government's role in 'working for peace between Israel and Palestine'.[110] The debate about whether to go to war in Iraq was not primarily about how to deal with Islamism or its violent strains, or about how to temper broader anti-Western sentiment in the Arab world. Rather, the strands of the debate included the extent to which Saddam posed an immediate threat, whether war was a justifiable means of dealing with that threat and whether it was right to act without international support. Therefore, the policy debate was not orientated around accommodationist and confrontationalist poles. Nonetheless, strong elements of the accommodationist perspective could be heard in the case against the war. Leading the caucus against the war, Labour MP Peter Kilfoyle talked about the Israeli-Palestinian issue in the context of 'the underlying causes that have given us the terrorism and the situation in Iraq in the first place'. Conservative MP Richard Ottaway agreed that, 'Failure to solve the Israel-Palestine conflict is at the root of the discontent in the Arab world.'[111] Jeremy Corbyn from the Labour benches and Michael Ancram on the Conservative benches both claimed that Israel was in some manner responsible for discord across the Middle East.[112] As in September 2002, other members reversed the causality. Labour MP Clive Soley stated, 'if we want a settlement in the Middle East, particularly of the Palestine-Israel situation, we also have to deal with Saddam Hussein.'[113] Another Labour MP, Hugh Bayley, claimed that both these linkages were true.[114] Furthermore, the double standards argument remained prominent. The most high-profile opponent of the war was Robin Cook. He resigned from the government in order to vote against. In his speech, he said:

> I welcome the strong personal commitment that the prime minister has given to Middle East peace, but Britain's positive role in the Middle East does not redress the strong sense of injustice throughout the Muslim world at what it sees as one rule for the allies of the US and another rule for the rest.[115]

The argument that attacking Iraq would increase Islamic anger, and therefore act as a 'recruiting sergeant' for Al Qaeda and increase the threat of terrorism, was a more prominent feature of the debate than it had been in September 2002. John Denham, who resigned as a Home Office Minister over the war, argued that military action would fuel more terrorism. Liberal Democrat MP Lembit

Opik argued that an attack on Iraq might cause terrorism against the United Kingdom. His argument was dismissed by Jack Straw who responded: 'I am afraid I do not accept that the way to oppose terrorists is to appease tyrants.' There were some arguing in favour of the war who claimed that what really angered Muslims was not Iraq, but the Israeli-Palestinian issue.[116] This was the same argument the Prime Minister had made in February. Blair himself said, 'I do not believe that there is any other issue with the same power to reunite the world community than progress on the issues of Israel and Palestine.'[117] Two hundred and seventeen MPs voted against the war, 139 of them were Labour.[118]

Once the war was underway, Blair continued pushing the US for greater commitment on the peace process. At a meeting in Northern Ireland on 9 April, Bush gave his British counterparts hope by stating that he was willing to 'expend the same amount of energy in the Middle East' as Blair had in Northern Ireland.[119] However, as Condoleezza Rice later admitted, such levels of US commitment were not followed through while the Bush administration remained focused on the Iraq War for the duration of its first term.[120]

On 29 April 2003, two British Muslims carried out a suicide bombing in the Mike's Place bar across from the Tel Aviv beach front. This event enhanced awareness in Britain of the increase in radicalization of Muslims in the United Kingdom. On the surface, this might have created more basis for bad feeling between the two countries, but behind the scenes, the incident led to the start of better intelligence cooperation between Britain and Israel.[121] Francis Cornish recalled that prior to 9/11, there was useful information sharing on regional, 'non-Israel issues', such as Iran and Iraq. However, he also recalled that there were tensions over Israeli intelligence operations that related to British citizens. The Mike's Place bombers were not the first British citizens to attempt to carry out terrorism in Israel. In January 2001, Israeli authorities arrested British-Lebanese citizen Jihad Shuman who was believed to be planning a terror attack on behalf of Hezbollah. The British government protested the detention of Shuman without trial and accused Shin Bet of torturing him.[122] Shuman was eventually tried and sentenced, but the incident was an indication of tension over Israeli security activities as they pertained to British citizens. The improved cooperation after the Mike's Place bombing was continued after the bombings carried out in Istanbul in November 2003, in which the British Embassy and a number of synagogues were attacked by the same terror cell.[123]

But whereas the Mike's Place attacks created a basis for better bilateral cooperation in intelligence and security, other incidents involving British citizens were simultaneously undermining relations. On 2 May 2003, James Miller, a British cameraman, was killed by a shot fired by an Israeli soldier in Gaza. The incident came three weeks after a peace activist, Tom Hurndall, was fatally wounded after being shot by an Israeli soldier. Another British citizen, UN official Iain Hook, was hit and killed by Israeli fire in November 2002 in the West Bank. British government dissatisfaction at the Israeli investigations into these incidents, fuelled by the campaigns of the victim's families, was another source of strain on the bilateral relationship.[124]

Further disagreement focused on the construction of Israel's security barrier in the West Bank. The proposal to build a barrier to protect Israel and the major settlements from infiltration by terrorists was approved by the Israeli government in 2002, with construction accelerating in 2003. The route of the barrier, designed to also protect the controversial settlement blocs, and in some cases tracts of undeveloped land around them, drew heavy international criticism, including from the United Kingdom.[125] The United States also pressured Israel over the route of the fence, even reducing slightly their annual loan guarantees to Israel because of dissatisfaction over its route.[126] Palestinians complained that in many cases the barrier cut them off from their agricultural land, divided communities, or inhibited their free movement, especially entering Jerusalem. They claimed that rather than being motivated by security considerations, the barrier was intended to annex pieces of the West Bank to Israel. As construction developed in 2003, British officials protested to their Israeli counterparts.[127]

Britain's intense focus on the Israeli-Palestinian arena drew increasingly vociferous anger from the Israeli government. In 2002, it had been Palestinian representative in the United Kingdom, Afif Safieh, complaining that Britain was the Palestinian's 'weak link' in Europe. In April 2003, Blair was berated as being too pro-Palestinian by the Israelis. Following an interview in which Blair said that achieving a two-state solution was as important as toppling Saddam, Sharon's close aide Dov Weissglass told *Israel Radio*, 'We regret that Great Britain is pushing itself out of involvement in the peace process as a result of extreme positions it has adopted.'[128] On 15 May, Prime Minister Sharon publicly attacked the British government in the *Jerusalem Post*, accusing it of 'unnecessary intervention' in Israel's affairs. Rather than enhancing relations between Britain and Israel, Britain's desire to see progress in the peace process as a counterpart to confronting Iraq brought UK–Israel bilateral relations to their lowest point of any time during Blair's term in office.

The Israeli-Palestinian Arena Becomes 'The Issue'

Blair's post-Iraq strategy in the War on Terror

After the fall of Baghdad, Blair spoke with increasing force about the centrality of the Israeli-Palestinian issue in combating terrorism. On 17 July 2003, Blair made a passionate, personally written speech to both houses of the US Congress.[1] It was an important articulation of Blair's beliefs about how to fight the War on Terror in the wake of the Iraq War.[2] He depicted the conflict as a battle of ideas against a fanatical strain of religious extremism that had mutated from the faith of Islam. He declared that the battle could not be won by military force alone. Blair argued that victory could only be secured by advancing the cause of liberty. He rejected the idea that freedom, democracy and human rights were Western values, and declared that, 'The spread of freedom is the best security for the free.'[3] He argued that the accusations of 'American imperialism' or 'a war on Muslims' would be undermined by the promotion of prosperity and democracy in Iraq and Afghanistan. In this context, he also stressed the centrality of the Israeli-Palestinian issue, saying:

> There is one cause terrorism rides upon, a cause they have no belief in but can manipulate. I want to be very plain: This terrorism will not be defeated without peace in the Middle East between Israel and Palestine. Here it is that the poison is incubated. Here it is that the extremist is able to confuse in the mind of a frighteningly large number of people the case for a Palestinian state and the destruction of Israel, and to translate this moreover into a battle between East and West, Muslim, Jew and Christian. May this never compromise the security of the state of Israel. The state of Israel should be recognized by the entire Arab world, and the vile propaganda used to indoctrinate children, not just against Israel but against Jews, must cease. You cannot teach people hate and then ask them to practice peace. But neither can you teach people peace except by according them dignity and granting them hope. Innocent Israelis

suffer. So do innocent Palestinians. The ending of Saddam's regime in Iraq must be the starting point of a new dispensation for the Middle East: Iraq, free and stable; Iran and Syria, who give succour to the rejectionist men of violence, made to realize that the world will no longer countenance it, that the hand of friendship can only be offered them if they resile completely from this malice, but that if they do, that hand will be there for them and their people; the whole of region helped toward democracy. And to symbolize it all, the creation of an independent, viable and democratic Palestinian state side by side with the state of Israel. What the president is doing in the Middle East is tough but right . . . And why has a resolution of Palestine such a powerful appeal across the world? Because it embodies an even-handed approach to justice.[4]

This speech could be interpreted as a version of the Palestine first position.[5] It certainly showed Blair's willingness to challenge the Sharon government and press for peace on terms which it was not clear Israel was ready to accept. However, Blair's logic remained distinct from those who believed that the Israeli-Palestinian conflict, or Western support for Israel, was the root cause of the threat facing the West from violent strains of Islamist extremism. He maintained that the grievances claimed by extremists against America and the West were false. He argued that the Israeli-Palestinian issue was exploited by the extremists to incubate their ideology of hatred against the West. Resolving the conflict would disprove these false accusations against the West, demonstrate Western commitment to justice and act as a wider symbol of the possibility of freedom for the whole region. Therefore for Blair, in contrast to many on the left of his party, establishing peace between Israel and the Palestinians was a necessary but not sufficient condition for defeating terrorism. Furthermore, Blair remained even-handed about the conflict itself. He did not equate commitment to resolving the conflict with putting pressure only on Israel. It was also particularly important that Blair made clear and consistent statements that while he wished to see the creation of a Palestinian state in Gaza and the West Bank, this could only come about in the context of arrangements that credibly met Israel's significant security concerns.

Repairing the damage with Israel

Blair had alienated the Israeli government in the run-up to the Iraq War by pushing the US to advance the peace process through the Roadmap. However,

Blair continued to believe the best way to promote British influence in the Israeli-Palestinian arena was through an approach that maintained good relations with both sides. After the publication of the Roadmap, Blair made efforts to repair relations with Israel. He gave a lengthy interview to the Hebrew language daily *Yediot Ahronot* in April 2003 and renewed an invitation for Sharon to come to London. In mid-May, he welcomed Foreign Minister Silvan Shalom to Number Ten,[6] and in June he met with Finance Minister Binyamin Netanyahu.[7] The situation was helped by the Roadmap gaining some diplomatic momentum. Yasser Arafat finally accepted the appointment of Mahmoud Abbas, also known as Abu Mazen, as Prime Minister of the Palestinian Authority at the end of April. On 4 June 2003, Bush chaired a summit in Aqaba, Jordan in which Sharon and Abbas committed themselves to the Roadmap, though Israel did so with a series of conditions.[8] At the end of June, Palestinian factions agreed to a ceasefire, and Israel agreed to some troop redeployments, the release of some prisoners and allowing more Palestinian workers into Israel.[9]

On 14 July, Sharon travelled to London and held an intimate dinner in the flat at Number Ten Downing Street with only Blair, David Manning and Sharon's adviser Dov Weissglass in attendance. Manning recalled such a personal welcome as 'rather exceptional'.[10] Though Britain reportedly rejected an Israeli demand to cut ties with Arafat,[11] Manning recalled it as a positive meeting.[12] It was not just Blair who was interested in repairing bilateral relations. Lord Levy believed that the Israelis, even when they disagreed with what Blair was trying to do in the Middle East, always appreciated that Blair was 'a solid friend of Israel'.[13] Furthermore, the Israelis respected Blair's influence in Washington. Levy stated that:

> Because of the perceived closeness of the relationship between Blair and Bush because of Iraq, they were always more wary on dealings with Blair and therefore me. Because they always wanted brownie points within Washington and not negative points within Washington, so therefore, if you like, perhaps the perceived influence was greater than it was.[14]

The progress on the ground that began at the end of June was short-lived. Violence resumed in August with Palestinian suicide bombings and other attacks, and Israeli incursions and targeted killings against Hamas and Islamic Jihad leaders, which also led to Palestinian civilian deaths. At the beginning of September 2003, Mahmoud Abbas resigned, having failed to gain the authority from Arafat to reform Palestinian security services and confront militants.[15] Another PLO veteran, Ahmed Qureia, also known as Abu Ala, was made Prime

Minister designate in his place. On 11 September 2003, the Israeli security cabinet decided 'in principle' to expel Arafat, but deferred acting on the decision. The decision drew criticism from the United Kingdom among other members of the UN Security Council, including the United States. The French called for an international force to be sent to the region.[16]

In the following months, Blair maintained pressure on President Bush to do more. In mid-November, Bush made an official state visit to the United Kingdom during which he made a firm call for Israel to cease settlement construction and criticized the security barrier. He echoed Blair's speech to Congress, saying that a Palestinian state alongside a secure Israel would 'remove an occasion and excuse for hatred and violence in the broader Middle East'.[17] However, Condoleezza Rice later admitted with regard to the Roadmap that, 'so much was caught up now in Iraq and trying to move that forward that I think we lost a little momentum.'[18] Blair too was distracted by major domestic political challenges, including inquiries into the flawed intelligence relating to the Iraq War, and controversial domestic reforms in health and education.

British support for efforts to fill the diplomatic void

In the absence of sustained US diplomatic leadership, a number of unofficial 'track two' initiatives were undertaken, bringing together Israeli and Palestinian interlocutors to look for ways forward. Among the most high profile was the Geneva Initiative – a set of negotiations led by former Israeli and Palestinian officials, which led to the creation of a draft Israeli-Palestinian peace accord. Blair was one of many international leaders who warmly welcomed this event, issuing a statement of support a few days before Colin Powell wrote to the founders of the initiative to praise their efforts.[19] However, Blair was typically cautious to take a position that got too far ahead of the US diplomatic agenda. He sought to stress the initiative's compatibility with the Roadmap, saying, 'The roadmap never described a settlement, just how to get there. So imaginative thinking about the endgame doesn't cut across it – it complements it.' Powell met with the drafters of the accord in December and took a similar line.[20]

British parliamentarians were also working to promote track two dialogue. In December 2003, the backbench parliamentary group Labour Friends of Israel (LFI), with the support of the Foreign Office, organized a conference at Ditchley in Oxfordshire. Israeli and Palestinian politicians attending included Ariel

Sharon's son Omri, and Yasser Arafat's security adviser Jibril Rajoub, along with UK Middle East Minister Baroness Symons and backbench members of LFI.

Meanwhile, the UK government was continuing to work behind the scenes to promote Palestinian security development. A security plan was drafted by high-ranking Palestinian security official Abed Allun, with British MI6 officers in Jerusalem. Allun was Chief of Staff to Palestinian security chief Mahmoud Dahlan, who had spent time in the United Kingdom and had developed a close relationship with British officials.[21] It was a comprehensive plan to address terrorism, including prevention of smuggling into Gaza, which would stop the firing of mortars and Qassam rockets. In December 2003, at a conference in Athens, Labour MK Ephraim Sneh, and senior Israeli journalists and security experts Ze'ev Schiff and Ehud Ya'ari, received a copy of the plan.[22]

According to Sneh, Ehud Ya'ari translated the security plan from Arabic and the three of them showed the plan to Sharon. But the Israeli Prime Minister ignored it. Rather than trying to coordinate with the Palestinians, he was planning a radical unilateral approach. Despite Sharon's dismissal of the plan, the United Kingdom continued to work with the Palestinians on security reform. Indeed, Blair's focus on Palestinian reform was a source of frustration for the Palestinians.[23] Blair told journalists at a Number Ten press conference in January 2004:

> I have been critical of certain aspects of Israeli policy, but I do honestly believe that it is impossible to get this process restarted unless there is a credible [Palestinian Authority] security plan that allows people to believe genuinely that every attempt is being made to stop the support of terrorism.[24]

Various leaked documents published by *Al Jazeera* and *The Guardian* show that British efforts to guide and support Palestinian security forces continued over the course of 2004.[25] However, it proved difficult for British security officers to bring about real progress with the internally divided Palestinian Authority still dominated by Arafat.[26] According to a leaked US Embassy telegram, senior Israeli officials, in private discussion with US counterparts, expressed their admiration for Blair, but their dim view of Britain's security role with the Palestinians.[27]

Backing Sharon's revolution and the revolt of the fifty-two

In December 2003, Ariel Sharon made a dramatic and largely unexpected speech at an annual policy conference in Herzliya, in which he announced that without progress on the Roadmap, Israel would implement a plan to unilaterally disengage from the Palestinians.[28] He proposed the removal of some settlements in order to 'reduce as much as possible the number of Israelis located in the heart of the Palestinian population'. It was a remarkable reversal for a leader who had personally promoted the establishment of settlements throughout the Gaza Strip and the West Bank for the very purpose of inhibiting any future withdrawal, which he had long argued would unacceptably compromise Israel's security. At Herzliya, Sharon pitched his proposal as a security move and not as a political one. He told the Israeli people that disengagement would reduce friction between Israel and the Palestinians and maximize security. Underneath this rationale was another consideration, which was that Jews would soon become a minority in the area between the Mediterranean Sea and the Jordan River. To secure Israel's future as a democratic state with a Jewish majority meant ending, as far as possible, Israel's occupation of Palestinian population areas.[29]

Sharon's Herzliya address was turned into a concrete proposal to withdraw from Gaza and part of the Northern West Bank. Sharon planned a trip to Washington in April 2004 to present his plan to Bush and seek his endorsement. A few days before the trip, Sharon's office announced that Blair had expressed favour for Sharon's plan in a phone conversation between the two. Again Blair's adaptability and practicality was being demonstrated. Jonathan Powell recalled that, 'Tony was being pretty pragmatic about it. It was better to have some progress than no progress.'[30]

At Sharon's meeting with President Bush in Washington on 14 April, Bush expressed support for the unilateral withdrawal. Bush also provided a letter to Sharon endorsing the principle that a final agreement would not mean a full return to the pre-1967 armistice lines and would take into account 'already existing major Israeli population centres'.[31] Blair gave his public backing for Sharon's disengagement plan the next day, in a joint White House press conference with Bush.[32] He subsequently made the case for backing the disengagement plan with other international leaders.[33]

Blair's support for disengagement greatly concerned many in the British political elite, including retired Foreign Office officials. Watching the Blair-Bush press conference at home on television, former British Ambassador to Libya, Oliver Miles, thought that by endorsing the disengagement, Blair had also endorsed Bush's recognition of the settlement blocs. He felt that, 'The abandonment of the position of principle that the settlements are illegal was a very important step which in effect meant that the Roadmap had been junked and we were left without a policy.'[34] Miles was concerned by how 'through mechanisms which I don't altogether understand and it's to do with the nature of the Israel lobby in America and so on, and various other factors, Likud were able to impose their vision of Israel's interests in America'. He found it 'mysterious' how the Israeli right 'had such a grip on American policy and through American policy also on British policy.'[35]

He organized a public letter to the Prime Minister, signed by 52 retired Foreign Office officials, criticizing his Middle East policy. The letter described the 'Israel/Palestine conflict' as 'a problem which, more than any other, has for decades poisoned relations between the West and the Islamic and Arab worlds.'[36] It described the Sharon plan, supported by Bush, as a policy that was 'one-sided and illegal and which will cost yet more Israeli and Palestinian blood'. Blair's support for it was 'abandoning the principles which for nearly four decades have guided international efforts to restore peace in the Holy Land and which have been the basis for such successes as those efforts have produced.'[37] Among the signatories was former British Ambassador to Israel, Francis Cornish. Despite having sympathies for Israel, he signed because:

> It disturbs me that successive Israeli governments have been able to argue we are not expanding settlements that are within the boundary, and then you find the boundary has moved out to here, and to there. So I was angry . . . It seemed to me to be intellectually lazy to keep on emphasising the extreme importance of making some progress on this thing then failing to exert pressure on some of the key bits where we could and which would be important to making an atmospheric difference.[38]

However, one of his predecessors, Andrew Burns, rejected the letter, and shared Blair's pragmatism. He thought, 'A proposition that unilateral withdrawal from Gaza was the wrong thing was pretty silly since we were clearly trying to get Israel out of Gaza.'[39]

The concerns of the retired officials were shared within Whitehall, in Parliament, and by other European leaders. According to a report in the *Guardian*, an assessment from the Department for International Development stated that the unilateral disengagement was not in line with the Roadmap and that, 'There is now a medium to high probability that there will be a lack of effective international engagement on the Middle East peace process due to other international priorities in 2004.' It added that, 'the EU, by contrast, remains focused, but has limited influence.'[40] Some 159 MPs, 119 of them Labour, signed an Early Day Motion criticizing the disengagement plan and Bush's support for it, and the Bush letter acknowledging that the settlement blocks would stay part of Israel.[41] French President Jacques Chirac typified the criticism of many in the international community for the Sharon plan. He said in late April, 'Only a negotiated agreement can allow Israelis and Palestinians to live side-by-side in peace and security. Every other procedure is doomed to failure.'[42]

Defending his position in the Commons on returning to Britain, Blair argued that rather than running contrary to the Roadmap, 'disengagement from occupied territory can be an opportunity to return to it.'[43] In particular, he saw a new opportunity for the international community to work with the Palestinians on security, economic and political reform. He reasserted once again that, 'The reason we are not in the Roadmap is perfectly simple – the basic security measures that are supposed to be taken under the Roadmap have not yet been taken.'[44] The Quartet eventually affirmed the Bush-Blair position of supporting disengagement in early May.[45] Indeed, Sharon's determined implementation of the disengagement ultimately brought widespread praise and for a short period a notable improvement in Israel's international standing.

As well as being unimpressed with the disengagement plan, Chirac objected to the broader Middle East initiative that President Bush launched at a G8 summit chaired by the US in Sea Island, Georgia the following month. The 'Broader Middle East and North Africa Project' aimed to promote political reform and democratization in the Arab world. While Blair was supportive, Chirac voiced scepticism, and stressed that returning to the Roadmap, rather than promoting reform, was the way to dispel hostility in the Middle East towards the West. Key US Arab allies, including Egypt, declined invitations to attend the summit.[46]

With the US preparing for presidential elections in the second half of 2004, expectations for a significant change in the US approach to the peace process declined. The likelihood of US engagement was also kept low by the continuing disarray within the PA and the refusal of Yasser Arafat to allow significant security reforms. In the absence of Palestinian security reform, Israeli military actions in Palestinian areas remained intensive. A series of Israeli operations, in conjunction with the security barrier, succeeded in greatly reducing terror attacks in Israel. However, the Palestinian death count in 2004, including many civilians, was considerably higher than in 2003. Palestinian fatalities were 112 in May, 113 in September and 144 in October. Israeli fatalities were 70, including civilians and security forces, in the whole of 2004.[47]

In the summer, there were calls from senior backbench Labour MPs for sanctions against Israel. Gerald Kaufman wrote in the *Guardian* in July that, 'Economic sanctions and an arms ban against Israel are the only way of breaking the impasse.'[48] He focused particular criticism on the security barrier, which had just been declared illegal by a ruling of the International Court of Justice. A *Guardian* editorial on 22 July backed the call for sanctions, stating that, 'If, in the real world, nothing will change until the battle for the White House is over, the case for economic sanctions against Israel will start to build inexorably.'[49] John Denham, who had resigned as a Home Office Minister over the Iraq War, wrote in the *Guardian* in the beginning of October: 'Israeli policy can be influenced by a clear external challenge. Many people are already questioning whether Israel's preferential trade agreement with the EU, which depends on that country's human rights record, can still be justified.'[50]

Though Kaufman was one of the Labour Party's most vociferous critics of Israel, neither he nor Denham were identified as usual suspects of the hard left of the party. Kaufman believed that in calling for sanctions he was echoing the views of the majority of Labour MPs.[51] The weight of backbench opinion against Israel was demonstrated in January 2004, when 205 MPs signed an Early Day Motion condemning the security barrier and calling on 'the British Government to bring all available pressure to bear on Israel to cease building this Wall.'[52]

While significant numbers of MPs expressed their views by signing EDMs, the groups of pro-Israel and pro-Palestinian MPs within the Labour Party who were sufficiently concerned to regularly speak in the chamber on these issues were small. As former Foreign Office special adviser Malcolm Chalmers put it, 'Most of all, the predominant view of most Labour MPs is that they wish the problem would go away.'[53] However, those MPs who were actively engaged in the issue were sharply divided and would seek to make their points during the regular session in the parliamentary calendar when Foreign Office ministers would take questions from MPs. MPs sympathetic to the Palestinian cause frequently condemned Israeli security policies, settlement construction and the security barrier. Israel-sympathetic MPs stressed Israel's security concerns, the shortcomings in the Palestinian Authority and the problem of incitement against Israel and Jews in the Arab world.[54] The bitterness with which the Israeli-Palestinian arena divided Labour MPs was illustrated by the reaction to Israel's assassination of Hamas leader Sheikh Ahmed Yassin in March 2004 by an airstrike. Labour MP Louise Ellman recalled that after a series of speakers had condemned the attack, when she got up to defend Israel, she was hissed by members of her own party.[55]

Just as in 2002, at the Labour Party conference at the end of September 2004, Blair felt the need to address the issue directly in his speech. He made revival of the peace process 'a personal priority', adding, 'Two states, Israel and Palestine, living side by side in an enduring peace would do more to defeat this terrorism than bullets alone can ever do.'[56]

The death of Arafat and the re-election of Bush: An opportunity

President Bush was re-elected at the beginning of November 2004. In a statement congratulating him, Blair stressed the priority he placed on the Middle East peace process in the context of the US–UK relationship. He declared that this was a critical time to bring the world together to fight global terrorism and that it was necessary to pursue, 'peace in the Middle East between Israel and Palestine'. He said, 'the Middle East peace process is the single most pressing political challenge in our world today.'[57] He also emphasized the importance of rebuilding US–EU relations. These were key issues on the agenda, as well as the important bilateral issues relating to Iraq and Afghanistan, when Blair flew to Washington for a summit with the President on 11 November.

As Blair made the trip, Yasser Arafat died in a Paris hospital at the age of 75, having fallen ill a few days earlier. Arafat was an iconic figure. During his life, the Palestinian national movement was inseparable from Arafat's image and persona. He had succeeded in winning international recognition and support for the Palestinian cause, the establishment of a self-governing Palestinian Authority, and acceptance even from Israel of the proposal to establish a Palestinian state in Gaza and the West Bank. But the Palestinian Authority he created was a corrupt and inept institution, rather than a state in waiting, and Arafat was unwilling to make the compromises necessary to reach a final status accord with Israel. His decision to ride the wave of the Second Intifada, rather than stamp it out, convinced the US administration, and Blair, that he was a roadblock to meaningful progress. The implication of his personal involvement in the *Karine-A* arms shipment in January 2002, in particular, proved a fatal blow to the credibility of his claims that he was not responsible for Palestinian violence. The attempts to circumvent Arafat though the appointment of a Prime Minister had failed, with Arafat unwilling to cede any significant power and accept the role of a figurehead. His death, therefore, presented new opportunities for the peace process.

At the end of their meeting, Blair and Bush issued a five-point joint statement on the Middle East peace process. According to the account of Anthony Seldon, the points were drafted by Blair.[58] They were a recommitment to the two-state vision, support for Palestinian elections, the mobilization of international support for the development of Palestinian institutions, support for Israel's disengagement plan and rapid progress on the Roadmap.[59] None of this was new. More significant was that Bush committed himself 'to use the next four years to spend the capital of the United States' on the creation of a Palestinian state.[60]

This was a welcome commitment from the British perspective, but they had heard similar commitments at the Northern Ireland summit a year and a half earlier and been disappointed. However, the death of Arafat and the disengagement plan were two significant developments on the ground that changed the situation. Another change was that Bush appointed Condoleezza Rice as Secretary of State in place of Colin Powell. According to the account of Bob Woodward, Rice had come to believe in the importance of the Palestinian issue and wanted assurances that it would be a focus before she would agree to take on the job. Powell had also been committed to the issue, but he was an isolated figure in the administration whose voice had frequently been crowded out. Rice, on the other hand, was a trusted close confidant of the President.[61]

With the US elections over and Arafat gone, Blair planned another event in London to move the peace process forward. When Blair visited Israel and the Palestinian Territories just before Christmas, he was accused by one British journalist of focusing on the peace process to distract attention away from the ongoing problems of insurgency in Iraq.[62] It was an accusation echoed by some in Israel.[63] Though Blair denied this, his envoy Lord Levy accepted that

> Politicians are motivated by many reasons. To have a high profile event on your own terms which is a success obviously has a tick in many boxes . . . Was there a genuine motivation that could help the Palestinian cause? I think there was . . . Was there rolled up into that equation some benefits for Blair and UK PLC? I'm sure there were. But why not? That's politics.[64]

In a press conference with Sharon, Blair stated the goals of the London meeting were to develop, in anticipation of the disengagement, 'a clear plan for the Palestinian side in respect of the measures necessary for the political institutions, economic transparency and security.'[65] Sharon expressed his support for the event, and declared that by mutual agreement, Israel would not attend. Blair stressed that a conference to negotiate final status issues was an area where the US had to take the lead, but in supporting Palestinian development, the wider international community could play a role. It was essentially a rerun of the January 2003 meeting which the Palestinians had been prevented from travelling to. David Manning recalled that it was a consistent belief of Blair's that, 'It's no good telling the Israelis to negotiate with the Palestinians if there is nobody to negotiate with and they have no structures. We have to help them to see that they need structures and help them to build them.'[66]

In the same press conference, Blair put great stress on the importance of the Palestinian state being democratic, tying into the broader theme of democracy promotion being promoted by both Bush and Blair. This was a central theme of Blair's annual foreign policy speech to the Lord Mayor's Banquet in mid-November and for President Bush's inaugural speech in January 2005. Bush publicly praised a book on this subject by Israeli politician and former Soviet dissident Natan Sharansky.[67] Sharansky argued that the promotion of freedom and democracy was a necessary precursor to peace in the Middle East, including in the Israeli-Palestinian arena.[68]

Ariel Sharon, on the other hand, showed no significant interest in democratization in the Palestinian arena or the wider Middle East, and likely thought it 'wishful thinking'.[69] To the extent that he was concerned about the Palestinian leadership, his interest was in whether it was willing and able to reign in Palestinian armed groups and stop attacks on Israelis, not its democratic mandate. From the end of 2003, he was focused on a unilateral path of disengagement that was rooted in an assumption that there was no effective Palestinian negotiating partner. The death of Arafat and the resulting Palestinian elections did not divert him from his path. He paid lip-service to the democratization agenda championed by Blair and acquiesced only reluctantly to the US demand to facilitate parliamentary elections in the Palestinian territories when this meant the participation of Hamas.[70] Blair, for his part, was willing to try and take the scattered political, strategic and diplomatic agendas of the various players, however disconnected, and try and weave them rhetorically into a consistent set of measures to bring progress. This was reflected in the five points he drafted for his joint statement with Bush in November 2004, which embraced the Roadmap, disengagement and Palestinian reform all together.

Mahmoud Abbas was elected the President of the PA on 9 January 2005. In early February 2005, he met Sharon at a summit in Sharm el Sheikh and declared a joint ceasefire. There followed a dramatic reduction in violence and a series of confidence-building measures, including the release of hundreds of Palestinian prisoners and the withdrawal of Israeli forces from some Palestinian towns.[71]

As in 2003, British attempts to take a leading role in the peace process put strains on the UK–Israel bilateral relationship. Behind the scenes, the Israelis worked directly with British officials on the text of the document that the London conference was intended to produce.[72] However, according to Israeli official Roey Gilad, there was a disagreement in the text between Sharon's personal adviser Dov Weissglass and Nigel Sheinwald, who had replaced David Manning in 2003 as Blair's foreign policy adviser. Israeli officials did not get their way in the final document.[73] Lord Levy recalled the incident as an attempt by Weissglass to 'scupper' the agenda. He believed that, 'Nothing like that would ever take place without the Israelis putting their viewpoint and creating waves', and that this was simply, 'all part of the game.'[74]

The meeting went ahead on 1 March with Mahmoud Abbas leading the Palestinian delegation and foreign ministers attending from 30 states, including Condoleezza Rice. In his opening speech at the event, Blair reiterated his line that the Israeli-Palestinian conflict was 'the single most pressing political challenge'. He added:

> Right round the world this is the issue that causes as much misunderstanding, division, concern, worry as virtually any other in the whole of the international community and if we are able to make progress on it, that is relevant and of interest of course primarily to the Palestinian people, to the Israeli people. It is also a major part of ensuring the security and stability of countries like Britain, of the European Union, of the whole of the rest of the world.[75]

This was a further development in Blair's rhetoric on the Israeli-Palestinian conflict. Not only did he put greater weight than ever before on the importance of this issue in creating international discord, but he also highlighted its direct effect on the security of Britain and other states.

The event was attended by US Army General William Ward, newly appointed by Rice to 'assist the Palestinian Authority to consolidate and expand their recent efforts on security and encourage resumption of Israeli-Palestinian security coordination.'[76] The appointment put the US back in the lead on the agenda of Palestinian security reform. It was among the first tangible steps of a new, more proactive American approach of the kind that Blair had been seeking. With Arafat gone, the US re-engaging and Israel planning to get out of Gaza, it was the most hopeful moment in the Israeli-Palestinian arena in five years. It was a window of opportunity to generate momentum, not by bringing greater pressure on Israel as many in the Labour Party demanded, but by pressing the agenda which Blair argued was critical for progress, namely reforming Palestinian political and security institutions.

The Israeli-Palestinian Issue and Domestic Counter-Radicalization

Foreign policy meets domestic security

On 6 April 2004, Cabinet Secretary Sir Andrew Turnbull wrote to John Gieve, Permanent Secretary of the Home Office, and other senior officials, inviting them to a cross-departmental discussion on 'Relations with the Muslim Community'. He wanted, in particular, to address the problem that, 'There is a feeling that parts of the Muslim community, particularly younger men, are disaffected.' The agenda of the meeting was to assess the problem and possible responses.[1] These included:

> Foreign Policy – should our stance (eg on MEPP or Kashmir) be influenced more by these concerns? How do we communicate our foreign policy to the Muslim community? Where are they getting their information and opinions from?[2] [Parenthesis in the original.]

This is a clear indication that at the highest levels of government, policy makers were weighing whether British policy in the Israeli-Palestinian arena ought to be reconsidered, as part of a strategy to prevent radicalization of British Muslims.

This chapter examines the extent to which fears about the radicalization of Muslims in Britain impacted on the formulation of foreign policy, in particular, with regard to the Israeli-Palestinian issue. Previous chapters have shown that the Prime Minister rejected the argument that Western foreign policies fuelled a justified sense of grievance that was the cause of Islamic extremist violence. However, he did believe in trying to build a coalition of support from moderate Muslim states for the War on Terror, including by stepping up efforts to resolve the Israeli-Palestinian conflict. The desire to gain the support of Muslims also applied to the British Muslim community. The role of building bridges with British Muslims, in particular to overcome concerns over British involvement in the War on Terror, was taken on by the Foreign Office. In the years after 9/11, there was an increasing concern within government that some British Muslims were becoming radicalized, in some cases to the point of plotting violent attacks within the United Kingdom. Concerns within government included the possibility that British policy, in particular with regard to the War on Terror, was contributing to the radicalization.

The debate about the radicalization of British Muslims mirrored the debate about the radicalization of Muslims overseas. It was focused on the question of whether radicalization was driven by a hate-filled ideology spread on the back of anti-Western propaganda, that had to be confronted and defeated, or whether it was driven by genuine grievances, including Britain's approach to the Israeli-Palestinian conflict, that could be to some extent accommodated.

British Muslims and the Israeli-Palestinian issue in the first term

The Muslim Council of Britain (MCB) was launched in 1997 as a body to represent British Muslim views to government. The organization had strong support from then-Home Secretary Jack Straw, himself MP to 25,000 Muslim constituents. This support continued when Straw moved to the Foreign Office.[3] It became the primary organization that officials and ministers across Whitehall departments referred to for a representative Islamic voice.[4]

While the main focus of the MCB's concerns was domestic issues such as legislation on race relations, it also had a strong foreign policy agenda.[5] The organization was highly critical of US airstrikes in Sudan and Afghanistan in 1998.[6] When Tony Blair addressed an MCB event for the first time in 1999, he spoke about Kosovo, but remarkably, did not mention the Israeli-Palestinian issue at all.[7] However, speaking in response, the MCB's leader, Iqbal Sacranie, called on Blair to bring 'the courageous, moral and humanitarian stand' he had taken on Kosovo to bear on the issues of 'Palestine, Jammu and Kashmir and the continuing suffering of the civilian population of Iraq'.[8]

The Israeli-Palestinian issue became an increasingly important feature of the MCB's foreign policy agenda as the issue became higher profile. Sacranie wrote to Robin Cook in 1999 urging the FCO not to allow the status of Jerusalem to be changed.[9] In October 2000, shortly after the outbreak of the Second Intifada, Sacranie wrote in a British Islamic journal:

Despite their many differences and political persuasions, Muslim scholars are united and resolute about one issue. They agree that the question of Palestine and the status of Jerusalem is the foremost international concern on the agenda of Muslims . . . The Muslim Council of Britain, therefore, views the illegal occupation of Jerusalem as a Muslim issue and not as a Palestinian issue.[10]

He went to on to commit that the MCB would 'exert all its moral, financial and political influence upon the British government to pressure Israel into accepting a fair and just solution of the Jerusalem issue'. The MCB not only subscribed to an exclusively Palestinian narrative with regard to the conflict, but also lobbied against the banning of Hamas and Palestinian Islamic Jihad under the Terrorism Act 2000.[11]

The 2001 general election was the first in which the MCB mobilized British Muslims to vote on 'Islamic issues'. With the Second Intifada dominating news from the Middle East, the MCB election campaign literature called on candidates to pledge their support for 'suffering Muslims in Palestine, Kashmir, Chechnya and Iraq'.[12] An editorial in the *Muslim News* in March 2001 claimed that it was the 'Palestinian intifadah' that had 'provided the wakeup call for Muslims to become more involved in politics'.[13]

Government relations with British Muslims after 9/11

All major Muslim organizations in the United Kingdom condemned the 9/11 attacks, though some radical groups either praised them or tried to dismiss them as a Zionist plot.[14] After 9/11, the government acted urgently against Islamic extremists in the United Kingdom by passing the Anti-Terrorism, Crime and Security Act 2001. This enabled the government to detain individuals on British soil who were considered dangerous, but who could not be deported on human rights grounds.[15] At that time, the British security services were principally concerned about foreign Islamic radicals, based in the United Kingdom, who might be plotting attacks overseas. It took some time for UK security services to focus on the radicalization of British Muslims and the threat they might pose.[16]

Nonetheless, the government was keen to avoid a backlash against British Muslims and was also aware of the concerns of British Muslims about the War on Terror. As a result of 9/11, Muslim leaders perceived that there was a sea change in the level of interaction between British Muslims and the government. Senior MCB activist Inayat Bunglawala recalled:

We saw a lot more invites [to meet with government] after 9/11 . . . Once the MCB started making those contact with senior officials the MCB became a lot more confident about writing to senior ministers and making their views known on issues that they believed that they had a duty to convey . . . You saw British Muslims become increasingly – it was not the MCB it was a grass roots phenomenon – becoming more politicised because the war in Afghanistan followed shortly after and many people had strong views about that. People wanted us to convey those views.[17]

The marked increase in the politicization of British Muslims, particularly of the younger generation, was noticed by MPs with large Muslim constituencies. Lorna Fitzsimons, MP for Rochdale from 1997 to 2005, which had an 18% Muslim population, recalled:

Nobody talked prior to 9/11 about Palestine . . . They talked about Kashmir if they talked about anything . . . After 9/11 it gradually became the topic, but the topic for the young, not the old.[18]

Mike Gapes MP, whose constituency of Ilford South was 20% Muslim, recalled:

I've got some 19 year old or 17 year old kid in Ilford who feels that he personally is under attack because of what is happening in Gaza, or what is happening in Afghanistan or what is happening in Iraq, or because he's watched Al Jazcera.

There was an early recognition within the Foreign Office in the wake of 9/11 of the concerns of British Muslims about UK foreign policy. Britain's involvement in the war in Afghanistan was opposed by the MCB. In an attempt to win British Muslim support for the war, the government produced a pamphlet entitled, 'Never Again'. The publication quoted Muslim leaders who condemned the September 11 attacks and included photographs of Tony Blair meeting Yasser Arafat.[19] This illustrated the Foreign Office belief that showing Britain's commitment to the Palestinians was an important part of its public diplomacy with British Muslims in the context of the War on Terror. Middle East Minister Ben Bradshaw told the Commons on 27 November 2001:

We recognise the importance of a solution in the Middle East in terms of public opinion in the Arab and Muslim worlds, and we recognise the importance of public opinion in the Arab and Muslim worlds not just in international relations, but in our domestic politics.[20]

Former British Ambassador to Israel Andrew Burns, who retired from the Foreign Office in 2003, regarded the heightened need to take account of domestic Muslim opinion in Britain after 9/11 and 7/7 as a 'sea change'.[21]

Intensification of FCO engagement with British Muslims

The desire of the government to engage with 'moderate' Muslims became even more intense in the run-up to the Iraq War. By February 2003, the FCO was trying to engage more directly with a range of British minority communities, but was making a particular effort with the Muslim community. It held a seminar entitled, 'Domestic Echoes of Foreign Policy', in which representatives of ethnic minorities were given the opportunity to voice frank views in conversation with officials and policy makers.[22] The policy agenda was led by the FCO Minister responsible for the Middle East Mike O'Brien.

According to an unpublished, internal FCO summary of the event, 'Mike O'Brien recognized that issues such as Iraq and Palestine resonate strongly with Britain's Muslims' and that the FCO should do more represent Britain's multicultural society.[23] One of the proposals to come out of the seminar was that, 'Communities should be involved in the formulation of policy for the long term. Enduring partnerships should in this way create trust.' The extent to which foreign policy was open to change based on the concerns of specific ethnic groups was left open. According to the FCO summary:

> It is important to be clear from the outset that consultation exercises are not guaranteed to change the UK's foreign policy. On the other hand, as the head of PaNDU [Partnerships and Networks Development Unit] said, they are also not guaranteed *not* to change policy.

March 2003 saw the establishment of the Partnerships and Networks Development Unit (PaNDU) with a remit to 'broaden and widen engagements with a range of stakeholders from the media, business and civil society, to assist in the formulation and delivery of UK foreign policy and the improvement of FCO services.'[24] Relations with the Muslim Community were defined as one of the key priorities for this new unit.[25] Based on the outcome of the 'Domestic Echoes' seminar, PaNDU produced a ten-point action plan which included:

A new programme of policy meetings in London, and around the UK, led by
FCO Minister Mike O'Brien with the minority ethnic communities on building
bridges with mainstream Islam. The aim will be to test out ideas and policy, and
develop new ideas.[26]

The foreign policy message that the government's principal Muslim interlocutor,
the MCB, was feeding into the government at the time was very clear. At the
outbreak of the Iraq War, the MCB issued a statement saying, 'This war appears
to be part of a plan to redraw the map of the Middle East in accordance with
the agenda of Zionists and American neo-Conservatives.' It added, 'Rather than
starting a new inferno in Iraq, our energies would have been better spent in
extinguishing the existing fire in Palestine.'[27]

Over the course of 2003, the FCO, led by Mike O'Brien, tried to strengthen
its relationship with the British Muslim Community. The Foreign Office
was already involved in activities such as sponsoring the British Haj delegation,
which former Foreign Office Special Adviser Malcolm Chalmers described
frankly as a way of winning 'brownie points' with the British Muslim
community.[28]

'Full scale engagement with British Muslims on foreign policy'

The war in Iraq added a greater sense of urgency to the FCO's agenda to engage
with British Muslims. In April 2003, Mike O'Brien approved a strategy document
for 'Building Bridges with Mainstream Islam'. An unpublished document setting
out the strategy opened with the words 'Muslim resentment towards the West
is worse than ever,' with Britain as well as the US now seen by many Muslims
as 'Crusader States.'[29] The document reported that the minister was 'concerned'
that the department's 'work on engaging with Islam has therefore been knocked
back'. The document determined that, 'A further effort is therefore required to
address Muslim resentment' by presenting the government's position clearly and
rebuilding trust. It added in that context, 'We also need to take full advantage
of political developments on the Palestinian issue' presumably in reference to
the publication of the Roadmap. The document then directly linked the need
to engage with moderate Muslims with the need to counter-radicalization,

stating: 'The main areas of resentment and the drivers behind the recruitment by extremist organisations . . . are directly related to Muslim foreign policy concerns.' This acceptance of the idea that foreign policy was the root of resentment among British Muslims and was fuelling extremism marked a turning point. The goal of Foreign Office engagement with British Muslims was shifting from addressing concerns of a group of British citizens about aspects of its policy, to countering the threat of extremism.

The means set out to rebuild trust with British Muslims included, 'Demonstrating how HMG [Her Majesty's Government] is active on key issues of concern . . . both past and present on primarily Palestine but also Kosovo, Chechnya and Kashmir.' The strategy also called for, 'Full scale engagement with British Muslims on foreign policy. This includes laying down the challenge to British Muslims, of suggesting pragmatic solution to their concerns.' It is clear from this document that the Foreign Office agenda of outreach to British Muslims was increasingly orientated not just to explaining or defending British foreign policy, but in giving British Muslims a direct role in shaping it.

In a leaked Foreign Office document from November 2003, the ongoing programme of work in the 'Building Bridges' strategy is described.[30] The activities included ministerial outreach to Muslims around the country. Future planned activities included programmes designed to better understand the concerns of young Muslims, in particular, over foreign policy, to better communicate British foreign policy to these groups, and to promote 'mainstream' Islam. One of the key challenges was seen as the problem of getting 'mainstream' Muslims to talk to government and overcoming a stigma associated with dealing with government. Events in Iraq and Palestine are described as an 'inevitable hindrance' to the work.[31]

Did the outreach to British Muslims actually influence policy? A speech by Mike O'Brien to the House of Commons on the eve of the Iraq War had a tone that reflected the perspective of the MCB. He referred repeatedly to the 'injustice done to the Palestinian people'[32] and declared that getting the US engaged was vital for 'ensuring that Prime Minister Sharon is delivered to the peace table'.[33] It was a very different tone from that used by the Prime Minister.

It is difficult to measure the extent to which O'Brien's choices of words on the peace process were influenced by his agenda to build bridges with the British Muslim community. Malcolm Chalmers was sceptical that British Muslim opinion made much difference on British policy in the Israeli-Palestinian arena.

However, he acknowledged that ministers who had a lot of contact with Muslims were more sensitive to Islamic opinion in their choice of words.[34] Mike O'Brien had clear concerns about the resentment of Muslims towards the West, and his approach to building bridges with British Muslims included making them feel listened to on questions of foreign policy. Given that fact, it is hard to imagine that this did not impact on his choice of words as Middle East Minister in referring to the Israeli-Palestinian arena. However, because of the dominance of the Prime Minister, there was limited scope for the Foreign Office to shift policy in a more pro-Palestinian direction in order to accommodate the concerns of British Muslims.

It is important to stress that there was no straightforward divide between the Foreign Office and the Prime Minister's Office. The views of individual ministers played an important role and not all ministers in the Foreign Office agreed with O'Brien's approach. Another junior Foreign Office Minister, Denis MacShane, believed that British Muslims were not doing enough to distance themselves from violent extremism. In November 2003, shortly after bomb attacks against British targets in Istanbul, he called on British Muslims to be clearer in their condemnation of the acts of 'terrorists'. He asserted that Muslims in the United Kingdom had to make a choice between non-violent, democratic political means and 'the way of the terrorists'. He said in a speech, 'I hope we will see clearer, stronger language that there is no future for any Muslim cause anywhere in the world that validates, or implicitly supports, the use of political violence in any way.'[35] He subsequently said his remarks were intended to counter 'anti-Israel rhetoric' and hostility to India among British Muslims.[36] He found himself isolated after his remarks, with senior members of government distancing themselves from them. Even though Blair had stressed in his speech to both Houses of Congress a few months earlier the need to fight a battle of ideas against a fanatical strain of religious extremism,[37] there was no appetite in Whitehall to apply the same confrontational rhetoric to Islamist sympathizers in the British Muslim community.[38]

MacShane's words reflected a completely different approach from the policy led by Mike O'Brien. The emphasis of the 'building bridges' strategy was on avoiding alienation or anger among British Muslims over British foreign policy which might lead them to sympathize with radical extremists. In contrast, MacShane was asking British Muslims to distance themselves unreservedly from extremist violence of all kinds, regardless of what disagreements there may be over policy.

Increasing threat from violent
British Islamists to the United Kingdom

There had been only isolated cases of British Muslims planning or perpetrating extremist violence prior to 9/11.[39] However, over the course of 2002, British security services became increasingly aware of threats to the United Kingdom from radical Islamists within Britain.[40] The first major case after 9/11 was a plot by Algerian asylum seekers to poison Londoners with ricin, uncovered by the police in early 2003. Shortly after, the Mike's Place bombing was carried out by two British suicide bombers in Tel Aviv. This was one of a number of incidents involving British citizens that led the government to put greater attention on extremism and radicalization among young British Muslims.[41] In September 2003, Metropolitan Chief Commissioner Sir John Stevens cited the Mike's Place attack when asserting that a suicide bombing in the United Kingdom was 'inevitable'.[42]

However, it took some time for the government to focus on domestic radicalization within the context of its counter-terrorism strategy. In the first year after 9/11, the Home Office-led counter-terrorism strategy was focused on targeting threatening individuals and their supporters and disrupting their activities. Though there was an acknowledgement of the need to tackle the 'root causes of terrorism', these were perceived principally to be areas overseas with social, economic or political problems. With regard to the United Kingdom, there was recognition of the need to improve cultural understanding, but no agenda to counter the radicalization of British Muslims.[43]

By early 2003, the counter-terrorism strategy, known as 'Contest', had evolved to a policy with four strands: Prevent, Pursue, Protect and Prepare. Hazel Blears recalled that, 'in the early days, particularly post-9/11 and post-7/7 the emphasis was on Pursue and Protect.'[44] These were the elements of the strategy focused on disrupting terrorist activities. 'Prevent' was intended to address the causes of terrorism by 'working to resolve international disputes' and 'seeking to ensure all our citizens feel fully part of our civil society'.[45] According to Blears, it was initially the least developed aspect of the strategy.[46] As part of the early version of 'Prevent', the Home Office set up a programme of ministerial visits 'to listen to the concerns of Muslim communities'.[47] Issues of relevance to the Home Office were not primarily related to foreign policy, but to policing issues such as the use of stop and search powers against young Muslim men.[48] In 2003, it was the Foreign Office which was more active in its engagement with British Muslims, based increasingly on concerns about radicalization.

Officials focus on foreign policy as a 'key driver'

On 11 March 2004, 191 people were killed in the Madrid train bombings. This was the first major Islamist terror attack in Europe, and it graphically illustrated the potential threat to British cities. Three weeks later, Operation Crevice carried out by the Metropolitan Police prevented a plot by a group of young, British, Muslim men to carry out large-scale bombings in the United Kingdom. The targets were believed to include the Ministry of Sound nightclub in London, the Bluewater shopping centre, synagogues and infrastructure.[49]

In the days following, concerns about extremism among British Muslims were discussed by the cabinet, leading Sir Andrew Turnbull to write to his senior civil service colleagues inviting them to discuss how to address the security challenges emerging from sections of the British Muslim population. It is clear from Turnbull's letter that the question was not just how foreign policy was communicated or explained to British Muslims, but the formation of the policy itself.[50]

Hazel Blears subsequently denied that the government's engagement with British Muslims involved 'capitulating to the position that because some people don't like our foreign policy therefore we must change it in order to protect our country.'[51] She denied that any of her cabinet colleagues were inclined to change foreign policy to appease 'a particular strand of political thought'. However, she acknowledged that on the question of the extent to which policy should be adapted to accommodate Muslim opinion, there was within the cabinet,

> always a spectrum of views, because they are highly political, highly contested [issues] and also dependent on people's personal experience – sometimes in their constituencies, when they have got a very large Muslim community and they are subject to intense pressures.[52]

Jonathan Powell also acknowledged that there was a range of views within government on this question. According to Powell, 'Tony took quite a strong view against the notion that we should somehow tailor our foreign policy to pander to people who were threatening violence.' However he recalled, 'There were people in government, certainly lots of commentators, who took the view that we were radicalizing part of the Islamic community by the decisions we took on foreign policy but I don't think Tony accepted that.'[53]

As a result of the discussions in the cabinet, the Home Office and Foreign Office worked together on a joint strategy document for the Prime Minister entitled, 'Young Muslims and Extremism' to analyse the causes of radicalization. The two policy goals defined in the document were to isolate extremists and support moderates and to prevent young Muslims from becoming involved in terrorism or extremism.[54] When defining the problem in the document summary, top of a list of factors which 'may attract some to extremism' was:

> Anger: a perception of 'double standards' in British foreign policy, where democracy is preached but oppression of the 'Ummah' (the one nation of belicvers) is practised or tolerated e.g. in Palestine, Iraq, Afghanistan, Kashmir, Chechnya'.[55]

The main document expanded this point by stating:

> Perceived Western bias in Israel's favour over the Israel/Palestine conflict is a key long term grievance of the international Muslim community which probably influences British Muslims.[56]

Despite the fact that the news in April 2004 had been dominated by the US offensive in Fallujah,[57] it is remarkable that the issue of Palestine was listed first, ahead of the issues of Iraq and Afghanistan, where British troops were actually engaged.

The paper recommended policies designed to improve understanding of the causes of extremism, combat recruitment of young British Muslims by terrorist organizations and combat Islamophobia. The document recommended, in essence, a continuation of the Foreign Office approach to building bridges with mainstream Islam, through engaging with British Muslims and trying to address their concerns. Addressing Muslim concerns about foreign policy featured prominently among the measures the document stated were being taken forward by the Home Office and the Foreign Office.[58]

On 18 May 2004, Permanent Secretary of the Foreign Office Sir Michael Jay, wrote to the cabinet secretary to offer his own thoughts on this issue of radicalization.[59] He noted that other colleagues had 'flagged up' the issues of discrimination, disadvantage and exclusion. He however, was keen to emphasize that, 'another recurring theme is the issue of British foreign policy, especially in the context of the Middle East Peace Process and Iraq'. He noted that the

> Experience of both Ministers and officials working in this area suggests that the issue of British foreign policy and the perception of its negative effect on Muslims globally plays a significant role in creating a feeling of anger and impotence among especially the younger generation of British Muslims.[60]

He stressed that he was concerned that anger at British foreign policy, 'seems to be a key driver behind recruitment by extremist organisations'.[61]

A joint internal Home Office and Foreign Office document from June 2004 shows how ideas about the relationship between radicalization and foreign policy were solidifying across departments. The document acknowledged that while government understanding of the drivers of religious extremism was limited, 'There is some evidence that international (foreign policy) concerns play a more important role that domestic/socioeconomic ones in radicalizing views (and perhaps actions) of some young Muslims (e.g. FCO/MORI focus groups).'[62]

Working on the assumption that foreign policy was a 'key driver' in radicalization, the Foreign Office continued to take a lead on engaging with British Muslims on questions of foreign policy. In September 2004, the Engaging with the Islamic World Group was formed.[63] It aimed to address the communication of government policy to Muslims in the United Kingdom and overseas.[64] The Foreign Office increasingly saw engaging with Muslims at home and abroad as intertwined. It was believed that many British Muslims, for example, used foreign news sources such as Al Jazeera. The FCO tried to ensure their spokesmen appeared on those channels.[65] The aim of this new FCO division, according to Malcolm Chalmers, was 'not to get the majority to agree that it was right to invade Iraq but to persuade them they should engage through the democratic process and not by blowing people up.'

The agenda to engage with Muslims both at home and abroad led to a difference of opinion within government about who the government should and should not be talking to.[66] In 2004, this question focused primarily on Muslims overseas. There was a sharp divide within government about how to relate to influential foreign Islamic clerics with views most in Britain considered extreme. In April 2004, Mike O'Brien hosted at the Foreign Office Fazlur Rahman, a Pakistani politician and Deobandi preacher who had reportedly blamed Jews for the 9/11 attacks. The Foreign Office defended the decision by saying: 'If you are going to engage, you can't always engage with people you agree with.'[67]

A more public controversy flared up a few months later when London Mayor Ken Livingstone invited Muslim Brotherhood leader Yusuf al-Qaradawi to London. Al-Qaradawi was regarded as a clerical authority by Hamas and was a vocal supporter of suicide bombing in Israel. He was granted a visa by the Foreign Office. The Prime Minister publicly disagreed with the decision, telling the Commons on 7 July 2004: 'We are totally opposed, as is everyone, to people coming to this country and using their visit as a platform to express views in support of terrorism or extremism of any sort.'[68]

The MCB defended the invitation of al-Qaradawi. Sadiq Khan, then chair of their legal affairs committee, told the Home Affairs Select Committee in November 2004, 'There is a consensus among Islamic scholars that Mr al-Qaradawi is not the extremist that he is painted as being by selective quotations from his remarks.'[69]

As well as defending the view of overseas preachers regarded by many as extreme, the MCB encouraged government departments to exercise self-censorship when talking about the conjunction of Islamism and violence. Sadiq Khan told the Home Affairs Select Committee in November 2004, 'We find it offensive when before the word "terrorism" the word "Islamic" or "Muslim" is inserted. It does not help.'[70] Blair had taken this line in the immediate wake of 9/11, and it was accepted by ministers across government. Hazel Blears told the same committee in March 2005:

> In the Home Office, ministers, all our officials, we are very, very keen to be very careful about the language that we use. We do not talk about Muslim terrorism, we do not talk about Islamic terrorism, we talk specifically about international terrorism associated with al-Qaeda.

Islamic foreign policy concerns at the ballot box

Apart from a counter-radicalization agenda, there was also a political and electoral consideration for some Labour MPs to consider the views of British Muslims. The desire of many British Muslims to punish the Labour government for the Iraq War was reflected in voting in local and European elections in 2003 and 2004.[71] The Liberal Democrats, who had opposed the war, gained from Labour.

In the General Election in 2005, the MCB again encouraged Muslims to vote on Muslim issues. Alongside a wide range of domestic issues, the MCB's election publication, 'Electing to Deliver' focused on Palestine as a key foreign policy issue, even ahead of Iraq. It declared:

> Our conduct in this [Middle East] region has been emotive to all. Palestine and its peoples should be offered no less than a resolution to their grievances . . . The

opportunity of a viable Palestinian state cannot be actualised if Israel is allowed to persist with its relentless ethnic cleansing of Palestine.[72]

The Muslim Brotherhood-aligned Muslim Association of Britain, an MCB affiliate, explicitly endorsed candidates that should receive the Muslim vote. Another Islamic campaign group, the Muslim Public Affairs Committee (MPAC), went further still, placing teams in specific constituencies to campaign against targeted candidates.[73]

Both the Liberal Democrats and Labour made specific efforts to target Muslim voters.[74] One attempt to court Muslim voters by Mike O'Brien brought accusations of anti-Semitism. In an article in *Muslim Weekly* in January 2005, he wrote: 'What will Michael Howard do for British Muslims? Will his foreign policy aim to help Palestine? Will he promote legislation to protect you from religious hatred and discrimination? Will he give you the choice of sending your children to a faith school?'[75] In the same article, O'Brien singled out a Jewish Liberal Democrat MP, Evan Harris, for failing to back new legislation against religious discrimination. O'Brien subsequently denied any anti-Semitic intent.[76]

One of the main thrusts of the lengthy article was attempting to establish Blair's and the Labour government's pro-Palestinian credentials, stressing that Blair had declared the creation of a Palestinian state to be a 'personal priority'. The article continued:

> The reality is that the only way a Palestinian state will be created is if Israel is prepared to concede land it currently occupies on the West Bank and Gaza. Whether we in Britain like it or not, the reality of the modern world is that only the Americans can influence Israel. And it seems only Tony Blair has any influence with the Americans.

The implication was that Blair's policy was to use his influence with the US to persuade them to make Israel concede Gaza and the West Bank. This was at best a very slanted representation of Blair's position. As has been discussed in previous chapters, Blair did consider the Israeli-Palestinian issue a priority and pressed the US to give it greater attention. However, he had not adopted the position that the resolution to the problem lay simply in forcing Israel to give up Gaza and the West Bank, rather his focus was on trying to get the Palestinians to reform. Regardless of whether O'Brien had any intent to deliberately play up Howard's and Harris's Jewishness, he was certainly trying to court the Muslim vote by spinning Blair and Labour as pro-Palestinian.

In a separate case, the Liberal Democrats were accused of an anti-Semitic attack on a Labour MP to attract the Islamic vote. A number of Labour MPs in seats with large Muslims constituencies were specifically targeted by MPAC. In Rochdale, Lorna Fitzsimons was branded a 'Jewish, Zionist' MP, because of her support for Israel and the Iraq War. She was not in fact Jewish. The campaign was orchestrated in coordination with the local Liberal Democrat candidate and it contributed to overturning a 6000 Labour majority and the Liberal Democrats taking the seat by 444 votes. MPAC's campaign was branded as 'virulent and racist' by Trevor Phillips, the Chair of the Commission for Racial Equality,[77] and MPAC was later accused of inciting hatred towards Jews by a 2006 All Party Parliamentary Enquiry into Antisemitism and banned from student campuses by the National Union of Students.[78]

Even more dramatic was the victory of George Galloway, representing the Respect Party, in the Bethnal Green and Bow Constituency. The constituency, which was 40% Muslim, was held with a 10,000 majority by Labour and represented by Oona King, an MP with an African-American father and Jewish mother, who had voted in favour of the Iraq War. The Respect party was an offshoot of the Stop the War campaign which built on its anti-war and anti-Zionist platform. King complained that she faced anti-Semitic abuse throughout the campaign.[79]

Most of the seats with large Muslim concentrations remained Labour. Rochdale and Bethnal Green and Bow were exceptions. Nonetheless, there is evidence of an accentuated swing across the country in the Muslim vote from Labour to the Liberal Democrats.[80] Dozens of Labour MPs would have been keenly aware of the foreign policy concerns of a large number of their Muslim constituents.

7/7 changes the rules of the game

The debate over how to address Islamist extremism became far more prominent in the wake of the July 2005 London bombings. Four British Muslims committed the attacks, killing 56 people on three tube trains and a bus in central London. Despite the fact that the security services had been warning of the likelihood of an attack in the United Kingdom for some time, the attacks came as a severe shock to the Prime Minister and his team. Powell recalled that they were particularly shaken to discover that the perpetrators were born and brought up in the

United Kingdom.[81] He recalled the debate within government about how to balance the different approaches to the problem:

> There was a long debate in government after that about how best to address it. And you've got people on both sides, some wanting rather too much relativism from my point of view – in other words lots of understanding and not doing anything – and others who just wanted to crack down. And there had to be combination of the two and it went back and forwards a lot of times.

The bombings fuelled the argument that Britain's foreign policy, particularly the war in Iraq, and also support for Israel, had made Britain more at risk from terrorism. This argument was supported by the testimony of the bombers. In messages recorded before the attacks, the ringleader, Mohammad Sidique Khan, claimed that his motivation was Western foreign policy towards Muslims. Al Qaeda number two Ayman Zawahiri appeared on Khan's video testimony saying: 'The lands and interests of the countries which took part in the aggression against Palestine, Iraq and Afghanistan, are targets for us all.'[82] Another of the bombers, Shezad Tanweer, said in a video testimony released in 2006:

> What you have witnessed now is only the beginning of a string of attacks that will continue and become stronger until you pull your forces out of Afghanistan and Iraq and until you stop your financial and military support to America and Israel.[83]

The day after the bombings, the *Guardian* ran an op-ed by the left-wing intellectual Tariq Ali, arguing that, 'The real solution lies in immediately ending the occupation of Iraq, Afghanistan and Palestine ... As long as western politicians wage their wars and their colleagues in the Muslim world watch in silence, young people will be attracted to the groups who carry out random acts of revenge.'[84]

The same day the paper published an article by former Foreign Secretary Robin Cook, in which he ascribed to the bombers, 'an obsessive fundamentalist identity', but at the same time warned that the current strategy of the West was making the situation worse. He wrote, 'The more the west emphasises confrontation, the more it silences moderate voices in the Muslim world who want to speak up for cooperation.'[85]

In a *New Statesman* article two weeks after the bombings, left-wing journalist John Pilger went much further, describing the attacks as 'Blair's Bombs'. He argued that terrorism was the result of humiliation in the Islamic world due to the policies of the US and Britain.[86] The argument was not confined to left critics of the government. A version of it was also made by British intelligence services in the months leading up to 7/7. A Joint Intelligence Committee (JIC) assessment dated 13 April 2005 asserted that the war in Iraq had 'reinforced the determination of terrorists who were already committed to attacking the West and motivated others who were not.' It added that 'the Iraq conflict had had a motivating effect on the UK extremist community, which was likely to continue into the future.'[87]

Blair acknowledged in his memoirs that it was 'a nightmare of an argument to deal with because, of course, at one level, if you don't fight these people, it's possible that you don't feature so much on their hate list.' 'But', he added, 'what does that say about how your foreign policy is determined?' In his public statements in the wake of the bombings, Blair, not surprisingly, rejected any suggestion that his policies to defeat terrorism had inadvertently resulted in the attacks on London. He dismissed out of hand any argument that gave justification for the attacks or implied there were legitimate grievances. When challenged at the end of July with the proposition that the bombings were because of the Iraq War, he responded:

> We are not having any of this nonsense about it is to do with what the British are doing in Iraq or Afghanistan, or support for Israel, or support for America, or any of the rest of it. It is nonsense, and we have got to confront it as that. And when we confront it as that, then we will start to beat it.[88]

This statement directly contradicted the basis on which the FCO had been engaging with British Muslims for over two years. Rather than acknowledge any need for a change in foreign policy, Blair announced measures to reduce the tolerance for extremism in Britain. In a press conference on 5 August, he declared, 'the rules of the game have changed.'[89] His proposals focused on containing or deporting extremists active in the United Kingdom along with efforts to better integrate sections of the Islamic community and proposals to close mosques where extremism was promoted. He called for the proscription of Hizb ut-Tahrir and other fringe Islamist groups in Britain which had been associated with the radicalization of British Muslims.

In the same press conference, he accepted that terrorists used issues such as Palestine to recruit, but rejected their claimed justifications as 'an obscenity'. At the same time, he acknowledged that 'a lasting settlement . . . would remove a lot of the charge of double standards that is used across the Arab and the

Muslim world'.[90] Was there a tension between believing that resolving the Israeli-Palestinian issue would help defeat terrorism and rejecting that British support for Israel was a cause of terror on the streets of London? Jonathan Powell explained the way in which Blair saw the distinction, saying:

> There are two different things here. One is: Would you change your foreign policy because of a terror threat at home? No you wouldn't. You would stick to what your foreign policy should be. Just because some people at home don't like your policy in Iraq, doesn't give them justification for blowing up people in the United Kingdom. In the case of the Middle East, we were not suggesting any concessions should be made, rather that a reinforced effort should be made to resolve it, because it was a very useful stick for Al Qaeda to beat the West with.[91]

In a speech in March 2006, Blair separated the notion that issues such as Israel-Palestine created a fertile ground for recruitment to extremism, which he accepted, from 'the notion that we have "caused" such recruitment or made terrorism worse', which he rejected.[92] Blair asserted that defeating terrorism meant defeating its ideology, including its anti-Americanism, its pre-feudal attitude to government and its attitudes to women and other faiths. The way to defeat the ideology of 'radical Islam' was to:

> reject the thought that somehow we are the authors of our own distress; that if only we altered this decision or that, the extremism would fade away. The only way to win is: to recognise this phenomenon is a global ideology; to see all areas, in which it operates, as linked; and to defeat it by values and ideas set in opposition to those of the terrorists.[93]

He acknowledged that this was a stance that ran against the attitudes of many in his party and his counterparts in Europe, who believed that US and UK policy had fuelled the threat of violence.

Blair rejected this, but still believed in engaging with British Muslims to build a common front against extremism. He recorded in his memoirs that he had 'real doubts about some of the leaders of the [Muslim] community and how they were confronting – or rather not confronting – this extremism, but it wasn't the time to entertain such doubts.'[94] Instead, as in the aftermath of 9/11, Blair took a lead after the 7/7 attacks in reaching out to British Muslims, welcoming a statement from the MCB in his remarks on the day of the bombings and seeking to engage British Muslims in the response. He chaired a meeting of Muslim organizations at Downing Street on 19 July.

Following this, the Home Office Minister responsible for counter-terrorism, Hazel Blears, appointed seven working groups made up of Muslim community representatives and others to address the problem of extremism among British Muslims. At the same time, Home Office Ministers Hazel Blears and Paul Goggins went on a 'listening tour' of Muslim communities to hear views on the causes of radicalization. According to an unpublished, internal Home Office summary, complaints from British Muslims included media stereotyping, government language and legislation, problems with mosques and religious leaders and shortcomings in education within the community. However, one of the most consistent assertions raised by young Muslims and communal leaders in most of the cities visited was that British foreign policy angered young British Muslims and was a factor in radicalizing young people. The areas of foreign policy mentioned explicitly were Palestine and Iraq.[95]

The 'Tackling Extremism and Radicalisation' working group was chaired by senior MCB official Inayat Bunglawala. He recalled that the MCB felt a responsibility to stress the role of foreign policy in radicalization, saying:

> The MCB had been making clear for a while that we regarded aspects of foreign policy as contributing to worsening the whole issue of violent extremism . . . When the July 7 attacks occurred and it was found that four British Muslims had perpetrated these acts the MCB condemned the attacks while also making clear that we believed that for a resolution of this issue of violent extremism, we needed to revisit some of these policies, and look at the way these policies are contributing to undermining our national security.[96]

This theme did not just come from within the working groups. An internal document to guide the 'Tackling Extremism and Radicalisation' working group was produced by the Home Office and Foreign Office. The FCO official involved was Mockbul Ali, a Muslim political appointee chosen by Mike O'Brien to be the Foreign Office's Islamic affairs adviser.[97] At the top of a list of bullet points explaining radicalization was the statement: 'Foreign Policy: there is anger over perceived double standards in British foreign policy and the perception of Islamophobia in policing and counter-terrorism policy.'[98] This was in addition to a summary list of 'Emerging Themes from Hazel Blears and Paul Goggins Ministerial Visits' which included the bullet point: 'Widespread anger and concern over foreign policy, stop and search and counter-terrorism policy.'[99]

Mockbul Ali was reinforcing the point that foreign policy was a factor in radicalizing young British Muslims, which was being pressed by the MCB. This was at the same time as the Prime Minister was publicly and firmly rejecting that approach. The foreword of the final Preventing Extremism Together report, which was signed by the convenors of all seven groups, asserted that, 'the solutions lie in the medium to longer-term issues of tackling inequality, discrimination, deprivation and inconsistent government policy, and in particular foreign policy.'[100]

The question over the role British foreign policy was playing in the radicalization of British Muslims, and the implications for policy formation, had now become a clear source of discord within the government, and between government and its favoured representatives from the Muslim community. The Chair of the Home Affairs Select Committee, John Denham, challenged the Home Secretary on this in a select committee hearing in September 2005. He charged that there was a:

> tension in government between fighting what could be described as the evil ideology which leads directly to terrorism and engaging in the broader issues of concern which may lead to anger or alienation amongst young Muslims in particular.[101]

Denham himself was a leading figure of the Labour soft left, who resigned from his ministerial role over the Iraq War.[102] He told the *Spectator* magazine after the 7/7 bombings that government policy was failing to take account of the concerns of British Muslims. He said in an interview, 'It is no exaggeration to say that Israeli policy in the occupied territories is not simply a matter of foreign policy — it is a matter for British domestic security policy too,' adding that 'we may well need to . . . be prepared to change the emphasis of our foreign policy in order to safeguard our own security.'[103] Denham returned to government as Secretary of State for Communities and Local Government in 2009.

Shortly after the publication of the Preventing Extremism Together report in October 2005, Home Secretary Charles Clarke set out a very different approach. It was a clear sign that it was the increasingly confrontationalist agenda set by the Prime Minister, and not the accommodationist approach urged by Denham and the 'Tackling Extremism' working groups, that was now setting the tone for government policy. Clarke emphasized the need to strengthen the integration of individuals of all faiths into the democratic culture and to use the law to criminalize extremists and their supporters. He explicitly rejected the link with foreign policy, declaring:

There is not some particular government policy decision, or even some overall policy stance, which we could change and thus somehow remove our society from the al-Qaeda firing line. Their nihilism means that our societies would only cease to be a target if we were to renounce all those values of freedom and liberty which we have fought to extend over so many years. Our only answer to this threat must be to contest and then to defeat it.[104]

Which Muslims to engage with in the United Kingdom?

While MCB figures took a prominent role in the Home Office's counter-radicalization consultation exercise, questions were asked in the media about the organization's own claims to be representing moderate Islam. A BBC Panorama documentary broadcast on 21 August 2005 accused the MCB of being dominated by leaders who subscribed to a narrow politicized version of Islam inspired by the Islamist Jamaat-e-Islami party founded by Maududi in Pakistan. It criticized the refusal of the MCB to participate in Holocaust Memorial Day, a decision made because the event did not deal with the suffering of other peoples, including in Palestine. It also drew attention to the respect accorded by MCB Secretary General Iqbal Sacranie to Hamas founder Sheikh Yassin at a memorial ceremony for him after his assassination by Israel in 2004.[105]

Questions were also raised both inside and outside government about the suitability of the Foreign Office's Islamic issues adviser Mockbul Ali. An official in the Engaging with the Islamic World Group, Derek Pasquill, became concerned that Ali was, like the MCB, promoting political Islam of the type inspired by the Muslim Brotherhood and Jamaat-e-Islami as mainstream.[106] He leaked documents to journalist Martin Bright highlighting his concerns over the advice given by Ali, and the support for engagement with Islamists among other sections of the Foreign Office. These included a document by Ali, dated 14 July 2005, which stated that Yusuf al-Qaradawi should not be excluded from the United Kingdom. Ali described al-Qaradawi as 'key in promoting mainstream Islam' and warned that excluding him would damage relations with Muslims abroad and in the United Kingdom.[107] Ali was able to draw on the assessment of the Metropolitan Special Branch Muslim Contact Unit who declared that:

Sheikh Qaradawi has a positive Muslim community impact . . . His support for Palestinian suicide bombers adds credibility to his condemnation of Al Qaeda in those sections of the community susceptible to the blandishments of Al Qaeda terrorist propaganda.[108]

This was despite al-Qaradawi's defence of suicide bombings against Israeli civilians and the fact that when al-Qaradawi came to the United Kingdom in 2004, the Prime Minister had said he did not consider individuals who defended acts of terrorist violence in Palestine welcome. Blair reiterated his position ever more clearly in August 2005 when he said:

> Anybody who is coming from abroad into our country and coming here to say suicide bombing is a good thing, these people are heroes, that they should do more of it and all the rest of the appalling rubbish that we've heard, they shouldn't come into Britain, and if they are here, they should leave.[109]

This was yet more evidence of two divergent mindsets operating within government at the same time. The Prime Minister's comments did not close the issue. A year later, the Foreign Office attracted more controversy for approving a visa for Bangladeshi politician and cleric, Delwar Hossain Sayeedi, who was quoted as saying that Britain and the United States 'deserved all that is coming to them' for overturning the Taliban in Afghanistan.[110]

However, the Prime Minister's declaration after 7/7 that the 'rules of the game have changed' marked a turning point in the way in which the government treated the claimed link between radicalization and British foreign policy. The government, led by the Prime Minister, began to turn against the recommendations of the MCB on how to maintain good relations with British Muslims. In March 2006, Blair explicitly rejected the advice that had been given to Ministers not to use the term 'Islamist extremist'. He said, 'To say his religion is irrelevant is both completely to misunderstand his motive and to refuse to face up to the strain of extremism within his religion that has given rise to it.'[111] This marked a new readiness on the part of the Prime Minister to link violent extremism against the West to a broader ideological strain within Islam.

In June 2006, the government renewed its counter-terrorism strategy and redefined the Prevent strand. Home Office Minister Hazel Blears acknowledged the shift in thinking around this time. She said:

> I think the country went through a big shock on 9/11 and then an even bigger shock on 7/7 when we realised that this wasn't simply international that this was very much here at home . . . Then there was an increasing recognition of it not just being about . . . the softer side of everybody feeling part of the country . . . But

also that there was need to tackle the ideology. And that the way in which the extremists draw, particularly young people, in is by having a political ideology which uses a religion as a front for it. And I think there is a clearer recognition – certainly I personally feel this very strongly – that unless you battle on ideology you won't be able to discredit and isolate the people who are the biggest threat to this country.[112]

Ruth Kelly, the minister who took responsibility for the Prevent policy stream in 2006, agreed that prior to the 7/7 bombings, 'People did not understand [radicalization] properly at that time and we were on a steep learning curve and certainly the bombings really focused people's minds.'[113]

Whereas before 7/7, Prevent had been about trying to resolve destabilizing conflicts abroad and making British Muslims feel listened to at home, the new strategy document defined two additional aspects. The first was, 'Deterring those who facilitate terrorism and those who encourage others to become terrorists.' The second was 'Engaging in the battle of ideas – challenging the ideologies that extremists believe can justify the use of violence, primarily by helping Muslims who wish to dispute these ideas to do so.'[114] Gone was the sensitivity about putting Islam and terrorism in the same sentence. The document stated:

> The principal terrorist threat is currently from radicalised individuals who are using a distorted and unrepresentative interpretation of the Islamic faith to justify violence. Such people are referred to here as Islamist terrorists.[115]

In a section addressing the question, 'How does radicalisation occur?', the link between Western foreign policies and radicalization was described as being based on a version of history and recent events that 'is highly negative and partial in its interpretation of past interactions between Islam and the West.' The document added:

> Some argue that the West does not apply consistent standards in its international behaviour . . . In particular, this applies to perceptions of relations with Israel and the approach to the Middle-East Peace Process, where the UK is actively committed to a two-state solution, with a viable Palestinian state alongside a secure Israel.[116]

Part of the revised Prevent stream of the strategy was the FCO 'doing more to explain' British Foreign Policy, including, the government commitment to, 'a Palestinian state alongside a secure Israel' and British support for the development of Palestinian institutions.[117]

The implication was that the sense of grievance that Muslims held towards the West was not justified, but based on a false and propagandized version of the facts. The new description of Prevent emphasized defending Britain's foreign policy rather than making foreign policy with an eye to the concerns of specific faith communities or the fear of radicalization.

Ruth Kelly breaks the government link with the MCB

Prior to 7/7, the Home Office's Prevent agenda and the Foreign Office's policy of building bridges with Muslims had been managed by junior ministers. After declaring that the 'rules of the game had changed', Blair imposed his own vision on the issue. His view developed that it was up to Muslim communities themselves to address the problem of extremism in their midst. He told the House of Commons Liaison Committee in July 2006:

> You can only defeat it if there are people inside the community who are going to stand up ... [and say] 'The whole sense of grievance, the ideology, is profoundly wrong. There may be disagreements that you have with America, with the UK, with the Western world but none of it justifies not merely the methods but also the ideas which are far too current within parts of the community.' My view is that until you challenge that at its root you are always going to be left in the situation ... where people kind of say, and I am putting it maybe in a harsher way than I mean to but I am doing it to make a point, 'Look: we understand why you feel like this and we can sympathise with that but you are wrong to do these things.' You are not going to defeat it like that. You are only going to defeat it if you say, 'You are wrong to feel those things.'[118]

In a government reshuffle in May 2006, Blair created a new Department for Communities and Local Government. He appointed Ruth Kelly as its Secretary of State, with responsibility for working with Muslim communities to prevent extremism. In his letter of appointment to Kelly, Blair wrote that, 'local communities need to be able to challenge robustly the ideas of those extremists who seek to undermine our way of life.'[119]

The issue retained its high profile over the summer of 2006, after the police uncovered a plot by British Muslim extremists to blow up transatlantic airliners.[120] In response to the arrests, which took place during the Second Lebanon War, a group of British Muslims, including members of the House of Commons and

Lords, wrote to Blair. While they sought to distance themselves from extremists, they simultaneously expressed sympathy with their professed causes, claiming:

> The debacle of Iraq and now the failure to do more to secure an immediate end to the attacks on civilians in the Middle East not only increases the risk to ordinary people in that region, it is also ammunition to extremists who threaten us all.[121]

Three out of the four Muslim Labour MPs signed the letter, as did three of four Muslim members of the House of Lords. It was the kind of response the Prime Minister had criticized in his evidence to the Liaison Committee, and was out of touch with the new direction of government policy. Ruth Kelly did not accept that foreign policy was the root cause of the problem. She said:

> There would always have been something that they could turn to in attempt to justify what they were trying to do and actually foreign policy was not the root cause of these problems. Not to say they didn't feature in the debates and in propaganda used to try and woo young people because obviously they did but it was the not the fundamental cause of the issue. And I was quite clear about that and that caused some tension with some of the groups that we were talking to who said the government doesn't listen to them on foreign policy and it was all to do with foreign policy.[122]

Kelly said she was influenced by the publication of documents from the Engaging with the Islamic World Group leaked to journalist Martin Bright, which had shown the tendency in the Foreign Office to engage constructively with Islamists. She found the Prevent stream of the counter-terrorism strategy within the Home Office had been underfunded and underdeveloped. She attempted to build up a department that would better understand the British Muslim community and the causes of extremism.

In the autumn of 2006, Kelly announced that government attention and resources would be shifted to local grass roots projects instead of 'gateway organisations' such as the MCB. Kelly felt the MCB had not done enough to confront extremism. In a speech on 11 October, she stated:

> It is not good enough to merely sit on the sidelines or pay lip service to fighting extremism. That is why I want a fundamental rebalancing of our relationship with Muslim organisations from now on . . . In future, I am clear that our strategy of funding and engagement must shift significantly towards those organisations that are taking a proactive leadership role in tackling extremism

and defending our shared values. It is only by defending our values that we will prevent extremists radicalising future generations of terrorists.[123]

She also criticized the MCB's boycott of Holocaust Memorial Day.

Until that point, certain ministers, including Jack Straw and Mike O'Brien, had promoted the MCB as the primary representative body for British Muslims. Kelly's policy change was a declaration that this approach would no longer be followed. She acknowledged that this decision was a source of sharp disagreement and was 'vehemently debated' in Cabinet committees.[124]

As her time in the post wore on, Kelly's position on the role of foreign policy in radicalization became more nuanced. In April 2007, she said:

> The Prime Minister has continually stressed that our foreign policy has not caused terrorism. He is right. John Reid said that terrorism pre-dates both 7/7 and 9/11 – and he is right. But we do need to recognise the central role that Iraq now plays in violent extremists' arguments . . . [B]eing honest enough to recognise how foreign policy is used as a motivating factor in radicalisation will help us tackle the threat. This does not mean that any one particular group should determine foreign policy. Foreign policy must continue to be decided on democratically and in Britain's interests. It does, however, mean being prepared to have the debate. It does mean pointing out the truths that cut through the violent extremists' arguments.[125]

Kelly was acknowledging that foreign policy was used in the arguments of the extremists. However, the approach remained orientated to defending British policy and undermining the narrative of the extremists that British or Western policies were anti-Islamic or that there was a clash of civilizations between Islam and the West.[126]

Until the end of Blair's premiership, the confrontationalist mindset remained dominant in Britain's counter-radicalization agenda. Blair had not imposed himself on the issue of domestic radicalization prior to 7/7, allowing increasingly obvious gaps to open up between his own view of the need to avoid compromises with extremists and the more accommodationist approach dominating Whitehall. After 7/7, Blair's own views with regard to radical Islam hardened and he made them far more explicit, consequently ensuring that policy across departments had a far more confrontational bent.

Blair Confronts 'Radical Islam'

The hardening of Blair's position on the Middle East

By the time Blair was re-elected in 2005, he was intimately familiar with the Israeli-Palestinian arena. Foreign Office special adviser Malcolm Chalmers said of him:

> He knew the details of some issues including the Middle East peace process as well as the foreign office civil servants, because he had been dealing with it for ten years, whereas they had only been dealing with it for six months because they had just been moved from the Uruguay desk or something.[1]

In a series of speeches and writings in 2006 in the midst of the Second Lebanon War, Blair expressed more clearly than before his understanding of the relationship between the Israeli-Palestinian conflict and the threat of Islamist extremism. Already aware that he was approaching the end of his premiership, he was concerned less with political expediency and more with leaving a foreign policy legacy.[2]

In a speech in Los Angeles during the Second Lebanon War, Blair argued that there was an arc of extremism in the Middle East which threatened the moderate Islamic world as well as the West. A struggle between what he called 'reactionary Islam' and 'moderate, mainstream Islam' was taking place, he argued, in every country in the region. He linked Islamist violence in Afghanistan, Indonesia and Iraq to the violence taking place in Lebanon and Gaza, and even to the bombings in London. Rather than criticize Israel for its military actions in southern Lebanon, he expressed sympathy for its predicament. He declared:

> 9/11 in the US, 7/7 in the UK, 11/3 in Madrid, the countless terrorist attacks in countries as disparate as Indonesia or Algeria, what is now happening in Afghanistan and in Indonesia, the continuing conflict in Lebanon and Palestine, it is all part of the same thing. What are the values that govern the future of the world? Are they those of tolerance, freedom, respect for difference and diversity

or those of reaction, division and hatred? My point is that this war can't be won in a conventional way. It can only be won by showing that our values are stronger, better and more just, more fair than the alternative.[3]

Nonetheless, he once again identified the Israeli-Palestinian issue as a central feature of the campaign against extremism. By resolving the Israeli-Palestinian conflict, he believed, a critical blow would be struck against the forces of extremism in the region. Resolving the conflict would not only take away a stick that Al Qaeda used to beat the West, but would symbolically disprove the notion of an inevitable clash of civilizations. He acknowledged that:

It can be very irritating for Israel to be told that this issue is of cardinal importance, as if it is on their shoulders that the weight of the troubles of the region should always fall. I know also their fear that in our anxiety for wider reasons to secure a settlement, we sacrifice the vital interests of Israel.

He declared that he would 'never put Israel's security at risk'. At the same time, he declared:

The real impact of a settlement is more than correcting the plight of the Palestinians. It is that such a settlement would be the living, tangible, visible proof that the region and therefore the world can accommodate different faiths and cultures, even those who have been in vehement opposition to each other. It is, in other words, the total and complete rejection of the case of reactionary Islam. It destroys not just their most effective rallying call, it fatally undermines their basic ideology.

As part of his effort to promote his world view before leaving office, he subsequently published a pamphlet summarizing his key foreign policy themes.[4] In an age of globalization and interdependence, it argued, it was imperative that foreign policy be activist, not isolationist. Developing threats of global extremism and terror had to be pre-empted, and it was wrong to believe that if the threats were ignored that they would not develop.

Islamic extremists, Blair claimed, had attacked the West, not because of a justified set of grievances, but to provoke a confrontation that would win Muslims over to their cause. The fundamental struggle was not, he believed, 'a clash between civilisations: it is a clash about civilisation. It is the age-old battle between progress and reaction, between those who embrace in the modern world, and those who reject its existence.' The way to win this struggle for hearts and minds, Blair wrote, was fighting for global progressive values, including by tackling global poverty, especially in Africa, by protecting the environment, and by promoting fair trade. 'Most of all,' he declared, 'we need to re-energize the Middle East Peace Process between Israel and Palestine – and we need to do it in a dramatic and profound manner.' This would be a total rejection of 'radical Islam' which would 'destroy not just their most effective rallying call, but fatally undermine their basic ideology.'[5]

The position articulated by Blair in 2006 marked an evolution in his position on the nature of the threat from Islamic extremism. In the wake of 9/11, Blair had rejected the suggestion that the Al Qaeda attacks were motivated by a justified grievance against the West. However, he was reluctant to link Al Qaeda with Palestinian armed groups, which he saw as acting in the context of a specific dispute that could potentially be resolved. By 2006, he regarded what he called 'reactionary Islam' to be a unified, anti-liberal ideological movement. This was a far more explicitly confrontationalist position, in that it regarded expressions of 'reactionary Islam' across the world to be 'all part of the same thing'. In a speech in London in March 2006 he declared that, 'The struggle against terrorism in Madrid or London or Paris is the same as the struggle against the terrorist acts of Hezbollah in Lebanon or the PIJ in Palestine or rejectionist groups in Iraq.'[6] This was as close as Blair came to articulating the view that Israel was the front line in the War on Terror.

While adopting an increasingly confrontationalist interpretation with regard to the nature of the threat, Blair continued to argue that an important blow could be struck against that ideology by resolving the Israeli-Palestinian conflict. However, unlike many others in his party and in his government, he did not express the view that Western support for Israel was a source of justified grievance that fuelled terrorism. Furthermore, he did not believe that advancing a solution to the conflict meant withdrawing support for Israel or dismissing Israel's security concerns. The distinctiveness of Blair's position, and the division between himself and others within his party and his government on these issues, were confirmed by Blair's response to the challenges that arose in his third term.

The Hamas dilemma

After Blair's re-election in June 2005, he ensured during the UK's 2005 presidency of the G8 that the Palestinian reform programme he had been championing since 2002 remained on the international agenda.[7] Blair believed that the Israeli withdrawal from the Gaza Strip created an opportunity for Palestinian institutional development with international support and funding. At the Gleneagles summit in July 2005, he secured a $9bn commitment from the G8 to support the Palestinian Authority following Israel's disengagement from Gaza.[8] The implementation of the disengagement in August 2005 created a further opportunity for the European Union to get directly involved in promoting Palestinian institutional development. An 'Agreement on Movement and Access' between Israel and the Palestinian Authority, brokered in November 2005, created an EU 'Border Assistance Mission'. Under the agreement, Israel allowed the Palestinians to control their side of the Gaza-Egypt border, with the oversight of EU monitors.[9] This significant upgrade in the EU involvement in the conflict was a symbol of improved relations between Israel and the European Union brought about by the implementation of the disengagement plan. A few months prior to the disengagement, Israel and the European Union agreed to significantly broaden the scope of their relations with the signing of the EU-Israel Action Plan.[10]

However, the relatively optimistic atmosphere around the disengagement was changed completely by the jarring and unpleasant shock caused by the election of Hamas. A key demand of Bush from 2002, incorporated into the Quartet backed Roadmap, was a call for new elections in the PA. While a Palestinian presidential election went ahead in January 2005, shortly following the death of Arafat, the last parliamentary election for the Palestinian Legislative Council (PLC) had been in 1996. After Abbas's election, in early 2005, he negotiated with Hamas to declare a hudna (temporary truce) with Israel, for which one of Hamas's conditions was entry into the PLO and the Palestinian electoral process.[11] While Israel was opposed to Hamas participation in elections, the United States decided not to interfere and pressed Israel to cooperate. Supporting an election in which Hamas, an armed extremist Islamist group, would participate – as Secretary of State Rice explicitly recognized – exposed an inherent contradiction in US policy, being consistent with Bush's agenda to promote democracy, but incongruous with the War on Terror.[12] However, President Bush supported Hamas participation in the belief that Palestinians would vote for the 'peace' platform of Mahmoud Abbas and defeat Hamas,[13] an assumption that was shared in the United Kingdom.[14]

The Palestinian electorate, however, had not read the script. Hamas took advantage of Fatah's disarray to win the election in January 2006 and form a government with a senior Hamas figure, Ismail Haniya, as Prime Minister. This created a major dilemma for Western powers. Hamas had earned the right to form the government of the PA on the basis of an election backed by the United States and the European Union. Hamas was, however, designated as a terrorist group by both the European Union and the United States. Blair had called for international support for political, economic and security reform in the PA in the belief that this would create the grounding for Israel to reduce its hold on Gaza and the West Bank. But could the United States and European Union maintain normal relations with a PA run by Hamas? If not, what was the fate of the Palestinian reform agenda and the billions of dollars pledged for Palestinian economic regeneration?

Whether to talk to Hamas had been a highly controversial topic in the United Kingdom even before the election. While the UK government did not equate Hamas with Al Qaeda, as Bush had done in his 2002 State of the Union speech, Hamas's military wing was listed as a proscribed terrorist organization in the United Kingdom in early 2001.[15] Despite this, British MI6 agent Alistair Crooke, working from his position in the EU envoy's office, was heavily involved in negotiating the Palestinian hudna, with Islamic Jihad, Hamas and militant factions of Fatah in 2003.[16] While he worked within an EU context, he regularly briefed his British colleagues of his contacts with Hamas.[17] However, in the middle of June 2003, the United States put pressure on the European Union to take tougher action against Hamas.[18] Jack Straw led a campaign to have Hamas proscribed in its entirety at the European Union level. The 'Izz al din al Qassam brigades', regarded as the 'military wing' of Hamas, were already subject to an EU asset freeze. Despite having overseen the banning of only the 'military wing' of Hamas in the United Kingdom as Home Secretary in 2001, in 2003, Straw declared: 'There's increasing evidence now that Hamas' political and military wings are very extensively intertwined.'[19] In face of French opposition, the move was eventually approved by the EU Council in September 2003, after the hudna of the summer of 2003 collapsed with a suicide bus bombing in Jerusalem. The collapse of the hudna also led to the removal of Crooke from his post. He later asserted: 'I was removed from my job in the European Union because I was told this is not the way to fight the "War on Terror" – by talking to groups like Hamas.'[20]

The debate about talking to Hamas formed part of a wider policy discussion about how to relate to Islamists in the Arab world. A hint at the nature of this debate among European policy makers was provided by a leaked Foreign Office document summarizing a roundtable of EU officials and experts which took place in Paris on 1 June 2005. The discussion was on the question of 'Engaging with Islamists in the Arab World.' According to the document, Frances Guy, the head of the Foreign Office's Engaging with the Islamic World group, defined the question as, '(i) should Western governments be speaking to Islamists?;

(ii) if so, to whom; and (iii) how?'. The framework for the discussion was set out
by a dichotomy defined by French academic Olivier Roy who:

> began by assessing that previous Western policy towards Islamists – containment
> and repression – had been a failure. The argument that authoritarianism would
> create a secular society which would in turn lead to democracy had been proven
> wrong. Now we had regimes incapable of reform, which actually increased the
> appeal of Islamism. If the West was now interested in reform, it had to consider
> how to integrate Islamists into the political system.[21]

Retired British official, Basil Eastwood, was among those at the discussion
advocating engagement. He was one of a group of retired European and American
officials who formed the 'Arab-American-European Dialogue' to engage with
Arab Islamists and persuade their governments to do the same. Eastwood's
view regarding Islamists was that it was wrong to think of all Islamists as violent
and that, 'if you want to prevent them sliding across this spectrum of Islamism
towards the violent extreme you have to engage with them.'[22] The group fed the
outcomes of their discussions to their respective foreign ministries. According to
Eastwood, the US State Department was uncomfortable with the idea of talking
to Islamists, whereas the British Foreign Office was 'open-minded' and 'happy
to receive the bits of paper'. Eastwood recalled that at the roundtable in Paris,
the position of the Danish government, which was ready to work with officials
who had been democratically elected, including Hamas members, found wide
approval.

Indeed, this was the approach that had already been adopted in practice by
the Foreign Office in the first half of 2005, after Hamas affiliates were elected to
local government positions. Despite the EU proscription of Hamas, which Straw
himself had promoted, in February 2005, Straw softened his position. According
to an unpublished Foreign Office note, he 'agreed that officials could maintain
low-profile working-level contacts in Lebanon and the Occupied Territories
with Hezbollah and Hamas politicians not implicated in violence.'[23]

Remarkably, this decision came despite the fact that Blair had privately
promised Condoleezza Rice the same month that he would proscribe the
political wings of both Hamas and Hezbollah. According to leaked cables sent
by officials in the US Embassy in London in February 2005, though a letter had
been drafted in the Foreign Office to be sent from Foreign Secretary Straw to
Home Secretary Charles Clarke requesting the proscription, the Foreign Office
hesitated to send it. The FCO's Counter Terrorism Policy Directorate (CTPD)

was 'pressing for Straw to take "a tough line" with Clarke,' but the Middle East and North Africa Directorate was 'considering proscriptions' implications to the Middle East peace process.'[24] The Home Office, the department with the legal power to proscribe organizations, had concerns about legal challenges against proscription. According to the US cable, American officials received encouragement from both the CTPD and Blair's foreign policy adviser to 'weigh-in' to the internal policy debate by directly encouraging both the Foreign Office and the Home Office to act.

Contacts between British officials and Hamas members were reported by the media on the eve of a visit to Israel by Straw in June 2005, and Straw was forced to admit publicly that UK officials had met 'with two elected Hamas mayors not personally implicated in violence'. He claimed that these contacts were routine courtesy calls by mid-level officials to the local mayor on visiting a West Bank town.[25] The government then suspended such contacts.[26]

Within Whitehall, the internal debate about proscription of the political wings of Hamas and Hezbollah rumbled on without conclusion, even after the toughening of the government's attitude towards radical Islamist groups following 7/7. According to leaked emails between Foreign Office officials, Straw met with Clarke on 28 August 2005. Despite having softened the Foreign Office's non-contact policy with Hamas and Hezbollah only months earlier, Straw now called on Clarke to proscribe both Hamas and Hezbollah in full under the Terrorism Act. He apparently cited 'recent evidence suggesting that that there was no distinction between the political and the military wings'. However, the input from the UK's intelligence agencies was that neither Hamas nor Hezbollah had changed significantly since the decision taken in 2001 to proscribe only the military wing. The decision to proscribe only part of each had been a political one taken by Straw himself as Home Secretary in 2001.[27] Charles Clarke consequently feared that changing the terms of the proscription without any supporting evidence that the nature of the organization had changed, would be vulnerable to a legal challenge.[28] The government was trapped by the decision Straw himself had made four years earlier to distinguish artificially the military and political wings of Hamas for political purposes.[29]

The victory of Hamas, running as 'Change and Reform', in the January 2006 Palestinian Legislative Council elections, made the dilemma of whether or not to talk to Hamas much more acute. The Quartet's response was defined in a statement on 30 January 2006, five days after the Palestinian election. The Quartet declared that, 'all members of a future Palestinian Government must be committed to non-violence, recognition of Israel, and acceptance of previous agreements and obligations, including the Roadmap.[30] These conditions were comparable to those that had paved the way for international recognition of the PLO in the late 1980s. The formation of a Hamas-led PA government also complicated the EU's funding relationship with the PA. The European Union could not directly fund a government run by an organization on its list of proscribed terrorist organizations. It therefore suspended both funding to the PA and meetings with its officials, except for the presidency under Mahmoud Abbas. Continued financial support was channelled through a 'Temporary International Mechanism' designed to bypass Hamas and divert funding for essential services through the office of the president.[31] This was a major setback for the Palestinian reform agenda.

Basil Eastwood's view was that the Israeli position, which was opposed to any kind of accommodation with Hamas, was decisive, because that determined the US position. This in turn determined the British and European positions, at a time when the Europeans did not want another major foreign policy fallout with the United States after the Iraq War.[32] Malcolm Chalmers, Jack Straw's special adviser at the time, acknowledged that there was considerable pressure from Israel and the United States not to talk to Hamas. However, he believed that it was in fact the position of Fatah that was decisive.[33] He recalled:

> The UK is only one player, you have all the members of the European Union, you've got the US. Not least you've got Fatah, and Fatah asking for us not recognise this government . . . I think some of those people calling for greater recognition of Hamas don't always understand . . . For the UK government to back relations with Hamas when Fatah were saying no, I think would be pretty incredible.

Mike Gapes, Chair of the House of Commons Foreign Affairs Select Committee, similarly recalled that when his committee recommended in 2007 that the government engage with moderate elements within Hamas, there was a very negative reaction from Fatah and the PLO. They feared legitimacy being granted to their Islamist rivals.[34] Tensions between the rival Palestinian factions became increasingly violent over the course of 2006 and 2007. There were 84 fatalities from violence between rival Palestinian factions in January and February 2007.[35]

According to Chalmers, given the international consensus around the Quartet conditions, there was no serious debate about whether or not to adopt them in UK government circles. However, there was a debate on the degree of flexibility with which they should be applied. On the surface, Blair made clear his position that the conditions should mean no contact with Hamas, when he gave evidence to the Ad Hoc Liaison Committee of MPs in February 2006. In spite of his commitment to bolstering the capabilities of the PA, he declared:

> We will not be able to have contact with an Hamas-led government unless it is clear that they are prepared to forswear that part of their constitution that says they want rid of the State of Israel and that they are prepared to embrace democratic and not violent means of achieving an independent, viable Palestinian state.[36]

However, Jack Straw was explicit about wanting a more flexible approach. In April 2006, he indicated that he viewed Hamas compliance with Quartet demands as a matter of degrees, rather than a clear line that Hamas had to cross. During a visit to Saudi Arabia, he said: 'Hamas now leads the government and we would like to have normal relations with them as we have had with previous governments . . . This requires movement by them as well as by us.'[37] Blair was forced to deny there was a change in the Quartet criteria at his monthly press conference a few days later.[38] Malcolm Chalmers acknowledged that:

> Jack certainly, both domestically and in the region was very much coming from the point of view that we should talk to a wide range of people and he thought it was daft when you dug yourselves into a hole when you didn't talk to people with who you disagree with fundamentally. We talked to those people in Northern Ireland and in the end it helped us get to a solution and that was very much his viewpoint. Blair maybe wasn't quite as convinced as Jack was.

Straw had enjoyed a complex personal history in his approach to the Islamist movement. As Home Secretary, he appeared to leave open the door to dialogue with Hamas by proscribing only the 'military wing' of Hamas, despite UK intelligence agencies recognizing no such distinction between military and political wings in the movement. Then as Foreign Secretary he had promoted the proscription of the movement in its entirety at EU level. Then after the election of Hamas mayors, he had allowed officials to meet with them. He then reversed that position once it had been uncovered. Finally, after the election of Hamas in national elections, he advocated a more open posture to Hamas once again. According to Straw's account, his greater willingness to engage with Hamas was the cause of a sharp phone conversation with Blair, in which the Prime Minister insinuated Straw was influenced by his Muslim constituents, a charge Straw denied. Straw also linked his eventual dismissal from the job of Foreign Secretary to differences with Blair over the Middle East, though this was denied by Jonathan Powell, who maintained Straw had simply been in the job too long.[39]

Straw was not alone in dissenting publicly from a strict non-contact policy. From the moment Hamas was elected, there were backbench Labour MPs, such as Labour Middle East Council Chair Richard Burden, who were willing to meet with Hamas.[40] The dissatisfaction with the non-contact policy within Parliament grew over the following year and a half. In January 2007, the House of Commons International Development Select Committee criticized the non-contact policy. The committee called for pressure to be put on Hamas to change its policies, 'through dialogue and engagement rather than isolation.'[41] In the summer of 2007, the Foreign Affairs Select Committee similarly called on the government to 'urgently consider ways of engaging politically with moderate elements within Hamas as a way of encouraging it to meet the three Quartet principles.' In July 2007, 128 MPs signed an Early Day Motion arguing that supporting Mahmoud Abbas 'should not preclude contact with Hamas.'[42]

While Blair remained firm in public that there would be no UK bilateral contact with Hamas, and committed to the United States in private that Britain would proscribe the organization in full, the policy of non-contact was never absolute. The government acknowledged in the summer of 2006 that British officials were attending multilateral forums, including at the UN, at which Hamas representatives were present.[43] Though Blair talked in increasingly Manichean terms about the need to support moderate Islam over radical Islam, he was open-minded about the possibility of Hamas being able to enter the peace process. In the Los Angeles speech discussed at the beginning of this chapter, where he described the struggle between moderate and radical Islam, he made a distinction between 'moderate' elements within Hamas, and the 'militant' and 'hardline' elements backed by Iran and Syria.[44] This shows that Blair did not believe that Hamas was monolithic and immovably committed to 'reactionary Islam'. He believed there were moderate elements within the movement who had failed to seize the initiative.

Number Ten also took an active interest in British NGOs engaging in dialogue with Hamas.[45] One such group was 'Forward Thinking', an organization established to work with 'hard-line' groups on both sides of the Israeli-Palestinian conflict to promote better understanding.[46] Number Ten was directly involved in ensuring the approval of visas for Hamas officials to visit the United Kingdom in 2006, including Ahmed Yusef, a senior adviser to Hamas Prime Minister Ismail Haniya, and senior spokesman Ghazi Hamad. The granting of visas by the British government to Hamas representatives prompted complaints from the US.[47] The Hamas representatives tried to promote the idea of a long-term hudna with Israel as a substitute for the recognition of Israel demanded by the Quartet.[48] There were no formal meetings with British officials, but there were informal contacts with UK officials in private forums.[49] In addition, Forward Thinking's Director, Oliver McTernan, met regularly with British officials and ministers to brief them on his experiences with the individuals he met.[50]

In making the case for engaging with Hamas, he was supported by recently retired Foreign Office official Jeremy Greenstock, who was the UK's Ambassador to the UN, and then in Iraq. Greenstock's view was that:

> Engagement with Hamas – again to use the very rough parallel . . . of Northern Ireland – to try and encourage them to think diplomatically and politically rather than militantly, was possible and was advisable and in due course would produce results.[51]

His view was further articulated in an article in January 2009, when he wrote:

> The more thoughtful strand of thinking in Hamas recognises the need for a political process and is ready to engage in the search for a durable solution to the conflict with Israel . . . Hamas, which in fact has no deep-rooted argument with the West or Christianity, no political alliance with Tehran or Hezbollah, no respect for al-Qaida and no 'charter' for the destruction of Israel in its political programme, just wants the Israeli occupation to end.[52]

Tony Blair's chief of staff Jonathan Powell recalled that he did speak to individuals who talked with Hamas, but stressed that he did not set up any official channels to Hamas. He recalled this as a matter of regret, saying, 'In retrospect we should have done more to encourage Israel and the United States to have at least a secret channel of communication with Hamas in the way we had done with the IRA. So I think we made a mistake in not pushing that harder.'[53]

Another close aide to Blair who favoured an open-minded approach to engaging with Hamas was Lord Levy, who said, 'At some stage you are going to have some sort of dialogue with Hamas movement – they are a political movement that won an election – if you want to make progress in having a two-state solution. I don't think one needs to be a rocket scientist to work that out.'[54] However, he stressed that despite his views, he did not have permission to meet Hamas individuals and, respectful of the government's policy, did not seek it.

It is clear from this that the UK government, including Blair and some of his most senior personal aides, was open-minded about whether Hamas had the potential to play a constructive role in the peace process. Chalmers asserted that. 'Both Blair and Straw wanted to find a way through which would allow some sort of national unity government and Hamas to be brought into the process.'[55] During a visit to the region in September 2006, Blair said the international community should work with a Palestinian unity government including Hamas if it accorded with Quartet requirements.[56]

However, while Straw was inclined to relax the three Quartet conditions, Blair was not. He did not come close to reversing the non-contact policy and did not initiate a backchannel with Hamas. Rather, he hoped for Hamas to move in the direction of the Quartet's demands and was disappointed that 'moderate' elements within the organization failed to make progress in this respect. For Blair, to have changed the non-contact policy would have driven a wedge between US and UK policy. The British position was influenced by that of the United States and Israel, who were opposed to contact with Hamas. However, according to David Manning, Blair was firm in accepting the position and that 'the preoccupation was, "don't do something that's going to undermine the Palestinian leadership."'[57] This was consistent with Blair's strong belief in the need to bolster moderate Islam against radical Islam.

Whether or not Hamas might moderate and accept the Quartet terms remained an open question for the UK government throughout 2006. However, in December 2006, violent clashes between Hamas and Fatah forces in Gaza peaked and Abbas called for new presidential and parliamentary elections to resolve the problem.[58] In a joint press conference in Ramallah, Blair promptly threw full support behind Abbas as a man of moderation and criticized Hamas for failing to accept international principles and holding back the Palestinian people.[59]

Fatah and Hamas did manage to form a short-lived national unity government from March to June 2007 under intense Saudi pressure. This created further complications for EU policy makers, making it much harder to simultaneously support Abbas and maintain a non-contact policy with his Hamas partners in government. The shared platform of the new government showed some movement on the part of Hamas towards the Quartet's three conditions but it did not meet them. While it pledged to 'honour the legitimate international decisions and agreements signed by the Palestinian Liberation Organisation', rather than renouncing violence, it asserted that all forms of 'resistance' were legitimate. It called for the establishment of a Palestinian state 'over all the lands occupied in 1967', but without explicitly accepting Israel's right to exist within pre-67 borders.[60] This mixed picture prompted a mixed response within the European Union, with some states wanting to maintain the policy of no contact and others prepared to deal with all elements in the new government immediately. According to leaked cables from US officials in London, British officials described to their US counterparts that the UK position on this spectrum was 'in the middle', and that they were waiting 'to judge the NUG [national unity government] on its actions.'[61]

Ultimately, the European Union continued to demand a clear recognition of Israel, but European foreign ministers agreed to extend contacts to moderate PA ministers.[62] Lord Levy, with permission from Number Ten, met with the independent foreign minister of the unity government, Ziad Abu Amr, in Ramallah in April 2007.[63] Non-EU states Russia and Norway went further, by granting meetings to senior Hamas representatives. The headache was ultimately taken away from British and EU policy makers by the collapse of the national unity government in June 2007 and a violent coup by Hamas forces in the Gaza Strip in which they ejected forces loyal to their Fatah rivals. Abbas retaliated in the West Bank by dissolving the unity government and appointing his own team of bureaucrats to run the PA. With the creation of two rival authorities – a Hamas-run authority in the Gaza Strip and an Abbas-run authority in the West Bank – Britain and the EU threw its support behind Abbas and maintained the non-contact policy with Hamas.

The Second Lebanon War

While not strictly within the Israeli-Palestinian arena, Blair's handling of the Second Lebanon War deserves close attention. Blair's response to the crisis was the starkest illustration of the gulf in world view between himself and other parts of the policy-making community. According to Blair's own account in his memoirs, 'It showed how far I had swung from the mainstream of conventional Western media wisdom and from my own people.' It is also important to note that Blair believed the conflict was linked to the Israeli-Palestinian issue as part of the wider struggle 'that affected the whole of the Middle East and the religion of Islam'. But as when discussing the links between Iraq and the Middle East peace process, Blair did not explain the linkage in a very clear and systematic way. Rather, various themes can be drawn out from this memoirs. According to Blair, the Israeli-Palestinian conflict itself was a manifestation, rather than the cause, of the 'wider struggle between the strain of religious extremism in Islam and the rest of us'. The conflict was used as a source of friction because Jerusalem is sacred in Islam and the occupation of that land by Jews 'invoked every dimension of Muslim victimhood from the Crusades onwards'. At the same time, Blair believed, with progress in the Israeli-Palestinian arena, 'each tunnel – in a region full of dark tunnels – suddenly acquired some light at the end of it'. But without progress, according to Blair, 'bad things happen,' of which the conflict in Lebanon was 'another example'.[64]

In January 2006, Prime Minister Sharon suffered a stroke which left him in an irreversible coma. Israeli general elections took place in March 2006. The election was won by Kadima, a new party formed by Sharon before his incapacitation, and led by his deputy, Ehud Olmert. The party won on a platform of continuing the process of unilateral withdrawal from isolated settlements in the West Bank, if an agreement with the Palestinians was not possible. It was a position that won guarded support from Blair.[65] Kadima formed a coalition with the Labour Party as their main partner. In June 2006, shortly after the formation of the government, a cross-border raid from Gaza into Israel by a coalition of terror groups including Hamas led to the capture of a young IDF conscript, Gilad Shalit. In response, Israel launched a series of military offensives into Gaza to secure the release of the soldier. The Israeli Air Force targeted infrastructure, including Gaza's power plant, and the offices of Hamas ministers.[66]

Amidst Israeli military activity in Gaza, on 12 July, Hezbollah forces in southern Lebanon, operating under the cover of Katyusha rocket fire, launched an incursion into Israel. In the resulting skirmish, eight Israeli soldiers were killed and two were captured. Israel decided to launch a major military response, and Prime Minister Ehud Olmert declared his intention to return the soldiers and to crush Hezbollah.[67] The Israel Air Force targeted Hezbollah strongholds in the border area and in cities including Beirut, as well as bridges and other infrastructure in southern Lebanon. Hezbollah launched hundreds of rockets daily at Israeli population centres across northern Israel, including the major port city of Haifa.

At a debate of the UN Security Council on 14 July 2006, France and Russia criticized Israel's military response as disproportionate. However, the United Kingdom, along with the United States, withheld direct criticism, with the

British calling for Israeli restraint. Blair publicly took the view that simply criticizing Israel's response or calling for a ceasefire would not resolve the problem. He told a press conference the same day that, 'this situation isn't going to be resolved by whatever we say as international leaders, it will only be resolved by what we do.'[68] World leaders at the G8 in Russia issued a joint statement on the escalating conflict. British officials, along with the French, the Americans and the Russians, took a central role. Blair was personally involved, in particular, in avoiding a call for an immediate ceasefire.[69] Blair was also caught embarrassingly on microphone privately offering to George Bush to travel to the region to prepare the ground for a mission by Rice. The offer was rebuffed by Bush.[70]

Blair was accused at the time, along with the Americans, of trying to create more time for Israel to deal a 'fatal blow' to Hezbollah.[71] In reality, Blair wanted to end the fighting, hence his offer to Bush to travel personally to the region to prepare the ground for a US-brokered ceasefire. But Blair feared that it was impossible to demand an unconditional ceasefire from Israel in a manner that was balanced. Blair sympathized with the position of Israeli Prime Minister Ehud Olmert. He recalled: 'I knew if I were him I would regard it as impossible to stop unless Hezbollah did too; or unless they were beaten; or, which is what finally occurred, Lebanon took enough pain that Hezbollah would not feel they could do it again.'[72] He also did not want the international community to press for a situation that would return things to the way they were, but rather sought a change in the status quo through the presence of an international force. Condoleezza Rice recalled that Blair was of the opinion that 'you couldn't let Hezbollah benefit from what they had done' and that Blair 'wasn't prepared to sacrifice the quality of the ceasefire for the speed'.[73]

Speaking in the Commons on 18 July, Blair made clear his view that the immediate causes of the violence in the Gaza Strip and southern Lebanon arenas were 'acts of extremism by militant groups that were, as the G8 said unanimously, without any justification'.[74] He drew links not only between the conflicts in Gaza and Lebanon, but also with the threats facing British forces in Iraq as being part of a single struggle in the region. Blair drew a direct link between Iranian arms supplied to Hezbollah and those being used against British forces in Iraq. According to Lord Levy, Blair believed the Iranians had pushed Hezbollah to trigger the conflict to distract international attention from their nuclear programme which was facing increased scrutiny at the time.[75]

Blair told the Commons:

> All over the Middle East there are those who want to modernise their nations, who believe as we do in democracy and liberty and tolerance. But ranged against them are extremists who believe the opposite, who believe in fundamentalist states and war not against Israel's actions but against its existence. In virtually every country of the region, including on the streets of Baghdad, such a struggle is being played out.[76]

This was one of Blair's firmest expositions of the confrontationalist stance with regard to Israel's role in the West's relationship with Islamist extremism. In his view, the extremists who had provoked the escalations of violence in both Gaza and Lebanon were part of a coalition that was not only opposed to Israel but that was also against 'democracy and liberty and tolerance'.

According to Jonathan Powell, Blair was also influenced by the same pragmatic considerations that had dictated his approach to the Israeli-Palestinian arena in the previous nine years. He recalled Blair's view was:

> If you adopt a declaratory policy and start calling for things that you know are going to be ineffective but are going to make you feel better you will give up your ability to change things and that's a mistake . . . He opted for, "I'll bear the political pain of not calling for a ceasefire in order to be able to influence events on the ground and stop the fighting. I am more interested in stopping the fighting than in getting good marks for what I say publicly."[77]

Alongside Blair in this crisis was a new Foreign Secretary, Margaret Beckett, who Blair had appointed in place of Straw in May 2006. According to Beckett, Blair warned her that Cook and Straw had lost Israel's confidence early and never won it back.[78] Blair told her that if the United Kingdom were to press Israel for a ceasefire, Olmert would conclude that Britain had joined the list of nations that had no appreciation for Israel's strategic or military isolation and Britain would lose whatever influence it had. According to Malcolm Chalmers, Beckett agreed with Blair. He recalled:

> I think her view very clearly was that calling for a ceasefire would not have produced one. It would have been read by the Israelis as a call for unilateral ceasefire and the Europeans who were pushing for this in the strongest form were doing it because that was their own electorates wanted. It wasn't something that would have made a difference on the ground.[79]

According to his aide Sally Morgan, Blair was also concerned, as ever, not to publicly cross the Americans in a way that he felt would undermine his influence with them.[80] Israel's then Ambassador to the UN, Dan Gillerman, recalled that the United States appeared content to give Israel diplomatic space to try and fundamentally weaken Hezbollah.[81] UN official Terje Rød-Larsen testified that behind closed doors, many Arab leaders were also keen to see Hezbollah beaten, seeing them as a dangerous proxy of Iran.[82] This marked a significant new development in regional dynamics, reflecting the growth in Arab concern over Iran and its support for violent Islamist groups. Few in the Foreign Office believed the destruction of Hezbollah was possible.[83] Beckett nonetheless stood firm by the Prime Minister's position at an international conference in Rome, at which she opposed calls for an immediate ceasefire.

The Prime Minister's reluctance to call for an immediate ceasefire and to criticize Israel's actions as disproportionate left him, according to biographer Anthony Seldon, 'as isolated internationally as he had been on Iraq'.[84] There was widespread concern about the scale of destruction wrought by Israel's offensive. Middle East Minister Kim Howells visited southern Lebanon and northern Israel ten days into the conflict and told the press, 'These have not been surgical strikes and it is very, very difficult, I think, to understand the kind of military tactics that have been used.'[85] However, consistent with Blair's approach, the Foreign Office's pressure on Israel was applied largely behind the scenes. Chalmers recalled:

> We had the Israeli ambassador in a couple of times, asking him lots of questions about why hit this and why hit that. Reports from our embassy coming in terms of what was being hit in Beirut . . . and the Israeli Ambassador was pretty uncomfortable . . . We weren't saying we would do something. We were saying we are supporting you publicly and it's hard when you are destroying things when there doesn't seem any reason for doing so.[86]

As well as international pressure on the UK's position, Foreign Office ministers and the Prime Minister came under increasing domestic pressure to call for an immediate ceasefire, including from backbench MPs and in the Cabinet. The general public were moved by television coverage of the destruction and civilian casualties.[87] Jack Straw told Blair in private he was making a fundamental mistake,[88] and broke ranks by publicly describing Israel's actions as 'disproportionate'.[89] David Manning, who by this time was Britain's Ambassador to the United States, also thought Blair was making a mistake.[90]

Blair, however, remained absolutely steadfast in his view. His position provoked a very negative reaction from Palestinians. Rosemary Hollis quoted a senior Palestinian intellectual writing to her at the time: 'The mad, blind and stupid Israeli military elephant is joined with the donkey in Washington and the monkey in London – people are very, very angry and bleeding.'[91] Hamas Prime Minister Ismail Haniya wrote in the *Guardian* at the beginning of September:

> The last decade has witnessed the most unfair and one-sided British policy towards the region since the creation of the state of Israel in our homeland close to 60 years ago. The problem has been the unquestioning attachment of Tony Blair's government to the Clinton and then Bush administrations, which have seen the Middle East through Israeli eyes only.[92]

Many Labour MPs were also angry with Blair's stance. One hundred Labour MPs signed an open letter to John Prescott, who was acting prime minister while Blair was technically on holiday, demanding a recall of Parliament to discuss the Middle East.[93] MPs from all parties signed another letter to Jack Straw as leader of the house, also calling for Parliament to be recalled. This letter specifically criticized the failure to call for an immediate ceasefire and the decision to allow US planes which were resupplying Israel to land at Prestwick. These acts had 'given the impression that the UK has assumed a tacitly active and less than impartial role in the conflict'.[94]

This letter was yet another stark illustration of the difference in world view between Blair and his critics within the Labour Party, and the lack of understanding among the MPs of what their own leader believed. Blair was criticized for not being impartial in the conflict, but an analysis of his position shows he had little intention of being impartial. As he had made quite clear in his Los Angeles speech, Blair saw the region defined by a struggle between 'reactionary Islam' and the values of 'tolerance, freedom and respect'. Such a world view could not but imply favour to Israel in a conflict with Hezbollah. For Blair, peace in the region was vital, and stopping the fighting highly desirable, but it could not be at the expense of granting victories to the extremists in the region.

A revealing leaked US Embassy cable shows the extent of the pressure generated on the government by Blair's position. It reported the comments of the then head of the Middle East and North Africa department at the FCO, Peter Gooderham, in a confidential meeting with a US Embassy official on 10 August.

Gooderham reiterated the intense domestic pressure HMG in general and PM Tony Blair in particular are under to resolve the crisis as soon as possible. The PM is determined to resist this pressure until a durable, lasting solution is in place. In the meantime, the UK is seeking to stave off some criticism by focusing on facilitating humanitarian relief, especially fuel supplies. Gooderham noted that UK embassy officials in Washington had been in touch with various parts of the Administration August 9 on this issue.[95]

Though Blair believed that avoiding public policy gaps with the United States was the best way to maintain British influence, the extent to which Blair exposed himself domestically illustrates the extent to which he was acting on his own conviction. Stephen Twigg said with regard to Blair's position on the conflict, 'If he were simply acting in terms of what he thought pragmatically he had to do he would not have taken the stances he did. So I think there was an element of real personal conviction there.'[96]

While Blair resisted calling for an immediate ceasefire in public, he worked actively to try and promote the grounds for a ceasefire that would not simply return the situation to the status quo. As the conflict ran into August, Britain became increasingly involved in trying to bring about a UN resolution that would create the framework for a ceasefire. Beckett flew to the UN in New York on 10 August in order to put pressure on her international counterparts to make sure an agreement was reached, and believed her efforts contributed to reaching an agreement.[97]

Blair's Middle East policy and the September 2006 coup

Blair's Director of Strategic Communications at the time, Ben Wegg-Prosser, believed that for many MPs, 'Lebanon was the straw that broke the camel's back' in turning them against Blair's leadership.[98] Blair himself believed it 'probably did me more damage than anything since Iraq'.[99] However, the significance of the Lebanon conflict should not be overstated. Blair's position was already weakened in 2006 by a series of domestic political crises and divisive public sector reforms. He had already hinted that he would not serve the full term by telling the Parliamentary Labour Party (PLP) that he would allow 'ample time' for a successor to come in to the role. Close aides claim that Blair had already determined he would go before the 2007 party conference.[100] However, the distance between Blair and his party and much of the public over the Second Lebanon War created the political backdrop for a section of the Parliamentary Labour Party to force Blair to announce when his premiership would end. In the view of James Purnell, 'You could make a quite a good argument to say that without his support for the war in Lebanon he might have had an extra year of Ministerial [office] – he may or he may not – but the coup would not have happened without Lebanon.'[101]

In early September 2006, Siôn Simon MP gathered signatures from a clique of usually loyal Labour MPs, who had entered Parliament in 2001, for a letter calling on Blair to resign. The letter coincided with a series of coordinated PPS resignations. Blair was forced to announce that he would stand down as Prime Minister before the next Labour Party conference.[102] It is significant to note that Simon and the other organizers of the letter were not from the left of the party. Several were closely affiliated to Labour Friends of Israel and were in fact relatively sympathetic to Blair and his position. Those involved were not among the 100 Labour MPs who had called for the recall of Parliament during the conflict. As Stephen Twigg noted,

> So many people involved in the plot were LFI people . . . Tom Watson, Siôn Simon, Chris Bryant, Iain [Wright] himself who was chair [of LFI] . . . I think that it became a hook for people but I'm not sure I can think of anyone who became anti-Blair because of Lebanon . . . It obviously didn't help him in what was going to be a very difficult time for him anyway. But do I think that the events of September '06 would have happened if the Lebanon War hadn't happened, I think they probably still would have done.[103]

Whether or not the backbench rebellion was ultimately triggered by the Second Lebanon War, it is clear that Blair paid a heavy political cost for acting out of personal conviction. He could have called for an immediate ceasefire and thereby avoided some of the domestic political criticism he faced.

The calls for him to resign in the wake of the conflict showed that even MPs who were usually sympathetic to Blair's world view were deeply concerned about the damage done to the government's standing by Blair's apparent indifference to public opinion. A poll conducted by Populus, published in *The Times* newspaper on 6 September, found that 73% agreed with the statement: 'the British Government's foreign policy, especially its support for the invasion of Iraq and refusal to demand an immediate ceasefire by Israel in the recent war against Hezbollah in Lebanon, has significantly increased the risk of terrorist attacks on Britain.'[104]

The need for Blair to respond to the concerns of his party was in evidence at the Labour Party conference a few weeks later, at which he declared:

> From now until I leave office I will dedicate myself, with the same commitment I have given to Northern Ireland, to advancing peace between Israel and Palestine. I may not succeed. But I will try because peace in the Middle East is a defeat for terrorism.[105]

Blair's commitment to the issue was genuine, but these kinds of personal pledges were reserved for Labour Party audiences. Blair committed in his 2004 party conference speech to make the Middle East peace process a 'personal priority'. At that point, he was odds with much of the party in backing Sharon's disengagement plan. He had also caused friction with the United States in his 2002 party conference speech by calling for the revival of final status negotiations by the end of the year. He had made this call at a time when such a development was completely unrealistic, while under extreme domestic political pressure in relation to the Iraq War.[106] In each case, Blair glossed over the deep difference in view between himself and the bulk of his party over the causes of the conflict, by stressing his personal commitment to resolving it.

Blair made another attempt to articulate his view of the Middle East in his annual foreign policy address at the Lord Mayor's banquet in November 2006. In this speech, he described a 'whole Middle East strategy' for addressing the UK's core foreign policy concern, which was the ongoing violence in Iraq. Blair argued that solving the violence in Iraq meant also addressing other regional problems. He declared:

> We should start with Israel/Palestine. That is the core. We should then make progress on Lebanon. We should unite all moderate Arab and Moslem voices behind a push for peace in those countries but also in Iraq.[107]

The purpose of addressing 'Israel/Palestine' was not to remove legitimate sources of grievance which cause terrorism. Rather Blair, claimed, it was a strategy to confront Iran and take away the sources of tension that they used to 'paint us, as they did over the Israel/Lebanon conflict, as the aggressors, inflame the Arab street and create political turmoil in our democratic politics'.

By describing the Israeli-Palestinian conflict as the 'core', Blair would likely have hoped to further calm the anger in his party and in the country over the position he took on the Second Lebanon War. However, the point of the strategy was not to force Israel to change its behaviour, as many in his party would have liked, but to undermine Iran. Blair kept his rhetoric focused on addressing the conflict. He did not revert to the idea that the key to resolving the conflict was to put more pressure on Israel to make concessions. In a subsequent interview with *Al Jazeera*, he described his purpose as presenting Iran and Syria with a clear choice, by stressing that good relations with the West depended on those countries being 'part of the solution'. He stressed further that, 'The only way you're going to get there is not if we suddenly start distancing ourselves from Israel because Israel's got to be part of this solution.'[108]

Blair's personal engagement in the region reflected this approach. The scope for significant progress in the Israeli-Palestinian arena was limited, not only by the violence that had been sparked in Gaza and southern Lebanon, but also by the division within the Palestinian polity. Nonetheless, he travelled to the region in September and December of 2006. On each occasion he sought a balanced position and focused on persuading Prime Minister Olmert and President Abbas to meet.[109]

While Blair made personal efforts to act on his 'whole Middle East strategy', he did not lose sight of the fact that US leadership remained key. Blair continued to promote the message in the United States that resolving the conflict was central to addressing the troubles in the region and undermining extremism. In November 2006, he testified before the Baker-Hamilton Inquiry, a US Congressional inquiry on Iraq chaired by former Secretary of State James Baker and former Democrat Congressman Lee Hamilton. He told the inquiry a positive strategy on the peace process would get 'moderate Muslim countries to support a new Iraq' and would 'take away the issue which was most exploited by extreme elements around the region', for radicalizing moderate Muslim opinion.[110]

The effort to push the United States to be more constructive on the peace process continued to be pursued also through other channels in government. According to Malcolm Chalmers, just as Blair and Straw had tried to work with Colin Powell to circumvent the more hawkish elements in the US administration, so Beckett did with Condoleezza Rice. He recalled:

> There is never a monolithic Washington anyway. Sometimes the State Department would find it very helpful when Margaret would say to Condi look you have to give us something here. And Condi would find it very helpful to go back

to say to the more hard line folk, the [then US Deputy National Security Advisor] Elliott Abrams of this world, and say, 'we've go to make some progress.'[111]

Blair's efforts to persuade the United States to be more proactive in relaunching peace talks continued during his visit to Washington in December 2006. At this time, the United States was starting to increase its engagement. Rice visited the region at the end of November 2006. She pushed for Israeli steps to improve movement and access in the West Bank and told reporters that the administration would look to support security forces loyal to Abbas.[112] However, the situation did not change significantly until the collapse of the Palestinian unity government in June 2007. This led to the creation of a Hamas government in the Gaza Strip and a separate Fatah-led government under the authority of Mahmoud Abbas in the West Bank. The clear division between the 'moderates' and 'extremists' in the Palestinian camp created an opportunity for the United States and the European Union to renew full-fledged support for the government of Abbas while continuing to maintain the non-contact policy with Hamas.

This development coincided with Blair's departure from Government. Shortly prior to his resignation as Prime Minister, Blair agreed with the US administration to take on the job of Quartet envoy.[113] Blair's role was to assist with the Abbas-led government on the development of their economy and political institutions. He likely sought a more direct role in brokering peace talks. However, the United States by this stage was finally initiating its own process of final status negotiations under the direct leadership of Rice. She saw the resumption of final status talks as a way of bolstering the moderate camp. Blair's new role in garnering Israeli and international support for the moderate Abbas government in the West Bank was entirely consistent with the agenda for the region Blair had been articulating throughout his third term. His decision to devote so much of his time to this issue demonstrated his continued and genuine belief in the issue's centrality. It was furthermore an expression of his belief in the need to work for the victory of moderates over radicals in the region. His willingness to focus on Palestinian reform also reflected his long-held belief that a competent PA was a necessary condition for Israeli concessions which could compromise her security.

After Blair

The extent to which Blair was isolated in his views about Islamism was apparent even before he left office. Middle East Minister Kim Howells told the Foreign

Affairs Select Committee in April 2007 that using language such as 'arc of extremism' was 'unhelpful'. It was a point with which the committee agreed.[114] In January 2009, David Miliband, who replaced Margaret Becket as Foreign Secretary, wrote in the *Guardian* that 'terrorist groups' in the Middle East such as Hezbollah, Lashkar-e-Taiba and the Sunni and Shia insurgents in Iraq were 'as diverse as the 1970s European movements of the IRA, Baader-Meinhof, and Eta'.[115] Miliband was a key adviser to Blair on domestic policy before entering Parliament and was regarded as like-minded politically. Despite this, the views he expressed on the relations between the Islamic world and the West were diametrically opposed to Blair's in many respects.

In May 2009, Miliband made a speech to the Oxford Centre for Islamic Studies in which he expanded on his position. Miliband called for 'rejecting the lazy stereotypes and moving beyond the binary division between moderates and extremists'. He implicitly rejected the democratization agenda, declaring that, 'there can be no single answer to the question of how we should live.' Whereas Blair rejected post-colonial guilt when he came into office, Miliband struck an apologetic tone, speaking about 'the prejudices that British history generates', including the fact that 'decisions taken many years ago in King Charles Street are still felt on the landscape of the Middle East and South Asia'. Whereas Blair at the end of his term had spoken of a single struggle across the Middle East between moderation and extremism, Miliband criticized the way that, 'Organizations with different aims, values and tactics were lumped together.' Whereas Blair had rejected a policy towards the Islamic world premised on addressing supposed grievances against the West, Miliband called for a 'shared effort to address the grievances, socioeconomic and political, that are perceived to keep Muslims down, and in fact do'. Whereas Blair sought a policy to confront the evil ideology of radical Islam, Miliband called for building coalitions even with groups 'whose aims we do not share, whose values we find deplorable, whose methods we think dubious', so long as they were committed to non-violence.[116]

This new approach coincided with a number of concrete policy steps in the Israeli-Palestinian arena, aimed to put greater pressure on Israel, which had the result of cooling diplomatic relations between the two countries. Towards the end of 2008, Britain promoted measures at EU level to increase pressure on Israel over settlement construction.[117] During Israel's Operation Cast Lead in Gaza in 2009, the UK branded Israel's actions as disproportionate, in contrast to the position taken by Blair during the Second Lebanon War.[118] In March 2009, shortly before elections in Lebanon, Britain announced publicly that it had dropped its policy of non-contact with Hezbollah and allowed its officials to meet with Hezbollah figures.[119] According to leaked cables from US officials, this decision had actually been taken in September 2008, and the timing of the public announcement, driven by the demand from MPs for clarification of the position, came to the United States as an unwelcome surprise.[120] In any event, it was a decision that boldly illustrated the extent to which Blair's confrontational approach to Hezbollah and other violent Islamist groups had left office with him.

Conclusions

Findings

The calculations in UK policy-making in the Israeli-Palestinian arena changed as a result of 9/11. Prior to 9/11, British interests related to its desire to promote regional stability and maintain good relations, influence and trade links with all sides. After 9/11, the question of how to address the threat of Islamist violence came to the forefront of foreign and domestic security policy and the UK's position on the Israeli-Palestinian arena became linked to this larger question. In this new context, the distinctive world view and political approach of the primary decision maker, Tony Blair, which showed marked differences from many in his own party, became a key factor in determining policy.

When the Labour Party came to power in 1997, it inherited a legacy of British involvement in the Middle East, with a combination of strong pro-Arab and pro-Israel traditions among the political elite. There was a high priority on maintaining influence and commercial interests in the Arab world, particularly with the Gulf States. At the same time, there was a tradition of support for Zionism and a view of Israel as a strategic ally of Western interests in the region. Britain was also affected by its unique position poised between its membership of the European Union and its special relationship with the United States. There was an institutional legacy of Arabism in the FCO, albeit in decline, but also a history of Prime Ministers who had impacted British policy in the Israeli-Palestinian arena through their personal views and connections with the issues.

The issue of political Islam was not a pre-eminent concern prior to Labour coming to power and was not commonly linked to the Israeli-Palestinian issue. Nonetheless, the roots of both accommodationist and confrontationalist tendencies were present in the Labour Party which came to power in 1997. The British left, especially after 1967, underwent a general shift from supporting Zionism to closely identifying with the Palestinian cause. Under the leadership of Blair, however, New Labour consciously distanced itself from the 'soapbox' causes of the left, including a pro-Palestinian stance. Blair rejected post-colonial guilt, was firmly Atlanticist and believed in the promotion of liberal democracy. This informed a broadly sympathetic attitude to Israel, as did his positive relationship with British Jews. At the same time, a suspicion of the United States and its power, and deep sympathy for the Palestinian cause remained present in the Labour grass roots and PLP. The growing politicization of British Muslims concentrated in Labour-held constituencies provided an additional bottom-up pressure on some Labour MPs to lean in a pro-Palestinian direction.

In Labour's first term, the most important determinants of British policy in the Israeli-Palestinian arena were the situation on the ground, the legacy of British involvement in the region and the personal politics of Blair. Britain accepted US leadership in promoting the peace process, while also seeking to play a more active role in keeping with New Labour's perception of Britain as a force for good in the world and as part of a more active European foreign policy. Blair in his first term placed a high priority on the Israeli-Palestinian conflict and showed considerable personal interest in playing a role in the peace process. Overall, Blair developed greater confidence on the international stage and articulated a foreign policy doctrine of liberal interventionism led by the United States. International concerns about the Israeli-Palestinian issue rose with the collapse of the peace process and the outbreak of the Second Intifada. However, while there were increasing concerns about the threat of violence from extreme Islamist groups during Blair's first term, this was not a pre-eminent concern, and not generally linked to the Israeli-Palestinian issue.

After 9/11, British policy in the Israeli-Palestinian arena was shaped not only by events within that sphere, but also by developments in Britain's policies to address the threat of violent extremism. In the immediate wake of 9/11, there was a broad consensus in the British policy-making elite that making progress on the Israeli-Palestinian peace process should be an important component of the response. However, there were different understandings of how the Israeli-Palestinian conflict related to the challenge of stopping attacks against the West. These were rooted in different understandings of the nature of the threat posed by the Al Qaeda, like-minded groups and their supporters. Those leaning towards the accommodationist perspective tended to see American and Western support for Israel as emblematic of unjust Western policies and double standards in the region. Reconsidering those policies, therefore, would help to remove a source of anger.

The Prime Minister was consistent from the immediate aftermath of 9/11 until the end of his period in government that violence directed against the West was not due to any justified grievance. In the wake of 9/11, he spoke of Al Qaeda and other similar extremist groups as being motivated by an anti-liberal ideology that was repudiated by most Muslims. However, he accepted that they exploited the Israeli-Palestinian conflict to inculcate hatred against the West. For Blair, therefore, in the wake of 9/11, a renewed effort on the Israeli-Palestinian issue would help build a coalition of support within the Arab world for fighting the war between 'civilization' and 'terror'. He also believed that solving the Israeli-Palestinian conflict would be a catalyst for reform in the region. Blair believed that as a result of 9/11, the pieces of the international order had been thrown into the air and he saw an opportunity to change the status quo. In particular, he hoped the United States could be persuaded to re-engage in the issue, after the Bush administration had largely rejected the role of peacemaker undertaken by Clinton. Blair believed it was a vital element of the response to 9/11 to win hearts and minds in the Arab and Islamic world.

Britain's approach to the Israeli-Palestinian conflict in this context was defined by the Prime Minister. In contrast to many in his party and other European leaders, he consistently resisted placing the weight of blame on Israel amidst the escalating violence of the Second Intifada, even in the wake of Operation Defensive Shield in April 2002. This reflected Blair's sympathy for Israel's right to self-defence.

It is important to stress that 9/11 and the War on Terror were not the only reasons that British policy makers were concerned with the Israeli-Palestinian conflict. Blair was committed to the issue on a personal level throughout his term in office. The high levels of violence of the Second Intifada attracted grave concerns across the political spectrum and would no doubt have done so even without 9/11 or the War on Terror. The Palestinian cause in any case had a hold on the left which Blair could not ignore even if he wanted to. Similarly, 9/11 did not significantly change events on the ground in the Israeli-Palestinian arena. However, in the wake of 9/11, and because of British involvement in the wars in Afghanistan and Iraq, the Israeli-Palestinian issue took on added salience. As a result of 9/11, for the first time since the end of the Mandate, British policy towards the Israeli-Palestinian issue was considered by policy makers to impinge directly on Britain's own national security.

Blair's principal method of promoting progress in the Israeli-Palestinian dispute was attempting to persuade the United States to be more proactive. In this he was only sporadically successful. For most of Blair's premiership, the Bush administration was much less concerned with building coalitions of international support for the War on Terror than Blair. They also tended to see Israel's fight against Palestinian militancy only through the prism of terrorism and believed little progress was possible with the Palestinian leadership under Arafat. Influenced by neoconservative thinking, the Bush administration saw the promotion of democracy as a prerequisite for lasting peace. Blair largely agreed with this and became a very active promoter of international support for Palestinian reform. At the same time, he continued to try and persuade the United States to do more to establish the conditions for the peace process to be resumed. He had an impact at certain moments, including the publication of the Roadmap in 2003. However, he failed to persuade the United States to put consistent effort into proactively changing the situation on the ground.

Blair wanted to see greater US effort in the peace process and believed in trying to build a consensus with the Arab world. However, he shared Bush's view that Arafat was not credible. This helps explain why Blair did not withdraw support from the US-led war in Iraq, despite the lack of significant progress in the Israeli-Palestinian arena, even though the Whitehall policy machine widely believed until mid-2002 that support for the war was conditional on improvements in the Israeli-Palestinian arena. Fear of the supposed threat of Iraqi WMD drove his decision-making, though he also believed removing Saddam would trigger wider regional change. He continued to believe that progress in the Israeli-Palestinian peace process would improve the diplomatic backdrop against which to pursue Saddam. He also came under considerable domestic political pressure to focus attention on the peace process in the run-up to the Iraq War. Both these considerations led Blair to pressure the United States to publish the Roadmap.

The domestic political pressure also forced Blair to take positions on the Israeli-Palestinian issue that satisfied the pro-Palestinian sentiments of his party grass roots but were out of step with US policy. More than once, Blair apparently tried to deflect criticism of his foreign policy from within the Labour Party by putting heavy emphasis on his commitment to the Israeli-Palestinian issue in annual party conference speeches. This was despite the fact his underlying assumptions about the nature of the conflict and how to resolve it remained distinct from large parts of his party. In the run-up to the Iraq War in particular, this caused strains in UK–Israel bilateral relations.[1] Allowing clear policy gaps between himself and the United States, and allowing British relations with Israel to be publicly strained, was at variance within Blair's own political instincts.

After the defeat of Saddam in the Iraq War, Blair increasingly spoke about the primacy of the Middle East peace process in the War on Terror and its importance to him personally. The belief that resolving the Israeli-Palestinian conflict would help in the effort to address Islamist extremist violence was widespread, as was the belief that this was the most important issue to address in combating extremism. However, Blair's position was distinctive, in that it stressed the paramount importance of the Israeli-Palestinian conflict, while simultaneously resisting the idea that Israel was primarily to blame.

His rhetoric about the importance of the Israeli-Palestinian conflict continued to be influenced at times by domestic political concerns, particularly within his own party, both about the Iraq War and about the ongoing violence in the Israeli-Palestinian arena. However, Blair never accepted the logic of those who put the weight of blame for the conflict, and for Islamic anger against the West, on Israel and her backers in the United States. Blair's language at times may have given the impression that he was ready to pay for the Iraq War by forcing Israel to concede on its core interests. But in essence, he never abandoned his basic sympathy for Israel's predicament. In policy terms, his focus on the Israeli-Palestinian issue did not translate to significantly greater pressure on Israel to make concessions, as many in his party would have liked. Instead, he focused on the need for Palestinian political and security reform, which he saw as a prerequisite for a meaningful political process which would be supported by Israel and the United States. In this regard, Blair saw the death of Arafat, and Ariel Sharon's disengagement plan, as opportunities to make progress. He declared his support for Israel's unilateral disengagement from Gaza in the face of considerable domestic and international opposition.

Blair's controversial policies in Iraq and in the Israeli-Palestinian arena were sources of concern for those in the Foreign Office engaged with reaching out to Islamic opinion in Britain and around the world. In the months following 9/11, the FCO began efforts to allay concerns of British Muslims who might perceive the War on Terror as anti-Muslim. In the period of rising tensions before the invasion of Iraq, this developed into a policy of giving British Muslims a voice in foreign policy, including with regard to the Middle East.

Around the time of the Iraq War, the agenda to 'Build Bridges with Mainstream Islam' became motivated not just by principles of inclusivism and public diplomacy, but a desire to prevent radicalization, with the FCO adopting a strategy which called for 'full scale engagement with British Muslims on foreign policy'.[2] Senior officials in Whitehall accepted an idea which the Prime Minister consistently rejected, that British foreign policy, including in the Israeli-Palestinian arena, was a 'key driver' in radicalization.[3] This led officials to consider whether policy on the Middle East peace process should be changed in response to the concerns about radicalization in the United Kingdom. Furthermore, Foreign Office ministers, under the advice of British Muslim representative groups and appointed Islamic affairs advisers, engaged openly with Islamist leaders whose views, such as support for Palestinian suicide bombers, were regarded as unacceptable and extreme by most people in Britain. This was despite the Prime Minister explicitly stating his opposition to such contacts.

Blair put a stop to this approach to domestic counter-radicalization after 7/7. Following the London bombings, Blair's language about the threat of Islamist violence evolved. He spoke more readily in the confrontationalist mode about 'radical Islam' as a unified ideology that had to be confronted. Whereas in the immediate aftermath of 9/11 he drew a distinction between Al Qaeda and Palestinian terrorism, after 7/7, he linked the conflict in Afghanistan to the violence in Gaza and Lebanon as part of a global struggle over the 'values that govern the future of the world'.[4] After 7/7, Blair rejected outright the idea that the radicalization of British Muslims was due to British foreign policy and declared that the 'rules of the game have changed'.[5] In concrete policy terms, this marked a decrease in tolerance for Islamist sympathies in the United Kingdom. Blair argued that defeating terrorism meant defeating the anti-Western, anti-liberal ideology of 'radical Islam'. The government announced a 'fundamental rebalancing' of government relations with British Muslim groups.[6] This meant a shift away from the Muslim Council of Britain which had promoted Islamist preachers like Yussuf al-Qaradawi as mainstream.

Blair's belief in the need to bolster moderates against extremists both at home and abroad informed his firm support for a policy of non-contact with Hamas, despite initial open-mindedness about the ability of the organization to join the camp of the moderates. However, this approach was not followed at all times consistently by the FCO, and a personal commitment Blair made to the United States to proscribe the Hamas political wing ultimately went unfulfilled, apparently due to fears in the Home Office of legal challenges.

More controversially, Blair's refused to call for an immediate ceasefire in the Second Lebanon War; a position that was consistent with his belief that Israel was acting in self-defence against an element of the 'arc of extremism', and that preventing Hezbollah from gaining an advantage in the conflict was paramount. This issue more than any other exposed the gap between Blair's views and those of his party and much of the public, who believed Israel's actions were indefensible and that Britain's failure to condemn them made the United Kingdom more at risk from terrorism. So sharply did this issue divide Blair from his party and public opinion that it triggered a coup which forced Blair to announce when he intended to leave office.

Blair's Guildhall speech of 2006, in which he described the Israeli-Palestinian conflict as the 'core' of a whole Middle East strategy, could be interpreted as a concession to those who saw Israel, and the West's support for her, as the cause of Islamic anger against the West. In fact, Blair never made this concession. The speech was an attempt to take his long-held view that dealing with the Israeli-Palestinian issue was an important part of tackling extremism into a process for dealing with the problems in the region. Blair stressed that the central problem was the radicalism promoted and exploited by Al Qaeda and Iran.

To some extent, the level of Blair's rhetorical commitment to resolving the Israeli-Palestinian conflict seemed motivated politically by a desire to offset internal party criticism of his handling of the Second Lebanon War. However, Blair genuinely felt that the Israeli-Palestinian question was a key priority issue that should be addressed. This was confirmed by his personal decision immediately after resigning as Prime Minister to take up the post of Quartet envoy dealing directly with the Israeli-Palestinian issue.

The broadly confrontationalist stance that Blair arrived at by the end of his term was firmly rejected by the Labour government after he left office. David Miliband in particular, as Foreign Secretary, articulated a sharply contrasting view, calling for engagement with all regardless of their beliefs and for efforts to address Islamic grievances against the West. This corresponded with a policy of exerting greater pressure on Israel with regard to the Israeli-Palestinian conflict.

Wider implications and ongoing questions

The findings of this thesis support the view that the beliefs and world views of individual leaders matter when it comes to foreign policy decisions. With regard to Britain's policy in the Israeli-Palestinian arena in the wake of 9/11, the underlying world view of the Prime Minister was critical to determining policy outcomes. There are sharply contrasting views of Israel in the West: for some an agent of imperialism or colonial oppressor which engenders hatred of the West, for others a state on the front line in the battle for liberal democracy against anti-liberal radicalism. The view of Israel in the West is impacted to a considerable degree by what Israel does and by events in the region. The credibility of Israel's claim to be on the front line of Western states against extremism is heavily affected by the extent to which it is seen to behave according to Western liberal standards. But the way Israel is viewed by policy makers in the West is also affected by the broader world views those individuals carry with them, quite independent of the knowledge or experience they may have of the conflict itself. This study of British policy in the Israeli-Palestinian arena in the wake of 9/11 has exemplified this. Divergent world views, even within the same political party, can generate very different policy preferences. At times this can lead to a situation in which different parts of the same government simultaneously pursue inconsistent policies based on very different assumptions about the nature of the problem and how to address it.

What this book has not done, is attempt to ascertain whether any of the supposed linkages between the Israeli-Palestinian issue, and relations between the Islamic world and the West are correct. While Blair and his critics disagreed about the nature of the linkage, they all agreed that links existed and were important. What they were all equally guilty of, was rarely describing their view of how these issues were linked in anything more than the vaguest and most generalizing terms. Would Islamic anger against the West be lessened by Western governments forcing Israel to evacuate the West Bank? Would resolution of the Israeli-Palestinian conflict take away the primary source of 'poison' in relations between the West and the Islamic world? Would it help overpower the ideology of anti-Western radicals and pave the wave for a transformative modernization of the region? Is it meaningful to talk about Islamism, radical Islam or Islamic extremism as unified phenomena which demands a universal policy response? Clear and consistent approaches to these questions built on evidence and a deep understanding of the region remain elusive among policy makers.

Yet more than a decade on from 9/11, the question of the relationship between the Israeli-Palestinian conflict and the challenge of Islamism remained highly salient and highly controversial. The centre left Israeli government of Ehud Olmert, which made considerable efforts to reach a final status accord with the Palestinians in 2008, failed to do so and gave way to a centre-right and far more conservative Israeli government under Benjamin Netanyahu. Meanwhile, the Palestinian division between the Hamas-ruled Gaza Strip and the Fatah-dominated Palestinian Authority in the West Bank only became more entrenched.

After leaving office, Blair remained an important voice on these issues as the representative of the Quartet. He continued to work to develop the institutional capacity of the Palestinian Authority led by Mahmoud Abbas and Palestinian Prime Minister Salam Fayyad in the West Bank, and to keep his distance from the Hamas authority in the Gaza Strip. In the Postscript to his memoirs, published in 2010, he criticized an approach that implied respect for the narrative that 'sees Islam as the victim of the scornful West' and described extremism as a 'strain within Islam', that can 'only actually be eliminated by those within Islam'.[7] When Hamas and Fatah tried again to form a national unity government in 2011, Blair cast doubt on the readiness of Hamas to renounce its extremist views or its support for terrorism. He criticized Hamas Prime Minister Ismail Haniyeh's description of Bin Laden after the Al Qaeda leader's death as a 'holy warrior'. Blair said, 'If this [agreement] meant that Hamas were changing . . . this would be positive, but you only have to look at the reaction from Haniyeh [to the death of Bin Laden] to have the obvious response and question marks.'[8]

However, new administrations on both sides of the Atlantic continued to wrestle with the same questions and to develop their own answers. In its first year, the Obama administration explicitly sought to reset US relations with the Arab and wider Islamic world, accepting the notion that the Israeli-Palestinian issue was one of the key sources of disagreement and stating that resolving it was a US national security interest. Obama did not buy into the confrontationalist view that Israel was on the right side of a bipolar struggle between extremists and moderates. In a keynote speech in Cairo in June 2009, Obama struck an accommodationist note, saying that, 'tension has been fed by colonialism that denied rights and opportunities to many Muslims.'[9] The US National Security Strategy published in May 2010 defined the primary threat to the United States, not as an arc of extremism, but far more narrowly, as a 'specific network, al-Qa'ida, and its terrorist affiliates'.[10] Israeli leaders have continued to make the case that Israel is an ally of the United States against extremism. Netanyahu told an audience in the United States in March 2010, 'For decades, Israel served as a bulwark against Soviet expansionism. Today it is helping America stem the tide of militant Islam.'[11] But Israeli Ambassador to the US. Michael Oren was forced to acknowledge in an article for *Foreign Policy* in 2011 that, 'an increasingly vocal group of foreign-policy analysts insists that support for the Jewish state, including more than $3 billion in annual military aid, is a liability,' which was 'the primary source of Muslim anger at the United States.'

The British Conservative party, the dominant player in the coalition government which replaced Labour in 2010, expressed a range of views on this subject. William Hague, in his first major speech as Foreign Secretary, made a clear link between the success of the counter-terrorism drive in Afghanistan and Pakistan and perceptions in the Islamic world of Britain and America's role in the Middle East peace process.[12] The implication was that Islamic public opinion would be taken more seriously in the formation of British policy in the Israeli-Palestinian arena. However in early 2011, David Cameron stated his position that though foreign policy issues including 'Palestine' were contributory factors fuelling what he termed 'Islamist extremism', 'the root lies in the existence of this extremist ideology', which would persist even if those issues were resolved.[13]

The dramatic political changes in the region brought about by the Arab Spring changed the context for the debate. At the height of the War on Terror, the fear was that real or imagined grievances against the West would push recruits and supporters into the arms of Al Qaeda. With the onset of the Arab Spring and the death of Bin Laden, the focus shifted to the threat that popular anti-Western sentiment would aid radical and anti-Western political parties and leaders in the newly competitive and pluralized Arab political space. The threat of Western allied regimes succumbing to popular Islamist movements became a reality, most notably in Egypt, the most populous Arab state. The Arab Spring made Arab publics more volatile and their views more important. Though the principal demands of Arab grass roots protest movements related to economic and political opportunity, standing up to the West and Israel inevitably became important sources of legitimacy for all political actors. This has been particularly important in Egypt, whose peace treaty with Israel is the cornerstone for any wider peace process, but whose public is deeply hostile to Israel and whose Islamist parties are ideologically opposed to Israel's existence.

For Western powers, public diplomacy in the Arab world has become more important, as they now strive to build sustainable diplomatic, strategic and trade relations with states whose political systems are based on popular mandate, rather than on authoritarian rule. The economic problems in the United States and Europe have made the trade aspects of these relationships all the more important.[14] In 2011, the United Kingdom was the single largest overseas investor in Egypt. British officials continued to see the Israeli-Palestinian arena as an important factor in this equation. Senior Foreign Office Official Mark Lyall Grant no doubt reflected a widespread Foreign Office view when stating at a public meeting at Chatham House in June 2011 that, 'Israel-Palestine remains the main poison in the well between the West and the Islamic world.' This belief continued to undercut Israel's case that it is an even more important strategic ally to the West, given the uncertain political future and strategic orientation of other Western allies in the region.

Looking to the future, therefore, it seems that the nature of the connection between the Israeli-Palestinian conflict and relations between the Islamic world and the West will continue to be a subject of disagreement among policy makers. How policy makers understand this relationship looks set to impact on their approach to the Israeli-Palestinian conflict for at least as long as that conflict persists.

Notes

Introduction

1 R. Satloff and T. Blair, "2010 Scholar-Statesman Award Dinner," *Washington Institute for Near East Policy*, 5/10/2010. Accessed 8/10/2010. http://www. washingtoninstitute.org/html/pdf/BlairScholarStatesman.pdf.

2 J. Taylor and C. Jasparo, "Editorials and Geopolitical Explanations for 11 September," *Geopolitics* 8, no. 3 (2003).

3 N. Lochery, *Loaded Dice: The Foreign Office and Israel* (London: Continuum Books, 2007), 220.

4 Q. Wiktorowicz and J. Kaltner, "Killing in the Name of Islam: Al-Qaeda's Justification for September 11," *Middle East Policy* 10, no. 2 (2003); G. Kepel, *The War for Muslim Minds* (Cambridge, Massachusetts: Harvard University Press, 2004), 2.

5 Wiktorowicz and Kaltner, "Killing in the name of Islam."

6 *Leaked Letter from Sir Michael Jay to Sir Andrew Turnbull on 'Relations with the Muslim Community'*, (Observer, 18/5/2004). Accessed 1/6/2010. http://politics. guardian.co.uk/foi/images/0,9069,1558170,00.html.

7 T. Blair, "Prime Minister's Downing Street Press Conference," *National Archives*, 26/7/2005. Accessed 1/5/2010. http://webarchive.nationalarchives.gov. uk/20070701080624/http://pm.gov.uk/output/Page7999.asp.

8 T. Blair, *A Journey* (London: Hutchinson, 2010).

9 R. Miller, *Inglorious Disarray: Europe, Israel and the Palestinians* (London: Hurst & Company, 2011); R. Hollis, *Britain and the Middle East in the 9/11 Era* (London: Wiley-Blackwell, 2009); Lochery, *Loaded Dice*; J. Rynhold and J. Spyer, "British Policy in the Arab–Israeli Arena 1973–2004," *British Journal of Middle Eastern Studies* 34, no. 2 (2007).

10 Rynhold and Spyer, "British Policy in the Arab-Israeli Arena."

11 Hollis, *Britain and the Middle East*: 75, 136.

12 Miller, *Inglorious Disarray: Europe, Israel and the Palestinians*: 170.

13 For a review of some of these arguments, see S. Azubuike, "The 'Poodle Theory' and the Anglo-American 'Special Relationship'," *International Studies* 42, no. 2 (2005). See also J. Powell, *The New Machiavelli: How to Wield Power in the Modern World* (London: Bodley Head, 2010), 261.

14 D. Coates, J. Krieger, and R. Vickers, *Blair's War* (Cambridge: Polity Press, 2004), 97.

15 L. Freedman, "The Special Relationship, Then and Now," *Foreign Affairs* 85, no. 3 (2006): 71. See also I. Parmar, " 'I'm Proud of the British Empire': Why Tony Blair Backs George W. Bush," *The Political Quarterly* 76, no. 2 (2005).

16 On the distinction between confrontationalist and accommodationist interpretations of political Islam, see F. A. Gerges, *America and Political Islam: Clash of Cultures or Clash of Interests?* (Cambridge: Cambridge University Press, 1999). This distinction is discussed in more detail in Chapter 4.

17 C. Hill, *The Changing Politics of Foreign Policy* (Basingstoke: Palgrave MacMillan, 2003).

18 According to Goldstein and Keohane, 'ideas influence policy when the principled or causal beliefs they embody provide road maps that increase actor's clarity about goals or ends-means relationships, when they affect outcomes of strategic situations in which there is no unique equilibrium, and when they become embossed in political institutions. J. Goldstein and R. O. Keohane, *Ideas and Foreign Policy: Beliefs, Institutions, and Political Change* (Ithaca: Cornell University Press, 1993), 3.

19 M. Bevir and R. A. W. Rhodes, "Interpretive Theory," in *Theory and Methods in Political Science, Second Edition*, ed. D. Marsh and G. Stoker (Basingstoke: Palgrave MacMillan, 2002), 140.

20 F. Devine, "Qualitative Methods," in *Theory and Methods in Political Science*, ed. D. Marsh and G. Stoker (Basingstoke: Palgrave Macmillan, 2002).

21 See, for example, Hollis, *Britain and the Middle East*: 185; R. Hinnebusch, *The International Politics of the Middle East* (Manchester: Manchester University Press, 2003), 1.

22 See M. Tessler, *A History of the Israeli–Palestinian Conflict* (Bloomington: Indiana University Press, 1994).

23 O. Roy and C. Volk, *The Failure of Political Islam* (Cambridge, MA: Harvard University Press, 1994), ix; see also N. Ayubi, *Political Islam: Religion and Politics in the Arab World* (London: Routledge, 1991).

24 G. E. Fuller, "The Future of Political Islam," *Foreign Affairs* 81, no. 2 (2002).

Chapter 1

1 E. Monroe, *Britain's Moment in the Middle East, 1914–1971* (London: Chatto & Windus, 1981).

2 A. Shlaim, 'The Balfour Declaration and its Consequences,' in *More adventures with Britannia: personalities, politics and culture in Britain*, ed. W. R. Louis (London: IB Tauris, 1998).

3 R. Miller, 'British Anti-Zionism Then and Now,' *Covenant Global Jewish Magazine* 1, no. 2 (2007).

4 Ibid.; D. Cesarani, 'Anti-Zionism in Britain, 1922–2002: Continuities and Discontinuities,' *Journal of Israeli History* 25, no. 1 (2006).

5 W. Laqueur, *The Israel-Arab Reader: A Documentary History of the Middle East Conflict* (Harmondsworth: Penguin, 1970), 33.

6 Ibid., 36.

7 Ibid., 39.

8 Tessler, *History of the Israeli–Palestinian Conflict*: 242–4.

9 W. Laqueur, *A History of Zionism* (New York: Schocken, 2003), 528–33.

10 W. R. Louis, *The British Empire in the Middle East, 1945–1951* (Oxford: Oxford University Press, 1984).

11 R. Ovendale, *Britain, the United States, and the Transfer of Power in the Middle East* (London: Leicester University Press, 1996).

12 Louis, *The British Empire in the Middle East*: 24.

13 E. Kedourie, *The Chatham House Version, and Other Middle-Eastern Studies* (London: Weidenfeld & Nicolson, 1970).

14 Laqueur, *The Israel-Arab Reader*: 311.

15 T. Segev, *One Palestine Complete; Jews and Arabs Under the British Mandate* (London: Abacus, 2001), 492.

16 Tessler, *History of the Israeli-Palestinian Conflict*.

17 Ovendale, *Britain, the United States, and the Transfer of Power*.

18 Lochery, *Loaded Dice*: 86.

19 Ibid., 36.

20 Ibid.

21 Ovendale, *Britain, the United States, and the Transfer of Power*.

22 Monroe, *Britain's Moment in the Middle East, 1914–1971*: 95ff.

23 Lochery, *Loaded Dice*: 42.

24 Ibid., 56.

25 A. Shlaim, 'The Protocol of Sevres, 1956: Anatomy of a War Plot,' *International Affairs* 73, no. 3 (1997).

26 Ovendale, *Britain, the United States, and the Transfer of Power*: 162ff.

27 Ibid., 182ff.

28 Lochery, *Loaded Dice*: 68.

29 Ibid.

30 Ibid., 95.

31 M. Gat, *Britain and the Conflict in the Middle East, 1964–1967: The Coming of the Six-Day War* (Westport, CT: Greenwood Publishing Group, 2003), 63.

32 Lochery, *Loaded Dice*.

33 Gat, *Britain and the Conflict in the Middle East*: 8.

34 Lochery, *Loaded Dice*: 99.

35 Gat, *Britain and the Conflict in the Middle East*: 242.

36 M. Gat, 'Britain and the Occupied Territories after the 1967 War,' *Middle East Review of International Affairs* 10, no. 4 (2006).

37 Tessler, *History of the Israeli-Palestinian Conflict*: 468.

38 Lochery, *Loaded Dice*: 138.

39 Ibid., 141.

40 Ibid., 142.

41 Ibid.

42 Miller, *Inglorious Disarray: Europe, Israel and the Palestinians*: 37.

43 Ibid., 33.

44 H. Wilson, *The Chariot of Israel: Britain, America, and the State of Israel* (London: Weidenfeld and Nicolson and M. Joseph, 1981), 380.

45 Rynhold and Spyer, 'British Policy in the Arab-Israeli Arena,' 148.

46 Miller, *Inglorious Disarray: Europe, Israel and the Palestinians*: 73–6.

47 Lochery, *Loaded Dice*: 183.

48 E. J. Evans, *Thatcher and Thatcherism* (London: Routledge, 2004), 94.

49 'The European Community's Venice Declaration,' *Knesset*, 13/6/1980. Accessed 1/5/2010. http://www.knesset.gov.il/process/docs/venice_eng.htm.

50 Lochery, *Loaded Dice*: 187.

51 Rynhold and Spyer, 'British Policy in the Arab-Israeli Arena.'

52 Tessler, *History of the Israeli-Palestinian Conflict*: 590–9.

53 Lochery, *Loaded Dice*: 190.

54 A. Bermant, 'Triumph of Pragmatism over Principle: Margaret Thatcher and the Arab-Israel Conflict' (PhD Diss, UCL, 2012).

55 O. Miles, interview with author, Oxford, 13/6/2007.

56 Hollis, *Britain and the Middle East*: 23.

57 Lochery, *Loaded Dice*: 193.

58 Rynhold and Spyer, 'British Policy in the Arab-Israeli Arena,' 150.

59 Ibid.

60 Tessler, *History of the Israeli-Palestinian Conflict*: 700.

61 J. Rynhold, *The Failure of the Oslo Process: Inherently Flawed or Flawed Implementation?* (Begin-Sadat Center for Strategic Studies, Bar-Ilan University, 2008); D. Ross, *The Missing Peace: The Inside Story of the Fight for Middle East Peace* (New York: Farrar Straus & Giroux, 2005), 89; S. Avineri, 'Rabin's Strategy: Understanding Security and the Limits of Power,' in *Striving for Peace; The Legacy of Yitzhak Rabin* (London: Labour Friends of Israel, 2005).

62 A. Burns, interview with author, London, 12/6/2007; M. Gilbert, *Israel: A History* (London: Doubleday, 1998), 556.

63 Lochery, *Loaded Dice*: 202.

64 H. Sachar, *Israel and Europe: An Appraisal in History* (New York: Vintage Books, 1998), 341.

65 M. Gilbert, interview with author, London, 12/6/2007.

66 Lochery, *Loaded Dice*: 209.

67 F. Cornish, interview with author, Taunton, 20/6/2008.

68 B. Eastwood, interview with author, by telephone, 1/9/2008.

69 J. Greenstock, interview with author, London, 25/2/2009.

70 R. O. Miles, interview by M. McBain, *Churchill Archives Centre, British Diplomatic Oral History Programme, DOHP*, 27/8/2004. Accessed 10/10/2012. http://www. chu.cam.ac.uk/archives/collections/BDOHP/Miles_Oliver.pdf.

71 J. Kampfner, *Blair's Wars* (London: Free Press, 2004), 183.

72 Lochery, *Loaded Dice*: 231.

73 T. Blair, 'Speech at the Lord Mayor's Banquet,' *National Archives*, 10/11/1997. Accessed 1/6/2010. http://webarchive.nationalarchives.gov.uk/20070701080624/ http://pm.gov.uk/output/Page1070.asp.

74 Burns, interview.

75 FIA/FCO/Information Relating to Arabic Language Training in the FCO, 7/8/2008.

76 Cornish, interview.

77 Burns, interview.

78 R. Gilad, interview with author, London, 6/6/2007.

79 R. Gidor, interview with author, Jerusalem, 20/3/2007.

80 Eastwood, interview.

81 Hollis, *Britain and the Middle East*.

82 Ibid., 169.

83 J. Purnell, interview with author, London, 7/6/2007.

84 J. Dumbrell, *A Special Relationship: Anglo-American Relations in the Cold War and After* (Basingstoke: Palgrave Macmillan, 2001).

85 P. Hennessy, *The Prime Minister: The Office and its Holders Since 1945* (London: Penguin Books, 2001), 88.

86 Hollis, *Britain and the Middle East*: 33–6.

87 D. Reynolds, 'A "Special Relationship"? America, Britain and the International Order Since the Second World War,' *International Affairs* (*Royal Institute of International Affairs 1944-*) (1985).

88 Rynhold and Spyer, 'British Policy in the Arab-Israeli Arena.'

89 D. Ross and D. Makovsky, *Myths, Illusions, and Peace: Finding a New Direction for America in the Middle East* (New York: Viking, 2009).

90 E. Stephens, *US Policy Towards Israel: The Role of Political Culture in Defining the 'Special Relationship'* (Portland, OR: Sussex Academic Press, 2006).

91   J. Rynhold and J. Spyer, 'British Policy Towards the Middle East in the Post-Cold War Era 1991–2005: A Bridge Between the US and the EU?,' in *Britain and the Middle East* eds Z. Levey and E. Podeh (Brighton: Sussex University Press, 2008). R. Kampeas, 'Rifkind: French in Mideast are "Romantic" But Do Not Advance Peace,' *Associated Press*, 23 October 1996.

92   B. Soetendorp, 'The EU's Involvement in the Israeli-Palestinian Peace Process: The Building of a Visible International Identity,' *European Foreign Affairs Review* 7(2002).

93   Sachar, *Israel and Europe*: 353.

94   Ibid., 354.

95   'Mr Fatchett to Visit Israel and Occupied Territories: 14–16 January,' *FCO Daily Bulletin*, 9/1/1998.

96   C. Hill, 'Renationalizing or Regrouping? EU Foreign Policy Since 11 September 2001,' *JCMS: Journal of Common Market Studies* 42, no. 1 (2004).

97   Rynhold and Spyer, 'British Policy towards the Middle East.'

98   Wilson, *Chariot of Israel*: 54.

99   G. Alderman, *Modern British Jewry* (New York: Oxford University Press, 1998).

100 A. Julius, *Trials of the Diaspora: A History of Anti-Semitism in England* (Oxford: Oxford University Press, 2010).

101 C. Shindler, 'The Place of Israel in British Jewish Identity,' in *Israel, the Diaspora and Jewish Identity*, eds D. Ben-Moshe and Z. Segev (London: Sussex Academic Press, 2007).

102 D. Graham and J. Boyd, *Committed, Concerned and Conciliatory: The Attitudes of Jews in Britain* (London: Institute for Jewish Policy Research, 2010).

103 Alderman, *Modern British Jewry*.

104 'About Us,' *BICOM*. Accessed 1/5/2010. http://www.bicom.org.uk/about/about-us.

105 Burns, interview.

106 A. Shlaim, *Lion of Jordan: The Life of King Hussein in War and Peace* (London: Penguin, 2008), 446.

107 A fervent debate is ongoing among scholars, and among European Muslims, about the sociological or political causes of this development, and about the role and status of Muslims in the West. See Kepel, *The War for Muslim Minds.*, B. Tibi, *Political Islam, World Politics and Europe: Democratic Peace and Euro-Islam Versus Global Jihad* (Oxon: Routledge, 2008); O. Roy, *Globalized Islam: The Search for a New Ummah* (New York: Columbia University Press, 2006).

108 D. Rich, 'British Muslims and UK Foreign Policy,' in *Britain and the Middle East*, eds Z. Levey and E. Podeh (Brighton: Sussex Academic Press, 2007).

109 Ibid.; S. Brighton, 'British Muslims, Multiculturalism and UK Foreign Policy: 'Integration' and 'Cohesion' In and Beyond the State,' *International Affairs* 83, no. 1 (2007).

110 H. A. Hellyer, 'British Muslims: Past, Present and Future', *The Muslim World* 97, no. 2 (2007).

111 Rich, 'British Muslims and UK Foreign Policy', 323.

112 I. Bunglawala, interview with author, by telephone, 3/8/2009.

113 Rich, 'British Muslims and UK Foreign Policy'.

114 L. Fitzsimons, interview with author, 9/7/2007, London.

115 Miles, interview.

116 Rich, 'British Muslims and UK Foreign Policy', 328.

117 A. McRoy, *From Rushdie to 7/7: The Radicalisation of Islam in Britain* (London: The Social Affairs Unit, 2006), 15.

Chapter 2

1 C. Shindler, *Israel and the European Left: Between Solidarity and Delegitimisation* (New York: Continuum, 2012), 84–5.

2 Cesarani, 'Anti-Zionism in Britain'.

3 J. Edmunds, *The Left and Israel: Party-Policy Change and Internal Democracy* (Basingstoke: Macmillan, 2000).

4 Shindler, *Israel and the European Left*: 129.

5 Wilson, *Chariot of Israel*: 124.

6 R. H. S. Crossman, *Palestine Mission: A Personal Record* (New Hampshire: Ayer Publishing, 1977), 166–8.

7 Edmunds, *The Left and Israel: Party-Policy Change and Internal Democracy*: 31.

8 A. Johnson, 'Ernest Bevin's Third Force Memos', *Democratia*, no. 8 (2007): 127; Shindler, *Israel and the European Left*.

9 A. Radosh and R. Radosh, *A Safe Haven: Harry S. Truman and the Founding of Israel* (New York: Harper, 2009), 254.

10 Edmunds, *The Left and Israel: Party-Policy Change and Internal Democracy*: 40.

11 M. Phythian, *The Labour Party, War and International Relations, 1945–2006* (London: Routledge, 2007), 58.

12 Edmunds, *The Left and Israel: Party-Policy Change and Internal Democracy*: 42–63.

13 Shindler, *Israel and the European Left*: 196.

14 Edmunds, *The Left and Israel: Party-Policy Change and Internal Democracy*: 63.

15 B. Cohen, 'A Discourse of Delegitimisation: The British Left and the Jews', *New European Extremism/JPR*, 2004. Accessed 22/2/2011. http://www.axt.org.uk/HateMusic/Cohen_essay_October_04.pdf.

16 Cesarani, 'Anti-Zionism in Britain'. J. Edmunds, *The Left's Views on Israel: From the Establishment of the Jewish State to the Intifada – PhD Thesis* (London: LSE, 1997), 116.

17 Wilson, *Chariot of Israel*: 332.

18 Sachar, *Israel and Europe*: 177–8.

19 Edmunds, *The Left and Israel: Party-Policy Change and Internal Democracy*: 75–6.

20 Cesarani, 'Anti-Zionism in Britain.' As Colin Shindler has shown, the brand of left-wing anti-Zionism that rejected Jewish national rights and associated Zionism with imperialism had deep roots in Britain, long predating the establishment of Israel. C. Shindler, 'The Road to Utopia: The Origins of Anti-Zionism on the British Left,' *Middle East Review of International Affairs* 14, no. 2 (2010).

21 J. Edmunds, 'The British Labour Party in the 1980s: The Battle Over the Palestinian/Israeli Conflict,' *Politics* 18, no. 2 (2002).

22 B. Rubin and J. C. Rubin, *Yasir Arafat; A Political Biography* (London: Continuum, 2003), 67.

23 Miller, *Inglorious Disarray: Europe, Israel and the Palestinians*: 74.

24 Edmunds, 'The British Labour Party in the 1980s.'

25 G. Kaufman, interview with author, London, 19/6/2007.

26 Shindler, *Israel and the European Left*: 244.

27 Edmunds, *The Left's Views on Israel*: 142.

28 J. Naughtie, *The Accidental American: Tony Blair and the Presidency* (Basingstoke: Pan Books, 2005), 109.

29 Shindler, *Israel and the European Left*: 247.

30 J. Freedland, interview with author, London, 10/9/2008.

31 Edmunds, *The Left and Israel: Party-Policy Change and Internal Democracy*: 90.

32 Tessler, *History of the Israeli-Palestinian Conflict*: 700.

33 Julius, *Trials of the Diaspora*: 455.

34 Phythian, *The Labour Party, War and International Relations, 1945–2006*.

35 Edmunds, *The Left and Israel: Party-Policy Change and Internal Democracy*: 105.

36 A. Rawnsley, *Servants of the People: The Inside Story of New Labour* (London: Penguin Books, 2001), xiv.

37 J. Rentoul, *Tony Blair: Prime Minister* (London: Warner Books, 2001).

38 Ibid.

39 P. Stephens, *Tony Blair: The Making of a World Leader* (New York: Viking, 2004).

40 A. Seldon, *Blair* (London: Free Press, 2004).

41 Rentoul, *Tony Blair*.

42 Ibid., 202.

43 Ibid., 528–9.

44 Ibid., 44.

45 Ibid., 348.

46 Stephens, *Tony Blair*: 25.

47 T. Blair, *Address Given at the Labour Friends of Israel Annual Lunch, 15th June 2004* (London: Labour Friends of Israel, 2004).

48 D. Macintyre, *Mandelson and the Making of New Labour* (London: HarperCollins, 1999), 311–15; J. Cronin, *New Labour's Pasts; The Labour Party and its Discontents* (Harlow: Pearson, 2004), 2.

49 Rentoul, *Tony Blair*: 252–7.

50 Ibid., 434.

51 Ibid., 192.

52 Blair, 'Speech at the Lord Mayor's Banquet'.

53 T. Blair, *The Third Way: New Politics for the New Century* (London: Fabian Society, 1998), 381.

54 Seldon, *Blair*: 381.

55 S. Twigg, interview with author, London, 17/6/2008.

56 See, for example, P. G. Cerny and M. Evans, 'Globalisation and Public Policy Under New Labour,' *Policy studies* 25, no. 1 (2004); M. Watson and C. Hay, 'The discourse of globalisation and the logic of no alternative: rendering the contingent necessary in the political economy of New Labour,' *Policy & Politics* 31, no. 3 (2003).

57 P. Williams, *British Foreign Policy Under New Labour, 1997–2005* (Basingstoke: Palgrave Macmillan, 2005), 5.

58 Ibid., 24.

59 Blair, *A Journey*: 224.

60 L. M. Levy, *A Question of Honour: Inside New Labour and the True Story of the Cash for Peerages Scandal* (London: Simon and Schuster, 2008), 91–2.

61 M. Levy, interview with author, London, 1/9/2008.

62 Levy, *A Question of Honour*.

63 Rentoul, *Tony Blair*.

64 A. Campbell, *The Blair Years* (London: Hutchinson, 2007).

65 Levy, interview.

66 Levy, *A Question of Honour*: 151.

67 Levy, interview.

68 J. Purnell, interview with author, London, 7/7/2009.

69 A. Hood, interview with author, London, 4/6/2007.

70 F. Cornish, interview with author, Taunton, 20/6/2008.

71 Levy, interview.

72 Hood, interview.

73 Blair, *Address Given at the Labour Friends of Israel Annual Lunch*.

74 T. Blair, 'Speech to Labour Friends of Israel Conference Reception,' 26/9/2006. Accessed 17/2/2008. www.lfi.org.uk/news.

75 Cornish, interview.

76 D. Manning, interview with author, London, 5/9/2008.

77 G. Brown, 'Speech at the Knesset, Israel,' *Labour*, 21/7/2008. Accessed 1/5/2011. http://www.labour.org.uk/gordon_brown_speech_to_the_knesset, 2008-07-21.

78 J. Frazer, 'Mandelson on Judaism, Lord Levy and his JC dad,' *Jewish Chronicle*, 22/7/2010. Accessed 1/5/2011. http://www.thejc.com/lifestyle/lifestyle-features/36025/mandelson-judaism-lord-levy-and-his-jc-dad.

79 Kampfner, *Blair's Wars*.

80 Freedland, interview. See also the comparable comments of Bryan Gould quoted in P. Seyd and P. Whiteley, *New Labour's Grassroots* (Basingstoke: Palgrave Macmillan, 2002), 168.

81 Kampfner, *Blair's Wars*.

82 Williams, *British Foreign Policy Under New Labour, 1997–2005*.

83 Blair, 'Speech at the Lord Mayor's Banquet' 24.

84 *New Labour – Because Britain Deserves Better, Labour Party Manifesto 1997* (London: Labour Party, 1997).

85 Blair, 'Speech at the Lord Mayor's Banquet'.

86 M. Gapes, *Hansard* Column 994, 4/2/1998.

87 From the author's own experience, Labour Friends of Israel and Labour Middle East Council officers were barely welcome at each other's parliamentary events between 2004 and 2006.

88 S. Simon, 'Israel Goes Orthodox,' *Spectator*, 13/9/1997.

89 Twigg, interview.

90 R. Blackhurst, 'A New Force in British Politics,' *New Statesman*, 26/7/2004.

91 Twigg, interview.

92 L. Fitzsimons, interview with author, London, 9/7/2007.

93 Rentoul, *Tony Blair*: 567.

94 R. Heffernan, 'Labour's New Labour Legacy: Politics after Blair and Brown,' *Political Studies Review* 9, no. 2 (2011).

95 M. Bright, interview with author, London, 21/6/2007.

96 C. Short, *An Honourable Deception?: New Labour, Iraq and the Misuse of Power* (London: The Free Press, 2004).

97 C. Short, *Hansard* Column 468, 21/2/1991.

98 P. Cockburn, 'Clare Short Faces a Barrage of Criticism From Israel After Speech,' *Independent*, 11/7/1997, 1997.

99 J. Kampfner, *Robin Cook* (London: Phoenix, 1999).

100 Rawnsley, *Servants of the People*: 168.

101 *Census 2001: Religion in Westminster Parliamentary Constituencies* (London: Office for National Statistics, 2003).

102 R. Pigott, 'Jewish Population on the Increase' *BBC News*, 1/5/2010. Accessed 21/5/2008. http://news.bbc.co.uk/2/hi/uk_news/7411877.stm.

103 *Census 2001: Religion in Westminster Parliamentary Constituencies*.

104 I. Bunglawala, interview with author, by telephone, 3/8/2009.

Chapter 3

1 Hennessy, *The Prime Minister*: 392.

2 Rawnsley, *Servants of the People*.

3 *Review of Intelligence on Weapons of Mass Destruction* (London: House of Commons, 14/7/2004). Accessed 15/10/2012. http://www.archive2.official-documents.co.uk/document/deps/hc/hc898/898.pdf.

4 M. Foley, *The British Presidency: Tony Blair and the Politics of Public Leadership* (Manchester: Manchester University Press, 2000), 316–17.

5 Hollis, *Britain and the Middle East*: 59.

6 Ibid., 61.

7 Ibid., 63.

8 A. Burns, interview with author, London, 12/6/2007.

9 Hollis, *Britain and the Middle East*: 180.

10 Burns, interview; P. Hain, *The End of Foreign Policy?: Britain's Interests, Global Linkages and Natural Limits* (London: Royal Institute of International Affairs, 2001).

11 R. Cook, 'Speech on the Government's Ethical Foreign Policy,' *Guardian*, 12/5/1997. Accessed 1/6/2010. http://www.guardian.co.uk/world/1997/may/12/indonesia.ethicalforeignpolicy.

12 Burns, interview; Rawnsley, *Servants of the People*: 170.

13 Hollis, *Britain and the Middle East*: 38.

14 P. Williams, 'The Rise and Fall of the Ethical Dimension: Presentation and Practice in New Labour s Foreign Policy,' *Cambridge Review of International Affairs* 15, no. 1 (2002).

15 A. Hood, interview with author, London, 4/6/2007.

16 Burns, interview.

17 F. Cornish, interview with author, Taunton, 20/6/2008.

18 Ibid.

19 D. Fatchett, *Hansard* Column 1003, 4/2/1998.

20 T. Blair, *Hansard* Column 17, 24/2/1998.

21 'Blair: Israeli Settlement is "Illegal," Algiers Needs "Transparency" and "Islamic Threat is Nonsense",' *Mideast Mirror*, 27/1/1998.

22 R. Kagan, 'The Benevolent Empire,' *Foreign Policy* (Summer 1998).

23 Hollis, *Britain and the Middle East*: 73.

24 'Diplomatic Disaster,' *The Times*, 18/3/1998.

25 Cornish, interview.

26 B. Tsur, 'Britain's Cook Praises Peace Moves,' *Jerusalem Post*, 25/10/1999.

27 Cornish, interview.

28 Rentoul, *Tony Blair*: 405–6.

29 J. Powell, *Great Hatred, Little Room: Making Peace in Northern Ireland* (London: Bodley Head, 2008), 147.

30 Hood, interview.

31 A. Pierce and C. Walker, 'Middle East "Can Learn from the Ulster Talks"', *The Times*, 18/4/1998.

32 D. Manning, interview with author, London, 5/9/2008.

33 *World Report 1999 – Israel, The Occupied West Bank, Gaza Strip, and Palestinian Authority Territories* (New York: Human Rights Watch, 1999).

34 D. Fatchett, *Hansard* Column 143, 12/5/1998.

35 Ross, *The Missing Peace*: 384.

36 L. Freedman, 'Will the Buck Stop with Blair?', *The Times*, 21/4/1998.

37 Seldon, *Blair*: 370.

38 S. M. Condron, 'Justification for Unilateral Action in Response to the Iraqi Threat: A Critical Analysis of Operation Desert Fox', *Military Law Review* 161(1999).

39 *Hansard* Column 899ff, 17/2/1998.

40 T. Dalyell, G. Galloway, *Hansard* Column 910, 17/2/1998.

41 Seldon, *Blair*: 388.

42 T. Blair, *Hansard* Column 613, 16/11/1998.

43 T. Blair, 'PM's Statement on Iraq strikes, Full Text', *BBC News*, 16/12/1998. Accessed 1/5/2012. http://news.bbc.co.uk/2/hi/events/crisis_in_the_gulf/texts_ and_transcripts/236932.stm.

44 Seldon, *Blair*: 392.

45 Rentoul, *Tony Blair*: 521.

46 Ibid., 523.

47 Seldon, *Blair*: 400.

48 Ibid.

49 T. Blair, 'Speech on the Doctrine of the International Community at the Economic Club, Chicago', *National Archives*, 24/4/1999. Accessed 1/5/2010. http://webarchive. nationalarchives.gov.uk/20070701080624/http://pm.gov.uk/output/Page1297.asp.

50 L. Freedman, interview with author, London, 18/6/2008.

51 Freedman, interview.

52 Naughtie, *The Accidental American: Tony Blair and the Presidency*; Powell, *The new Machiavelli: how to wield power in the modern world*: 265.

53 The speech was included in an anthology of writings said to underpin Neoconservative thought edited by Irwin Stelzer. I. Stelzer, *Neoconservatism* (London: Atlantic, 2004).

54 Blair, 'Speech on the Doctrine of the International Community at the Economic Club, Chicago'.

55 J. Powell, interview with author, by telephone, 7/7/2009.

56 T. H. Kean et al., *The 9/11 Commission Report: Final Report of the National Commission on Terrorist Attacks Upon the United States* (Washington, DC: US General Printing Office, 2004).

57 T. Blair, *Hansard* Column 705, 2/9/1998.

58 J. Burke and B. Whitaker, 'Focus: A Year of Living Dangerously: Caveman Terrorist Spooks the West,' *Observer*, 3/1/1999.

59 'Document 11: Leaked Internal FCO Email Exchanges on Hamas, Hezbollah and Hizb-ut-Tahrir of 30–31/8/2005,' in *When Progressives Treat with Reactionaries; The British State's Flirtation with Radical Islam*, ed. M. Bright (London: Policy Exchange, 2006).

60 I. Burrell, 'Tamil Tigers and Hezbollah Banned by Terrorism Act,' *Independent*, 1/3/2001.

61 'MCB Says "Terrorist List" is Ill-Conceived', *Muslim Council of Britain*, 2/3/2001. Accessed 7/8/2009. http://www.mcb.org.uk/media/pr/020301a.html.

62 T. Lloyd, *Hansard* Column 690, 20/4/1999.

63 N. Lochery, 'Present and Post-Blair British Middle East Policy, The Annual Madame Madeleine Feher European Scholar Lecture No. 9,' (The Begin Sadat Center for Strategic Studies, 2007).

64 'Barak is "Beacon of Hope",' *The Times*, 24/11/1999.

65 E. Sneh, interview with author, Jerusalem, 16/4/2007.

66 Burns, interview.

67 Cornish, interview.

68 Ibid.

69 Levy, *A Question of Honour*: 155–6; 'Mordechai Warns Arafat Not to Declare a State in May 1999, and Suffice With "Autonomy-Plus",' *Mideast Mirror*, 16/4/1998.

70 Cornish, interview.

71 O. Miles, interview with author, Oxford, 13/6/2007.

72 C. Gillan, *Hansard* Column 962, 20/7/1999; R. Spring, *Hansard* Column 710, 27/2/2001.

73 Cornish, interview; B. Eastwood, interview with author, by telephone, 1/9/2008.

74 C. Meyer, *DC Confidential* (London: Weidenfeld & Nicolson, 2005), 80.

75 Eastwood, interview.

76 Ross, *The Missing Peace*: 535.

77 Blair cancelled a trip to Moscow scheduled for the beginning of October. Blair's Labour Party Conference speech on 26 September barely touched on foreign policy. See Rawnsley, *Servants of the People*.

78 Hollis, *Britain and the Middle East*: 82.

79 'London Calls on Israel to Reconsider Level of Force,' *Agence France Presse*, 8/10/2000.

80 R. Cook, *Hansard* Column 147, 7/11/2000.

81 'Statistics – Fatalities,' *B'tselem*. Accessed 1/5/2010. http://www.btselem.org/english/statistics/casualties.asp.

82 Ross, *The Missing Peace*: 758.

83 B. Wilson, *Hansard* Column 737W, 1/3/2001.

84 R. Cook, *Hansard* Column 147, 7/11/2000.

85 R. Cook, *Hansard* Column 462, 12/12/2000.

86 Cornish, interview.

87 T. Blair, *Hansard* Column 963, 29/11/2000.

88 Powell, interview.

89 Lochery, *Loaded Dice*: 219.

90 G. Galloway, 'Session 2000–01, EDM 303, Election of Ariel Sharon,' *www.parliament.uk*, 7/2/2001. Accessed 1/5/2012. http://www.parliament.uk/edm/2000-01/303.

91 J. Murphy, *Hansard* Column 709, 27/2/2001.

92 *Foreign Affairs Committee, Strategic Export Controls: Annual Report for 1999 and Parliamentary Prior Scrutiny, Third Report of 2000–2001 Session* (London: House of Commons, 6/3/2001). Accessed 15/10/2012. http://www.publications.parliament.uk/pa/cm200001/cmselect/cmfaff/212/212fa02.htm.

93 Ibid.

94 Ibid.

95 House of Commons Defence, Foreign Affairs, International Development and Trade and Industry Committees, *Oral Evidence Given by R. Cook*, 30/1/2001 2001. Accessed 10/10/2012. http://www.publications.parliament.uk/pa/cm200001/cmselect/cmfaff/212/1013007.htm.

96 'Annual Strategic Export Controls Reports,' *Foreign and Commonwealth Office*. Accessed 1/5/2009. http://www.fco.gov.uk/en/about-us/publications-and-documents/publications1/annual-reports/export-controls1.

97 Cornish, interview.

98 Ibid.

99 Levy, interview.

100 A. Crooke, 'Bottom-up Peacebuilding in the Occupied Territories,' interview by A. Byrne, *Conflicts Forum*, 11/2007. Accessed 1/5/2010. http://conflictsforum.org/2007/bottom-up-peacebuilding-in-the-occupied-territories/.

101 I. H. Daalder and J. M. Lindsay, *America Unbound* (Washington: Brookings Institution, 2003), 66.

102 *Report of the Sharm el-Sheikh Fact-Finding Committee* (Washington: Meridian International Center, 30/4/2001).

103 Ross, *The Missing Peace*: 786.

104 A. La Guardia, 'Blair Backs Sharon's Ceasefire Appeal,' *Daily Telegraph*, 25/6/2001.

105 B. Bradshaw, *Hansard* Column 121W, 17/7/2001.

106 The very high tensions between the US and Saudi Arabia prior to 9/11 were described by US Ambassador to Saudi Arabia at the time Robert Jordan, at a seminar held by the Washington Institute for Near East Studies on July 15, 2009. R. Jordan and S. Henderson, 'Policy Forum – Who Will Be the Next King of Saudi Arabia . . . And Does It Matter?,' *Washington Institute for Near East Policy*, 15/7/2009. Accessed 1/5/2010. http://www.washingtoninstitute.org/templateC05. php?CID=3090.

107 R. Kaiser and D. Ottaway, 'Saudi Leader's Anger Revealed Shaky Ties; Bush's Response Eased a Deep Rift On Mideast Policy; Then Came Sept. 11,' *Washington Post*, 10/2/2002.

Chapter 4

1 J. L. Esposito, *The Islamic Threat; Myth or Reality?* (New York: Oxford University Press, 1995), 53ff; K. Armstrong, *Islam; A Short History* (London: Phoenix, 2001). 130; N. R. Keddie, *An Islamic Response to Imperialism: Political and Religious Writings of Sayyid Jamāl al-Dīn al-Afghānī* (Los Angeles: University of California Press, 1968).

2 Ayubi, *Political Islam.*

3 S. Qutb, *Milestones (Ma 'alim fil Tariq)* (Indianapolis: American Trust Publications, 1990).

4 Ayubi, *Political Islam.*

5 Ibid., 134ff.

6 Gerges, *America and Political Islam*: 42.

7 Ayubi, *Political Islam*: 146. Hinnebusch, *The International Politics of the Middle East*: 192.

8 N. R. Keddie, *Modern Iran: Roots and Results of Revolution* (New Haven & London: Yale University Press, 2006), 192, 238.

9 Gerges, *America and Political Islam*: 79.

10 F. Halliday, 'The Politics of "Islam" – A Second Look,' *British Journal of Political Science* 25, no. 3 (1995).

11 Gerges, *America and Political Islam.*

12 Ibid., 45.

13 J. Burke, *Al Qaeda* (London: Penguin, 2004), 111.

14 Kepel, *The War for Muslim Minds.*

15 'Bin Laden's Declaration of War against the Americans Occupying the Land of the Two Holy Places,' *PBS Newshour*, 1/8/1996. Accessed 22/4/2012. http://www.pbs. org/newshour/terrorism/international/fatwa_1996.html?print.

16 R. S. Wistrich, *Hitler's Apocalypse: Jews and the Nazi Legacy* (London: Weidenfeld & Nicolson, 1985), 175; B. Lewis, *The Jews of Islam* (London: Routledge & Kegan Paul, 1984).

17 R. L. Nettler, *Past Trials and Present Tribulations: A Muslim Fundamentalist's View of the Jews* (Oxford Pergamon, 1987). These anti-Semitic influences are prevalent in the rhetoric of many Islamist groups, and not the least in Palestinian Islamist groups. The charter of Hamas is replete with anti-Semitic references. Though the anti-Semitism of Hamas is animated by its struggle with Israel, the rhetoric is rooted in the Muslim Brotherhood. See M. Maqdsi, 'Charter of the Islamic Resistance Movement (Hamas) of Palestine,' *Journal of Palestine Studies* 22, no. 4 (1993). Anti-Semitism is also deeply rooted in Shia Islamism, see R. Khomeini, *Islamic Government* (New York: Manor Books, 1979).

18 B. Milton-Edwards, 'Political Islam and the Palestinian-Israeli Conflict,' *Israel Affairs* 12, no. 1 (2006): 69.

19 Ibid.

20 Armstrong, *Islam; A Short History*: 81.

21 Kepel, *The War for Muslim Minds*: 2.

22 The thesis is widely credited in this way. See, for example, D. Philpott, 'The Challenge of September 11 to Secularism in International Relations,' *World Politics* 55, no. 1 (2003); F. B. Adamson, 'Global Liberalism Versus Political Islam: Competing Ideological Frameworks in International Politics,' *International Studies Review* 7, no. 4 (2005).

23 S. P. Huntington, *The Clash of Civilizations and the Remaking of World Order* (London: The Free Press, 2002), 212.

24 Ibid., 110.

25 B. Lewis, 'The Roots of Muslim Rage,' *The Atlantic Monthly* Sept 1990.

26 Ibid.

27 Huntington, *The Clash of Civilizations and the Remaking of World Order*: 114. For another example of this view of Islamic civilization, see E. Kedourie, *Democracy and Arab Political Culture* (London: Frank Cass, 1994), 7.

28 Huntington, *The Clash of Civilizations and the Remaking of World Order*: 212.

29 S. P. Huntington, Interviewed by M. Steinberger, *The Observer*, 21/10/2001. Accessed 15/10/2012. http://www.guardian.co.uk/world/2001/oct/21/afghanistan.religion2.

30 Gerges, *America and Political Islam*: 90–7.

31 'Blair: Israeli Settlement is "Illegal," Algiers Needs "Transparency" and "Islamic Threat is Nonsense".'

32 'EU deplores "dangerous" Islam jibe,' *BBC News*, 27/9/2004. Accessed 22/4/2012. http://news.bbc.co.uk/2/hi/middle_east/1565664.stm.

33 F. Halliday, *Islam and the Myth of Confrontation: Religion and Politics in the Middle East* (London, NY: I.B.Tauris, 2003); Esposito, *The Islamic Threat; Myth or Reality?*: 199.

34 Tibi, *Political Islam, World Politics and Europe: Democratic Peace and Euro-Islam Versus Global Jihad.*

35 B. Lewis et al., 'The MESA Debate – The Scholars, the Media, and the Middle East,' *Journal of Palestine Studies* 16, no. 2 (1987).

36 S. Murden, *Islam, the Middle East, and the New Global Hegemony* (London: Lynne Rienner Publishers, 2002), 37.

37 Esposito, *The Islamic Threat; Myth or Reality?*: 250.

38 Murden, *Islam, the Middle East, and the New Global Hegemony*; Williams, *British Foreign Policy Under New Labour, 1997–2005.*

39 F. Fukuyama, *The End of History and the Last Man* (New York: Free Press, 1992).

40 Murden, *Islam, the Middle East, and the New Global Hegemony.*

41 F. Fukuyama, 'After the "End of History",' *Open Democracy*, 2/5/2006. Accessed 1/4/2011. http://www.opendemocracy.net/content/articles/PDF/3496.pdf.

42 Ibid.

43 Fukuyama, *The End of History and the Last Man*: 45–6.

44 Ibid., 76.

45 M. E. Brown, S. M. Lynn-Jones, and S. E. Miller, *Debating the Democratic Peace* (Cambridge, MA: The MIT Press, 1996).

46 Murden, *Islam, the Middle East, and the New Global Hegemony*: 28.

47 Williams, *British Foreign Policy Under New Labour, 1997–2005.*

48 Blair, 'Speech on the Doctrine of the International Community at the Economic Club, Chicago'.

49 W. Kristol and R. Kagan, 'Towards a Neo-Reaganite Foreign Policy,' *Foreign Affairs* (1996).

50 I. Stelzer, 'Neoconservatives and their Critics,' in *Neoconservatism*, ed. I. Stelzer (London: Atlantic Books, 2004), 22.

51 M. Boot, 'Myths About Neconservatism,' in *Neoconservatism*, ed. I. Stelzer (London: Atlantic Books, 2004), 46.

52 E. Abrams et al., 'Letter to President Clinton on Iraq,' *Project for the New American Century*, 26/1/1998. Accessed 1/5/2010. http://www.newamericancentury.org/lettersstatements.htm.

53 T. J. Lynch, 'Kristol Balls: Neoconservative Visions of Islam and the Middle East,' *International Politics* 45, no. 2 (2008).

54 Ibid.

55 Ross and Makovsky, *Myths, Illusions and Peace.*

56 B. Woodward, *Plan of Attack* (London: Pocket Books, 2004), 21.

57 Julius, *Trials of the Diaspora*: 484.

58 J. Muravchik, 'The Neoconservative Cabal,' in *Neoconservatism*, ed. I. Stelzer (London: Atlantic Books, 2004), 251. See also M. Friedman, *The Neoconservative Revolution: Jewish Intellectuals and the Shaping of Public Policy* (Cambridge: Cambridge University Press, 2005).

59 Muravchik, 'The Neoconservative Cabal.'; Julius, *Trials of the Diaspora*: 483.

60 Boot, 'Myths About Neconservatism,' 45.

61 The centrality of these players is born out in the detailed account of Bob Woodward. Woodward, *Plan of Attack*.

62 D. Waxman, 'From Jerusalem to Baghdad? Israel and the War in Iraq,' *International Studies Perspectives* 10, no. 1 (2009).

63 P. Berman, 'Interrogating Terror and Liberalism,' in *Global Politics After 9/11, The Democratiya Interviews*, ed. A. Johnson (London: Foreign Policy Centre, 2007).

64 P. Berman, 'Terror and Liberalism,' *The American Prospect*, 21/10/2001.

65 Gerges, *America and Political Islam*: 31.

66 Esposito, *The Islamic Threat; Myth or Reality?*: 196.

67 Ibid., 204.

68 G. E. Fuller and I. O. Lesser, *A Sense of Siege: The Geopolitics of Islam and the West* (Boulder; Oxford: Westview, 1995), 5.

69 Shindler, *Israel and the European Left*: 274.

70 F. Halliday, 'The Left and the Jihad,' Accessed 22/7/2012. http://www. opendemocracy.net/globalization/left_jihad_3886.jsp.

71 R. Del Sarto, 'Israeli Identity as Seen through European Eyes,' in *Integration and Identity: Challenges to Europe and Israel*, eds S. Avineri and W. Weidenfeld (1999); T. Greene, 'Between the Crescent and the Star: British Policy in the Israeli Palestinian Arena in the Wake of 9/11' (PhD Diss, UCL, 2011), 59–65.

72 Sachar, *Israel and Europe*: xi.

73 B. Kimmerling, *The Invention and Decline of Israeliness* (Berekely: University of California Press, 2001), 2.

74 E. Barak, 'Security and Counter-Terrorism,' in *Re-Ordering the World*, ed. M. Leonard (London: The Foreign Policy Centre, 2002), 92.

75 Murden, *Islam, the Middle East, and the New Global Hegemony*: 34; Gerges, *America and Political Islam*: 36.

76 Ross and Makovsky, *Myths, Illusions and Peace*: 91.

77 R. Perle et al., *A Clean Break: A New Strategy for Securing the Realm* (Jerusalem and Washington: The Institute for Advanced Strategic and Political Studies, 1996).

78 Ibid.

79 J. J. Mearsheimer and S. M. Walt, *The Israel Lobby and US Foreign Policy* (London: Penguin Books, 2008), 62.

80 Ibid., 64.

81 See Chapter 8.

82 R. Vickers, *The Labour Party and the World: The Evolution of Labour's Foreign Policy, 1900–51* (Manchester: Manchester Univ Press, 2003), 12.

83 Phythian, *The Labour Party, War and International Relations, 1945–2006*.

84 Edmunds, *The Left and Israel: Party-Policy Change and Internal Democracy*: 96.

85 Gerges, *America and Political Islam*: 42.

86 M. Kennard, 'Tony Benn on the EU, Cuba and Islam,' *Comment Factory*, 18/6/2010. Accessed 1/5/2011. http://www.thecommentfactory.com/tony-benn-on-the-eu-cuba-and-islam-3185/.

87 N. Cohen, *What's Left?: How Liberals Lost Their Way* (Fourth Estate, 2007), 346.

88 M. Bright, interview with author, London, 21/6/2007; D. Hirsh, 'Anti-Zionism and Antisemitism: Cosmopolitan Reflections,' *The Yale Initiative for the Interdisciplinary Study of Antisemitism Working Paper Series* (2007): 49.

89 S. Moore, 'Tough, Tough Talk by a Weak, Weak Man,' *Sunday Mail*, 16/9/2001.

90 P. Oborne, 'Israel's Actions Affect our Security,' *Spectator*, 24/9/2005.

91 C. Short, 'Our Patrons Say. . .' *Skies are Weeping*, 15/10/2005. Accessed 1/5/2010. http://weepingskies.blogspot.com/.

92 Gerges, *America and Political Islam*.

Chapter 5

1   Hennessy, *The Prime Minister*.

2   D. Kavanagh, 'The Blair Premiership,' in *The Blair Effect 2001–05*, eds A. Seldon and D. Kavanagh (Cambridge: Cambridge University Press, 2005); Hennessy, *The Prime Minister*: 536.

3   Seyd and Whiteley, *New Labour's Grassroots*.

4   Heffernan, 'Labour's New Labour Legacy: Politics after Blair and Brown.'

5   T. Bentley et al., *A Vision for the Democratic Left* (London: Compass, 2003).

6   L. Baston and S. Henig, 'The Labour Party,' in *The Blair Effect 2001–05*, eds A. Seldon and D. Kavanagh (Cambridge: Cambridge University Press, 2005).

7   P. Hennessy, 'Informality and Circumscription: The Blair Style of Government in War and Peace,' *The Political Quarterly* 76, no. 1 (2005).

8   C. Short, *Hansard* Column 36, 12/5/2003.

9   Hennessy, *The Prime Minister*: 523.

10 J. Dickie, *The New Mandarins: How British Foreign Policy Works* (London: IB Tauris & Co Ltd, 2004), 92–3.

11 J. O. Kerr, interview by M. McBain, *Churchill Archives Centre, British Diplomatic Oral History Programme*, 6/4/2004. Accessed 1/6/2012. http://www.chu.cam.ac.uk/archives/collections/BDOHP/Kerr.pdf.

12 M. Chalmers, interview with author, London, 2/9/2008.

13 FIA/FCO/0340-09/Telegram from Tel Aviv Ambassador to London on US Terrorist Attacks/11/9/2001.

14 *Review of Intelligence on Weapons of Mass Destruction*, (London: House of Commons, 14/7/2004). Accessed 15/10/2012. http://www.archive2.official-documents.co.uk/document/deps/hc/hc898/898.pdf.

15 The contents of this memo have been described in a number of places. See T. Blair, interview, PBS Frontline, 8/5/2002. Accessed 1/6/2010; http://www.pbs.org/wgbh/pages/frontline/shows/campaign/interviews/blair.html. D. Balz and B. Woodward, 'A Pivotal Day of Grief and Anger; Bush Visits Ground Zero and Helps Move the Country From Sorrow to War,' *Washington Post*, 30/1/2002; Campbell, *The Blair Years*: 564; Meyer, *DC Confidential*: 191; T. Blair, Interviewed by PBS Frontline, *PBS Frontline*, 8/5/2002. Accessed 1/6/2010. http://www.pbs.org/wgbh/pages/frontline/shows/campaign/interviews/blair.html; Powell, *The new Machiavelli: how to wield power in the modern world*: 50.

16 A. Seldon, P. Snowdon, and D. Collings, *Blair Unbound* (London: Simon & Schuster UK, 2007), 49.

17 Campbell, *The Blair Years*: 563.

18 T. Blair, *Hansard* Column 616, 14/9/2001.

19 T. Blair, Interviewed by K. Ahmed, *The Observer*, 14/10/2001. Accessed 15/10/2012. http://www.guardian.co.uk/politics/2001/oct/14/afghanistan.terrorism1.

20 *Review of Intelligence on Weapons of Mass Destruction*.

21 T. Blair, Interviewed by C. Moore, J. Keegan and G. Jones, *The Daily Telegraph*, 25/10/2001. Accessed 15/10/2012. http://www.telegraph.co.uk/news/worldnews/asia/afghanistan/1360429/Interview-with-the-Prime-Minister.html.

22 Campbell, *The Blair Years*: 564.

23 T. Blair, 'September 11 Attacks: Prime Minister's Statement,' *Prime Minister's Office*, 11/9/2001. Accessed 1/5/2010. http://www.number10.gov.uk/Page1596.

24 Blair, *A Journey*: 347–8.

25 T. Blair, 'PM's Meeting with Leaders of the Muslim Communities in Britain,' *Prime Minister's Office*, 27/9/2001. Accessed 1/5/2010. http://www.number10.gov.uk/Page1605.

26 J. Powell, interview with author, by telephone, 7/7/2009.

27 M. Levy, interview with author, London, 1/9/2008.

28 Campbell, *The Blair Years*: 565.

29 Ibid., 570.

30 D. Manning, interview with author, London, 5/9/2008.

31 Blair, *A Journey*: 387.

32 N. Chomsky, *World Orders Old and New* (London: Pluto Press, 1997), 204.

33 Stephens, *Tony Blair*: 201.

34 L. Freedman, interview with author, London, 18/6/2008.

35 T. Blair, 'Speech by the Prime Minister at the 2001 Labour Party Conference,' *Guardian*, 2/10/2001. Accessed 1/5/2010. http://www.guardian.co.uk/ politics/2001/oct/02/labourconference.labour6.

36 Dickie, *The New Mandarins*: 93.

37 Kerr, interview by M. McBain.

38 Seldon, Snowdon, and Collings, *Blair Unbound*: 54.

39 Campbell, *The Blair Years*: 581; Stephens, *Tony Blair*: 203.

40 T. Blair and B. al-Assad, 'Transcript of Joint Press Conference: Prime Minister Blair and President Assad,' *National Archives*, 31/10/2001. Accessed 1/5/2010. http://webarchive.nationalarchives.gov.uk/20070701080624/http://pm.gov.uk/ output/Page1637.asp.

41 S. Goldenberg and P. Wintour 'Blair Defuses Israel's Anger After Straw Remark Threatens Talks,' *Guardian*, 26/9/2001.

42 A. La Guardia and P. Bishop, 'Straw's Trip to Teheran Infuriates Israelis,' *Daily Telegraph*, 25/9/2001.

43 Ibid.

44 E. Owen, 'Egos, Gaffes and Hissy Fits – the Art of Diplomacy,' *London Evening Standard*, 25/9/2009.

45 E. Sneh, interview with author, 16/4/2007, Jerusalem.

46 'FIA/FCO/0340-09/Telegram from Tel Aviv Ambassador to London on US Terrorist Attacks/11/9/2001.'

47 R. Gidor, interview with author, Jerusalem, 20/3/2007.

48 T. Blair, *Hansard* Column 325–6, 5/12/2001.

49 J. Straw, *Hansard* Column 341, 5/12/2001.

50 I. Black, P. Wintour, and D. Hencke, 'War in the Gulf: Straw Distances UK From Threats to Syria and Iran,' *Guardian*, 3/4/2003. 'War Briefings – Day 27,' *Scotsman*, 15/4/2003.

51 H. Keinon, 'Sharon Sets Up Peace Team With Peres,' *Jerusalem Post*, 2/11/2001.

52 T. Blair and Y. Arafat, 'Press Conference: PM and President Arafat,' *Prime Minister's Office*, 2/11/2001. Accessed 10/2/2012. http://collections.europarchive.org/ tna/20011108193912/http://pm.gov.uk/news.asp?NewsId=2916&SectionId=32.

53 Hollis, *Britain and the Middle East*: 142.

54 Blair and al-Assad, 'Transcript of Joint Press Conference: Prime Minister Blair and President Assad.'

55 B. Woodward, *Bush at War: Inside the Bush White House* (London: Pocket Books, 2003).

56 Daalder and Lindsay, *America Unbound*: 83–5.

57 Woodward, *Bush at War*: 30.

58 Ross and Makovsky, *Myths, Illusions and Peace*: 92–4.

59 G. W. Bush, 'Address to a Joint Session of Congress and the American People,' *White House*, 20/9/2001. Accessed 1/5/2010. http://georgewbush-whitehouse. archives.gov/news/releases/2001/09/20010920-8.html.

60 Ibid.

61 R. Jervis, 'Understanding the Bush Doctrine,' *Political Science Quarterly* 118, no. 3 (2003); Daalder and Lindsay, *America Unbound*: 195–7.

62 G. W. Bush, 'CNN Live Event/Special; Target: Terrorism – Bush Meets With Congressional Leaders,' *CNN*. Accessed 16/8/2009. http://transcripts.cnn.com/ TRANSCRIPTS/0110/02/se.15.html.

63 P. Reeves, 'Sharon Appeals to America not to "Appease" Arabs,' *Independent*, 5/10/2001.

64 Manning, interview.

65 Bush, 'Address to a Joint Session of Congress and the American People'.

66 G. W. Bush, 'The President's State of the Union Address,' *White House*, 29/1/2002. Accessed 1/5/2010. http://georgewbush-whitehouse.archives.gov/news/ releases/2002/01/20020129-11.html.

67 Daalder and Lindsay, *America Unbound*: 168–9.

68 Blair, Interviewed by C. Moore, J. Keegan and G. Jones.

69 Manning, interview.

70 Powell, interview.

71 Dickie, *The New Mandarins*: 191; Meyer, *DC Confidential*: 190.

72 Blair, T., *Hansard* Column 604ff, 14/9/2001.

73 Seldon, Snowdon, and Collings, *Blair Unbound*: 49.

74 Manning, interview.

75 Meyer, *DC Confidential*: 232.

76 Woodward, *Bush at War*: 113–14.

77 G. W. Bush and T. Blair, 'Remarks by President Bush And Prime Minister Tony Blair of Great Britain in Press Availability,' *White House*, 8/11/2001. Accessed 1/5/2010. http://georgewbush-whitehouse.archives.gov/news/ releases/2001/11/20011108-1.html.

78 G. W. Bush, 'Remarks by the President to United Nations General Assembly,' *White House*, 10/10/2001. Accessed 1/5/2010. http://georgewbush-whitehouse. archives.gov/news/releases/2001/11/20011110-3.html; ibid.

79 G. W. Bush, 'Speech on United States Position on Terrorists and Peace in the Middle East,' *US Department of State*, 19/11/2001. Accessed 1/5/2010. http://2001– 2009.state.gov/secretary/former/powell/remarks/2001/6219.htm.

80 'The Government of Israel Views with Grave Severity the Terrorist Attacks Last Evening,' *Israeli Prime Minister's Office*, 13/12/2001. Accessed 1/5/2010. http://www.pmo.gov.il/PMOEng/Archive/Speeches/2001/12/Speeches4676.htm

81 Powell, interview.

82 Blair, T., *Hansard* Column 331–2, 5/12/2001.

83 Straw, T., *Hansard* Column 334, 5/12/2001.

84 D. Macintyre and A. Grice, 'Campaign Against Terrorism: No Link Between Iraq and Terror Attacks, Says Straw,' *Independent*, 21/12/2001.

85 G. W. Bush and A. Sharon, 'Remarks by the President and Prime Minister Sharon of Israel in Photo Opportunity,' *White House*, 7/2/2002. Accessed 1/5/2010. http://georgewbush-whitehouse.archives.gov/news/releases/2002/02/20020207-15.html.R. Cheney, 'The Vice President Appears on Fox News Sunday ' *White House*, 27/1/2002. Accessed 1/5/2010. http://georgewbush-whitehouse.archives.gov/vicepresident/news-speeches/speeches/vp20020127-1.html; Hollis, *Britain and the Middle East*: 95.

Chapter 6

1 Woodward, *Bush at War*: 49.

2 Daalder and Lindsay, *America Unbound*: 130.

3 Iraq Inquiry, *Oral Evidence Given by P. Rickets*, 24/11/2009. Accessed 1/5/2010. http://www.iraqinquiry.org.uk/transcripts/oralevidence-bydate/091124.aspx.

4 *Review of Intelligence on Weapons of Mass Destruction*.

5 T. Blair, 'The West's Tough Strategy on Iraq is in Everyone's Interests; Why Saddam is Still a Threat to Britain,' *Express*, 6/3/2002.

6 Campbell, *The Blair Years*: 608; R. Cook, *Point of Departure* (London: Simon & Schuster, 2003).

7 Naughtie, *The Accidental American: Tony Blair and the Presidency*: 83.

8 D. Blunkett, *The Blunkett Tapes: My Life in the Bear Pit* (London: Bloomsbury, 2006), 359.

9 A. Mahon, EDM 927 (2001–2002) – Military Action Against Iraq, 4/3/2002.

10 *PM/02/019/Memo from Jack Straw to Tony Blair/25/3/2002*, (Iraq Inquiry). Accessed 1/9/2012. http://www.iraqinquiry.org.uk/media/50151/straw-to-blair-25march2002-letter.pdf.

11 *Letter from PS/Sir Richard Dearlove's Private Secretary to Sir David Manning/3/12/2001*, (Iraq Inquiry). Accessed 15/10/2012. http://www.iraqinquiry.org.uk/media/52012/2001-12-03-Dearlove-Private-Secretary-to-Manning-letter-and-attachments.pdf.

12 M. Smith, 'Ministers Were Told Premier Was Seen as Stooge,' *Daily Telegraph*, 24/9/2004. *Leaked Memo from Cabinet Office Overseas and Defence Secretariat – Iraq: Options Paper*, (Downing Street Memo(s), 8/3/2002). Accessed 1/5/2010. http://downingstreetmemo.com/docs/iraqoptions.pdf.

13 Iraq Inquiry, *Oral Evidence Given by J. Sawyers*, 10/12/2009. Accessed 1/5/2010. http://www.iraqinquiry.org.uk/media/40668/20091210amsawers-final.pdf.

14 Leaked Memo from David Manning to Tony Blair, *Downing Street Memo(s)*, 14/3/2002. Accessed 1/5/2010. http://downingstreetmemo.com/manningtext.html.

15 Meyer, *DC Confidential*: 241.

16 T. Blair and R. Cheney, 'Transcript of Doorstep Given by the Prime Minister Tony Blair and US Vice President Dick Cheney, London,' *National Archives*, 11/3/2002. Accessed 1/5/2010. http://webarchive.nationalarchives.gov.uk/20070701080624/http://pm.gov.uk/output/Page1704.asp.

17 Woodward, *Plan of Attack*: 112.

18 I. Black, 'EU Backs Arafat With Call for Poll,' *Guardian*, 9/2/2002.

19 'French Non Paper on the Revival of A Dynamics of Peace in the Middle-East of February 2002,' *Bitterlemons*. Accessed 6/9/2009. http://www.bitterlemons.org/docs/french.html.

20 S. Goldenberg, 'Straw Calls on Arafat to Rein in Terror,' *Guardian*, 14/2/2002. On his return, Straw repeated the message, see J. Straw, 'No Military Solution,' *Guardian*, 26/2/2002.

21 T. Blair, *Hansard* Column 32, 18/3/2002.

22 'Statistics – Fatalities'.

23 *Report of the Secretary-General Prepared Pursuant to General Assembly Resolution ES-10/10*, (United Nations, 30/7/2002). Accessed 1/5/2010. http://daccess-dds-ny.un.org/doc/UNDOC/GEN/N02/499/57/IMG/N0249957.pdf?OpenElement.

24 'The Battle for the Truth,' *Guardian*, 17/4/2002.

25 G. W. Bush, 'President to Send Secretary Powell to Middle East,' *White House*, 4/4/2002. Accessed 1/5/2010. http://georgewbush-whitehouse.archives.gov/news/releases/2002/04/20020404-1.html.

26 Meyer, *DC Confidential*: 244.

27 Leaked Memo from Cabinet Office Overseas and Defence Secretariat – Iraq: Options Paper.

28 Kerr, interview by M. McBain.

29 B. Keller, 'The Sunshine Warrior,' *New York Times Magazine*, 22/9/2002; Waxman, 'From Jerusalem to Baghdad? Israel and the War in Iraq.'; Meyer, *DC Confidential*: 236.

30 Blair, *A Journey*: 369, 88, 401.

31 Ibid., 388.

32 Ibid., 387, 673.

33 *S187/02/Memo from J. Powell to Prime Minister/19/7/2002*, (Iraq Inquiry). Accessed 14/10/2012. http://www.iraqinquiry.org.uk/media/50772/Powell-to-Blair-19July2002-minute.pdf.

34 *Leaked Text of Cabinet Office Briefing Paper – Iraq: Conditions for Military Action (A Note by Officials)*, (Michael Smith, 21/7/2002). Accessed 1/5/2010. http://www.michaelsmithwriter.com/memos.html.Meyer, *DC Confidential*: 246.

35 *PM/02/042/Memo from J. Straw to Prime Minister/8/7/2002*, (Iraq Inquiry). Accessed 14/10/2012. http://www.iraqinquiry.org.uk/media/50793/Straw-to-Blair-Iraq-Contingency-Planning-8July2002.pdf.

36 *Minute from Edward Chaplin, Director MENA to PS/Foreign Secretary/12/7/2002*, (Iraq Inquiry). Accessed 14/10/2012. http://www.iraqinquiry.org.uk/media/52492/chaplin-ps-foreign-sec-military-action-2002-07-12.pdf.

37 Iraq Inquiry, *Oral Evidence Given by J. Powell*, 18/1/2010. Accessed 1/5/2010. http://www.iraqinquiry.org.uk/media/44184/20100118pm-powell-final.pdf.

38 Blair, *A Journey*.

39 M. Levy, interview with the author, London, 1/9/2008.

40 Seldon, Snowdon, and Collings, *Blair Unbound*: 102.

41 J. Powell, interview with the author, by telephone, 7/7/2009.

42 M. Shaviv, 'Language of Diplomacy,' *Jerusalem Post*, 22/3/2002.

43 J. Freedland, interview with the author, London, 10/9/2008.

44 Freedland, interview.

45 R. Burden, 'Session 2001–2002, EDM 1106, Israeli Incursions Into Palestinian Land,' *www.parliament.uk*, 10/4/2002. Accessed 15/10/2012.

46 Hirsh, 'Anti-Zionism and Antisemitism: Cosmopolitan Reflections.'

47 T. Blair, *Hansard* Column 23, 10/4/2002.

48 J. Kampfner, 'The Expired Mandate – Radio 4 Documentary,' *BBC Radio 4*, 1/8/2002. Accessed 1/5/2010. http://news.bbc.co.uk/hi/english/static/audio_video/programmes/analysis/transcripts/middle_east.txt.

49 Woodward, *Bush at War*: 326.

50 Kerr, interview by M. McBain. See also Meyer, *DC Confidential*: 245.

51 Jordan and Henderson, 'Policy Forum – Who Will Be the Next King of Saudi Arabia . . . And Does It Matter?'.

52 A. Crooke, 'Talking to Terrorists,' *BBC Radio 4*, 15/7/2007. Accessed 1/5/2010. http://conflictsforum.org/2007/talking-to-terrorists/.

53 Daalder and Lindsay, *America Unbound*: 135.

54 Iraq Inquiry, *Oral Evidence Given by C. Meyer*, 26/11/2009. Accessed 1/5/2012. http://www.iraqinquiry.org.uk/media/44184/20100118pm-powell-final.pdf.

55 Powell, interview.

56 Campbell, *The Blair Years*: 626.

57 Levy, interview.

58 *Oral Evidence Given by J. Sawyers.*

59 Campbell, *The Blair Years*: 627.

60 Meyer, *DC Confidential*: 248.

61 Leaked Text of Cabinet Office Briefing Paper – Iraq: Conditions for Military Action (A Note by Officials).

62 Blair, *A Journey*: 405.

63 T. Blair, 'Prime Minister's Press Conference,' *National Archives*, 3/9/2002. Accessed 1/5/2010. http://webarchive.nationalarchives.gov.uk/20070701080624/http:/pm.gov.uk/output/Page3001.asp.

64 Kerr, interview by M. McBain. See also Review of Intelligence on Weapons of Mass Destruction.

65 Blair, *A Journey*: 407.

66 Ibid., 408.

67 Campbell, *The Blair Years*: 635.

68 Iraq Inquiry, *Oral Evidence Given by D. Manning*, 30/11/2009. Accessed 1/5/2012. http://www.iraqinquiry.org.uk/media/40459/20091130pm-final.pdf.

69 *Communiqué Issued by the Quartet, New York*, (UNISPAL, 17/9/2002). Accessed 17/9/2002. http://unispal.un.org/unispal.nsf/udc.htm.

70 Campbell, *The Blair Years*: 639; Short, *An Honourable Deception?*: 150.

71 T. Blair, *Hansard* Column 6, 24/9/2002.

72 Straw, J., *Hansard* Column 26, 24/9/2002. Straw also pointed out the technical distinction between Chapter Six resolutions relating to the peace process and Chapter Seven resolutions relating to Iraq.

73 A. Tyrie, *Hansard* Column 113, 24/9/2002.

74 F. Maude, *Hansard* Column 52; R Key, *Hansard* Column 84, 24/9/2002.

75 N. Soames, *Hansard* Column 59, 24/9/2002.

76 *Hansard* Column 154, 24/9/2002.

77 T. Blair, 'At Our Best When at Our Boldest, Speech at the Labour Party Conference,' *City University, London*, 1/10/2002. Accessed 1/5/2010. http://www.staff.city.ac.uk/p.willetts/IRAQ/TB011002.HTM.

78 Seldon, Snowdon, and Collings, *Blair Unbound*: 79.

79 Kampfner, *Blair's Wars*: 212; Short, *An Honourable Deception?*: 152.

80 This view is also accepted in Phythian, *The Labour Party, War and International Relations, 1945–2006*: 143.

81 Freedland, interview.

82 Miller, *Inglorious Disarray: Europe, Israel and the Palestinians*: 170.

83 Waxman, 'From Jerusalem to Baghdad? Israel and the War in Iraq.'

84 Julius, *Trials of the Diaspora*: 484.

85 S. Farrell, 'Arafat Rejects Prime Minister Plan,' *The Times*, 3/10/2002; C. McGreal,
    'Former Mossad Chief Holds Secret Talks with Palestinian Official,' *Guardian*,
    3/10/2002.

86 J. Straw, *Hansard* Column 652W, 8/7/2002.

87 E. Sneh, interview with the author, Jerusalem, 16/4/2007; O. Blackman, 'We
    Won't Arm Israel; Exclusive Blair Curbs Export of Military Equipment,' *Mirror*,
    27/8/2002.

88 R. Gilad, interview with the author, London, 6/6/2007.

89 Sneh, interview; Levy, *A Question of Honour*: 195.

90 S. Weisman, 'No Mideast Plan Until Israel Holds Elections, Powell Says,' *New York
    Times*, 19/12/2002.

91 T. Blair, *Hansard* Column 538, 16/12/2002.

92 J. Straw, 'Interview by BBC Radio 4's Today Programme,' *Foreign and
    Commonwealth Office*, 6/1/2003. Accessed 18/9/2009. http://www.fco.gov.uk/
    resources/en/news/2003/01/fco_nit_060103_strawtodayisrael.

93 Interview with David Manning, 5/9/2008, London.

94 *The Outcomes of the London Conference on Palestinian Reform*, (Foreign and
    Commonwealth Office, 14/1/2003). Accessed 18/9/2009. http://unispal.un.org/
    UNISPAL.NSF/0/6285301BFE6F08C285256CB70054B9B5.

95 Manning, Interview.

96 S. Henderson, 'Policy Watch #738 – Bush and Blair: Tensions in the Relationship,'
    Washington Institute for Near East Policy, 2/4/2003.

97 S. Twigg, interview with the author, London, 17/6/2008.

98 A. La Guardia, 'Blair Snub for Netanyahu's Attempt to Isolate Arafat,' *Daily
    Telegraph*, 21/12/2002.

99 In a joint press conference with Tony Blair at Downing Street on December 16,
    President Assad implausibly claimed that the Palestinian groups only had 'press
    offices' in Damascus. T. Blair and B. al-Assad, 'Press Conference: Prime Minister
    Tony Blair and Syrian President al-Assad,' *National Archives*, 16/12/2002. Accessed
    8/11/2009. http://webarchive.nationalarchives.gov.uk/20070701080624/http://
    pm.gov.uk/output/Page1744.asp.

100 Sneh, interview.

101 T. Blair, 'Speech to Foreign Office Conference in London,' *Prime Minister's Office*,
    7/1/2003. Accessed 1/5/2010. http://www.number10.gov.uk/Page1765.

102 T. Blair, *Hansard* Column 34, 3/2/2003.

103 Manning, interview.

104 Levy, interview.

105 R. Phillips, 'Standing Together: The Muslim Association of Britain and the Anti-War Movement,' *Race & Class* 50, no. 2 (2008).

106 S. Walgrave and J. Verhulst, 'Government stance and internal diversity of protest: A comparative study of protest against the war in Iraq in eight countries,' *Social Forces* 87, no. 3 (2009).

107 Short, *An Honourable Deception?*

108 G. W. Bush, 'President Discusses Roadmap for Peace in the Middle East,' *White House*, 14/3/2003. Accessed 1/6/2010. http://georgewbush-whitehouse.archives.gov/news/releases/2003/03/20030314-4.html.

109 Powell, interview.

110 *Hansard* Column 760, 18/3/2003.

111 R. Ottoway, *Hansard* Column 878, 18/3/2003.

112 M. Ancram, *Hansard* Column 894; Corbyn, J., *Hansard* Column 879, 18/3/2003.

113 C. Soley, *Hansard* Column 814, 18/3/2003.

114 H. Bayley, *Hansard* Column 842, 18/3/2003.

115 R. Cook, *Hansard* Column 728, 17/3/2003.

116 C. Efford, *Hansard* Column 809, 18/3/2003.

117 T. Blair, *Hansard* Column 771, 18/3/2003.

118 'Blair Wins War Backing Amid Revolt,' *BBC News*, 19/3/2002. Accessed 1/5/2010. http://news.bbc.co.uk/2/hi/uk_news/politics/2862325.stm.

119 Campbell, *The Blair Years.*

120 Seldon, Snowdon, and Collings, *Blair Unbound*: 313.

121 R. Gidor, interview.

122 F. Cornish, interview with the author, Taunton, 20/6/2008.

123 Gidor, interview.

124 Ibid.

125 Even before the route was published, the Foreign Office took a negative view of the barrier, arguing that security could only be achieved through a peace process. M. O'Brien, *Hansard* Column 783W, 25/7/2002.

126 'Spokesman's Daily Press Briefing,' *US Department of State*, 26/11/2003. Accessed 1/5/2003. http://2001-2009.state.gov/r/pa/prs/dpb/2003/26718.htm.

127 M. O'Brien, *Hansard* Column 528W, 14/4/2003.

128 R. Tait, 'Blair's Peace Efforts Too Extreme, Says Israel,' *The Times*, 7/4/2003.

Chapter 7

1 Seldon, Snowdon, and Collings, *Blair Unbound*: 198.

2 Blair described it as 'one of the most important and, in my judgement, best speeches I made.' Blair, *A Journey*: 457.

3   T. Blair, 'Speech to the United States Congress,' *National Archives*, 17/7/2003.
    Accessed 27/9/2009. http://webarchive.nationalarchives.gov.uk/20070701080624/
    http://pm.gov.uk/output/Page4220.asp.

4   Ibid.

5   See Chapter 2.

6   R. Beeston, 'Britain and Israel Work to Rebuild Relations,' *The Times*,
    16/5/2003.

7   M. Woolfe, 'Fury as MPs Compare Palestinians' Treatment to Nazi Ghettos,'
    Independent, 20/6/2003.

8   *Israel's Response to the Roadmap*, (Knesset, 25/5/2003). Accessed 1/5/2010. http://
    www.knesset.gov.il/process/docs/roadmap_response_eng.htm.

9   'Chronological Review of Events Relating to the Question of Palestine, Monthly
    Media Monitoring Review, July 2003,' *UN Division for Palestinian Rights*,
    31/7/2003. Accessed 1/5/2010. http://unispal.un.org/UNISPAL.nsf/59c118f065c44
    65b852572a500625fea/f9e27e7ec25e1af285256d80005f4bdb?OpenDocument.

10 D. Manning, interview with the author, London, 5/9/2008.

11 M. Woolfe, 'Britain Rejects Ariel Sharon's Formal Request to Cut Ties with Yasser
    Arafat,' *Independent*, 15/7/2003.

12 Manning, interview.

13 M. Levy, interview with the author, London, 1/9/2008.

14 Levy, interview. As Middle East Minister, Mike O'Brien echoed the notion that
    Britain's closeness to the US, in conjunction with its role in the EU, added to the
    credibility of its voice in the region. See Kampfner, 'The Expired Mandate – Radio
    4 Documentary'.

15 I. Gilmore, 'Abbas Resignation Wrecks "Road Map",' *Sunday Telegraph*, 7/9/2003.
    Speaking in the Commons, Jack Straw blamed Abbas's resignation on a Hamas
    suicide bombing which killed 22 in Jerusalem in August, and on his power
    struggle with Arafat. J. Straw, *Hansard* Column 46, 8/9/2003.

16 'Chronological Review of Events Relating to the Question of Palestine, Monthly
    Media Monitoring Review,' *UN Division for Palestinian Rights*, 30/9/2003.
    Accessed 27/9/2009. www.unispal.un.org.

17 G. W. Bush, 'President Bush Discusses Iraq Policy at Whitehall Palace in London,'
    White House, 19/11/2003. Accessed 1/6/2010. http://georgewbush-whitehouse.
    archives.gov/news/releases/2003/11/20031119-1.html.

18 Seldon, Snowdon, and Collings, *Blair Unbound*: 313.

19 J. Keyser, 'Powell Praises Symbolic Israeli-Palestinian Peace Plan,' *Associated Press*,
    7/11/2003; ibid.

20 'Secretary Powell's Meeting with Drafters of Geneva Initiative,' *US Department of
    State*, 5/12/2003. Accessed 1/5/2011. http://domino.un.org/unispal.nsf/d80185e9f0
    c69a7b85256cbf005afeac/0b0495d12be5e95885256e16006d9c16?OpenDocument.

21 S. Bar, 'Gaza – The British Are Coming – Co-Opting Terrorists – AME Exclusive,' *Independent Media Review Analysis*, 11/4/2004. Accessed 1/5/2010. http://www. imra.org.il/story.php3?id=20410.

22 E. Sneh, interview with the author, Jerusalem, 16/4/2007.

23 C. McGreal, 'Palestinian PM Urges Blair to Play Fair: Qureia Accuses British Government of Double Standards Over Security,' *Guardian*, 7/2/2004.

24 T. Blair, 'Prime Minister's Press Conference,' *National Archives*, 15/1/2004. Accessed 1/5/2010. http://webarchive.nationalarchives.gov.uk/20070701080624/ http://pm.gov.uk/output/Page5157.asp.

25 *Palestine Papers/Fax from the Egyptian Embassy dated 5/1/2004*, (Guardian, 25/1/2011). Accessed 14/10/2012. http://www.guardian.co.uk/world/palestine-papers-documents/169.

26 E. Yaari, 'The Eastern Border,' *Jerusalem Report*, 5/4/2004.

27 *Wikileaks/04TELAVIV2335/Report from US Embassy Tel Aviv of 22/4/2004*, (Cablegate, 1/9/2011). Accessed 14/10/2012. http://www.cablegatesearch.net/cable. php?id=04TELAVIV2335&q=%3Duk.

28 A. Sharon, 'Herzliya Addess,' *Institute for Policy and Strategy*, 18/12/2003. Accessed 1/5/2010. http://www.herzliyaconference.org/Eng/_Articles/Article.asp? ArticleID=892&CategoryID=153.

29 J. Rynhold and D. Waxman, 'Ideological Change and Israel's Disengagement from Gaza,' *Political Science Quarterly* 123, no. 1 (2008).

30 J. Powell, interview with the author, by telephone, 7/7/2009.

31 *Exchange of Letters Between PM Sharon and President Bush*, (Israeli Ministry of Foreign Affairs, 14/4/2004). Accessed 1/5/2010. http://www.mfa.gov.il/ MFA/Peace+Process/Reference+Documents/Exchange+of+letters+Sharon-Bush+14-Apr-2004.htm.

32 G. W. Bush and T. Blair, 'Bush, Blair Discuss Sharon Plan; Future of Iraq in Press Conference,' *White House*, 16/4/2004. Accessed 1/5/2010. http://georgewbush-whitehouse.archives.gov/news/releases/2004/04/20040416-4.html.

33 Blair, *A Journey*: 516.

34 O. Miles, interview with the author, Oxford, 13/6/2007.

35 Ibid.

36 O. Miles et al., 'Ambassador's Letter to Blair,' *BBC*, 29/4/2004. Accessed 1/5/2010. http://news.bbc.co.uk/2/hi/uk_news/politics/3660837.stm.

37 Ibid.

38 F. Cornish, interview with the author, Taunton, 20/6/2008.

39 A. Burns, interview with the author, London, 12/6/2007.

40 P. Wintour, 'Alarm at US drift over Middle East, UK report reveals fears for future of Palestinians,' *Guardian*, 21/7/2004.

41 R. Burden; EDM 991 (2003–2004) – Impact of President Bush's statement on Israeli policy in the Occupied Territories; 19/4/2004.

42 N. Guttman and A. Benn, 'France's Chirac: Unilateral Gaza Pullout "Doomed to Failure," ' *Haaretz*, 29/4/2004.

43 T. Blair, *Hansard* Column 22, 19/4/2004.

44 Ibid.

45 *Middle East Quartet Communique*, (United Nations, 4/5/2004). Accessed 1/5/2010. http://www.un.org/News/dh/infocus/middle_east/quartet-comque-4may04.htm.

46 L. Elliott and D. Teather, 'Bush Opens New Rift over Middle East Plan ' *Guardian*, 10/6/2004.

47 'Statistics – Fatalities'.

48 G. Kaufman, 'The Case for Sanctions Against Israel: What Worked With Apartheid Can Bring Peace to the Middle East', *Guardian*, 12/7/2004.

49 'Israel's Wall: Obeying the Law', *Guardian*, 22/7/2004.

50 J. Denham, 'Time is Running out for Two States: Trade Pressure on Israel Would Help Blair Deliver his Middle East Pledge', *Guardian*, 1/10/2004.

51 G. Kaufman, interview with the author, London, 16/6/2007.

52 R. Burden, EDM 407 (2003–2004), Israel's separation wall, 13/1/2004.

53 M. Chalmers, interview with the author, London, 2/9/2008.

54 As Head of Policy and Research for Labour Friends of Israel from June 2004 until June 2006, the author briefed LFI-affiliated MPs for these exchanges.

55 L. Ellman, interview with the author, London, 6/6/2007.

56 T. Blair, 'Speech to the Labour Party Conference', *BBC News*, 28/9/2004. Accessed 1/5/2010. http://news.bbc.co.uk/2/hi/uk_news/politics/3697434.stm.

57 T. Blair, 'Statement on Bush's Re-election', *Guardian*, 4/11/2004. Accessed 10/10/2009. http://www.guardian.co.uk/world/2004/nov/04/uselections2004. usa13.

58 Seldon, Snowdon, and Collings, *Blair Unbound*: 317.

59 'US and UK Joint Statement Concerning the Middle East Peace Process', *White House*, 12/11/2004. Accessed 10/10/2009. http://georgewbush-whitehouse. archives.gov/news/releases/2004/11/20041112-3.html.

60 G. W. Bush and T. Blair, 'President and Prime Minister Blair Discussed Iraq, Middle East', *White House*, 12/11/2004. Accessed 10/10/2009. http://georgewbush-whitehouse.archives.gov/news/releases/2004/11/20041112-5.html.

61 B. Woodward, *State of Denial: Bush at War* (London: Simon and Schuster, 2007).

62 'Press Conference With the Israeli Prime Minister, Mr Ariel Sharon', *National Archives*, 22/12/2004. Accessed 11/5/2010. http://webarchive.nationalarchives.gov. uk/20070701080624/http://pm.gov.uk/output/Page6836.asp.

63 C. McGreal, 'Israel Wary of Blair Peace Initiative', *Guardian*, 8/12/2004.

64 Levy, interview.

65 'Press Conference With the Israeli Prime Minister, Mr Ariel Sharon'.

66 Manning, interview.

67 'Bush "Committed" to Winning War on Terror', *Washington Times*, 12/1/2005.

68 N. Sharansky and R. Dermer, *The Case for Democracy* (New York: Public Affairs, 2004).

69 C. Shindler, *A History of Modern Israel* (Cambridge: Cambridge University Press, 2008), 297.

70 T. Blair and A. Sharon, 'PM's Press Conference With the Israeli Prime Minister, Mr Ariel Sharon', *National Archives*, 22/12/2004. Accessed 11/5/2010. http://webarchive.nationalarchives.gov.uk/20070701080624/http://pm.gov.uk/output/Page6836.asp; 'Israel drops Hamas vote ban call', *BBC News*, 24/10/2005. Accessed 1/5/2011. http://news.bbc.co.uk/2/hi/middle_east/4371100.stm.

71 'Chronological Review of Events Relating to the Question of Palestine, Monthly Media Monitoring Review, February 2005', *UN Division for Palestinian Rights*, 3/5/2005. Accessed 1/5/2010. http://unispal.un.org/unispal.nsf/9a798adbf322aff38525617b006d88d7/3d752e1f646122b985256fb9006a5f20?OpenDocument.

72 Gilad, interview.

73 Ibid.

74 Levy, interview.

75 T. Blair and M. Abbas, 'Tony Blair/Mahmoud Abbas Press Conference Opening Remarks', *Prime Minister's Office*, 1/3/2005. Accessed 1/5/2010. http://www.number10.gov.uk/Page7237.

76 C. Rice, 'Remarks to the Press; Ben Gurion Airport; Tel Aviv, Israel', *US State Department*, 7/2/2005. Accessed 28/10/2009. http://2001-2009.state.gov/secretary/rm/2005/41936.htm.

Chapter 8

1 R. Winnett and D. Leppard, 'Leaked No 10 Dossier Reveals Al-Qaeda's British Recruits', *Sunday Times*, 10/7/2005.

2 Ibid.

3 T. Archer, 'Welcome to the Umma: The British State and its Muslim Citizens Since 9/11', *Cooperation and Conflict* 44, no. 3 (2009).

4 S. Twigg, interview with the author, London, 17/6/2008.

5 McRoy, *From Rushdie to 7/7*: 174.

6 'MCB Press Release – American Airstrikes Against Afghanistan and Sudan', *Muslim Council of Britain*, 21/8/1998. Accessed 11/2/2010. www.mcb.org.uk/media/archive/news210898.html.

7   T. Blair, 'Speech to the Muslim Council of Britain,' *National Archives*, 5/5/1999. Accessed 1/5/2010. http://webarchive.nationalarchives.gov.uk/20070701080624/http:/pm.gov.uk/output/Page1329.asp.

8   I. Sacranie, 'Secretary General's Address at Reception for Prime Minister,' *Muslim Council of Britain*, 5/5/1999. Accessed 1/5/2010. http://www.mcb.org.uk/media/speech_05_05_99.php.

9   McRoy, *From Rushdie to 7/7*: 174.

10 I. Sacranie, 'The Role of British Muslims in Bringing Justice to Palestine,' *Friends of Al Aqsa Journal* 3, no. 1 (2000). My attention was drawn to this article by Milton-Edwards, 'Political Islam and the Palestinian-Israeli Conflict.'

11 Burrell, 'Tamil Tigers and Hezbollah Banned by Terrorism Act.'

12 McRoy, *From Rushdie to 7/7*: 46.

13 Ibid.

14 Ibid., 38.

15 H. Blears, 'Speech on Homeland Security, Cityforum Opening Address,' *Home Office*, 28/10/2004. Accessed 1/5/2010. http://tna.europarchive.org/20061101012820/http://press.homeoffice.gov.uk/Speeches/speeches-archive/sp-homeland-security-1004.

16 P. Clarke, *Learning From Experience – Counter-Terrorism in the UK Since 9/11: The Colin Cramphorn Memorial Lecture* (London: Policy Exchange, 2007).

17 I. Bunglawala, interview with the author, by telephone, 3/8/2009.

18 L. Fitzsimons, interview with the author, London, 9/7/2007.

19 R. Winnett, 'Muslim Anger at British Leaflets,' *Sunday Times*, 2/12/2001.

20 B. Bradshaw, *Hansard* Column 819, 27/11/2001.

21 A. Burns, interview with the author, London, 12/6/2007.

22 FIA/FCO/0340-09/Report on the Domestic Echoes of Foreign Policy Seminar, 26/2/2003.

23 Ibid.

24 *Foreign Policy and the West Midlands; A Background Paper for the Foreign & Commonwealth Office's West Midlands Regional Seminar*, (Foreign and Commonwealth Office, 6/2003). Accessed 25/4/2009. http://www.fco.gov.uk/resources/en/pdf/pdf12/fco_localcommswmidlands.

25 M. Bright, 'Leak Shows Blair Told of Iraq War Terror Link: Top Official Warned in 2004 of British Muslim Anger; Secret Document Said UK Seen as "Crusader State",' *Observer*, 28/8/2006; ibid.

26 *Partnerships and Network Development Unit 10 Point Action Plan for 2003/4: The FCO and Minority Ethnic Communities – Following Seminar of 26 February 2003, 'Domestic Echoes of Foreign Policy'*, (Foreign and Commonwealth Office 3/2003). Accessed 1/5/2010. http://www.fco.gov.uk/resources/en/pdf/pdf12/fco_ethniccommactionplan.

27 'A Black Day in Our History – MCB News Release,' *Muslim Council of Britain*, 20/3/2003. Accessed 25/4/2009. http://www.mcb.org.uk/media/presstext.php?ann_id=33.

28 M. Chalmers, interview with the author, London, 2/9/2008, London.

29 FIA/FCO/0340-09/Strategy for Building Bridges with Mainstream Islam, 29/4/2003.

30 Winnett and Leppard, 'Leaked No 10 Dossier Reveals Al-Qaeda's British Recruits.'; *Leaked Foreign and Commonwealth Office and Home Office Paper – Young Muslims and Extremism*, (Global Security, 4/2004). Accessed 1/5/2010. http://www.globalsecurity.org/security/library/report/2004/muslimext-uk.htm.

31 Bright, 'Leak Shows Blair Told of Iraq War Terror Link.'

32 O'Brien, M., Hansard Column 184, 11/3/2003.

33 Ibid., Column 257.

34 Chalmers, interview.

35 G. Jones, 'Minister Urges "British Way" for Muslims,' *Daily Telegraph*, 22/11/2003.

36 G. Hurst, 'Muslim Fury as Minister Says: "Make Your Choice",' *The Times*, 22/11/2003.

37 See Chapter 7.

38 D. MacShane, 'Our Failure to Confront Radical Islam is There for All to See,' *Daily Telegraph*, 17/10/2006.

39 In 1998, a group of British Muslims in Yemen, allegedly associated with Abu Hamza's 'Supporters of Sharee'ah' group, was arrested on terrorist offenses. In 2000, two Muslim men were arrested – one later convicted – in Sparkbrook, accused of manufacturing explosives.

40 Clarke, Learning From Experience – Counter-Terrorism in the UK Since 9/11: The Colin Cramphorn Memorial Lecture.

41 Leaked Foreign and Commonwealth Office and Home Office Paper – Young Muslims and Extremism; Clarke, *Learning From Experience – Counter-Terrorism in the UK Since 9/11: The Colin Cramphorn Memorial Lecture.*

42 O. Bowcott, 'UK Suicide Bombings Inevitable,' *Guardian*, 4/9/2003.

43 Ibid.

44 H. Blears, interview with the author, Salford, 20/2/2009.

45 Blears, 'Speech on Homeland Security, Cityforum Opening Address.'

46 Blears, interview.

47 *Countering International Terrorism – The United Kingdom's Strategy – Cm 6888*, (London: The Stationery Office, 7/2006). Accessed 16/10/2012. http://www.official-documents.gov.uk/document/cm68/6888/6888.pdf.

48 'MCB Press Release – Police Using Stop & Search Practice Indiscriminately Against British Muslims,' *Muslim Council of Britain*, 2/7/2004. Accessed 11/2/2010. http://www.mcb.org.uk/media/presstext.php?ann_id=100.

49 *Intelligence and Security Committee, Could 7/7 Have Been Prevented? Review of the Intelligence on the London Terrorist Attacks on 7 July 2005*, (London: The Stationery Office, 5/2009). Accessed 15/10/2012. http://www.official-documents. gov.uk/document/cm76/7617/7617.pdf.

50 Winnett and Leppard, 'Leaked No 10 Dossier Reveals Al-Qaeda's British Recruits.'

51 Blears, interview.

52 Ibid.

53 J. Powell, interview with the author, by telephone, 7/7/2009.

54 Leaked Foreign and Commonwealth Office and Home Office Paper – Young Muslims and Extremism.; A leaked Joint Intelligence Committee document from April 2005 confirmed that intelligence services told the Prime Minister that 'Iraq is likely to be an important motivating factor for some time to come in the radicalisation of British Muslims.' 'D. Leppard, 'Iraq Terror Backlash in UK "For Years",' *Sunday Times*, 2/4/2006.

55 Leaked Foreign and Commonwealth Office and Home Office Paper – Young Muslims and Extremism.

56 Ibid.

57 'Press Muses Falluja Withdrawal,' *BBC News*, 30/4/2004. Accessed 1/5/2010. http:// news.bbc.co.uk/2/hi/uk_news/3672271.stm.

58 Leaked Foreign and Commonwealth Office and Home Office Paper – Young Muslims and Extremism.

59 Bright, 'Leak Shows Blair Told of Iraq War Terror Link.'

60 Leaked Letter from Sir Michael Jay to Sir Andrew Turnbull on 'Relations with the Muslim Community'.

61 Ibid.

62 FIA/FCO/0340-09/Joint Home Office and Foreign and Commonwealth Office Paper on Engaging With the Muslim Community, 6/2004.

63 *Engaging With the Islamic World Factsheet*, (Foreign and Commonwealth Office). Accessed 5/4/2009. http://collections.europarchive.org/tna/20080205132101/ www.fco.gov.uk/servlet/Front%3Fpagename=OpenMarket/Xcelerate/ShowPage& c=Page&cid=1153388310360.

64 *Foreign & Commonwealth Office Departmental Report: 1 April 2004 – 31 March 2005, Cm 6533*, (London: The Stationery Office, 6/2005).

65 Chalmers, interview.

66 Ibid.

67 'News Investigation: Young Islam: Hardline Youths Fuel Bitter Muslim Divide,' *Observer*, 4/4/2004.

68 T, Blair, *Hansard* Column 836, 7/7/2004.

69 House of Commons Home Affairs Committee, *Oral Evidence given by S. Khan*, 16/11/2004. Accessed 1/6/2010. http://www.publications.parliament.uk/pa/cm200405/cmselect/cmhaff/165/4111601.htm.

70 Ibid.

71 McRoy, *From Rushdie to 7/7*: 47.

72 'Electing to Deliver,' *Muslim Council of Britain*, 2005. Accessed 1/5/2010. http://www.mcb.org.uk/vote2005/index.php.

73 McRoy, *From Rushdie to 7/7*: 47.

74 J. Fisher et al., 'The General Election 2005: Campaign Analysis,' *London: Electoral Commission* (2005); P. Norris and C. Wlezien, 'Introduction: The Third Blair Victory: How and Why?,' *Parliamentary Affairs* 58, no. 4 (2005).

75 M. O'Brien, 'Labour and British Muslims: Can We Dream the Same Dream?,' *Muslim Weekly (London)*, 7–13/1/2005.

76 B. Cohen, 'Jerusalem Viewpoints No. 527 – Evaluating Muslims-Jewish Relations in Britain,' *Jerusalem Centre for Public Affairs*, 1–15/2/2005. Accessed 1/5/2010. http://www.jcpa.org/jl/vp527.htm.

77 Letter from Trevor Phillips to Simon Hughes, 'Re: Mail on Sunday Report on Rochdale Liberal Democrat Candidate, 27/4/2005,' provided to the author by a private individual.

78 S. Maher and M. Frampton, *Choosing our Friends Wisely* (London: Policy Exchange, 2009).

79 'Oona King Denounces Intimidation,' *BBC News*, 11/5/2005. Accessed 1/5/2010. http://news.bbc.co.uk/2/hi/4535885.stm.

80 R. Johnston, C. Pattie, and D. Rossiter, 'The Election Results in the UK Regions,' *Parliamentary Affairs* 58, no. 4 (2005).

81 Powell, interview.

82 Johnston, Pattie, and Rossiter, 'The Election Results in the UK Regions,' 67.

83 'Al Qaeda London Bombing Video Aired,' *Sky News*, 7/7/2006. Accessed 1/5/2010. http://news.sky.com/skynews/Home/Sky-News-Archive/Article/200806413531587.

84 T. Ali, 'The Price of Occupation,' *Guardian*, 8/7/2005.

85 R. Cook, 'The struggle against terrorism cannot be won by military means,' *Guardian*, 8/7/2005.

86 J. Pilger, 'Blair's Bombs,' *New Statesman*, 25/7/2005.

87 *JIC Assessment, International Terrorism: Impact of Iraq/13/4/2005*, (Iraq Inquiry). Accessed 15/10/2012. http://www.iraqinquiry.org.uk/media/52036/2005-04-13-JIC-assessment.pdf.

88 Blair, 'Prime Minister's Downing Street Press Conference, 26/7/2005'.

89 T. Blair, 'Prime Minister's Downing Street Press Conference,' *Prime Minister's Office*, 5/8/2005. Accessed 12/2/2010. http://www.number10.gov.uk/Page8041.

90 Ibid.

91 Powell, interview.

92 T. Blair, 'Not A Clash Between Civilisations, But a Clash About Civilisation – Speech by the Prime Minister,' *Foreign Policy Centre*, 21/3/2006. Accessed 1/5/2010. http://fpc.org.uk/events/past/clash-about-civilisation.

93 Ibid.

94 Blair, *A Journey*: 569.

95 Unpublished Spreadsheet Summarising Views Expressed During Ministerial Visits with Muslim Communities in Oldham, Burnley, Leicester, Bradford, Manchester, Leeds and Birmingham in August 2005, provided to the author by a private individual.

96 Bunglawala, interview.

97 Bright, interview; Archer, 'Welcome to the Umma: The British State and its Muslim Citizens Since 9/11.'

98 'Working Together to Prevent Extremism: Tackling Extremism and Radicalisation,' Home Office pack supporting Tackling Extremism and Radicalisation, 2005, provided to the author by a private individual.

99 Ibid.

100 Y. Islam et al., ' "Preventing Extremism Together" Working Groups,' 8–10/2005. Accessed 15/10/2012. http://www.communities.gov.uk/documents/communities/pdf/152164.pdf.

101 House of Commons Home Affairs Committee, *Oral Evidence Given by C. Clarke*, 13/9/2005. Accessed 1/5/2010. http://www.publications.parliament.uk/pa/cm200506/cmselect/cmhaff/462/5091301.htm.

102 Oborne, 'Israel's Actions Affect our Security.'

103 Ibid.

104 C. Clarke, 'Speech on Contesting the Threat of Terrorism,' *Heritage Foundation*, 21/10/2005. Accessed 1/5/2010. http://www.heritage.org/research/homelandsecurity/hl902.cfm.

105 M. Robinson, 'Response to MCB Complaints,' 30/9/2005. Accessed 1/5/2010. http://news.bbc.co.uk/2/hi/programmes/panorama/4297490.stm. See also Cesarani, 'Anti-Zionism in Britain.'

106 D. Pasquill, 'I Had No Choice But to Leak,' *New Statesman*, 17/1/2008.

107 'Document 6: Internal FCO Submission from Mockbul Ali to John Sawers Regarding Sheikh Yusuf al Qaradawi dated 14/7/2005,' in *When Progressives Treat with Reactionaries; The British State's Flirtation with Radical Islam*, ed. M. Bright (London: Policy Exchange, 2006).

108 Ibid.

109 Blair, 'Prime Minister's Downing Street Press Conference, 5/8/2005'.

110 B. Brogan, 'Extremist Linked Cleric Given Green Light to Enter Britain,' *Daily Mail*, 13/7/2006.

111 Blair, 'Not A Clash Between Civilisations, But a Clash About Civilisation – Speech by the Prime Minister'.

112 Blears, interview.

113 R. Kelly, interview with the author, London, 26/2/2009.

114 Countering International Terrorism – The United Kingdom's Strategy – Cm 6888.

115 Ibid., 6.

116 Ibid., 10.

117 Ibid., 15.

118 House of Commons Liaison Committee, *Oral Evidence given by T. Blair*, 6/7/2006. Accessed 15/10/2012. http://www.publications.parliament.uk/pa/cm200506/cmselect/cmliaisn/709/6070401.htm.

119 *Letter From the Prime Minister to Ruth Kelly*, (Department for Communities and Local Government, 9/5/2006). Accessed 1/5/2010. http://www.communities.gov.uk/archived/general-content/corporate/388681/prime-minister-letter.

120 B. Sherwood and S. Fidler, 'MI5 Tracked Group for a Year,' *Financial Times*, 10/8/2006.

121 'Full Text: Muslim Groups' Letter,' *BBC News*, 12/8/2006. Accessed 1/5/2010. http://news.bbc.co.uk/2/hi/uk_news/4786159.stm.

122 Kelly, interview.

123 R. Kelly, 'Speech on Britain: Our Values, Our Responsibilities,' *Department for Communities and Local Government*, 11/10/2006. Accessed http://webarchive.nationalarchives.gov.uk/+/http://www.communities.gov.uk/archived/speeches/corporate/values-responsibilities.

124 Kelly, interview.

125 R. Kelly, 'Speech at Muslim Cultural Heritage Centre,' 5/4/2007. Accessed http://www.communities.gov.uk/archived/general-content/corporate/formerministers/ruthkellyspeeches/.

126 Kelly, interview.

Chapter 9

1 M. Chalmers, interview with the author, London, 2/9/2008.

2 Seldon, Snowdon, and Collings, *Blair Unbound*: 481.

3 Ibid.

4 T. Blair, *A Global Alliance for Global Values* (London: Foreign Policy Centre, 2006).

5 Ibid., 30.

6 Blair, 'Not A Clash Between Civilisations, But a Clash About Civilisation – Speech by the Prime Minister'.

7   'Gleneagles 2005: Chairman's Summary,' *Prime Minister's Office*, 8/7/2005.
    Accessed 1/5/2010. http://www.pm.gov.uk/output/Page7883.asp.

8   'G8 Statement on Middle East Peace Process, Gleneagles Summit,' *G8*, 8/7/2005.
    Accessed 1/5/2010. http://www.g8.utoronto.ca/summit/2005gleneagles/mepp.pdf.

9   'Agreement on Movement and Access,' 15/11/2005. Accessed 1/5/2010. http://
    unispal.un.org/unispal.nsf/9a798adbf322aff38525617b006d88d7/c9a5aa5245d910
    bb852570bb0051711c/$FILE/Rafah%20agreement.pdf.

10 R. Del Sarto, 'Wording and Meaning(s): EU-Israeli Political Cooperation
    according to the ENP Action Plan,' *Mediterranean politics* 12, no. 1 (2007).

11 M. Herzog, 'Can Hamas be Tamed?,' *Foreign Affairs* 85 (2006).

12 C. Rice, 'Press Availability After Middle East Quartet Meeting,' *US State
    Department*, 20/9/2005. Accessed 14/11/2009. http://2001–2009.state.gov/
    secretary/rm/2005/53612.htm.

13 G. W. Bush and M. Abbas, 'President Welcomes Palestinian President Abbas to the
    White House,' *White House*, 26/5/2005. Accessed 15/11/2009. http://georgewbush-
    whitehouse.archives.gov/news/releases/2005/05/20050526.html.

14 Seldon, Snowdon, and Collings, *Blair Unbound*: 449.

15 See Chapter 3.

16 A. Crooke, interviewed by A. Mansour, *Al Jazeera*, 24/1/2007. Accessed 1/5/2010.
    http://conflictsforum.org/2007/interview-the-us-campaign-to-topple-the-
    palestinian-government/.

17 M. Levy, interview with the author, London, 1/9/2008.

18 Miller, *Inglorious Disarray: Europe, Israel and the Palestinians*: 178.

19 'Britain urges EU to blacklist Hamas Political Wing,' *Agence France Presse*,
    16/6/2003.

20 Crooke, interviewed by A. Mansour.

21 'Document 1: A. McKee's Summary of Paris Roundtable on Engaging with
    Islamists, 7/6/2005,' in *When Progressives Treat with Reactionaries: The British
    State's Flirtation with Radical Islam*, ed. M. Bright (London: Policy Exchange,
    2006).

22 B. Eastwood, interview with the author, by telephone, 1/9/2008.

23 FIA/FCO/0340-09/Excerpt From FCO Document of 2/6/2005 covering a note of
    7/5/2005.

24 *Wikileaks/05London1257/Report from US Embassy London on Taking Action
    Against Hezbollah and Hamas of 11/5/2005*, (Cablegate, 14/9/2011). Accessed
    15/10/2012. http://www.cablegatesearch.net/cable.php?id=05LONDON1257.

25 T. Butcher, 'Gaza Rocket Attack Puts Straw on Back Foot Over Hamas,' *Daily
    Telegraph*, 8/6/2005.

26 *Fourth Report from the Foreign Affairs Committee Session 2005–06, Foreign
    Policy Aspects of the War Against Terrorism: Response of the Secretary of State*

for Foreign and Commonwealth Affairs, (London: The Stationery Office, 9/2006). Accessed 15/10/2012. http://www.fco.gov.uk/resources/en/pdf/pdf18/ fco_4thfacresponse0506.

27 See Chapter 4.

28 'Document 11: Leaked Internal FCO Email Exchanges on Hamas, Hezbollah and Hizb-ut-Tahrir of 30–31/8/2005.'

29 See Chapter 3.

30 'Statement by Middle East Quartet: SG/2104, PAL/2042', *UN Secretary General*, 30/1/2006. Accessed 1/5/2010. http://unispal.un.org/UNISPAL.NSF/0/354568CCE 5E38E5585257106007A0834.

31 'After Mecca: Engaging Hamas – Middle East Report No. 62', *International Crisis Group* (2007).

32 Eastwood, interview.

33 Chalmers, interview.

34 M. Gapes, interview with the author, London, 2/3/2008.

35 'Statistics – Fatalities'.

36 House of Commons Liaison Committee, *Oral Evidence Given by T. Blair*, 7/2/2006. Accessed 1/5/2010. http://www.publications.parliament.uk/pa/cm200506/ cmselect/cmliaisn/709/6020701.htm.

37 A. La Guardia, 'Straw Softens Tone As He Offers Hamas Financial Lifeline', *Daily Telegraph*, 20/4/2006.

38 T. Blair, 'PM's Monthly Press Conference', *National Archives*, 24/4/2006. Accessed 1/5/2010. http://webarchive.nationalarchives.gov.uk/20070701080624/http:/ pm.gov.uk/output/Page9353.asp.

39 J. Straw, *Last Man Standing: Memoirs of a Political Survivor* (London: MacMillan, 2012).

40 Burden, R., *Hansard* Column 1463, 15/2/2006.

41 *International Development Committee, Development Assistance and the Occupied Palestinian Territories, Fourth Report of Session 2006–07*, (London: House of Commons, 31/1/2007). Accessed 15/10/2012. http://www. publications.parliament.uk/pa/cm200607/cmselect/cmintdev/114/114i.pdf.

42 R. Burden, EDM 1841 (2006–07) – Release of Alan Johnston, 4/7/2007.

43 K. Howells, *Hansard* Column 1003W, 12/6/2006.

44 T. Blair, 'Speech on the Middle East to the Los Angeles World Affairs Council', *Prime Minister's Office*, 1/8/2006. Accessed 1/5/2010. http://www.pm.gov.uk/ output/Page9948.asp.

45 O. McTernan, interview with the author, London, 14/9/2008.

46 'Middle East Initiative', *Forward Thinking*. Accessed 1/5/2010. http://www. forwardthinking.org/default.asp?id=15.

47   J. Powell, interview with the author, by telephone, 7/7/2009.

48   E. MacAskill and H. Sherwood, 'Hamas Touts 10-Year Ceasefire Plan Instead of Recognising Israel,' *Guardian*, 1/11/2006.

49   Private information.

50   McTernan, interview.

51   J. Greenstock, interview with the author, London, 25/2/2009.

52   J. Greenstock, 'Rebuilding Burned Bridges,' *Guardian*, 15/1/2009. Accessed 1/5/2010. http://www.guardian.co.uk/commentisfree/2009/jan/15/greenstock-gaza-israel-hamas-palestinians.

53   Powell, interview.

54   Levy, interview.

55   Chalmers, interview.

56   T. Blair and M. Abbas, 'Tony Blair and Palestinian President Mahmoud Abbas Met to Discuss Peace Efforts in the Middle East,' *National Archives*, 10/9/2006. Accessed 5/2/2010. http://webarchive.nationalarchives.gov.uk/20070701080624/http://pm.gov.uk/output/Page10045.asp.

57   D. Manning, interview with the author, London, 5/9/2008.

58   'Blair in the Middle East: FAQ,' *Guardian*, 18/12/2006.

59   T. Blair and M. Abbas, 'Press Conference with Palestinian President,' *National Archives*, 18/12/2006. Accessed 1/5/2010. http://webarchive.nationalarchives.gov.uk/20070701080624/http://pm.gov.uk/output/Page10648.asp.

60   'Programme of Palestinian National Unity Government,' *UNISPAL*, 17/3/2007. Accessed 1/6/2010. http://unispal.un.org/unispal.nsf/9a798adbf322aff38525617b006d88d7/8670ee789be79869852572c10058759a?OpenDocument.

61   *Wikileaks/07London1196/Report from US Embassy London on UK Views in Advance of March 30–31 Foreign Ministers Meeting (Gymnich) of 28/3/2007*, (Cablegate, 24/4/2011). Accessed 15/10/2012. http://www.cablegatesearch.net/cable.php?id=07LONDON1196&q=israel.

62   'EU Expands PA Contacts; Upsets Israel,' *Jerusalem Post*, 1/4/2007.

63   Levy, interview.

64   Blair, *A Journey*: 597–9.

65   T. Blair and E. Olmert, 'Joint Press Conference with Israeli PM Ehud Olmert,' *National Archives*, 13/6/2006. Accessed 1/5/2010. http://webarchive.nationalarchives.gov.uk/20070701080624/http://pm.gov.uk/output/Page9600.asp.

66   'Chronological Review of Events Relating to the Question of Palestine – Monthly Media Monitoring Review,' *UN Division for Palestinian Rights* 30/6/2006. Accessed 1/10/2010. http://unispal.un.org/unispal.nsf/9a798adbf322aff38525617b006d88d7/ca12e21fa366c920852571c500533c8d?OpenDocument.

67   E. Inbar, 'How Israel Bungled the Second Lebanon War,' *Middle East Quarterly*, Summer 2007.

68 T. Blair and S. Harper, 'Tony Blair Joint Press Conference with Canadian Prime Minister', *National Archives*, 14/7/2006. Accessed 1/5/2010. http://webarchive. nationalarchives.gov.uk/20070701080624/http://pm.gov.uk/output/Page9851.asp.

69 Seldon, Snowdon, and Collings, *Blair Unbound*: 469–71.

70 Hollis, *Britain and the Middle East*: 153.

71 E. MacAskill, S. Tisdall, and P. Wintour 'United States to Israel: You Have One More Week to Blast Hizbullah', *Guardian*, 19/7/2006.

72 Blair, *A Journey*: 597.

73 Seldon, Snowdon, and Collings, *Blair Unbound*: 467.

74 T. Blair, *Hansard* Column 151, 18/7/2006.

75 Levy, *A Question of Honour*.

76 T. Blair, *Hansard* Column 153, 18/7/2006.

77 Powell, interview.

78 Seldon, Snowdon, and Collings, *Blair Unbound*: 471.

79 Chalmers, interview.

80 Seldon, Snowdon, and Collings, *Blair Unbound*: 472.

81 E. Stourton, 'The Summer War in Lebanon: A Tragedy of Errors', *BBC Radio 4*, 3–10/4/2007. Accessed 18/7/2010. http://www.bbc.co.uk/radio4/news/summer_ war_lebanon.shtml.

82 Ibid.

83 Chalmers, interview.

84 Seldon, Snowdon, and Collings, *Blair Unbound*: 471.

85 D. Cracknell and H. Jaber, 'Minister Hits at Israel as Britons Flee', *Sunday Times*, 23/7/2006.

86 Chalmers, interview.

87 Stourton, 'The Summer War in Lebanon: A Tragedy of Errors'.

88 Seldon, Snowdon, and Collings, *Blair Unbound*: 473.

89 J. Oliver, 'Cabinet in Revolt as Straw Attacks Israeli Bombings', *Mail on Sunday*, 30/7/2006.

90 Seldon, Snowdon, and Collings, *Blair Unbound*: 475.

91 Hollis, *Britain and the Middle East*: 153.

92 I. Haniyeh, 'A Just Peace or No Peace', *Guardian*, 9/9/2006.

93 H. Mulholland and Agencies, 'More Than 100 Labour MPs Demand Recall of Parliament', *Guardian*, 11/8/2006.

94 M. Tempest and Agencies, 'Minister Brushes Aside Calls for Recall of Parliament', *Guardian*, 9/8/2006.

95 *Wikileaks/06London6861/Report from US Embassy London of 10/8/2006*, (Cablegate, 1/9/2011). Accessed 20/10/2012. http://www.cablegatesearch.net/cable. php?id=06LONDON5861&q=israel.

96 S. Twigg, interview with the author, 17/6/2008, London.

97 Chalmers, interview.

98 Seldon, Snowdon, and Collings, *Blair Unbound*: 481.

99 Blair, *A Journey*: 594.

100 Seldon, Snowdon, and Collings, *Blair Unbound*: 481.

101 J. Purnell, interview with the author, London, 9/7/2007.

102 Seldon, Snowdon, and Collings, *Blair Unbound*: 493.

103 Twigg, interview.

104 P. Riddell, 'Best Defence Against Terrorism is a Split with US, Say Voters,' *The Times*, 6/9/2006.

105 T. Blair, 'Speech to Labour Party Conference,' 26/9/2006. Accessed 1/5/2010. http://www.guardian.co.uk/politics/2006/sep/26/labourconference.labour3.

106 See Chapter 6.

107 T. Blair, 'World Affairs Speech to Lord Mayor's Banquet,' *Prime Minister's Office*, 13/11/2006. Accessed 1/5/2010. http://www.number10.gov.uk/archive/2006/11/PMs-world-affairs-speech-to-Lord-Mayors-Banquet-10409.

108 T. Blair, Interviewed by D. Frost, *Al Jazeera*, 11/12/2006. Accessed 1/5/2010. http://english.aljazeera.net/programmes/frostovertheworld/2006/11/2008525184756477907.html.

109 Blair and Abbas, 'Press Conference with Palestinian President'; Blair and Abbas, 'Tony Blair and Palestinian President Mahmood Abbas met to discuss Peace Efforts in the Middle East.'

110 'Press Briefing from the Prime Minister's Official Spokesman on Iraq Study Group – Middle East,' *National Archives*, 14/11/2006. Accessed 1/7/2010. http://webarchive.nationalarchives.gov.uk/20070701080624/http://pm.gov.uk/output/Page10421.asp.

111 Chalmers, interview.

112 C. Rice, 'Roundtable with the Travel Pool,' *US Department of State*, 30/11/2006. Accessed 1/5/2010. http://2001-2009.state.gov/secretary/rm/2006/77167.htm.

113 Seldon, Snowdon, and Collings, *Blair Unbound*: 577.

114 *House of Commons Foreign Affairs Committee, Global Security: The Middle East, Eighth Report of Session 2006–07*, (London: House of Commons, 25/7/2007). Accessed 15/10/2012. http://www.publications.parliament.uk/pa/cm200607/cmselect/cmfaff/363/363.pdf.

115 D. Miliband, '"War on Terror" Was Wrong,' *Guardian*, 15/1/2009.

116 D. Miliband, 'Our Shared Future: Building Coalitions and Winning Consent, Speech to the Oxford Center For Islamic Studies,' 21/5/2009. Accessed 1/6/2010. http://www.davidmiliband.info/speeches/speeches_09_06.htm.

117 D. Macintyre, 'Britain to Crack Down on Exports from Israeli Settlements; European Concern over West Bank Producers Bypassing Restrictions,' *Independent*, 3/11/2008.

118 T. Leonard, 'Nations Line Up To Condemn Attack on Gaza', *Daily Telegraph*,
     8/1/2009.
119 I. Black, 'UK Ready for Talks with Hezbollah', *Guardian*, 5/3/2009.
120 *Wikileaks/09London617/Report from US Embassy London, UK Announces*
     It Will Reengage With Hizballah, But Not Hamas, of 10/8/2006, (Cablegate,
     1/9/2011). Accessed 20/10/2012. http://www.cablegatesearch.net/cable.
     php?id=09LONDON617&q=hamas.

Conclusions

1   Henderson, 'Policy Watch #738 – Bush and Blair: Tensions in the Relationship.'
2   'FIA/FCO/0340-09/Strategy for Building Bridges with Mainstream Islam, 29/4/2003.'
3   Leaked Letter from Sir Michael Jay to Sir Andrew Turnbull on 'Relations with the
    Muslim Community'.
4   Blair, 'Speech on the Middle East to the Los Angeles World Affairs Council'.
5   Blair, 'Prime Minister's Downing Street Press Conference, 5/8/2005'.
6   Kelly, 'Speech on Britain: Our Values, Our Responsibilities'.
7   Blair, *A Journey*: 673.
8   'Hamas, Fatah face tough questions following unity deal', *BICOM*, 5/5/2011.
    Accessed 15/10/2012. http://www.bicom.org.uk/news-article/hamas-fatah-face-
    tough-questions-following-unity-deal/.
9   B. Obama, 'Speech in Cairo: A New Beginning', *White House*, 4/6/2009. Accessed
    1/6/2010. http://www.whitehouse.gov/issues/foreign-policy/presidents-speech-
    cairo-a-new-beginning.
10 *National Security Strategy*, (Washington: White House, 5/2010). Accessed
    15/10/2012. http://www.whitehouse.gov/sites/default/files/rss_viewer/national_
    security_strategy.pdf.
11 B. Netanyahu, 'Address at the AIPAC Policy Conference', *Israeli Prime Minister's*
    Office, 22/3/2010. Accessed 1/6/2010. http://www.pmo.gov.il/PMOEng/
    Communication/PMSpeaks/speechaipac220310.htm.
12 W. Hague, 'Speech on Britain's Foreign Policy in a Networked World', *Foreign and*
    Commonwealth Office, 1/7/2012. Accessed 3/10/2012. http://www.fco.gov.uk/en/
    news/latest-news/?view=Speech&id=22472881.
13 D. Cameron, 'Speech at Munich Security Conference', *Prime Minister's Office*,
    5/2/2011. Accessed 15/10/2012. http://www.number10.gov.uk/news/pms-speech-
    at-munich-security-conference/.
14 T. Greene, 'Shifting World, Shifting Priorities: a mid-term report on the UK
    coalition's relations with Israel', *Fathom*, no. 1 (2012).

Bibliography

Primary sources

Official internet sources for published or declassified documents

Foreign and Commonwealth Office (http://www.fco.gov.uk)
George W. Bush White House Webarchive (http://georgewbush-whitehouse.archives.
gov/)
Hansard Parliamentary Debates, House of Commons Publications and Select
Committee Inquiries (http://www.parliament.uk/business/publications)
House of Commons Early Day Motions Database (http://www.parliament.uk/edm)
Iraq Inquiry-Oral Evidence and Declassified Documents (http://www.
iraqinquiry.org.uk/)
Israeli Ministry of Foreign Affairs (http://www.mfa.gov.il)
Knesset (http://www.knesset.gov.il)
National Archives Webarchives – Archived Number Ten and Foreign and
Commonwealth Office Web sites (http://webarchive.nationalarchives.gov.uk/ and
http://collections.europarchive.org/tna/)
Number Ten/Prime Minister's Office (http://www.number10.gov.uk)
Official Documents – National Archives Site for Accessing Command Papers and
House of Commons Documents (http://www.official-documents.gov.uk/)
United Nations Information System on the Question of Palestine (UNISPAL) (http://
www.unispal.un.og)
US Department of State Webarchive for 2001–2009 (http://2001-2009.state.gov/)

Internet sources for leaked documents

Downing Street Memo(s) (http://downingstreetmemo.com/)
Palestine Papers-Al Jazeera Transparency Unit (http://www.ajtransparency.com/
Services/Search/default.aspx) and Guardian (http://www.guardian.co.uk/world/
palestine-papers)
Wikileaks – "Secret US Embassy Cables" (http://www.cablegatesearch.net/)

Published official documents

'Agreement on Movement and Access,' 15/11/2005. Accessed 1/5/2010. http://unispal.
un.org/unispal.nsf/9a798adbf322aff38525617b006d88d7/c9a5aa5245d910bb852570
bb0051711c/$FILE/Rafah%20agreement.pdf.

'Berlin European Council Declaration on the Middle East Peace Process,' *European
Parliament*, 24–25/3/1999. Accessed http://www.europarl.europa.eu/summits/
ber2_en.htm#partIV.

Communiqué Issued by the Quartet, New York. UNISPAL, 17/9/2002. Accessed
17/9/2002. http://unispal.un.org/unispal.nsf/udc.htm.

Countering International Terrorism – the United Kingdom's Strategy – Cm 6888. London:
The Stationery Office, 7/2006. Accessed 16/10/2012. http://www.official-documents.
gov.uk/document/cm68/6888/6888.pdf.

Engaging with the Islamic World Factsheet. Foreign and Commonwealth Office.
Accessed 5/4/2009. http://collections.europarchive.org/tna/20080205132101/www.
fco.gov.uk/servlet/Front%3Fpagename=OpenMarket/Xcelerate/ShowPage&c=Page
&cid=1153388310360.

'The European Community's Venice Declaration,' *Knesset*, 13/6/1980. Accessed
1/5/2010. http://www.knesset.gov.il/process/docs/venice_eng.htm.

Exchange of Letters between PM Sharon and President Bush. Israeli Ministry of Foreign
Affairs, 14/4/2004. Accessed 1/5/2010. http://www.mfa.gov.il/MFA/Peace+Process/
Reference+Documents/Exchange+of+letters+Sharon-Bush+14-Apr-2004.htm.

*Foreign Affairs Committee, Strategic Export Controls: Annual Report for 1999 and
Parliamentary Prior Scrutiny, Third Report of 2000–2001 Session*. London: House of
Commons, 6/3/2001. Accessed 15/10/2012. http://www.publications.parliament.uk/
pa/cm200001/cmselect/cmfaff/212/212fa02.htm.

*Foreign & Commonwealth Office Departmental Report: 1 April 2004 – 31 March 2005,
Cm 6533*. London: The Stationery Office, 6/2005.

*Foreign Policy and the West Midlands; a Background Paper for the Foreign
& Commonwealth Office's West Midlands Regional Seminar*. Foreign and
Commonwealth Office, 6/2003. Accessed 25/4/2009. http://www.fco.gov.uk/
resources/en/pdf/pdf12/fco_localcommswmidlands.

*Fourth Report from the Foreign Affairs Committee Session 2005–06, Foreign Policy
Aspects of the War against Terrorism: Response of the Secretary of State for Foreign
and Commonwealth Affairs*. London: The Stationery Office, 9/2006. Accessed
15/10/2012. http://www.fco.gov.uk/resources/en/pdf/pdf18/fco_4thfacresponse0506.

'G8 Statement on Middle East Peace Process, Gleneagles Summit,' *G8*, 8/7/2005.
Accessed 1/5/2010. http://www.g8.utoronto.ca/summit/2005gleneagles/mepp.pdf.

'Gleneagles 2005: Chairman's Summary,' *Prime Minister's Office*, 8/7/2005. Accessed
1/5/2010. http://www.pm.gov.uk/output/Page7883.asp.

House of Commons Foreign Affairs Committee, Global Security: The Middle East, Eighth Report of Session 2006–07. London: House of Commons, 25/7/2007. Accessed 15/10/2012. http://www.publications.parliament.uk/pa/cm200607/cmselect/cmfaff/363/363.pdf.

Intelligence and Security Committee, *Could 7/7 Have Been Prevented? Review of the Intelligence on the London Terrorist Attacks on 7 July 2005.* London: The Stationery Office, 5/2009. Accessed 15/10/2012. http://www.official-documents.gov.uk/document/cm76/7617/7617.pdf.

International Development Committee, *Development Assistance and the Occupied Palestinian Territories, Fourth Report of Session 2006–07.* London: House of Commons, 31/1/2007. Accessed 15/10/2012. http://www.publications.parliament.uk/pa/cm200607/cmselect/cmintdev/114/114i.pdf.

Israel's Response to the Roadmap. Knesset, 25/5/2003. Accessed 1/5/2010. http://www.knesset.gov.il/process/docs/roadmap_response_eng.htm.

Kean, T. H., L. Hamilton, R. Ben-Veniste, B. Kerrey, F. F. Fielding, J. F. Lehman, J. S. Gorelick, et al. *The 9/11 Commission Report: Final Report of the National Commission on Terrorist Attacks Upon the United States.* Washington, DC: US General Printing Office, 2004.

L 340/63/ Council Decision of 22 December 2003 Implementing Article 2(3) of Regulation (EC) No 2580/2001 on Specific Restrictive Measures Directed against Certain Persons and Entities with a View to Combating Terrorism and Repealing Decision 2003/646/EC – (2003/902/EC). Official Journal of the European Union, 22/12/2003. Accessed 10/10/2012. http://eur-lex.europa.eu/LexUriServ/LexUriServ.do?uri=OJ:L:2003:340:0063:0064:EN:PDF.

Letter from the Prime Minister to Ruth Kelly. Department for Communities and Local Government, 9/5/2006. Accessed 1/5/2010. http://www.communities.gov.uk/archived/general-content/corporate/388681/prime-minister-letter.

Middle East Quartet Communique. United Nations, 4/5/2004. Accessed 1/5/2010. http://www.un.org/News/dh/infocus/middle_east/quartet-comque-4may04.htm.

National Security Strategy. Washington: White House, 5/2010. Accessed 15/10/2012. http://www.whitehouse.gov/sites/default/files/rss_viewer/national_security_strategy.pdf.

The Outcomes of the London Conference on Palestinian Reform. Foreign and Commonwealth Office, 14/1/2003. Accessed 18/9/2009. http://unispal.un.org/UNISPAL.NSF/0/6285301BFE6F08C285256CB70054B9B5.

Partnerships and Network Development Unit 10 Point Action Plan for 2003/4: The FCO and Minority Ethnic Communities – Following Seminar of 26 February 2003, 'Domestic Echoes of Foreign Policy'. Foreign and Commonwealth Office 3/2003. Accessed 1/5/2010. http://www.fco.gov.uk/resources/en/pdf/pdf12/fco_ethniccommactionplan.

A Performance-Based Roadmap to a Permanent Two-State Solution to the Israeli-Palestinian Conflict. UNISPAL, 30/4/2003. Accessed 15/10/2012. http://unispal.un.org/unispal.nsf/0/6129B9C832FE59AB85256D43004D87FA.

'Programme of Palestinian National Unity Government,' *UNISPAL,* 17/3/2007. Accessed 1/6/2010. http://unispal.un.org/unispal.nsf/9a798adbf322aff38525617b006d88d7/8670ee789be79869852572c10058759a?OpenDocument.

Report of the Secretary-General Prepared Pursuant to General Assembly Resolution ES-10/10. United Nations, 30/7/2002. Accessed 1/5/2010. http://www.un.org/peace/jenin/

Report of the Sharm El-Sheikh Fact-Finding Committee. Washington: Meridian International Center, 30/4/2001.

Review of Intelligence on Weapons of Mass Destruction. London: House of Commons, 14/7/2004. Accessed 15/10/2012. http://www.archive2.official-documents.co.uk/document/deps/hc/hc898/898.pdf.

SN 150/1/98 Rev 1/ Cardiff European Council Presidency Conclusions. European Union, 16/6/1998. Accessed 15/10/2012. http://www.consilium.europa.eu/uedocs/cms_data/docs/pressdata/en/ec/54315.pdf.

'Statement by Middle East Quartet: SG/2104, Pal/2042', *UN Secretary General,* 30/1/2006. Accessed 1/5/2010. http://unispal.un.org/UNISPAL.NSF/0/354568CCE5E38E5585257106007A0834.

The United Kingdom and the Campaign against International Terrorism – Progress Report. Cabinet Office, 9/9/2002. Accessed 15/10/2012. http://webarchive.nationalarchives.gov.uk/ + /http://www.cabinetoffice.gov.uk/~/media/assets/www.cabinetoffice.gov.uk/publications/reports/sept11/coi%200809%20pdf.ashx.

'US and UK Joint Statement Concerning the Middle East Peace Process,' *White House,* 12/11/2004. Accessed 10/10/2009. http://georgewbush-whitehouse.archives.gov/news/releases/2004/11/20041112-3.html.

Oral evidence to official hearings

House of Commons Defence, Foreign Affairs, International Development and Trade and Industry Committees, *Oral Evidence Given by R. Cook,* 30/1/2001. Accessed 10/10/2012. http://www.publications.parliament.uk/pa/cm200001/cmselect/cmfaff/212/1013007.htm.

House of Commons Home Affairs Committee, *Oral Evidence Given by C. Clarke,* 13/9/2005. Accessed 1/5/2010. http://www.publications.parliament.uk/pa/cm200506/cmselect/cmhaff/462/5091301.htm.

House of Commons Home Affairs Committee, *Oral Evidence Given by S. Khan,* 16/11/2004. Accessed 1/6/2010. http://www.publications.parliament.uk/pa/cm200405/cmselect/cmhaff/165/4111601.htm.

House of Commons Liaison Committee, *Oral Evidence Given by T. Blair*, 6/7/2006. Accessed 15/10/2012. http://www.publications.parliament.uk/pa/cm200506/cmselect/cmliaisn/709/6070401.htm.

House of Commons Liaison Committee, *Oral Evidence Given by T. Blair*, 7/2/2006. Accessed 1/5/2010. http://www.publications.parliament.uk/pa/cm200506/cmselect/cmliaisn/709/6020701.htm.

Iraq Inquiry, *Oral Evidence Given by C. Meyer*, 26/11/2009. Accessed 1/5/2012. http://www.iraqinquiry.org.uk/media/44184/20100118pm-powell-final.pdf.

Iraq Inquiry, *Oral Evidence Given by D. Manning*, 30/11/2009. Accessed 1/5/2012. http://www.iraqinquiry.org.uk/media/40459/20091130pm-final.pdf.

Iraq Inquiry, *Oral Evidence Given by G. Hoon*, 19/1/2010. Accessed 1/5/2012. http://www.iraqinquiry.org.uk/transcripts/oralevidence-bydate/100119.aspx.

Iraq Inquiry, *Oral Evidence Given by J. Powell*, 18/1/2010. Accessed 1/5/2010. http://www.iraqinquiry.org.uk/media/44184/20100118pm-powell-final.pdf.

Iraq Inquiry, *Oral Evidence Given by J. Sawyers*, 10/12/2009. Accessed 1/5/2010. http://www.iraqinquiry.org.uk/media/40668/20091210amsawers-final.pdf.

Iraq Inquiry, *Oral Evidence Given by J. Straw*, 21/1/2010. Accessed 1/5/2012. http://www.iraqinquiry.org.uk/media/44190/20100121pm-straw-final.pdf.

Iraq Inquiry, *Oral Evidence Given by P. Rickets*, 24/11/2009. Accessed 1/5/2010. http://www.iraqinquiry.org.uk/transcripts/oralevidence-bydate/091124.aspx.

Iraq Inquiry, *Oral Evidence Given by T. Blair*, 29/1/2010. Accessed 1/5/2012. http://www.iraqinquiry.org.uk/transcripts/oralevidence-bydate/100129.aspx.

Speeches, press conferences and published interviews

Blair, T. *Address Given at the Labour Friends of Israel Annual Lunch, 15th June 2004.* London: Labour Friends of Israel, 2004.

—, 'At Our Best When at Our Boldest, Speech at the Labour Party Conference,' *City University, London*, 1/1/2002. Accessed 1/5/2010. http://www.staff.city.ac.uk/p.willetts/IRAQ/TB011002.HTM.

—, *A Global Alliance for Global Values.* London: Foreign Policy Centre, 2006.

—, Interviewed by C. Moore, J. Keegan and G. Jones, *The Daily Telegraph*, 25/10/2001. Accessed 15/10/2012. http://www.telegraph.co.uk/news/worldnews/asia/afghanistan/1360429/Interview-with-the-Prime-Minister.html.

—, Interviewed by D. Frost, *Al Jazeera*, 11/12/2006. Accessed 1/5/2010. http://english.aljazeera.net/programmes/frostovertheworld/2006/11/2008525184756477907.html.

—, Interviewed by K. Ahmed, *The Observer*, 14/10/2001. Accessed 15/10/2012. http://www.guardian.co.uk/politics/2001/oct/14/afghanistan.terrorism1.

—, Interviewed by PBS Frontline, *PBS Frontline*, 8/5/2002. Accessed 1/6/2010. http://www.pbs.org/wgbh/pages/frontline/shows/campaign/interviews/blair.html.

—, 'Not a Clash between Civilisations, but a Clash About Civilisation – Speech by the Prime Minister', *Foreign Policy Centre*, 21/3/2006. Accessed 1/5/2010. http://fpc.org.uk/events/past/clash-about-civilisation.

—, 'PM Welcomes Geneva Accord Middle East Initiative', *Prime Minister's Office*, 4/11/2003. Accessed 1/5/2010. http://www.number10.gov.uk/Page4765.

—, 'PM's Meeting with Leaders of the Muslim Communities in Britain', *Prime Minister's Office*, 27/9/2001. Accessed 1/5/2010. http://www.number10.gov.uk/Page1605.

—, 'PM's Monthly Press Conference', *National Archives*, 24/4/2006. Accessed 1/5/2010. http://webarchive.nationalarchives.gov.uk/20070701080624/http:/pm.gov.uk/output/Page9353.asp.

—, 'PM's Statement on Iraq Strikes, Full Text', *BBC News*, 16/12/1998. Accessed 1/5/2012. http://news.bbc.co.uk/2/hi/events/crisis_in_the_gulf/texts_and_transcripts/236932.stm.

—, 'Prime Minister's Downing Street Press Conference', *Prime Minister's Office*, 5/8/2005. Accessed 12/2/2010. http://www.number10.gov.uk/Page8041.

—, 'Prime Minister's Downing Street Press Conference', *National Archives*, 26/7/2005. Accessed 1/5/2010. http://webarchive.nationalarchives.gov.uk/20070701080624/http://pm.gov.uk/output/Page7999.asp.

—, 'Prime Minister's Press Conference', *National Archives*, 3/9/2002. Accessed 1/5/2010. http://webarchive.nationalarchives.gov.uk/20070701080624/http:/pm.gov.uk/output/Page3001.asp.

—, 'Prime Minister's Press Conference', *National Archives*, 15/1/2004. Accessed 1/5/2010. http://webarchive.nationalarchives.gov.uk/20070701080624/http://pm.gov.uk/output/Page5157.asp.

—, 'September 11 Attacks: Prime Minister's Statement', *Prime Minister's Office*, 11/9/2001. Accessed 1/5/2010. http://www.number10.gov.uk/Page1596.

—, 'Speech at the Lord Mayor's Banquet', *National Archives*, 10/11/1997. Accessed 1/6/2010. http://webarchive.nationalarchives.gov.uk/20070701080624/http://pm.gov.uk/output/Page1070.asp.

—, 'Speech at the Lord Mayor's Banquet', *National Archives*, 13/11/2000. Accessed 1/5/2010. http://webarchive.nationalarchives.gov.uk/20070701080624/http://pm.gov.uk/output/Page1535.asp.

—, 'Speech by the Prime Minister at the 2001 Labour Party Conference', *Guardian*, 2/10/2001. Accessed 1/5/2010. http://www.guardian.co.uk/politics/2001/oct/02/labourconference.labour6.

—, 'Speech on the Doctrine of the International Community at the Economic Club, Chicago', *National Archives*, 24/4/1999. Accessed 1/5/2010. http://webarchive.nationalarchives.gov.uk/20070701080624/http://pm.gov.uk/output/Page1297.asp.

—, 'Speech on the Middle East to the Los Angeles World Affairs Council,' *Prime Minister's Office*, 1/8/2006. Accessed 1/5/2010. http://www.pm.gov.uk/output/Page9948.asp.

—, 'Speech to Foreign Office Conference in London,' *Prime Minister's Office*, 7/1/2003. Accessed 1/5/2010. http://www.number10.gov.uk/Page1765.

—, 'Speech to Labour Friends of Israel Conference Reception,' *Labour Friends of Israel*, 26/9/2006. Accessed 17/2/2008. www.lfi.org.uk/news.

—, 'Speech to Labour Party Conference,' 26/9/2006. *Guardian*. Accessed 1/5/2010. http://www.guardian.co.uk/politics/2006/sep/26/labourconference.labour3.

—, 'Speech to the Labour Party Conference,' *BBC News*, 28/9/2004. Accessed 1/5/2010. http://news.bbc.co.uk/2/hi/uk_news/politics/3697434.stm.

—, 'Speech to the Muslim Council of Britain,' *National Archives*, 5/5/1999. Accessed 1/5/2010. http://webarchive.nationalarchives.gov.uk/20070701080624/http:/pm.gov.uk/output/Page1329.asp.

—, 'Speech to the United States Congress,' *National Archives*, 17/7/2003. Accessed 27/9/2009. http://webarchive.nationalarchives.gov.uk/20070701080624/http://pm.gov.uk/output/Page4220.asp.

—, 'Statement on Bush's Re-Election,' *Guardian*, 4/11/2004. Accessed 10/10/2009. http://www.guardian.co.uk/world/2004/nov/04/uselections2004.usa13.

—. *The Third Way: New Politics for the New Century.* London: Fabian Society, 1998.

—. 'The West's Tough Strategy on Iraq Is in Everyone's Interests; Why Saddam Is Still a Threat to Britain.' *Express*, 6/3/2002.

—, 'World Affairs Speech to Lord Mayor's Banquet,' *Prime Minister's Office*, 13/11/2006. Accessed 1/5/2010. http://www.number10.gov.uk/archive/2006/11/PMs-world-affairs-speech-to-Lord-Mayors-Banquet-10409.

Blair, T., and M. Abbas, 'Press Conference with Palestinian President,' *National Archives*, 18/12/2006. Accessed 1/5/2010. http://webarchive.nationalarchives.gov.uk/20070701080624/http://pm.gov.uk/output/Page10648.asp.

—, 'Tony Blair and Palestinian President Mahmoud Abbas Met to Discuss Peace Efforts in the Middle East,' *National Archives*, 10/9/2006. Accessed 5/2/2010. http://webarchive.nationalarchives.gov.uk/20070701080624/http://pm.gov.uk/output/Page10045.asp.

—, 'Tony Blair/Mahmoud Abbas Press Conference Opening Remarks,' *Prime Minister's Office*, 1/3/2005. Accessed 1/5/2010. http://www.number10.gov.uk/Page7237.

Blair, T., and B. al-Assad, 'Press Conference: Prime Minister Tony Blair and Syrian President al-Assad,' *National Archives*, 16/12/2002. Accessed 8/11/2009. http://webarchive.nationalarchives.gov.uk/20070701080624/http://pm.gov.uk/output/Page1744.asp.

—, 'Transcript of Joint Press Conference: Prime Minister Blair and President Assad,' *National Archives*, 31/10/2001. Accessed 1/5/2010. http://webarchive.nationalarchives.gov.uk/20070701080624/http://pm.gov.uk/output/Page1637.asp.

Blair, T., and Y. Arafat, 'Press Conference: PM and President Arafat,' *Prime Minister's Office*, 2/11/2001. Accessed 10/2/2012. http://collections.europarchive.org/ tna/20011108193912/http://pm.gov.uk/news.asp?NewsId=2916&SectionId=32.

Blair, T., and R. Cheney, 'Transcript of Doorstep Given by the Prime Minister Tony Blair and US Vice President Dick Cheney, London,' *National Archives*, 11/3/2002. Accessed 1/5/2010. http://webarchive.nationalarchives.gov.uk/20070701080624/ http://pm.gov.uk/output/Page1704.asp.

Blair, T., and S. Harper, 'Tony Blair Joint Press Conference with Canadian Prime Minister,' *National Archives*, 14/7/2006. Accessed 1/5/2010. http://webarchive. nationalarchives.gov.uk/20070701080624/http://pm.gov.uk/output/Page9851.asp.

Blair, T., and E. Olmert, 'Joint Press Conference with Israeli PM Ehud Olmert,' *National Archives*, 13/6/2006. Accessed 1/5/2010. http://webarchive.nationalarchives.gov. uk/20070701080624/http:/pm.gov.uk/output/Page9600.asp.

Blair, T., and A. Sharon, 'PM's Press Conference with the Israeli Prime Minister, Mr Ariel Sharon,' *National Archives*, 22/12/2004. Accessed 11/5/2010. http://webarchive. nationalarchives.gov.uk/20070701080624/http://pm.gov.uk/output/Page6836.asp.

Blears, H., 'Speech on Homeland Security, Cityforum Opening Address,' *Home Office*, 28/10/2004. Accessed 1/5/2010. http://tna.europarchive.org/20061101012820/http:// press.homeoffice.gov.uk/Speeches/speeches-archive/sp-homeland-security-1004.

Brown, G., 'Speech at the Knesset, Israel,' *Labour*, 21/7/2008. Accessed 1/5/2011. http:// www.labour.org.uk/gordon_brown_speech_to_the_knesset,2008-07-21.

Bush, G. W., 'Address to a Joint Session of Congress and the American People,' *White House*, 20/9/2001. Accessed 1/5/2010. http://georgewbush-whitehouse.archives.gov/ news/releases/2001/09/20010920-8.html.

—, 'CNN Live Event/Special; Target: Terrorism – Bush Meets with Congressional Leaders,' *CNN*, Accessed 16/8/2009. http://transcripts.cnn.com/TRANSCRIPTS/0110/02/se.15. html.

—, 'President Bush Calls for New Palestinian Leadership,' *White House*, 24/6/2002. Accessed 1/5/2010. http://georgewbush-whitehouse.archives.gov/news/ releases/2002/06/20020624-3.html.

—, 'President Bush Discusses Iraq Policy at Whitehall Palace in London,' *White House*, 19/11/2003. Accessed 1/6/2010. http://georgewbush-whitehouse.archives.gov/news/ releases/2003/11/20031119-1.html.

—, 'President Discusses Roadmap for Peace in the Middle East,' *White House*, 14/3/2003. Accessed 1/6/2010. http://georgewbush-whitehouse.archives.gov/news/ releases/2003/03/20030314-4.html.

—, 'President to Send Secretary Powell to Middle East,' *White House*, 4/4/2002. Accessed 1/5/2010. http://georgewbush-whitehouse.archives.gov/news/ releases/2002/04/20020404-1.html.

—, 'The President's State of the Union Address,' *White House*, 29/1/2002. Accessed 1/5/2010. http://georgewbush-whitehouse.archives.gov/news/ releases/2002/01/20020129-11.html.

—, 'Remarks by the President to United Nations General Assembly,' *White House*,
    10/10/2001. Accessed 1/5/2010. http://georgewbush-whitehouse.archives.gov/news/
    releases/2001/11/20011110-3.html.

—, 'Speech on United States Position on Terrorists and Peace in the Middle East,' *US
    Department of State*, 19/11/2001. Accessed 1/5/2010. http://2001-2009.state.gov/
    secretary/former/powell/remarks/2001/6219.htm.

Bush, G. W., and M. Abbas, 'President Welcomes Palestinian President Abbas to the
    White House,' *White House*, 26/5/2005. Accessed 15/11/2009. http://georgewbush-
    whitehouse.archives.gov/news/releases/2005/05/20050526.html.

Bush, G. W., and T. Blair, 'Bush, Blair Discuss Sharon Plan; Future of Iraq in Press
    Conference,' *White House*, 16/4/2004. Accessed 1/5/2010. http://georgewbush-
    whitehouse.archives.gov/news/releases/2004/04/20040416-4.html.

—, 'President and Prime Minister Blair Discussed Iraq, Middle East,' *White House*,
    12/11/2004. Accessed 10/10/2009. http://georgewbush-whitehouse.archives.gov/
    news/releases/2004/11/20041112-5.html.

—, 'Remarks by President Bush and Prime Minister Tony Blair of Great Britain in
    Press Availability,' *White House*, 8/11/2001. Accessed 1/5/2010. http://georgewbush-
    whitehouse.archives.gov/news/releases/2001/11/20011108-1.html.

Bush, G. W., and A. Sharon, 'Remarks by the President and Prime Minister Ariel Sharon
    of Israel in Photo Opportunity,' *White House*, 20/3/2001. Accessed 1/5/2010. http://
    georgewbush-whitehouse.archives.gov/news/releases/2001/03/20010320-3.html.

—, 'Remarks by the President and Prime Minister Sharon of Israel in Photo
    Opportunity,' *White House*, 7/2/2002. Accessed 1/5/2010. http://georgewbush-
    whitehouse.archives.gov/news/releases/2002/02/20020207-15.html.

Cameron, D., 'Speech at Munich Security Conference,' *Prime Minister's Office*, 5/2/2011.
    Accessed 15/10/2012. http://www.number10.gov.uk/news/pms-speech-at-munich-
    security-conference/.

Cheney, R., 'The Vice President Appears on Fox News Sunday', *White House*, 27/1/2002.
    Accessed 1/5/2010. http://georgewbush-whitehouse.archives.gov/vicepresident/
    news-speeches/speeches/vp20020127-1.html.

Clarke, C., 'Speech on Contesting the Threat of Terrorism,' *Heritage Foundation*,
    21/10/2005. Accessed 1/5/2010. http://www.heritage.org/research/
    homelandsecurity/hl902.cfm.

Cook, R., 'Speech on the Government's Ethical Foreign Policy,' *Guardian*, 12/5/1997.
    Accessed 1/6/2010. http://www.guardian.co.uk/world/1997/may/12/indonesia.
    ethicalforeignpolicy.

Hague, W., 'Speech on Britain's Foreign Policy in a Networked World,' *Foreign and
    Commonwealth Office*, 1/7/2012. Accessed 3/10/2012. http://www.fco.gov.uk/en/
    news/latest-news/?view=Speech&id=22472881.

Kelly, R., 'Speech at Muslim Cultural Heritage Centre,' 5/4/2007. Accessed
    1/5/2010. http://www.communities.gov.uk/archived/general-content/corporate/
    formerministers/ruthkellyspeeches/.

—, 'Speech on Britain: Our Values, Our Responsibilities,' *Department for Communities and Local Government*, 11/10/2006. Accessed 1/5/2010. http://webarchive. nationalarchives.gov.uk/+/http://www.communities.gov.uk/archived/speeches/ corporate/values-responsibilities.

Miliband, D., 'Our Shared Future: Building Coalitions and Winning Consent, Speech to the Oxford Center for Islamic Studies,' 21/5/2009. Accessed 1/6/2010. http://www. davidmiliband.info/speeches/speeches_09_06.htm.

Netanyahu, B., 'Address at the AIPAC Policy Conference,' *Israeli Prime Minister's Office*, 22/3/2010. Accessed 1/6/2010. http://www.pmo.gov.il/PMOEng/Communication/ PMSpeaks/speechaipac220310.htm.

Obama, B., 'Speech in Cairo: A New Beginning,' *White House*, 4/6/2009. Accessed 1/6/2010. http://www.whitehouse.gov/issues/foreign-policy/presidents-speech- cairo-a-new-beginning.

Powell, C., 'On-the-Record Briefing by C. Powell En Route from Louisville, Kentucky, to Washington, DC,' *US Department of State*, 19/11/2001. Accessed 1/5/2010. http://2001-2009.state.gov/secretary/former/powell/remarks/2001/6227.htm.

—, 'Secretary Colin L. Powell Press Availability with Danish Foreign Minister Per Stig Moeller, EU High Representative Javier Solana, and European Union Commissioner Chris Patten,' *US Department of State*, 18/12/2002. Accessed 1/5/2010. http://2001- 2009.state.gov/secretary/former/powell/remarks/2002/16100.htm.

Rice, C., 'Press Availability after Middle East Quartet Meeting,' *US State Department*, 20/9/2005. Accessed 14/11/2009. http://2001-2009.state.gov/secretary/ rm/2005/53612.htm.

—, 'Remarks to the Press, Ben Gurion Airport, Tel Aviv, Israel,' *US State Department*, 7/2/2005. Accessed 28/10/2009. http://2001-2009.state.gov/secretary/ rm/2005/41936.htm.

—, 'Roundtable with the Travel Pool,' *US Department of State*, 30/11/2006. Accessed 1/5/2010. http://2001-2009.state.gov/secretary/rm/2006/77167.htm.

Sharon, A., 'Herzliya Address,' *Institute for Policy and Strategy*, 18/12/2003. Accessed 1/5/2010. http://www.herzliyaconference.org/Eng/_Articles/Article. asp?ArticleID=892&CategoryID=153.

Straw, J., 'Interview by BBC Radio 4's Today Programme,' *Foreign and Commonwealth Office*, 6/1/2003. Accessed 18/9/2009. http://www.fco.gov.uk/resources/en/ news/2003/01/fco_nit_060103_strawtodayisrael.

Memoirs

Blair, T. *A Journey*. London: Hutchinson, 2010.
Blunkett, D. *The Blunkett Tapes: My Life in the Bear Pit*. London: Bloomsbury, 2006.
Campbell, A. *The Blair Years*. London: Hutchinson, 2007.
Cook, R. *Point of Departure*. London: Simon & Schuster, 2003.

Kerr, J. O., Interview by M. McBain, *Churchill Archives Centre, British Diplomatic Oral History Programme*, 6/4/2004. Accessed 1/5/2010. http://www.chu.cam.ac.uk/archives/collections/BDOHP/Kerr.pdf.

Levy, L. M. *A Question of Honour: Inside New Labour and the True Story of the Cash for Peerages Scandal*. London: Simon and Schuster, 2008.

Meyer, C. *DC Confidential*. London: Weidenfeld & Nicolson, 2005.

Miles, R. O., Interview by M. McBain, *Churchill Archives Centre, British Diplomatic Oral History Programme*, 27/8/2004. Accessed 10/10/2012. http://www.chu.cam.ac.uk/archives/collections/BDOHP/Miles_Oliver.pdf.

Powell, J. *Great Hatred, Little Room: Making Peace in Northern Ireland*. London: Bodley Head, 2008.

—. *The New Machiavelli: How to Wield Power in the Modern World*. London: Bodley Head, 2010.

Ross, D. *The Missing Peace: The inside Story of the Fight for Middle East Peace*. New York: Farrar Straus & Giroux, 2005.

Short, C. *An Honourable Deception?: New Labour, Iraq and the Misuse of Power*. London: The Free Press, 2004.

Straw, J. *Last Man Standing: Memoirs of a Political Survivor*. London: MacMillan, 2012.

Miscellaneous non-governmental documents

'Bin Laden's Declaration of War against the Americans Occupying the Land of the Two Holy Places,' *PBS Newshour*, 1/8/1996. Accessed 22/4/2012. http://www.pbs.org/newshour/terrorism/international/fatwa_1996.html?print.

'Electing to Deliver,' *Muslim Council of Britain*, 2005. Accessed 1/5/2010. http://www.mcb.org.uk/vote2005/index.php.

'French Non Paper on the Revival of a Dynamics of Peace in the Middle-East of February 2002,' *Bitterlemons*. Accessed 6/9/2009. http://www.bitterlemons.org/docs/french.html.

'Full Text: Muslim Groups' Letter,' *BBC News*, 12/8/2006. Accessed 1/5/2010. http://news.bbc.co.uk/2/hi/uk_news/4786159.stm.

New Labour – Because Britain Deserves Better, Labour Party Manifesto 1997. London: Labour Party, 1997.

Abrams, E., R. Armitage, W. Bennett, J. Bergner, J. Bolton, P. Dobriansky, F. Fukuyama, *et al.*, 'Letter to President Clinton on Iraq,' *Project for the New American Century*, 26/1/1998. Accessed 1/5/2010. http://www.newamericancentury.org/letterstatements.htm.

Bentley, T., A. Coote, C. Crouch, A. Gamble, S. Goss, L. Harker, D. Held, *et al. A Vision for the Democratic Left*. London: Compass, 2003.

Islam, Y., L. N. Ahmed, B. P. M. Uddin, I. Bunglawala, M. A. Aziz, N. Majid, and A. Ullah, ' "Preventing Extremism Together" Working Groups,' 8–10/2005. Accessed

15/10/2012. http://www.communities.gov.uk/documents/communities/pdf/152164. pdf.

Miles, O., S. B. Barder, P. Bergne, S. J. Birch, S. D. Blatherwick, G. H. Boyce, S. J. Bullard, *et al.*, 'Ambassador's Letter to Blair,' *BBC*, 29/4/2004. Accessed 1/5/2010. http://news. bbc.co.uk/2/hi/uk_news/politics/3660837.stm.

Trickett, J., 'Parliamentary Labour Party Letter to John Prescott Requesting Recall of Parliament,' 11/8/2006. Accessed 1/5/2010. http://image.guardian.co.uk/sys-files/ Politics/documents/2006/08/11/PrescotLetter.doc.

Unpublished documents and papers

Documents relating to the 'Preventing Extremism Together' working groups, 2005–2006. Provided to the author by a private individual.

Foreign and Commonwealth Documents, 2001–2005. Released to the author by the Foreign and Commonwealth Office under the Freedom of Information Act. Ref 0340-09.

Letter from Trevor Phillips to Simon Hughes, 'Re: Mail on Sunday Report on Rochdale Liberal Democrat Candidate, 27/4/2005.' Provided to the author by a private individual.

Newspapers, magazines and news services

Items were accessed either from the publication's or news service's website or from Lexis-Nexis database.

Agence France Presse

Associated Press

Al Jazeera

BBC News

CNN

Daily Mail (London)

Daily Telegraph (London)

Express (London)

Financial Times (London)

Guardian (London)

Haaretz

Huffington Post

Independent (London)

Jerusalem Post

Jerusalem Report

Jewish Chronicle (London)

London Evening Standard
Maariv
Mail on Sunday (London)
Mideast Mirror (London)
Mirror (London)
Muslim Weekly (London)
New Statesman (London)
New York Times
Observer (London)
PBS
Scotsman
Sky News
Spectator (London)
Sunday Mail (London)
Sunday Telegraph (London)
Sunday Times (London)
The Times (London)
Wall Street Journal
Washington Post
Washington Times

Secondary sources

Books, articles and other research papers

Abbas, T. 'Ethno-Religious Identities and Islamic Political Radicalism in the UK: A Case Study.' *Journal of Muslim Minority Affairs* 27, no. 3 (2007): 429–42.
Abdelal, R., Y. M. Herrera, A. I. Johnston, and R. McDermott. 'Identity as a Variable.' *Perspectives on Politics* 4, no. 04 (2006): 695–711.
Abrahamian, E. 'The US Media, Huntington and September 11.' *Third World Quarterly* 24, no. 3 (Jun 2003): 529–44.
Abrahamsen, R. 'Blair's Africa: The Politics of Securitization and Fear.' *Alternatives: Global, Local, Political* 30, no. 1 (2005): 55–81.
Abu-Amr, Z. 'Hamas: A Historical and Political Background.' *Journal of Palestine Studies* 22, no. 4 (1993): 5–19.
Adamson, F. B. 'Global Liberalism Versus Political Islam: Competing Ideological Frameworks in International Politics.' *International Studies Review* 7, no. 4 (2005): 547–69.
'After Mecca: Engaging Hamas – Middle East Report No. 62.' *International Crisis Group* (28/2/2007).

Ajami, F. 'On Nasser and His Legacy.' *Journal of Peace Research* 11, no. 1 (1974): 41.

—. 'The Summoning: "But They Said, We Will Not Hearken".' *Foreign Affairs* 72, no. 4 (1993): 2–9.

Alderman, G. *Modern British Jewry*. New York: Oxford University Press, 1998.

Allison, G. *Essence of Decision: Explaining the Cuban Missile Crisis*. Boston, MA: Little, Brown, 1971.

Al-Sayyid, M. K., B. Baktiari, M. Barnett, S. Hegasy, E. S. Hurd, E. Lust–Okar, D. Mednicoff, *et al.* 'The Impact of 9/11 on the Middle East.' *Middle East Policy* 9, no. 4 (2002): 75–101.

Archer, T. 'Welcome to the Umma: The British State and Its Muslim Citizens since 9/11.' *Cooperation and Conflict* 44, no. 3 (2009): 329–47.

Armstrong, K. *Islam; a Short History*. London: Phoenix, 2001.

Ashton, N. J. 'Britain, Israel, and the United States, 1955–58: Beyond Suez.' *International History Review* 27, no. 1 (Mar 2005): 197–9.

Asmus, R. D., and B. P. Jackson. 'Does Israel Belong in the EU and Nato.' *Policy Review*, no. 126 (Feb 2005): 47–56.

Avineri, S. 'Rabin's Strategy: Understanding Security and the Limits of Power.' In *Striving for Peace; the Legacy of Yitzhak Rabin*. 33–40. London: Labour Friends of Israel, 2005.

Ayubi, N. *Political Islam: Religion and Politics in the Arab World*. London: Routledge, 1991.

Azubuike, S. 'The "Poodle Theory" and the Anglo-American "Special Relationship".' *International Studies* 42, no. 2 (2005): 123.

Balfour-Paul, G. *The End of Empire in the Middle East*. Cambridge: Cambridge University Press, 1991.

Bar, S. 'Deterring Nonstate Terrorist Groups: The Case of Hizballah.' *Comparative Strategy* 26, no. 5 (2007): 469–93.

—, 'Gaza – the British Are Coming – Co-Opting Terrorists – AME Exclusive,' *Independent Media Review Analysis*, 11/4/2004. Accessed 1/5/2010. http://www.imra.org.il/story.php3?id=20410.

Barak, E. 'Security and Counter-Terrorism.' In *Re-Ordering the World*, edited by M. Leonard. 91–7. London: The Foreign Policy Centre, 2002.

Barber, B. *Jihad Vs. Mcworld*. London: Corgi, 2003.

Barder, B. 'Britain: Still Looking for That Role?'. *The Political Quarterly* 72, no. 3 (2001): 366–74.

Bar-Zohar, M. *Yaacov Herzog: A Biography*. London: Halban Publishers, 2005.

Bassi, C. '"The Anti-Imperialism of Fools': A Cautionary Story on the Revolutionary Socialist Vanguard of England's Post-9/11 Anti-War Movement.' *ACME: An International E-Journal for Critical Geographies* 9, no. 2 (2010): 113–37.

Baston, L., and S. Henig. 'The Labour Party.' In *The Blair Effect 2001–05*, edited by A. Seldon and D. Kavanagh. Cambridge: Cambridge University Press, 2005.

Beilin, Y. *Israel; a Concise Political History*. London: Weidenfeld and Nicolson, 1992.

Bell, D. S. A. 'Mythscapes: Memory, Mythology, and National Identity.' *The British Journal of Sociology* 54, no. 1 (2003): 63–81.

Ben-Porat, G. 'A New Middle East? Globalization, Peace and the Double Movement.' *International Relations* 19, no. 1 (2005): 39–62.

Ben-Rafael, E. 'Where Stands Israel?.' *Ethnic and Racial Studies* 27, no. 2 (Mar 2004): 310–16.

Berman, P. 'Interrogating Terror and Liberalism.' In *Global Politics after 9/11, the Democratiya Interviews*, edited by A. Johnson. 125–53. London: Foreign Policy Centre, 2007.

—. 'Terror and Liberalism.' *The American Prospect*, 21/10/2001.

Bermant, A. 'Triumph of Pragmatism over Principle: Margaret Thatcher and the Arab-Israel Conflict.' PhD Diss, University College London, 2012.

Bevir, M., and R. A. W. Rhodes. 'Interpretive Approaches to British Government and Politics.' *British Politics* 1, no. 1 (2006): 84–112.

—. 'Interpretive Theory.' In *Theory and Methods in Political Science, Second Edition*, edited by D. Marsh and G. Stoker. Basingstoke: Palgrave MacMillan, 2002.

Bew, J., G. Glickman, M. Frampton, J. Rogers, M. A. Hoare, G. Mailer, T. Harris, and M. Jamison. *The British Moment*. London: The Social Affairs Unit, 2006.

Beyoghlow, K. A. 'Gerges, Fawaz A. America and Political Islam: Clash of Cultures or Clash of Interests.' *American Political Science Review* 95, no. 1 (2001): 255–6.

Bialer, U. 'Sterling Balances and Claims Negotiations – Britain and Israel 1947–52.' *Middle Eastern Studies* 28, no. 1 (Jan 1992): 157–77.

Bilgrami, A. 'The Clash within Civilizations.' *Daedalus* 132, no. 3 (2003): 88–94.

Bluth, C. 'The British Road to War: Bush, Blair and the Decision to Invade Iraq.' *International Affairs* 80, no. 5 (2004): 871–92.

Boot, M. 'Myths About Neoconservatism.' In *Neoconservatism*, edited by I Stelzer. 43–52. London: Atlantic Books, 2004.

Brecher, M. *The Foreign Policy System of Israel: Setting, Images, Process*. Oxford: Oxford University Press, 1972.

Bright, M. *When Progressives Treat with Reactionaries: The British State's Flirtation with Radical Islamism*. London: Policy Exchange, 2006.

Brighton, S. 'British Muslims, Multiculturalism and UK Foreign Policy: "Integration" and "Cohesion" in and Beyond the State.' *International Affairs* 83, no. 1 (2007): 1–17.

Broad, M., and O. Daddow. 'Half Remembered Quotations from Mostly Forgotten Speeches: The Limits of Labour's European Policy Discourse.' *The British Journal of Politics & International Relations* 12, no. 2 (2010): 205–22.

Brown, M. E., S. M. Lynn-Jones, and S. E. Miller. *Debating the Democratic Peace*. Cambridge, MA: The MIT Press, 1996.

Bull, P. 'New Labour, New Rhetoric? An Analysis of the Rhetoric of Tony Blair.' In *Beyond Public Speech and Symbols: Explorations in the Rhetoric of Politicians and the Media*, edited by C. De Landtsheer and O. Feldman. 3–16. Westport: Praeger Publishers, 2000.

Bulley, D. 'Textualising British Politics: Deconstructing the Subject of British Foreign Policy.' *British Politics* 4, no. 3 (2009): 291–314.

Burch, M., and I. Holliday. 'The Blair Government and the Core Executive.' *Government and Opposition* 39, no. 1 (2004): 1–21.

Burke, J. *Al Qaeda*. London: Penguin, 2004.

Byrne, A., 'Bottom-up Peacebuilding in the Occupied Territories, Alastair Crooke Interviewed by Aisling Byrne,' *Conflicts Forum*, 11/2007. Accessed 1/5/2010. http://conflictsforum.org/2007/bottom-up-peacebuilding-in-the-occupied-territories/.

Cameron, F. 'The Islamic Factor in the European Union's Foreign Policy '. In *Islam, Europe's Second Religion: The New Social, Cultural and Political Landscape*, edited by S. Hunter. Westport: Praeger Publishers, 2002.

Cassels, A. *Ideology and International Relations in the Modern World*. London: Routledge, 1996.

Cerny, P. G., and M. Evans. 'Globalisation and Public Policy under New Labour.' *Policy studies* 25, no. 1 (2004): 51–65.

Cesarani, D. 'Anti-Zionism in Britain, 1922–2002: Continuities and Discontinuities.' *Journal of Israeli History* 25, no. 1 (2006): 131–60.

Chiozza, G. 'Is There a Clash of Civilizations? Evidence from Patterns of International Conflict Involvement, 1946–97.' *Journal of Peace Research* 39, no. 6 (Nov 2002): 711–34.

Chirot, D. 'A Clash of Civilizations or of Paradigms? Theorizing Progress and Social Change.' *International Sociology* 16, no. 3 (Sep 2001): 341–60.

Chomsky, N. *Hegemony or Survival: America's Quest for Global Dominance*. New York: Holt Paperbacks, 2004.

—. *World Orders Old and New*. London: Pluto Press, 1997.

Clarke, P. *Learning from Experience – Counter-Terrorism in the UK since 9/11: The Colin Cramphorn Memorial Lecture*. London: Policy Exchange, 2007.

Coates, D., J. Krieger, and R. Vickers. *Blair's War*. Cambridge: Polity Press, 2004.

Cohen, B., 'A Discourse of Delegitimisation: The British Left and the Jews,' *New European Extremism/JPR*, 2004. Accessed 22/2/2011. http://www.axt.org.uk/HateMusic/Cohen_essay_October_04.pdf.

—, 'Jerusalem Viewpoints No. 527 – Evaluating Muslims-Jewish Relations in Britain,' *Jerusalem Centre for Public Affairs*, 1–15/2/2005. Accessed 1/5/2010. http://www.jcpa.org/jl/vp527.htm.

Cohen, N. *What's Left?: How Liberals Lost Their Way*. London: Fourth Estate, 2007.

Coles, J. *Making Foreign Policy*. London: John Murray, 2000.

Condron, S. M. 'Justification for Unilateral Action in Response to the Iraqi Threat: A Critical Analysis of Operation Desert Fox.' *Military Law Review* 161 (1999): 115.

Cooper, R. *The Breaking of Nations*. London: Atlantic Books, 2003.

Coughlin, C. *American Ally: Tony Blair and the War on Terror*. London: Politico's Publishing, 2006.

Cronin, J. *New Labour's Pasts; the Labour Party and Its Discontents.* Harlow: Pearson, 2004.

Crooke, A., 'Talking to Terrorists,' *BBC Radio 4*, 15/7/2007. Accessed 1/5/2010. http://conflictsforum.org/2007/talking-to-terrorists/.

Curtis, M. 'Britain's Real Foreign Policy and the Failure of British Academia.' *International Relations* 18, no. 3 (2004): 275.

Daalder, I. H., and J. M. Lindsay. *America Unbound.* Washington: Brookings Institution, 2003.

Dabashi, H. 'For the Last Time: Civilizations.' *International Sociology* 16, no. 3 (Sep 2001): 361–8.

David Miller, A. 'The False Religion of Mideast Peace and Why I'm No Longer a Believer.' *Foreign Policy*, May/June 2010.

Del Sarto, R. *Contested State Identities and Regional Security in the Euro-Mediterranean Area.* New York; Basingstoke: Palgrave Macmillan, 2006.

—. 'Israeli Identity as Seen through European Eyes.' In *Integration and Identity: Challenges to Europe and Israel*, edited by S. Avineri and W. Weidenfeld. 59–79, 1999.

—. 'Wording and Meaning(s): EU-Israeli Political Cooperation According to the ENP Action Plan.' *Mediterranean politics* 12, no. 1 (2007): 59–75.

Devine, F. 'Qualitative Methods.' In *Theory and Methods in Political Science*, edited by D. Marsh and G. Stoker. Basingstoke: Palgrave Macmillan, 2002.

Dickie, J. *The New Mandarins: How British Foreign Policy Works.* London: IB Tauris & Co Ltd, 2004.

Dixon, R., and P. Williams. 'Tough on Debt, Tough on the Causes of Debt? New Labour's Third Way Foreign Policy.' *The British Journal of Politics & International Relations* 3, no. 2 (2001): 150–72.

Dover, R. 'The Prime Minister and the Core Executive: A Liberal Intergovernmentalist Reading of UK Defence Policy Formulation.' *The British Journal of Politics & International Relations* 7, no. 4 (2005): 508–25.

Dowty, A. 'Israeli Foreign Policy and the Jewish Question.' *Middle East* 3, no. 1 (1999).

Drezner, D. W. 'Ideas, Bureaucratic Politics, and the Crafting of Foreign Policy.' *American Journal of Political Science* 44, no. 4 (2000): 733–49.

Dumbrell, J. *A Special Relationship: Anglo-American Relations in the Cold War and After.* Basingstoke: Palgrave Macmillan, 2001.

Dunne, T., and N. J. Wheeler. 'Blair's Britain: A Force for Good in the World?'. In *Ethics, Interests and Foreign Policy*, edited by K. Smith and M. Light. Cambridge: Cambridge University Press, 2001.

Dyson, S. B. 'Personality and Foreign Policy: Tony Blair's Iraq Decisions.' *Foreign Policy Analysis* 2, no. 3 (2006): 289–306.

Edmunds, J. 'The British Labour Party in the 1980s: The Battle over the Palestinian/Israeli Conflict.' *Politics* 18, no. 2 (2002): 111–18.

—. 'The Evolution of British Labour Party Policy on Israel from 1967 to the Intifada.' *Twentieth Century British History* 11, no. 1 (2000): 23.

—. *The Left and Israel: Party-Policy Change and Internal Democracy.* Basingstoke: Macmillan, 2000.

—. *The Left's Views on Israel: From the Establishment of the Jewish State to the Intifada - Phd Thesis.* London: London School of Economics, 1997.

El Fadl, K. A., J. Cohen, and D. Chasman. *Islam and the Challenge of Democracy.* Princeton, NJ: Princeton University Press, 2004.

Esposito, J. L. 'Contemporary Images of Islam in the West.' *Revista De Occidente*, 188 (Jan 1997): 7–20.

—. *The Islamic Threat; Myth or Reality?* New York: Oxford University Press, 1995.

—. *Unholy War: Terror in the Name of Islam.* Oxford: Oxford University Press, 2002.

Esposito, J. L., and J. O. Voll. 'Islam and the West: Muslim Voices of Dialogue.' *Millennium-Journal of International Studies* 29, no. 3 (2000): 613–39.

Evans, E. J. *Thatcher and Thatcherism.* London: Routledge, 2004.

Findlay, A. M. *The Arab World.* London: Routledge, 1994.

Fisher, J., E. Fieldhouse, D. Denver, A. Russell, and D. Cutts. *The General Election 2005: Campaign Analysis.* London: Electoral Commission, 2005.

Foley, M. *The British Presidency: Tony Blair and the Politics of Public Leadership.* Manchester: Manchester University Press, 2000.

—. 'Presidential Attribution as an Agency of Prime Ministerial Critique in a Parliamentary Democracy: The Case of Tony Blair.' *British Journal of Politics & International Relations* 6, no. 3 (2004): 292–311.

Freedman, L. 'The Coming War on Terrorism.' *The Political Quarterly* 73 (2002): 40–56.

—. 'International Security: Changing Targets.' *Foreign Policy*, 110 (1998): 48–63.

—. 'The Special Relationship, Then and Now.' *Foreign Affairs* 85, no. 3 (2006): 61–73.

—. 'War in Iraq: Selling the Threat.' *Survival* 46, no. 2 (2004): 7–49.

—. 'Will the Buck Stop with Blair?' *The Times*, 21/4/1998.

Friedman, I. 'Arnold Toynbee: Pro-Arab or Pro-Zionist?'. *Israel Studies* 4, no. 1 (1999): 73–95.

—. *Palestine, a Twice-Promised Land?: The British, the Arabs & Zionism, 1915–1920.* New Brunswick: Transaction Publishers, 2000.

Friedman, M. *The Neoconservative Revolution: Jewish Intellectuals and the Shaping of Public Policy.* Cambridge: Cambridge University Press, 2005.

Frisch, H. 'Has the Israeli-Palestinian Conflict Become Islamic? Fatah, Islam, and the Al-Aqsa Martyrs' Brigades.' *Terrorism and Political Violence* 17, no. 3 (Spr–Sum 2005): 391–406.

Frost, M. 'Putting the World to Rights: Britain's Ethical Foreign Policy.' *Cambridge Review of International Affairs* 12, no. 2 (1999): 80–9.

Fukuyama, F., 'After the "End of History",' *Open Democracy*, 2/5/2006. Accessed 1/4/2011. http://www.opendemocracy.net/content/articles/PDF/3496.pdf.

—. *The End of History and the Last Man.* New York: Free Press, 1992.

Fuller, G. E. 'The Future of Political Islam.' *Foreign Affairs* 81, no. 2 (Mar–Apr 2002): 48–60.

Fuller, G. E., and I. O. Lesser. *A Sense of Siege: The Geopolitics of Islam and the West.* Boulder; Oxford: Westview, 1995.

Gaskarth, J. 'Discourses and Ethics: The Social Construction of British Foreign Policy.' *Foreign Policy Analysis* 2, no. 4 (2006): 325–41.

Gat, M. *Britain and the Conflict in the Middle East, 1964–1967: The Coming of the Six-Day War.* Westport, CT: Greenwood Publishing Group, 2003.

—. 'Britain and the Occupied Territories after the 1967 War.' *Middle East Review of International Affairs* 10, no. 4 (2006): 69.

George, B., T. Watson, and J. Roberts. *The British Labour Party and Defense.* New York: Praeger Publishers, 1991.

Gerges, F. A. *America and Political Islam: Clash of Cultures or Clash of Interests?* Cambridge: Cambridge University Press, 1999.

Gilbert, M. *Israel: A History.* London: Doubleday, 1998.

Goldstein, J., and R. O. Keohane. 'Ideas and Foreign Policy: An Analytical Framework.' In *Ideas and Foreign Policy: Beliefs, Institutions, and Political Change,* edited by J. Goldstein and R. O. Keohane. Ithaca, NY: Cornell University Press, 1993.

Gove, M. *Celsius 7/7.* London: Weidenfeld and Nicolson, 2006.

Graham, D., and J. Boyd. *Committed, Concerned and Conciliatory: The Attitudes of Jews in Britain.* London: Institute for Jewish Policy Research, 2010.

Greenberg, S. B. *Dispatches from the War Room: In the Trenches with Five Extraordinary Leaders.* New York: Thomas Dunne Books, 2009.

Greene, T. 'Between the Crescent and the Star: British Policy in the Israeli Palestinian Arena in the Wake of 9/11.' PhD Diss, University College London, 2011.

—. 'Shifting World, Shifting Priorities: A Mid-Term Report on the UK Coalition's Relations with Israel.' *Fathom*, 1 (Winter 2012): 40–9.

Greilsammer, I., and J. Weiler. *Europe's Middle East Dilemma: The Quest for a Unified Stance.* Boulder: Westview Press, 1987.

Hain, P. *The End of Foreign Policy?: Britain's Interests, Global Linkages and Natural Limits.* London: Royal Institute of International Affairs, 2001.

Haines, S. "A Word Full of Terror to the British Mind": The Blair Doctrine and British Defence Policy.' In *The Development of British Defence Policy: Blair, Brown and Beyond,* edited by D. Brown. Surrey: Ashgate Publishing, Ltd., 2010.

Halabi, Y. 'Orientalism and US Democratization Policy in the Middle East.' *International Studies* 36, no. 4 (1999): 375.

—. 'US Responses to Major Developments in the Arab-Islamic World.' *International Studies* 43, no. 4 (2006): 339.

Halliday, F. *Islam and the Myth of Confrontation: Religion and Politics in the Middle East.* London; NY: I.B.Tauris, 2003.

—, 'The Left and the Jihad,' Accessed 22/7/2011. http://www.opendemocracy.net/
    globalization/left_jihad_3886.jsp.

—. ' "Orientalism" and Its Critics.' British Journal of Middle Eastern Studies 20, no. 2
    (1993): 145–63.

—. 'The Politics of "Islam" – a Second Look.' British Journal of Political Science 25,
    no. 3 (1995): 399–417.

—. Two Hours That Shook the World. London: Saqi Books, 2002.

—. 'West Encountering Islam: Islamophobia Reconsidered.' In Islam Encountering
    Globalization, edited by A. Mohammadi. Oxon: Routledge Curzon, 2002.

Hamilton, K. 'Britain, France, and America's Year of Europe, 1973.' Diplomacy and
    Statecraft 17, no. 4 (2006): 871–95.

Haron, M. 'Britain and Israel, 1948–1950.' Modern Judaism 3, no. 2 (1983): 217–23.

Heffernan, R. 'Exploring (and Explaining) the British Prime Minister.' British Journal of
    Politics & International Relations 7, no. 4 (2005): 605–20.

—. 'Labour's New Labour Legacy: Politics after Blair and Brown.' Political Studies
    Review 9, no. 2 (2011): 163–77.

Heilbrunn, J. 'The Clash of Samuel Huntingtons.' American Prospect, 1/7/1998.

Hellyer, H. A. 'British Muslims: Past, Present and Future.' The Muslim World 97, no. 2
    (2007): 225–58.

Henderson, E. A. 'Mistaken Identity: Testing the Clash of Civilizations Thesis in Light
    of Democratic Peace Claims.' British Journal of Political Science 34 (Jul 2004):
    539–54.

Henderson, S. 'Policy Watch #738 – Bush and Blair: Tensions in the Relationship.'
    Washington Institute for Near East Policy, 2/4/2003.

Henderson, E. A., and R. Tucker. 'Clear and Present Strangers: The Clash of
    Civilizations and International Conflict.' International Studies Quarterly 45, no. 2
    (Jun 2001): 317–38.

Hennessy, P. 'Informality and Circumscription: The Blair Style of Government in War
    and Peace.' The Political Quarterly 76, no. 1 (2005): 3–11.

—. The Prime Minister: The Office and Its Holders since 1945. London: Penguin Books,
    2001.

Henry, C. M. 'The Clash of Globalisations in the Middle East.' In International Relations
    of the Middle East, edited by L. Fawcett. Oxford: Oxford University Press, 2005.

Hermann, M. G. 'Explaining Foreign Policy Behavior Using the Personal
    Characteristics of Political Leaders.' International Studies Quarterly 24, no. 1 (1980):
    7–46.

Hermann, M. G., and J. D. Hagan. 'International Decision Making: Leadership Matters.'
    Foreign Policy, 110 (1998): 124–37.

Herzl, T. The Jewish State. New York: American Zionist Emergency Council, 1946.

Herzog, M. 'Can Hamas Be Tamed?.' Foreign Affairs 85 (2006): 83–94.

Hill, C. The Changing Politics of Foreign Policy. Basingstoke: Palgrave MacMillan, 2003.

—. 'Renationalizing or Regrouping? EU Foreign Policy since 11 September 2001.' *Journal of Common Market Studies* 42, no. 1 (2004): 143–63.

Hinnebusch, R. 'Globalization and the Middle East: Islam, Economy, Society and Politics.' *Australian Journal of International Affairs* 57, no. 1 (Apr 2003): 143–4.

—. *The International Politics of the Middle East.* Manchester: Manchester University Press, 2003.

Hirsh, D. 'Anti-Zionism and Antisemitism: Cosmopolitan Reflections.' *The Yale Initiative for the Interdisciplinary Study of Antisemitism Working Paper Series* (2007).

Hoggett, P. 'Iraq: Blair's Mission Impossible.' *British Journal of Politics & International Relations* 7, no. 3 (2005): 418–28.

Hollis, R. *Britain and the Middle East in the 9/11 Era.* London: Wiley-Blackwell, 2009.

—. 'A Fateful Decision for Britain.' In *The Iraq War: Causes and Consequences*, edited by R. Fawn and R. Hinnebusch. Boulder, CO: Lynne Rienner Publishers, 2006.

—. 'The Israeli-Palestinian Road Block: Can Europeans Make a Difference?'. *International Affairs* 80, no. 2 (2004): 191–201.

Howorth, J. 'Britain, France and the European Defence Initiative.' *Survival* 42, no. 2 (2000): 33–55.

Hudson, V. M., and C. S. Vore. 'Foreign Policy Analysis Yesterday, Today, and Tomorrow.' *Mershon International Studies Review* 39, no. 2 (1995): 209–38.

Huntington, S. P. *The Clash of Civilizations and the Remaking of World Order.* London: The Free Press, 2002.

—. 'The Clash of Civilizations?'. *Foreign Affairs* 72, no. 3 (1993): 22–49.

—. 'If Not Civilizations, What? Samuel Huntington Responds to His Critics.' *Foreign Affairs* 72 (1993): 186–94.

—. 'The West Unique, Not Universal.' *Foreign Affairs* 75, no. 6 (1996): 28–46.

Hurd, E. S. 'The Political Authority of Secularism in International Relations.' *European Journal of International Relations* 10, no. 2 (Jun 2004): 235–62.

—. 'Political Islam and Foreign Policy in Europe and the United States.' *Foreign Policy Analysis* 3, no. 4 (2007): 345–67.

Hussein, E. *The Islamist.* London: Penguin Books, 2007.

Inbar, E. 'How Israel Bungled the Second Lebanon War.' *Middle East Quarterly* 14, no. 3 (Summer 2007): 57–65.

Inglehart, R., and P. Norris. 'The True Clash of Civilizations.' *Foreign Policy*, 135 (Mar–Apr 2003): 62–70.

Jervis, R. 'Understanding the Bush Doctrine.' *Political Science Quarterly* 118, no. 3 (2003): 365–88.

Joffe, J. 'A World without Israel.' *Foreign Policy* 146 (2005): 36–42.

Johnson, A. 'Ernest Bevin's Third Force Memos.' *Democratia*, no. 8 (Spring 2007).

—. 'Introduction: Towards a Decent Left.' In *Global Politics after 9/11: The Democratiya Interviews*, edited by A. Johnson. London: The Foreign Policy Centre, 2007.

Johnston, R., C. Pattie, and D. Rossiter. 'The Election Results in the UK Regions.' *Parliamentary Affairs* 58, no. 4 (2005): 786.

Jordan, J., and L. Boix. 'Al-Qaeda and Western Islam.' *Terrorism and Political Violence* 16, no. 1 (Spr 2004): 1–17.

Jordan, R., and S. Henderson, 'Policy Forum – Who Will Be the Next King of Saudi Arabia... And Does It Matter?,' *Washington Institute for Near East Policy*, 15/7/2009. Accessed 1/5/2010. http://www.washingtoninstitute.org/templateC05. php?CID=3090.

Julius, A. *Trials of the Diaspora: A History of Anti-Semitism in England*. Oxford: Oxford University Press, 2010.

Kaarbo, J. 'Prime Minister Leadership Styles in Foreign Policy Decision Making: A Framework for Research.' *Political Psychology* 18, no. 3 (1997): 553–81.

Kagan, R. 'The Benevolent Empire.' *Foreign Policy* 111 (Summer 1998): 24–35.

—. *Paradise and Power: America Versus Europe in the Twenty-First Century*. New York: Knopf, 2003.

Kamm, O. *Anti-Totalitarianism*. London: The Social Affairs Unit, 2005.

Kampfner, J. *Blair's Wars*. London: Free Press, 2004.

—, 'The Expired Mandate – Radio 4 Documentary,' *BBC Radio 4*, 1/8/2002. Accessed 1/5/2010. http://news.bbc.co.uk/hi/english/static/audio_video/programmes/ analysis/transcripts/middle_east.txt.

—. *Robin Cook*. London: Phoenix, 1999.

Kavanagh, D. 'The Blair Premiership.' In *The Blair Effect 2001–05*, edited by A. Seldon and D. Kavanagh. Cambridge: Cambridge University Press, 2005.

—. 'The Paradoxes of British Political Parties.' In *British Politics Today*, edited by Colin Hay. Cambridge: Polity Press, 2002.

Kavanagh, D., and A. Seldon. *The Powers Behind the Prime Minister: The Hidden Influence of Number Ten*. London: HarperCollins, 1999.

Keddie, N. R. 'The Future of Islam and the West: Clash of Civilizations or Peaceful Coexistence.' *International Journal of Middle East Studies* 32, no. 1 (Feb 2000): 180–3.

—. *An Islamic Response to Imperialism: Political and Religious Writings of Sayyid JamāL Al-DīN Al-AfghāNī*. Los Angeles: University of California Press, 1968.

—. *Modern Iran: Roots and Results of Revolution*. New Haven & London: Yale University Press, 2006.

Kedourie, E. *The Chatham House Version, and Other Middle-Eastern Studies*. London: Weidenfeld & Nicolson, 1970.

—. *Democracy and Arab Political Culture*. London: Frank Cass, 1994.

—. *Politics in the Middle East*. Oxford: Oxford University Press, 1992.

Keohane, D. 'The Absent Friend: EU Foreign Policy and Counter Terrorism.' *Journal of Common Market Studies* 46, no. 1 (2008): 125–46.

Kepel, G., 'Beyond the Clash of Civilizations,' *New York Times*, 11/3/2011. Accessed 1/4/2011. http://www.nytimes.com/2011/03/12/opinion/12iht-edkepel12.html.

—. *The Revenge of God: The Resurgence of Islam, Christianity, and Judaism in the Modern World*. Cambridge: Polity Press, 1994.

—. *The War for Muslim Minds*. Cambridge, MA: Harvard University Press, 2004.

Kettell, S. *Dirty Politics?: New Labour, British Democracy and the Invasion of Iraq*. London; New York: Zed Books, 2006.

Khomeini, R. *Islamic Government*. New York: Manor Books, 1979.

Kimmerling, B. *The Invention and Decline of Israeliness*. Berekely, CA: University of California Press, 2001.

Kristol, W., and R. Kagan. 'Towards a Neo-Reaganite Foreign Policy.' *Foreign Affairs* (July/August 1996).

Laqueur, W. *A History of Zionism*. New York: Schocken, 2003.

—. *The Israel-Arab Reader: A Documentary History of the Middle East Conflict*. Harmondsworth: Penguin, 1970.

Leiken, R. S. 'Europe's Angry Muslims.' *Foreign Affairs* 84, no. 4 (Jul–Aug 2005): 120–35.

Leonard, M. *Re-Ordering the World*. London: The Foreign Policy Centre, 2002.

Levey, Z. 'Israeli Foreign Policy and the Arms Race in the Middle East 1950–1960.' *Journal of Strategic Studies* 24, no. 1 (Mar 2001): 29–48.

Lewis, B. 'Freedom and Justice in the Modern Middle East.' *Foreign Affairs* (May/June 2005).

—. *The Jews of Islam*. London: Routledge & Kegan Paul, 1984.

—. *The Middle East*. London: Phoenix Press, 2004.

—. *The Multiple Identities of the Middle East*. London: Phoenix, 1999.

—. 'The Roots of Muslim Rage.' *The Atlantic Monthly* 266, no. 3 (Sept 1990): 47–60.

—. *Semites and Anti-Semites: An Inquiry into Conflict and Prejudice*. London: Weidenfeld and Nicolson, 1986.

—. 'The West and the Middle East.' *Foreign Affairs* 76, no. 1 (Jan–Feb 1997): 114–30.

—. *What Went Wrong?* London: Phoenix, 2002.

Lewis, B., C. E. Dodge, E. W. Said, L. Wieseltier, and C. Hitchens. 'The MESA Debate – the Scholars, the Media, and the Middle East.' *Journal of Palestine Studies* 16, no. 2 (1987): 85–104.

Light, M. 'Foreign Policy Analysis.' In *Contemporary International Relations: A Guide to Theory*, edited by M. Light and A. J. R. Groom. 93–108. London: Pinter Publishers, 1994.

Little, R., and M. Wickham-Jones. *New Labour's Foreign Policy: A New Moral Crusade?* Manchester: Manchester University Press, 2000.

Litvak, M. 'The Islamization of the Palestinian-Israeli Conflict: The Case of Hamas.' *Middle-Eastern-studies* 34 (1998): 148–63.

Lochery, N. *Loaded Dice: The Foreign Office and Israel*. London: Continuum Books, 2007.

—. 'The Netanyahu Era: From Crisis to Crisis, 1996–99.' *Israel Affairs* 6, no. 3 (2000): 221–37.

—. 'Present and Post-Blair British Middle East Policy, the Annual Madame Madeleine Feher European Scholar Lecture No. 9.' The Begin Sadat Center for Strategic Studies, 2007.

—. *Why Blame Israel?* London: Icon Books, 2005.

Louis, W. R. *The British Empire in the Middle East, 1945–1951.* Oxford: Oxford University Press, 1984.

Lynch, T. J. 'Kristol Balls: Neoconservative Visions of Islam and the Middle East.' *International Politics* 45, no. 2 (2008): 182–211.

Macintyre, D. *Mandelson and the Making of New Labour.* London: HarperCollins, 1999.

Maclean, D. *British Foreign Policy since Suez.* London: Hodder and Stoughton, 1970.

MacShane, D. *Globalising Hatred: The New Antisemitism.* London: Weidenfeld & Nicolson, 2008.

Maher, S., and M. Frampton. *Choosing Our Friends Wisely.* London: Policy Exchange, 2009.

Mandel, D. 'A Good International Citizen: H. V. Evatt, Britain, the United Nations and Israel, 1948–49.' *Middle Eastern Studies* 39, no. 2 (Apr 2003): 82–104.

Maqdsi, M. 'Charter of the Islamic Resistance Movement (Hamas) of Palestine.' *Journal of Palestine Studies* 22, no. 4 (1993): 122–34.

Marsh, D. 'Understanding British Government: Analysing Competing Models.' *The British Journal of Politics & International Relations* 10, no. 2 (2008): 251–68.

Mathiopoulos, M., and I. Gyarmati. 'Saint Malo and Beyond: Toward European Defense.' *The Washington Quarterly* 22, no. 4 (1999): 65–76.

Matlock, J. F. 'Can Civilizations Clash?'. *Proceedings of the American Philosophical Society* 143, no. 3 (1999): 428–39.

McLean, C., and A. Patterson. 'A Precautionary Approach to Foreign Policy? A Preliminary Analysis of Tony Blair's Speeches on Iraq.' *British Journal of Politics & International Relations* 8, no. 3 (2006): 351–67.

McRoy, A. *From Rushdie to 7/7: The Radicalisation of Islam in Britain.* London: The Social Affairs Unit, 2006.

Mearsheimer, J. J., and S. M. Walt. *The Israel Lobby and US Foreign Policy.* London: Penguin Books, 2008.

Miller, B. 'The Effects of Changes in the International Environment on the Future of the Middle East.' *Israel Affairs* 10, no. 1 & 2 (2004): 105–20.

Miller, R. 'British Anti-Zionism Then and Now.' *Covenant Global Jewish Magazine* 1, no. 2 (2007) http://www.covenant.idc.ac.il/en/vol1/issue2/miller_print.html (Accessed 28/1/2013).

—. *Inglorious Disarray: Europe, Israel and the Palestinians.* London: Hurst & Company, 2011.

Milton-Edwards, B. 'The Concept of Jihad and the Palestinian Islamic Movement.' *British Journal of Middle Eastern Studies* 19, no. 1 (1992): 48–53.

—. *Contemporary Politics in the Middle East.* Malden: Polity Press, 2006.

—. 'Political Islam and the Palestinian-Israeli Conflict.' *Israel Affairs* 12, no. 1 (January 2006): 65–85.

Moaddel, M., and K. Talattof. *Modernist and Fundamentalist Debates in Islam: A Reader.* New York: Palgrave Macmillan, 2002.

Monroe, E. *Britain's Moment in the Middle East, 1914–1971.* London: Chatto & Windus, 1981.

Muravchik, J. 'The Neoconservative Cabal.' In *Neoconservatism*, edited by I. Stelzer. 243–57. London: Atlantic Books, 2004.

Murden, S. *Islam, the Middle East, and the New Global Hegemony.* London: Lynne Rienner Publishers, 2002.

Murray, D. 'How the UK Arrived at the Present Situation Regarding Israel and Middle East Issues.' *Middle East Review of International Affairs* 14, no. 2 (June 2010): 4–7.

Naughtie, J. *The Accidental American: Tony Blair and the Presidency.* Basingstoke: Pan Books, 2005.

Netanyahu, B. *A Place among the Nations: Israel and the World.* London: Bantam, 1993.

Nettler, R. L. *Past Trials and Present Tribulations: A Muslim Fundamentalist's View of the Jews.* Oxford: Pergamon, 1987.

Norris, P., and R. Inglehart. 'Islamic Culture and Democracy: Testing the "Clash of Civilizations" Thesis.' *Comparative Sociology* 1, no. 3–4 (2002): 235–63.

Nye, J. S. 'The Decline of America's Soft Power – Why Washington Should Worry.' *Foreign Affairs* 83, no. 3 (May–Jun 2004): 16–20.

O'Malley, E. 'Setting Choices, Controlling Outcomes: The Operation of Prime Ministerial Influence and the UK's Decision to Invade Iraq.' *British Journal of Politics & International Relations* 9, no. 1 (2007): 1–19.

Ovendale, R. *Britain, the United States, and the Transfer of Power in the Middle East.* London: Leicester University Press, 1996.

Owen, E. 'Egos, Gaffes and Hissy Fits – the Art of Diplomacy.' *London Evening Standard*, 25/9/2009.

Paris, J., 'UK Counter-Radicalisation Strategy: Accommodation to Confrontation?,' *Henry Jackson Society*, 2/7/2008. Accessed 1/5/2010. www.henryjacksonsociety.org/ stories.asp?id=734.

Parmar, I. 'I'm Proud of the British Empire': Why Tony Blair Backs George W. Bush.' *The Political Quarterly* 76, no. 2 (2005): 218–31.

Pelletiere, S. C. *Landpower and Dual Containment: Rethinking America's Policy in the Gulf.* Carlisle, PA: Strategic Studies Institute, US Army War College, 1999.

Peres, S. *The New Middle East.* New York: Henry Holt, 1993.

Perle, R., J. Colbert, C. Fairbanks, R. Loewenberg, J. Torop, D. Wurmser, and M. Wurmser. *A Clean Break: A New Strategy for Securing the Realm.* Jerusalem and Washington: The Institute for Advanced Strategic and Political Studies, 1996.

Phillips, M. *Londonistan: How Britain Is Creating a Terror State Within.* London: Gibson Square, 2007.

Phillips, R. 'Standing Together: The Muslim Association of Britain and the Anti-War Movement.' *Race & Class* 50, no. 2 (2008): 101.

Philpott, D. 'The Challenge of September 11 to Secularism in International Relations.' *World Politics* 55, no. 1 (2003): 66–95.

—. *Revolutions in Sovereignty: How Ideas Shaped Modern International Relations.* Princeton, NJ: Princeton University Press, 2001.

Phythian, M. *The Labour Party, War and International Relations, 1945–2006.* London: Routledge, 2007.

Pipes, D. 'The Politics of Muslim Anti-Semitism.' *Commentary*, August 1981.

Piscatori, J. P. *Islam in a World of Nation-States.* Cambridge: Cambridge University Press, 1986.

Pryce-Jones, D. 'The Chatham House Version, yet Again.' *Middle East Quarterly* (2004).

Putnam, R. D. 'Diplomacy and Domestic Politics: The Logic of Two-Level Games.' *International Organization* 42, no. 03 (1988): 427–60.

Qutb, S. *Milestones (Ma 'Alim Fil Tariq).* Indianapolis: American Trust Publications, 1990.

Radosh, A., and R. Radosh. *A Safe Haven: Harry S. Truman and the Founding of Israel.* New York: Harper, 2009.

Ramadan, T. *Western Muslims and the Future of Islam.* Oxford: Oxford University Press, 2004.

Rawnsley, A. *The End of the Party.* London: Viking, 2010.

—. *Servants of the People: The inside Story of New Labour.* London: Penguin Books, 2001.

Rentoul, J. *Tony Blair: Prime Minister.* London: Warner Books, 2001.

Reynolds, D. 'A "Special Relationship"? America, Britain and the International Order since the Second World War.' *International Affairs (Royal Institute of International Affairs 1944-)* 62, no. 1 (1985): 1–20.

Rich, D. 'British Muslims and UK Foreign Policy.' In *Britain and the Middle East*, edited by Z. Levey and E. Podeh. 322–39. Brighton: Sussex Academic Press, 2007.

Richards, P. *Labour Looks to Israel – Essays on Politics, Society and Peace.* London: Labour Friends of Israel, 2005.

Riddell, P. *Hug Them Close: Blair, Clinton, Bush and the 'Special Relationship'.* London: Politico's Publishing, 2004.

—. *The Unfulfilled Prime Minister: Tony Blair's Quest for a Legacy.* London: Politico's Publishing, 2005.

Ross, D. B. 'Yasir Arafat.' *Foreign Policy* 131 (Jul–Aug 2002): 18.

Ross, D., and D. Makovsky. *Myths, Illusions, and Peace: Finding a New Direction for America in the Middle East.* New York: Viking, 2009.

Roy, O. *Globalized Islam: The Search for a New Ummah.* New York: Columbia University Press, 2006.

Roy, O., and C. Volk. *The Failure of Political Islam.* Cambridge, MA: Harvard University Press, 1994.

Rubin, B. *The Tragedy of the Middle East*. Cambridge: Cambridge Univesity Press, 2002.

Rubin, B., and J. C. Rubin. *Yasir Arafat; a Political Biography*. London: Continuum, 2003.

Rynhold, J. 'Cultural Shift and Foreign Policy Change.' *Cooperation and Conflict* 42, no. 4 (2007): 419.

—. *The Failure of the Oslo Process: Inherently Flawed or Flawed Implementation?*: Begin-Sadat Center for Strategic Studies, Bar-Ilan University, 2008.

Rynhold, J., and J. Spyer. 'British Policy in the Arab–Israeli Arena 1973–2004.' *British Journal of Middle Eastern Studies* 34, no. 2 (2007): 137–55.

—. 'British Policy Towards the Middle East in the Post-Cold War Era 1991–2005: A Bridge between the US and the EU?'. In *Britain and the Middle East*, edited by Z. Levey and E. Podeh. 283–310. Brighton: Sussex University Press, 2008.

Rynhold, J., and D. Waxman. 'Ideological Change and Israel's Disengagement from Gaza.' *Political Science Quarterly* 123, no. 1 (2008): 11–37.

Sachar, H. *Israel and Europe: An Appraisal in History*. New York: Vintage Books, 1998.

Sacranie, I. 'The Role of British Muslims in Bringing Justice to Palestine.' *Friends of Al Aqsa Journal* 3, no. 1 (2000): 21–3.

Said, E. W. *Orientalism*. London: Penguin, 2003.

—. *The Question of Palestine*. London: Vintage, 1992.

Saikal, A. *Islam and the West: Conflict or Cooperation?* Basingstoke: Palgrave Macmillan, 2003.

Salla, M. E. 'Political Islam and the West: A New Cold War or Convergence?'. *Third World Quarterly* 18, no. 4 (1997): 729–42.

Satloff, R., and T. Blair, '2010 Scholar-Statesman Award Dinner,' *Washington Institute for Near East Policy*, 5/10/2010. Accessed 8/10/2010. http://www.washingtoninstitute. org/html/pdf/BlairScholarStatesman.pdf.

Segev, T. *One Palestine Complete; Jews and Arabs under the British Mandate*. London: Abacus, 2001.

Seldon, A. *Blair*. London: Free Press, 2004.

Seldon, A., P. Snowdon, and D. Collings. *Blair Unbound*. London: Simon & Schuster UK, 2007.

Sen, A. K. 'The Right to One's Identity.' *Frontline*, 5–18/1/2002, 63–64.

Seyd, P., and P. Whiteley. *New Labour's Grassroots*. Basingstoke: Palgrave Macmillan, 2002.

Sharansky, N., and R. Dermer. *The Case for Democracy*. New York: Public Affairs, 2004.

Shindler, C. *A History of Modern Israel*. Cambridge: Cambridge University Press, 2008.

—. *Israel and the European Left: Between Solidarity and Delegitimisation*. New York: Continuum, 2012.

—. 'The Place of Israel in British Jewish Identity.' In *Israel, the Diaspora and Jewish Identity*, edited by D. Ben-Moshe and Z. Segev. London: Sussex Academic Press, 2007.

—. 'The Road to Utopia: The Origins of Anti-Zionism on the British Left.' *Middle East Review of International Affairs* 14, no. 2 (June 2010): 38–47.

Shlaim, A. 'The Balfour Declaration and Its Consequences.' In *More Adventures with Britannia: Personalities, Politics and Culture in Britain*, edited by W. R. Louis. London: IB Tauris, 1998.

—. *Lion of Jordan: The Life of King Hussein in War and Peace.* London: Penguin, 2008.

—. 'The Protocol of Sevres, 1956: Anatomy of a War Plot.' *International Affairs* 73, no. 3 (Jul 1997): 509–30.

Shlaim, A., P. Jones, and K. Sainsbury. *British Foreign Secretaries since 1945.* Newton Abbot: David & Charles, 1977.

Sicher, E. 'The Image of Israel and Postcolonial Discourse in the Early 21st Century: A View from Britain.' *Israel Studies* 16, no. 1 (2011): 1–25.

Soetendorp, B. 'The EU's Involvement in the Israeli-Palestinian Peace Process: The Building of a Visible International Identity.' *European Foreign Affairs Review* 7 (2002): 283–95.

Spyer, J. 'An Analytical and Historical Overview of British Policy toward Israel.' *MERIA* 8, no. 2 (2004): 80–102.

Stansky, P. 'Review: Anglo-Jew or English/British? Some Dilemmas of Anglo-Jewish History.' *Jewish Social Studies* 2, no. 1 (1995): 159–78.

Stelzer, I. *Neoconservatism.* London: Atlantic, 2004.

—. 'Neoconservatives and Their Critics.' In *Neoconservatism*, edited by I. Stelzer. 3–28. London: Atlantic Books, 2004.

Stephens, E. *US Policy Towards Israel: The Role of Political Culture in Defining the 'Special Relationship'.* Portland OR: Sussex Academic Press, 2006.

Stephens, P. *Tony Blair: The Making of a World Leader.* New York: Viking, 2004.

Stothard, P. *Thirty Days: A Month at the Heart of Blair's War.* London: Harper Collins, 2003.

Stourton, E. 'The Summer War in Lebanon: A Tragedy of Errors,' *BBC Radio 4,* 3–10/4/2007. Accessed 18/7/2010. http://www.bbc.co.uk/radio4/news/summer_war_lebanon.shtml.

Talatoff, K., and M. Moaddel. *Contemporary Debates in Islam: Modernism Versus Fundamentalism.* Basingstoke: Macmillan, 1999.

Taylor, J., and C. Jasparo. 'Editorials and Geopolitical Explanations for 11 September.' *Geopolitics* 8, no. 3 (2003): 217–52.

Tessler, M. *A History of the Israeli-Palestinian Conflict.* Bloomington: Indiana University Press, 1994.

—. 'Islam and Democracy in the Middle East – the Impact of Religious Orientations on Attitudes toward Democracy in Four Arab Countries.' *Comparative Politics* 34, no. 3 (Apr 2002): 337–54.

Theakston, K. 'New Labour and the Foreign Office.' In *New Labour's Foreign Policy: A New Moral Crusade*, edited by R. Little and M. Wickham-Jones. 112–27. Manchester: Manchester University Press, 2000.

Thorpe, A. *A History of the British Labour Party*. Basingstoke: MacMillan Press, 1997.

Tibi, B. *Political Islam, World Politics and Europe: Democratic Peace and Euro-Islam Versus Global Jihad*. Oxon: Routledge, 2008.

Tomlin, E. W. F. *Arnold Toynbee: A Selection from His Works*. Oxford: Oxford University Press, 1978.

Vickers, R. *The Labour Party and the World: The Evolution of Labour's Foreign Policy, 1900–51*. Manchester: Manchester University Press, 2003.

Walgrave, S., and J. Verhulst. 'Government Stance and Internal Diversity of Protest: A Comparative Study of Protest against the War in Iraq in Eight Countries.' *Social Forces* 87, no. 3 (2009): 1355–87.

Wallace, W. 'The Collapse of British Foreign Policy.' *International Affairs* 81, no. 1 (2005): 53–68.

—. 'Foreign Policy and National Identity in the United Kingdom.' *International Affairs* 67, no. 1 (1991): 65–80.

Wallace, W., and C. Phillips. 'Reassessing the Special Relationship.' *International Affairs* 85, no. 2 (2009): 263–84.

Wallerstein, I. *The Politics of the World-Economy: The States, the Movements, and the Civilizations*. Cambridge: Cambridge University Press, 1984.

Ward, H. 'Rational Choice.' In *Theory and Methods in Political Science, Second Edition*, edited by D. Marsh and G. Stoker. Basingstoke: Palgrave MacMillan, 2002.

Watson, M., and C. Hay. 'The Discourse of Globalisation and the Logic of No Alternative: Rendering the Contingent Necessary in the Political Economy of New Labour.' *Policy & Politics* 31, no. 3 (2003): 289–305.

Waxman, D. 'From Jerusalem to Baghdad? Israel and the War in Iraq.' *International Studies Perspectives* 10, no. 1 (2009): 1–17.

Wedeen, L. 'Beyond the Crusades: Why Huntington, and Bin Laden, Are Wrong.' *Middle East Policy* 10, no. 2 (2003): 54–61.

Wheeler, N. J., and T. Dunne. 'Good International Citizenship: A Third Way for British Foreign Policy.' *International Affairs* 74, no. 4 (1998): 847–70.

Wickham-Jones, M. 'Labour Party Politics and Foreign Policy.' In *New Labour's Foreign Policy: A New Moral Crusade*, edited by R. Little and M. Wickham-Jones. 93–111. Manchester: Manchester University Press, 2000.

Wiktorowicz, Q. *Radical Islam Rising*. Lanham, Maryland: Rowman and Littlefield, 2005.

Wiktorowicz, Q., and J. Kaltner. 'Killing in the Name of Islam: Al-Qaeda's Justification for September 11.' *Middle East Policy* 10, no. 2 (2003): 76–92.

Williams, P. *British Foreign Policy under New Labour, 1997–2005*. Basingstoke: Palgrave Macmillan, 2005.

—. 'The Rise and Fall of the Ethical Dimension: Presentation and Practice in New Labour's Foreign Policy.' *Cambridge Review of International Affairs* 15, no. 1 (2002): 53–63.

—. 'Who's Making UK Foreign Policy?'. *International Affairs* 80, no. 5 (2004): 909–29.

Wilson, H. *The Chariot of Israel: Britain, America, and the State of Israel*. London: Weidenfeld and Nicolson and M. Joseph, 1981.

Wistrich, R. S. *Antisemitism: The Longest Hatred*. London: Thames Methuen, 1991.

—. *Hitler's Apocalypse: Jews and the Nazi Legacy*. London: Weidenfeld & Nicolson, 1985.

Woodward, B. *Bush at War: Inside the Bush White House*. London: Pocket Books, 2003.

—. *Plan of Attack*. London: Pocket Books, 2004.

—. *State of Denial: Bush at War*. London: Simon and Schuster, 2007.

Yaari, E. 'The Eastern Border'. *Jerusalem Report*, 5/4/2004.

Yakobson, A., and A. Rubinstein. *Israel and the Family of Nations: The Jewish Nation-State and Human Rights*. Oxford: Routledge, 2008.

Youngs, R. 'European Approaches to Security in the Mediterranean'. *The Middle East Journal* 57, no. 3 (2003): 414–31.

Zakaria, F. 'Realism and Domestic Politics: A Review Essay'. *International Security* 17, no. 1 (1992): 177–98.

Index

www.ingramcontent.com/pod-product-compliance
Lightning Source LLC
Chambersburg PA
CBHW060149280326
41932CB00012B/1695